SO-BIE-846

791.530947 Kel
Kelly.
Petrushka.

The Lorette Wilmot Library
Nazareth College of Rochester

CAMBRIDGE STUDIES IN RUSSIAN LITERATURE

Petrushka
The Russian Carnival Puppet Theatre

CAMBRIDGE STUDIES IN RUSSIAN LITERATURE

General editor MALCOLM JONES

Editorial board ANTHONY CROSS, CARYL EMERSON
HENRY GIFFORD, G.S. SMITH, VICTOR TERRAS

Recent titles in the series

Marina Tsvetaeva
SIMON KARLINSKY

Bulgakov's last decade
J. A. E. CURTIS

Velimir Khlebnikov
RAYMOND COOKE

Dostoyevsky and the process of literary creation
JACQUES CATTEAU
translated by Audrey Littlewood

The poetic imagination of Vyacheslav Ivanov
PAMELA DAVIDSON

Joseph Brodsky
VALENTINA POLUKHINA

A complete list of books in the series will be found at the end of this volume.

Petrushka

The Russian Carnival Puppet Theatre

CATRIONA KELLY
Christ Church, Oxford

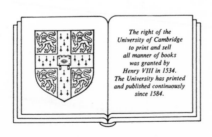

The right of the University of Cambridge to print and sell all manner of books was granted by Henry VIII in 1534. The University has printed and published continuously since 1584.

CAMBRIDGE UNIVERSITY PRESS

CAMBRIDGE

NEW YORK   PORT CHESTER

MELBOURNE   SYDNEY

DISCARDED
LORETTE WILMOT LIBRARY
NAZARETH COLLEGE

Published by the Press Syndicate of the University of Cambridge
The Pitt Building, Trumpington Street, Cambridge CB2 1RP
40 West 20th Street, New York, NY 10011, USA
10 Stamford Road, Oakleigh, Melbourne 3166, Australia

© Cambridge University Press 1990

First published 1990

Printed in Great Britain at the University Press, Cambridge

British Library cataloguing in publication data
Kelly, Catriona
Petrushka: the Russian carnival puppet theatre.
(Cambridge studies in Russian literature)
1. Russian puppet theatre
1. Title
791.5'3'0947

Library of Congress cataloguing in publication data
Kelly, Catriona.
Petrushka, the Russian carnival puppet theatre / Catriona Kelly.
p.   cm. – (Cambridge studies in Russian literature)
Includes bibliographical references.
ISBN 0 521 37520 7
1. Puppet theater – Soviet Union.
1. Title.
II. Title: Russian carnival puppet theatre.
III. Series.
PN1978.S6K45 1990
791.5'3'0947–dc20   89-17442 CIP

ISBN 0 521 37520 7

CE

791.530947
Kl

To A.K., A.K. and A.K.,
K.K. and M.K.
with love

Contents

Illustrations

Acknowledgements for illustrations

1, 3, 5, 10, private collection, Soviet Union; 2, 9, 11, 21, 22, author's own collection; 4, 20, Russian Centre Library, St Antony's College, Oxford; 6, 7, 15, 16, by kind permission of the Curators, Taylor Institution, Oxford; 8, by kind permission of the Bodleian Library, Oxford (shelf-mark 20589 c. 19); 12, by kind permission of Oxford University Press; 13, 14, private collection of Mr George Speaight, London, by kind permission of the owner; 17, by kind permission of the Ashmolean Museum, Oxford; 18, 19, private collection of Mr and Mrs Lobanov-Rostovsky, London, by kind permission of the owners.

Acknowledgements

I have been fortunate in the advice and help extended to me from all sides whilst working on this book; one of the great pleasures of writing it, indeed, was the range of people amongst Slavists and theatre specialists with whom it put me in touch. Amongst the former I would particularly like to thank Barbara Heldt, who read a first draft and made valuable suggestions; Jonathan Aves and Wendy Rosslyn, who read the manuscript at a later stage and suggested various alterations to the first and fourth chapters; and David Shepherd, who found time to go through the final draft despite a mass of other commitments. Gerry Smith was a source of many valuable bibliographical suggestions and encouraged the idea from an early stage; other very useful material came from Timothy Breen, Richard Davies, Paul Foote, Lindsey Hughes, Stephen Jones, Georgia Lagoumitzi, Patrick Newman, Adam Noble, Chris Pike, Tim Potts, Michael Pursglove, John Richmond, Don Roberts, Robert Russell, Nigel Thompson, David Walters and Faith Wigzell. Further enthusiastic and helpful comments were made by members of the Department of Russian Studies at the University of Manchester and the, sadly, now defunct Department of Russian Studies at the University of Reading. Amongst the experts on the popular theatre from whose knowledge I have especially benefited are Zoe Brooks of the Puppet Centre Trust, London; John Blundall of the Canon Hill Puppet Theatre in Birmingham; the staff of the Pollocks Toy Theatre Shop in London; and above all George Speaight, who placed his unique collection of materials on the puppet theatre at my disposal and who was also most generous with hospitality. I would also like to thank the following libraries and individuals: the staffs of the British Library, the National Art Library, the School of Slavonic and East European Studies, the Bodleian Library, Oxford, and especially Gregory Walker and C.C. Menzies, the Taylor Institution, especially David Howells, David Thomas, and Giles Barber, and Jackie Willcox of the Russian Centre Library, St Antony's College. My research on this book was supported financially by a Senior Scholarship and latterly a Junior Research Fellowship at Christ Church, Oxford: I am appreciative of the generosity of the Dean, Canons and Students of the college, and am grateful that they exercised more imagination about this project than the acquaintances who asked me, 'How on earth did you put *that* past *them*?' My writing of this book has been greatly helped by Ian Thompson's tolerance of carnivalesque reversals and upheavals in the domestic arena which must at times have seemed less than amusing; my parents Alexander and Margaret Kelly, and my sister Alison Davan Wetton have endured if not tolerated similar tribulations for a considerably longer period. Finally, I would like to thank two scholars in the Soviet Union from whose encyclopedic knowledge and very great kindness I have benefited over several years; my debt of gratitude is acknowledged, though hardly repaid, in the dedication.

Two section of the book have already appeared in rather different form: I should like to thank Macmillan Publishers, London, and the editors of the *Oxford Slavonic Papers*, for giving me permission to re-use this material.

I conclude by restating the traditional *mea culpa* formula: though this book has depended in large measure on collective creativity, I recognise that I, like every *balagan* operator, will be the one to face any rotten eggs.

A note on transliteration

The system used is British Standard 2979: 1958 without diacritics, as adopted by *Oxford Slavonic Papers*. It has the benefit of simplicity and familiarity, not requiring exceptions to be made for such well-known names as Yalta. Variant transliterations have of course been used in the titles of books or names of authors which differ on the title page of the original from this scheme (e.g. Iurii Lotman).

Unless otherwise stated all translations are my own.

Glossary

balagan Derived from the Persian *balahana*, balcony; perhaps cognate with English 'barbican'. It was originally used for warehouses or market sheds; from the early nineteenth century the word was transferred to the architecturally similar wooden constructions used as temporary theatres at fairs, and then (pejoratively) to the shows performed in them. Expressions like *balaganstvo* (*balagan*-ery) also had a contemptuous flavour.

chastushka Comic four-line rhyming verse, rather like a limerick.

Gaer Perhaps derived from the German *Geiger* (fiddler). 'The Russian Harlequin', as he called himself; a Hanswurst-like clown of ready wit and gross appetites, normally a servant who aids (or frustrates) his master's lustful intentions. Later generically (also in the feminine form, Gaerka) for a street clown.

gulyan'e (plural *gulyan'ya*), alternatively *narodnoe gulyan'e* A funfair, carnival or celebration; see the Introduction for detailed explanation.

intermediya (plural *intermedii*) A brief comic dramatic spectacle used as leavening before or between tragedies; cf. 'farce'; later performed individually in the 'democratic' (cheap and accessible to the populace) theatres and in the servants' theatres.

lubok A word used originally for a woodcut; later applied to any sort of print, including lithographs. They were sold at fairs and by peddlars wandering from village to village. *Lubochnaya kniga*, or lubok book (chapbook), was a term applied to cheap mass-circulation books.

raek Diminutive of *rai*, 'paradise'. Can mean *paradis* in the French sense, English 'the gods': the balcony in a theatre, but its standard fairground use was for a mobile peepshow (allegedly because the earliest displayed religious pictures of the Fall). Hence *raeshnyi stikh*, rhyming doggerel used by the operators of these shows and also by other fairground artistes (clowns and puppeteers).

school plays   Liturgical dramas performed by seminarians from the 1730s onwards, originally in Latin and later in Russian. Modelled on the Latin texts used by the Jesuits in Poland and the Ukraine for dissemination of the faith during the Counter-Reformation. (See also Karlinsky, *Russian Drama*, pp. 7–11.)

skomorokh   Etymology debated. The minstrel-buffoon entertainer of medieval Russia, later applied to any comic entertainer, including clowns at the fairground. (One of the Moscow popular theatres in the late nineteenth century was called the *Skomorokh* – see Doroshevich, *Sakhalin*, p. 130). The subject of many proverbs: 'Everyone can dance, but not like a *skomorokh*' (Dal', *Slovar' velikorusskogo yazyka*, IV, p. 203)

vertep (also called *betleika, szópka*)   Ukrainian, Belorussian and Polish miniature Christmas crib and hence a form of theatre in which Christmas crib figures are manipulated by rods in an open-fronted box (see also p. 54, illustration 6).

Abbreviations

Berkov: Berkov, P. N., *Russkaya narodnaya drama XVII–XX vekov: teksty p'es i opisaniya predstavlenii*, Moscow 1953.

FT: *Fol'klornyi teatr*, ed. A. F. Nekrylova and A. I. Savushkina, Moscow 1988 [actually 1989].

Grigorovich: Grigorovich, D. V., 'Peterburgskie sharmanshchiki', *Polnoe sobranie sochinenii v 12 tt*, St Petersburg 1896, I, pp. 5–29.

Mitcoff: Mitcoff, Elena (trans.), 'Petrushka', in Paul MacPharlin, *A Repertory of Marionette Plays*, New York 1929, pp. 291–300.

NP 1891: Anon., *Noveishii Petrushka, ili zabavnyi kloun*, pub. A. A. Ikonnikova, St Petersburg 1891.

P 1907: Anon., *Petrushka*, pub. A. D. Stupin, Moscow 1907.

P 1908: Anon., *Veselyi teatr Petrushki*, pub. I. D. Sytin, Moscow 1908.

P 1910: Anon., *Petrushka, narodnyi kukol'nyi geroi*, pub. E. Konovalov, Moscow 1910.

P 1915: Anon., *Petrushka, ulichnyi payats*, pub. Sytin, Moscow 1915.

RV: *Russkie vedomosti*, newspaper published Moscow 1863–1918.

Tarasov: Tarasov, G., *Petrushka v shkole i v pionerotryade*, Leningrad 1930.

TP: Eremin, Igor' and Tsekhnovitser, Orest, *Teatr Petrushki*, Moscow and Leningrad 1927.

VLB: Putintsev, A. M. (ed.), 'Van'ka, sovremennaya narodnaya kukol'naya komed'', *Voronezhskaya literaturnaya beseda*, I, 1925, 5–15.

Introduction

The Russian *Punch and Judy* show, *The Comedy of Petrushka*, was one of the most popular types of street theatre in Russia during the century between 1830 and 1930. It was known and performed in most Russian-speaking parts of the Russian Empire, from Odessa to Sakhalin, and its audience was composed of children and adults, rich and poor, peasants and proletariat, although its most characteristic spectators were the urban poor. 'The puppet theatres were more numerous [than any other type of entertainment] at the carnivals,' writes Yury Dmitriev; and Ivan Shcheglov confirms this:

No sir, Petrushka is not to be trifled with – he is still the fairground's favourite hero! Take a look, if you please; the thickest and most contented crowd is always the one by his booth; besides those standing, some of the more diminutive spectators are even sitting on other people's shoulders.[1]

The memoirs of painters, writers and other artists active around the turn of the century testify to the charm of *Petrushka*: Mstislav Dobuzhinsky, Sergey Yutkevich, Grigory Kozintsev, Andrey Bely and, most famously, Alexandre Benois, all did it homage (see particularly chapters 1 and 4).

Petrushka has considerable appeal also as an academic subject. All theatrical performances are necessarily ephemeral, popular theatrical performaces the more so, and we are confronted, as in all popular-cultural traditions, with 'the massive silences of the archives', in James Clifford's phrase.[2] But in the case of *Petrushka*, some artefacts have survived (a few puppets, for instance), which help to give some idea of what performances were like.[3] A series of variants of the show, mostly dating from the late nineteenth century, supplies verbal, as well as visual, material to work with. The *Petrushka* shows are some indication of the diversity of Russian popular culture, whilst conversely making its links with popular culture elsewhere in Europe clear, being a fascinating combination of Western European influences brought by Italian puppeteers, and the native comic tradition going back to the minstrels and buffoons of Old Russia.

I

The study of *Petrushka* can also make a contribution to the upsurge in interest in Russian urban popular culture, which has been manifested in particular by two excellent recent books, Anna Nekrylova's *Russkie narodnye gorodskie prazdniki*, on the Russian fairground, and Jeffrey Brooks' *When Russia Learned to Read*, on the cheap popular printed books of the late nineteenth century, and by A. M. Konechny's several articles and the exhibition on the Petersburg fairground which he organised at the Museum of the History of Leningrad in spring 1985.[4] The importance of the popular dramatic tradition cannot be overestimated, given the illiteracy which notoriously obtained in the Russian Empire.[5] The audiences for fairground and street theatre ran into millions; they outstripped by far the numbers who had access to printed material. At least until the late nineteenth century they were numerically the most important types of organised, professional entertainment. *Petrushka*, as a type of entertainment which was always nearly, and often entirely, free, reached particularly large numbers; and the place of its performance, directly among its audience, made it especially well suited to express the interests and frustrations of the urban poor. And until the 1860s it, the peepshows and the clowns' monologues were the only important types of spoken drama allowed on the fairground; most other shows were pageants and pantomimes with little dialogue.[6]

The importance of *Petrushka* extends outside its immediate context, for it inspired two traditions of drama outside the street. It was imitated by the high theatre: the Benois–Stravinsky ballet *Petrouchka* is arguably the most famous adaptation ever made of a Russian orally transmitted dramatic text. In the 1920s it, like other street genres, inspired many agitprop theatre spectacles and even whole agitprop theatre groups. And the significance of *Petrushka*, like other popular theatre genres, is explained by more than 'influence' in the sense of positive effect: throughout the nineteenth and twentieth centuries Russian high theatre, with very few exceptions, has striven to dissociate itself from popular entertainment, to be a rarified pastime for intellectuals. It is impossible to understand Russian drama if this struggle for dissociation is not taken into account; yet most commentators on the dramatic tradition have preserved the purview of Russian dramatists. Such insensitivity to the popular theatrical tradition is a flaw, for example, in Simon Karlinsky's recent book on Russian drama, which does an excellent job on reclaiming the minor works of the high theatre.[7]

My own interest in *Petrushka* came originally from my work on the high theatre, when I was studying neo-classical tragedies written by the Symbolists.[8] I began by asking myself why the Symbolists, whose enthusiasm for drama was proclaimed to derive from a desire to reach the masses (as in Vyacheslav Ivanov's essays on the theatre, for example), should have with few exceptions ignored the dramatic forms which would have made access to the masses most likely. When they did choose popular theatrical forms, many of them turned to non-Russian traditions, as Vsevolod Meyerhold did in his essay 'The Fairground Booth', which discusses the French and Italian medieval and Renaissance fairgrounds, but not the Russian fairground; or to Russian popular theatre of the distant past, as Aleksey Remizov did in his drama based on the 'School Plays'.[9] I then discovered that this contempt for or indifference to Russian popular theatre was very deep-rooted and by no means confined to the Symbolists. It led Mikhail Bakhtin, author of *François Rabelais and His World*, perhaps the best and most influential study of carnival in existence, to assert that Russia had never had carnivals in the Western sense:

The clearest, most classical carnival forms were preserved in Italy, especially in Rome. The next most typical carnivals were those of Paris. Next came Nuremburg, which adopted a more or less classical form at a somewhat later period. In Russia this process did not develop at all; the various aspects of folk merriment of a national or local character (shrove days, Christmas, fairs) remained unchanged. They offered none of the traits typical of Western European amusements. Peter the Great, as we know, tried to bring to Russia the later European style of the 'feast of fools' (for example, the election of the All-Clowns' Pope) and the pranks of the April fool, but these customs did not take root, and did not mix with local traditions.[10]

Bakhtin is right only in the two examples which he cites; a visit to any Russian fairground in the nineteenth or early twentieth century would have given him plenty of evidence that the rides, amusements and dramatic genres of the European fairground were represented in Russia, where they enjoyed popularity in no way inferior to their popularity in the West, and that, besides, carnival in an abstract sense – drunkenness, popular revelry, hedonism, and subversive celebration – was no less at home in Russia than elsewhere.

Bakhtin's indifference to Russian popular entertainments may have been prompted by prudence, given the date of his book on Rabelais.[11] There is no doubt that it is more benign than the crusading and hortatory attitude adopted by many of his compatriots. The difficulty of translating the term 'popular culture' into Russian is indicative of difference in attitude. And even if the coinage *popyulyarnaya kul' tura* were made, there would remain a problem, both aesthetic and political: the word *kul' tura* in Russian has not completed the meaning shifts which the word *culture* has accomplished in the West. As James Clifford has pointed out, since 1900 or so the word 'culture' has increasingly been used in a relativistic way, 'suggesting a world of separate, distinctive, and equally meaningful ways of life'; it has to a great extent lost its former sense of 'the outcome of a process of long development ... the basic, progressive movement of humanity'.[12] In the Soviet Union, however, belief in 'the basic, progressive movement of humanity' remains enshrined. Ethnographers use the word *kul' tura* to refer to intellectual activities only (in opposition to *byt*, or 'material culture'), and references to *kul' tura* in its relativistic meaning (such as 'meetings between two cultures') are found directly alongside references to *kul' tura* in a teleological or evolutionary sense ('the raising of cultural levels').[13] Though commentators now more readily admit the autonomy of popular culture, rather than dismissing it as existing on scraps discarded by the bourgeoisie (as Vsevolodsky-Gerngross did in 1929), commentary by Russian Soviet cultural observers remains all too often ethnocentric and imperialist (where relating to other cultures), elitist and hegemonic, dictated by the values of the cultural hegemony of educated intellectuals (where relating to their own).[14] The following passage, describing variations in living patterns between different groups of workers in the Urals before the Revolution, polarises 'bad' (not intellectualised) and 'good' (semi-intellectualised) workers:

Everything about the decoration – the crocheted [*garusnye*] napkins hung on the walls and scattered on the chests of drawers, the multitude of crudely glazed ceramic statuettes, shells and other such cheap fripperies, *lubok*-type lithographs on the walls, painted rugs of sacking from the market, primed and decorated with tasteless bouquets or 'fake parquet' – bears witness to the penetration of *petit-bourgeois* influences to the worker milieu ... The whole arrangement of the place in which the young worker lived indicated that he was a man with *fully developed cultural interests and requirements*. Besides the kind of furnishings typical for a highly skilled worker ... he had a writing desk with books and magazines on it ... there was a mass of quality literature in his trunk ... the walls were hung with pictures of writers in elaborate frames ... the room was lit with two high-powered kerosene lamps.[15]

A view of culture which is value-laden, if not teleological, is found more insidiously in writings which gesture towards ideological neutrality; in *The Semiotics of Russian Cultural History*, a collection of essays by Lotman, L. Ginzburg and Uspensky, examples are taken from high culture: the literary canon, fine art and the behaviour of the cultural elite.[16]

This is not to suggest that mistrust of popular culture is limited to critics in the Soviet Union. In the West, lip-service to relativism is certainly paid: as Carlo Ginzburg writes 'if only verbally we have now gone beyond ... the attitude which saw in the ideas, beliefs and world views of the lower classes nothing but an incoherent fragmentary mass of theories that had been originally worked out by the dominant classes perhaps many centuries before'.[17] There is now an exemplary corpus of work on Western popular culture, especially of the early modern period.[18] But as far as studies relating to Russia and the Soviet Union go, some battles won years ago in other subject areas remain as yet unfought. The following hilariously reactionary comments were made by a Western critic writing not, as one might suppose, in 1886, but in *1986*:

It is unhappily the case that the masses of the people – even in a political democracy, let alone an autocracy – make very minor contributions to political history. In a real sense it makes very little difference what the people happen to think at a given moment, whereas the values of the high culture as they affect the views of those in political power are very much worth analysing. It is difficult to see that the most intricate analyses of the readership, say, of detective novels and the ramifications of their plots could help scholars a hundred years in the future to understand the course of American History today.[19]

Even Rose Glickman, in her excellent study of women factory workers in the nineteenth century, *Russian Factory Women*, seems unaware of the realities of popular entertainment in Russian cities:

The squalor and poverty of the Russian workers' lives, the long hours of arduous labour for which they were so miserably remunerated, left them with little time, energy or money for recreation. Nor were amusements and social amenities readily accessible. The rich cultural offerings of the cities were inaccessible and possibly not much to their taste. Even simpler pleasures were hard to come by.[20]

Western studies of Russian popular culture have to date also been dogged by an occasionally unreflective adoption of quantitative methods of analysis and a tendency to treat the material of popular culture *uncritically*, as if it spoke for itself.[21] Central theoretical issues remain unresolved. There has, for example, been a reluctance to make any distinction between popular culture and culture for the people, mass entertainment, a lack of sense that 'it is absurd to equate "the culture produced by the popular classes" with "the culture imposed on the masses"'.[22] The distinction between cultural phenomena where the subordinate or popular classes were actively involved in and responsible for production, and those in which they were not, needs to be made, even if it is blurred in practice by the fact that members of the subordinate classes were capable of new interpretations and appropriations of the improving works designed for their consumption by outsiders. One theatre activist described with chagrin how a production of *Anna Karenina* drew vast crowds attracted not by the literary merits of the spectacle but by the prospect of seeing the heroine throw herself under the locomotive.[23]

Despite the importance of *Petrushka* as a popular-cultural genre, it too, like other kinds of Russian popular culture, has been the subject of dismissive hauteur on the one hand, non-commitment in theoretical terms on the other. The Soviet theatrical activist Tarasov writes:

Previously, when Petrushka was still very popular, few educated people paid him any attention. *Nor did he deserve that they should have done: the contents of his comedy were uninteresting, and the text was characterised by crudity and improper language.* (Tarasov 29; my emphasis)

Elsewhere we hear that *Petrushka* was 'the favourite spectacle of an *undemanding* public' (VLB 3; my emphasis). Even Nina Simonovich-Efimova, a puppeteer of great skill and so committed to her occupation that she was still finishing a costume for her own puppet theatre as she lay on her deathbed, wrote that 'it is impossible to reproach the *Petrushka* plays with anything *except a certain lack of content*'.[24]

Academic study of *Petrushka* has also been limited. There is no book on the subject in English, though Elizabeth Warner's *The Russian Folk Theatre* and Russell Zguta's *Russian Minstrels* have sections on it.[25] Even in Russian there has so far been no full-length study of the text, though several informative articles have appeared, amongst the best of which are those in the volume *Teatr Petrushki*, by Orest Tsekhnovitser and Igor' Eremin. The book was intended as a manual for practising puppeteers, but the articles on *Petrushka* are excellent scholarly studies; that by Eremin gives valuable information on textual variants. Recently this work has been supplemented by a series of articles written by the Soviet scholar Anna Nekrylova, who wrote her dissertation on *Petrushka*. Some factual areas, however, require elucidation: amongst these are the connection between Petrushka and Western European puppet theatre, and the fate of the text after the Revolution. The only source of information on the latter is Natalia Smirnova's book on the Soviet puppet theatre, which, however, concludes at 1932.[26]

In this book I hope to fill in some of the gaps left. I shall try to explain how the *Petrushka* street tradition was caught in a pincer movement between economic and cultural reforms in the 1930s; I shall also give a fuller account of its history and its links with the Western street glove-puppet theatre – the resemblance between Petrushka and Punch, Pulcinella, Polichinelle, Guignol. I shall give a more detailed description and analysis of the text than has been attempted before, and a fuller account of its audience and the circumstances in which it was performed. As important as these points of detail, however, is the need to clarify the theoretical principles according to which *Petrushka* is studied. Study of *Petrushka* has suffered, like other forms of popular culture, from a certain lack of direction. The studies have tended to be of a descriptive rather than an analytical character. Sometimes an overtly tendentious rhetoric is adopted (as by Smirnova); more often the material is marginalised by emphasising that it is of purely ethnographical interest. It has been accepted by one commentator after another that this text is 'folklore', and that the methods suitable for its study are structural analysis and speculation about distant ritual origins. Individual objections to and reservations about these approaches will be dealt with later; at the moment I shall simply give a broad outline of my own orientations.

I think it is as well to make clear why I prefer to describe *Petrushka* as a popular-cultural text, rather than a folkloric one, as it has been described by previous commentators. I do so not out of disrespect for the academic study of folklore, which has evolved methodologies vital in the recording, classification and interpretation of orally transmitted material; on these I shall myself draw. My objections are not operational, but ideological. Whilst aware of the dangers of the term 'popular culture', which Peter Burke has described as both too inclusive and too exclusive,[27] I am determined to use it for several important reasons. First, because I am studying it as part of the entire cultural system rather than as an autonomous phenomenon. The folklorist Dan Ben-Amos has argued that it is time folklore was accepted as 'a sphere of interaction in its own right'.[28] I respect this statement of scholarly independence; but, for my part, I intend to study *Petrushka* in conjunction with other material, not all of which can be accommodated by the most elastic definitions of folklore. By using the term 'popular culture', and opposing to it the term 'high culture', I also indicate my views of divisions within the cultural system, which are not, I believe, opposed in a clear-cut and mutually exclusive way. I avoid the word 'folklore' because it is easily and conventionally opposed to 'literature', as for example in Roman Jakobson and Pavel Bogatyrev's famous essay 'Die Folklore als eine besondere Form des Schaffens', where 'literature' (individual, original, transcendent of time and social convention and expectation) is in every way the mirror-image of 'folklore' (collective, conventional, ephemeral, or subordinate to time, and obedient to 'preventive censorship', that is, forced to cater to the whims of its audience).[29] It seems to me that an important conceptual confusion has arisen here, for an ideologically neutral distinction between oral and written discourse has been mapped onto a far from neutral division between intellectual and popular creation. Despite the difference in medium of transmission, a folk-tale has more in common with a chapbook or broadsheet than it does with an after-dinner speech in an Oxford college, however liberally laced with anecdotes the latter, and the reasons why, say, *War and Peace* is not seen to be ephemeral have to do with more than the manner of textual dissemination. In Russian culture, for a variety of historical reasons, the creations and values of the elite have been as dependent on oral transmission as have those of the people; yet in spite of – or even because of – this similarity, literature and other forms of high culture have, at least since Westernisation, been set apart and specially revered.[30]

The terms 'popular culture' and 'high culture' are meant also to give equal weight to both sides, since I believe that debate about primacy of one tradition or the other is empty and sterile. It is meaningless to argue about whether high cultural ideas 'sink down' into the popular classes or, conversely, folkloric traditions go 'upwards' into the educated classes.[31] The relationship is circular, and not just in individual cases or from epoch to epoch. Within a given culture at any moment, the popular tradition may articulate assumptions directly which are buried in high culture; whilst members of the cutural elite may draw on popular tradition as a form of escape, refuge or legitimation strategy.

The preference of 'popular culture' over 'folklore' indicates also a concern with immediate contexts and historical facts rather than with remote origins or with tradition. Dan Ben-Amos has argued that 'the traditional character of folklore is an analytical construct; it is a scholarly and not a cultural fact'.[32] I do not disagree; but I think that the use of the word 'tradition' has dangers. When Herbert Halpert, for example, gives a working definition of folklore as 'traditional cultural lore ... transmitted traditionally rather than by official sources; [consisting] of ideas which find various forms of expression, in sounds, actions, or objects',[33] it is possible to assume that he refers only to a process of communication, but often the word 'tradition' implies much more. A recent volume in the Penguin Folklore Library stated that the interests of its compilers were in 'how the inherent values or oral literature should be communicated for the benefit of humanity'; whilst, more recently still, a series of letters in the *Guardian* discussing the custom by which British children are encouraged to leave discarded milk teeth under their pillows for the 'tooth fairy' in exchange for small coins attracted a heated missive from a representative of the Folklore Society. The correspondent insisted that this was not folklore, but 'fakelore', and the writer concluded 'we seem better at preserving our old stones and bones than our traditional beliefs and customs'.[34] As this letter suggests, closely allied to respect for tradition is emphasis on the 'purity' of the folkloric text, which has led some folklorists to underestimate the cross-fertilisation from printed genres to oral genres, some others to despise the collection of material which is impure in a more specific sense, that is, obscene. Over the last thirty years attitudes amongst Western folklorists have become more pluralist, partly because of an impelling sense that if principles were too rigidly applied there would be nothing left to collect at all; but in the Soviet Union obscenity is still kept out of sight and outpourings of contempt for 'vulgar' or '*petit-bourgeois*' genres remain more frequent than study of or commentary on them.[35]

Petrushka is not particularly old and certainly not particularly pure; it offers little comfort to those in search of folk wisdom or traditional moral values, and by the exacting standards defined above can only be described as 'degenerate' unless much of the text is passed over in silence. In order to avoid critical reduction, therefore, we must use notions such as 'morals' or 'purity' with caution. Equally, we must

take the notion of context beyond the rather cosy family or extended
family circle which is posited in some studies of 'folklore'. Take this
description of a Scottish traveller–storyteller for example:

With Betsy [his daughter] dozing on his lap and Linda [his wife] lovingly
looking after Thomas, both my ten-year-old daughter Heather and I have sat
hours on end spellbound as Duncan has taken us into his special world of
wonder and magic.[36]

The introduction to a recently published collection of Irish folk-tales
describes a typical tale-telling beside a turf fire, where the warm
atmosphere of male bonding over whiskey is increased in effect by
its contrast with the 'wild night' raging outside.[37] Dan Ben-Amos'
statement that folklore is performed in 'small group situations' is
apparently more clinical, but depends just as much on a model of
social consensus and harmony.[38]

It is not my business to decide how adequate these idyllic pictures
are to the conditions in which rural popular culture operates or
operated; but I believe that urban popular entertainments belonged to
rather a different world. They were often defiant, constrained not so
much by 'preventive censorship' as by the desire to breach censorship.
The 'small groups' which watched them lacked the cohesion set down
by Dan Ben-Amos as a primary requirement for the transmission of
folklore, that 'the participants in the small group situation have to
belong to the same reference group, one composed of people of the
same age or of the same professional, local, religious or ethnic
affiliation'.[39] The groups watching fairground dramas were not
always united by all of these features (there was usually a variety of
ages and professions, if not of ethnos or creed); they were, moreover,
invariably divided by a feature ignored by Dan Ben-Amos, that of
gender. It was possible, as we shall see, for fairground performances to
single out certain members of the group (such as ethnic minorities or
women) for abuse, in order to reassure others (dominant ethnic
groups and men). The 'small-group' labelling cannot reflect such
contradictions and conflicts. Nor can it reflect the conflicts, which
were equally important on the fairground, between one 'small group'
and others; indeed, such conflicts are explicitly avoided in the statement 'the connotations of marginality and low socio-economic status
that were once associated with the term "folk" have been aban-
doned'.[40] The final reason for avoiding the term 'folklore', therefore,
is because it suggests a classless society; the watchers of *Petrushka*

were socio-economically deprived, they *were* culturally marginalised; they were not indifferently composed 'small groups', but members of the popular or *subordinate classes*. As we shall see, this term is itself a generalisation, a construct, but a more politically explicit one than 'the small group'. It is impossible not to agree with Carlo Ginzburg that 'a concept of class structure, however generally conceived, is still a big advance over classlessness'.[41]

The reason why I feel that it is important that the *Petrushka* texts should be removed from the domain of folklore and ethnography is not – heaven forbid – because I argue that they should be judged by high-literary criteria and will be redeemed when these are applied, nor is it that I am concerned to lament the popular theatre in a spirit of aestheticising nostalgia. Nor do I believe that the Russian carnival and street theatre had transcendentally subversive qualities which were invulnerable to the world outside. As in any other country, in Russian popular entertainment has always hovered between subversion and conformity, alternately encouraged by the 'bread and circuses' cast(e) of thought and put down by those fearing its seditious potential. The ecclesiastical authorities in Russia were consistently opposed to popular entertainment as practised there; the secular authorities were aware that it could be channelled for their purposes. The following quotations, selected from statements made by government and opposition in Russia over nearly two hundred years, indicate the swings in attitude:

People singing and dancing think no evil.   (Catherine II)

The Russian common people will understand that His Imperial Majesty entered the *balagan* precisely in order to take part in the merriment of his people.   (The reactionary Bulgarin)

Many frivolous visitors are persuaded that life consists in nothing other than these amusements. Even those in the farthest-flung provinces share this view. I leave the reader to judge how mistaken it is. But at the same time I, for my part, maintain that our life really is an endless holiday with music, national dancing and fireworks. The difference between my view and that of frivolous visitors is in essence insignificant and can be expressed by changing a word or two. They are convinced that our life *should* consist of endless festivities; but I maintain that it *does* consist of endless festivities.
                                        (The radical writer V. Sleptsov)

How, we venture to ask, do clowns amuse their public? With words, of course. And do they speak in public? They do. And so why does no one [in authority]

take account of what they say and do? Who has given them the right to speak like this? There is only one answer: they have given it to themselves.
(Anonymous article in *Dnevnik russkogo teatra*, 1880s, demanding the extension of theatrical censorship to clowns)

Circuses? Who needs them?
(N. M. Kishkin, representative of the Provisional Government, 1917)

Many people are convinced that we can overcome the difficulties and dangers of the present *panem et circenses* (with bread and spectacles). With bread – of course! As far as spectacles go, by all means let's have them – I've no objection. But at the same time we mustn't forget that spectacles are not genuine great art; they are, rather, a more or less attractive type of enter-tainment.   (Lenin)[42]

It is the fairground's dubious status in which I am interested. The fairground dramas were difficult for the authorities, for they always hovered at the bounds of acceptability, and much of the time went over the top. There was always a possibility that a large public gathering might turn from a celebration into a riot, a possibility foreseen by legislation classifying entertainment and social disorder together. Besides, they were offensive not only to political, but also to moral authority, manifesting what has been called 'the politics of hierarchy inversion as a ritual strategy on the part of subordinate groups'.[43] The word *inversion* is significant: the fairground genres did not undermine the idea of hierarchy, they set another up in its place. It is no great political change to have a fool as king if that fool-king comports himself as despotically as the authority he has replaced. Carnival genres lack the seamlessness, the intellectual coherence, of satire; they are offensive to educated liberals and reactionaries alike.

The carnival genres are untrustworthy, they tend to stab the enlightened sentimentalist in the back. Nonetheless I believe not that they invariably *were* a vehicle of political protest, but that they *could be*. This is why I have studied the demise of *Petrushka* and other street genres after 1917. I have shown how Bolshevik cultural policy was not dictated by admiration for popular culture, but by a commitment to making high culture accessible to the masses or by awareness of the popular culture as a short-term political instrument. I have shown how popular entertainment was centralised and regulated, and how the history of pre-revolutionary entertainment was adjusted to legiti-mise the process. For example, it is frequently asserted, as a reproach, that there were no 'professional' puppeteers before the Revolution.[44]

This does the street theatre a disservice; there certainly were, in the sense of people who earned their living by puppetry, though not in the sense that they had sinecured posts, with retirement pensions, in centralised state-run institutions. Given this mistrust of the raw material, it is no accident that most forms of street theatre are no longer extant in the Soviet Union, that genuine busking is rarely practised, and that the only fairground entertainment which has survived in anything like its pre-revolutionary form is the circus.[45]

Again, I stress that I do not want to whitewash the pre-revolutionary fairground tradition. It is clear from surviving descriptions that the showmen suffered hardships: semi-starvation, cold, homelessness, sickness and injury. The shows they gave were sometimes awful. This no doubt applied to the *Petrushka* show too, though it is worth bearing in mind that whilst any fool can get out on stage and affect to act, it takes a certain amount of skill and nerve to make puppets and perform with them, even at an execrable level.

The organisation of the book is chronological, beginning with *Petrushka*'s appearance in Russia, and concluding with the last recorded performances. The first three chapters discuss the character of the show as performed on the streets and the fairgrounds of Russia, the last two the literary and agitprop appropriations of the text. As the title of the book suggests, I shall use material about the fairground in general, and the other dramatic genres played there, in order to put *Petrushka* in context. The main points covered are as follows. Chapter 1 will deal with the history of the Russian fairground, with particular reference to the changes which occurred in the late 1830s, when foreign showmen, among them the puppeteers, began to be replaced by Russians; a brief description of the urban subordinate classes, from which the audience and performers of *Petrushka* were drawn, is also given. The subject of chapter 2 is the structure and comic devices of *Petrushka*, with a study of carnival elements in the text, of chapter 3 the links of *Petrushka* with the Western puppet theatre and with other types of Russian popular humour. Chapters 4 and 5 deal with appropriations of the text by outsiders, the earlier chapter with high culture and the carnival text, the later with *Petrushka* in the agit-prop theatre and with what happened to the street tradition.

One of the most difficult, but one of the most crucial, aspects of the subject is what to use as source material. Unfortunately, the best way of finding out what a street theatre show is like – watching it and talking to the showman – is not a possibility, since *Petrushka* showmen, if they still exist at all, are elusive. So one is in the questionable position of relying on recorded versions of the text.

The *Petrushka* texts began to be recorded in the late nineteenth century, as I stated earlier. But unfortunately the collection was at first not systematic. In the 1920s the Sokolov brothers published a manual containing excellent advice on how to record puppet theatre texts, but it came too late; within ten years the *Petrushka* tradition was gone.[46] Of all the thousands of performances given during the nineteenth century, only about thirty texts survive. The majority of these are still held in archives and are unlikely to be published in full. For this study, I had available to me the following texts: a text published in the nineteenth century, which appears in Grigorovich's sketch 'The Petersburg Organ-Grinders'; two texts recorded in the early twentieth century from the puppeteers Lashchenko (in 1902) and Shumsky (undated), published in the Soviet Union in 1953 and 1903 respectively, Berkov and Tarasov (the latter is unfortunately bowdlerised); five *Petrushka* texts published in cheap large print-run editions between 1891 and 1915; a post-revolutionary street text in the traditional mould, published in 1925; an English version of *Petrushka* of dubious authenticity, published in the USA in 1929.[47] This relatively scanty information I have supplemented by reference to quotations from and descriptions of unpublished versions in articles by Soviet scholars; and by accounts by educated observers, both Russian intellectuals and Western travellers.

This study of *Petrushka*, therefore, has the same drawbacks as many other studies of popular culture: it is dependent on material collected by outsiders. Many of them were superficial and unobservant in their descriptions; one comes across many accounts like the following from *Russkie vedomosti* in 1890:

From the Friday of Shrove Week the carnival at Devich'e Field has been especially lively because work at factories and in workshops came to an end on Thursday evening and working people are hastening to make use of the last days of Shrove which they have free, and to avail themselves of those *cheap entertainments which are available for them in abundance in the booths and theatres placed there. The same kind of entertainments are attracting a public made up of the grey masses* on Tsvetnoi Boulevard; here the crowds of people, especially in the evening, are sometimes so thick that it is hard to make one's way through them.[48]

The frustrations of reading such accounts, when what one needs is an enumeration of the 'cheap entertainments' which the genteel writer is too squeamish to record, are considerable. It is necessary to reconcile oneself with a collection of source material which is, at best, imperfect. Often one is dependent on hostile accounts, where popular culture is condemned, for any information about it at all. Undue despondency is unnecessary, however. It is worth bearing in mind Carlo Ginzburg's observation that 'the fact that a source is not "objective" . . . does not mean that it is useless'.[49] There are also important ways in which the various accounts complement each other. The Western travellers were less familiar with what they observed and could not give it a history, but on the other hand often described events in detail which native Russians were too blasé or contemptuous to record, or which they did not wish to record because they were concerned to present Russia as equal in high-cultural achievements to the countries of Western Europe, not to stress how quaintly folkloric it was. Since fewer of the Western travellers were engaged in pressing for social reforms in Russia, they tended to be more ready to admit that the subordinate classes occasionally had fun. Many Russian observers, on the other hand, belonged to the class which Peter Keating has termed 'social explorers': that is, full of good intentions to improve the hideous lot of their inferiors, and convinced that any light in the dark picture would threaten its propaganda effect.[50]

Most importantly, I am unrepentant about my use of educated sources since they represent the other side of cultural conflict, the marginalising, as well as the marginal sources. The statements of the 'social explorers' and commentators are to be looked *at*, as well as through; they do not so much help to fill the gaps in the history of popular culture as indicate how popular culture filled gaps for the observers, representing for some a nightmare drama of how the uncivilised masses were about to bring down the world, for others a source of easy charity and pity. This applies as much to non-fictional accounts, such as those by Gilyarovsky, as to the fictional accounts by Chekhov, Dostoevsky and Dal' – indeed, the distinction between fiction and non-fiction is often blurred, most especially in the genre of *ocherk*, or sketch. Finally, the written accounts of puppet-show observers can contribute as much to understanding the literary appropriations of *Petrushka* as they can to the history of its performance on the street.

I hope that this book will appeal to those generally interested in the street puppet theatre and in Russian cultural history as well as to Slavists. I have therefore translated all prose and puppet texts. Rather than strict literalism, I have attempted renderings which convey the puns and jokes of the original, and the doggerel in which it is partly written. Appendix A is a translation of the whole of one *Petrushka* street text, for the use of readers who know no Russian, and appendix B is a compendium of laws and regulations dealing with popular entertainment from before and after the Revolution.

Key terms which have been used in Russian throughout the text appear in a short glossary (*balagan*, etc.). Two terms deserve comment at a little greater length here: 'funfair' and 'carnival'. Russian has two terms which overlap with these: *yarmarka*, which actually means a trade fair, and *narodnoe gulyan' e*, literally 'a popular walking', from the verb *gulyat'*, which means to walk, to have a joy ride, to have fun, or to get drunk. (It can also be to skive off work, not necessarily doing any of these things.) The *yarmarki* were associated with buying and selling; they had a major economic role in Russia until they were abolished in the early 1930s. But the larger ones usually had funfairs attached. The words *narodnye gulyan'ya* might signify certain rustic entertainments, such as dancing round maypoles, or tearing round the countryside in a sledge, but the term was also used for the big seasonal funfairs which happened in towns and villages outside Russia. To save trouble, the English words funfair and carnival have been used interchangeably for the entertainments sections at the *yarmarki* and the urban funfairs; funfair refers to the rides, spectaculars, popular and popularising entertainments in general, carnival specifically to the popular acts and associated celebrations.

Throughout the book, whilst trying to be as informative as possible, I have borne in mind that *Petrushka* is funny and entertaining. I have tried to bring this across with ample quotation. At the same time, a valedictory or polemical tone has occasionally been unavoidable. Like the sixteenth century as described by Ginzburg, the era after the Revolution was one of 'renewed effort to achieve hegemony' and 'repression and effacement of popular culture'.[51] *Petrushka*, like most of the other fairground spectacles, went out of existence and has not reappeared. As Simon Dreiden wrote in 1955: 'These days old hunchback Petrushka warms his bruised and battered bones in peace, in the showcases of museums. New puppets have come to take his place. A new theatre has risen on the ashes of the *balagan*. New feelings and thoughts inspire the creations of Soviet artists.'[52] The old fairgrounds are gone, and have been succeeded by the technically superb but undisturbing entertainments of the centralised circuses and puppet theatres, and by the battered shooting-ranges, rusting dodgems and pseudo-rustic ice-cream parlours which make up organised popular entertainment, the misnamed 'attractions', in many Soviet provincial towns today. The argument of this book is not that the decarnivalisation of Soviet society is unique, nor that it is necessarily irreversible.[53] Rather, I am concerned to emphasise the process of struggle and conflict after which hegemony was achieved, to argue that it was not the result of a seamless and organic progress towards coherence and maturity, where 'life had introduced decisive correctives' making good the mistakes of the past.[54]

Postscript, June 1989

After I completed the manuscript of this book the anthology *Fol'klornyi teatr* (FT), the first important collection of Russian folk and popular theatre to appear in nearly forty years, was published in Moscow. It contains three previously unpublished texts of *Petrushka*, two recorded in or near Petersburg in 1896 and 1903, and one recorded in Troitse-Sergiev *posad*, near Moscow, in 1898. All three variants have been commented on and quoted by I. Eremin and A. F. Nekrylova in articles on *Petrushka*, but I have added two or three brief new observations to the discussion of variants and textual transmission in chapter 2. The new anthology is a popular rather than a scholarly edition: the three texts contain omissions, probably bowdlerisations, and there is little new information on the transcription history or on the biographies of the puppeteers.

1

Petrushka and the fairground

The Russian funfairs

Few things are as colourful and charming as a fairground at full tilt, overwhelming every sense with blaring music, deafening mechanical squeals, lurid colours and lights and the mingled smell of fast food and recently dried varnish. The Russian funfairs, though less elegant (it was said) than their Italian or French counterparts, were every bit as appealing. The sensual impressions they made, as Ivan Shcheglov, an activist in the People's Theatre movement, recalled in the late nineteenth century, were unforgettable:

> But inside the circle [of the fairground] – good heavens, what goes on inside the circle! You can hardly take it in, let alone describe it. First, the music – truly, the music alone could deprive someone who'd just arrived of his senses, because the point is that it's not *the* music, it's all sorts of music – several kinds together, and your ears are deafened simultaneously by a satanic compound of wind and strings, steam and barrel organs, accordions, with the classic squeal of 'Petrushka' rising above all, in place, as it were, of a tuning fork . . . And then there are the cries of the men and women selling things . . . They are shouting now quite differently from the way they usually shout in streets and markets, with a sort of special frenzy, until tears come into their eyes and they go hoarse.[1]

The Russian fairgrounds offered a range of entertainments equal to any in Europe: swings, roundabouts, roller-coasters, puppet shows, dancing bears, acrobatics and clowns inside wooden booths and on the street, Harlequinades and sleigh rides, stalls with drinks and gingerbread. Between the late eighteenth century and the Revolution a visit to these fairs was a nearly obligatory item on the itinerary of foreign visitors to Russia, and many of them have left vivid accounts of what they saw there. A German visitor wrote in the 1840s:

> There are booths with clever horses and stupid people doing tricks, with bears and boxers, apes and actors; there are big and little roundabouts, Russian swings and ordinary ones, and two ice hills as well, if the weather is still cold

enough at Easter; sellers of brandy, nuts and gherkins, Prenniks [= *pryaniki*, spiced gingerbread], and kvas [small beer made from fermented bread and water], *kislie shchi* [fizzy kvas] and spun sugar, apples and sausage, spice cakes and pig's tripe, carob, pickled herrings and rotten apples – and bread and cakes and music here, there and everywhere. You can see trick riding and beheadings followed by resurrections, giantesses and dwarfs, boring trans-formation scenes with a Taglioni look-alike; and lately entrepreneurial interests have brought in roundabouts with steam-boats and steam-trains, which have done very well despite the simple naivety of the general public.[2]

A more eloquent tribute still was made by Alexandre Benois, for whom, in emigration, the fairgrounds represented the lost world of his Russian childhood, where the sun always shone and food and drink were always abundant:

In front of us is the main avenue of the fairground. To our right stretches a row of massive structures, clad in freshly-planed, sweet-smelling pine-planks which sparkle in the sunlight. On the other side stand smaller huts of varied size, arranged higgledy-piggledy, at random ... And among the small huts are a few miserable little theatres, but for the most part the square on that side is covered with roundabouts, ice-hills and countless stalls where you can buy all sorts of tasty things to eat: gingerbread, nuts, pea-pods, lollies, bunches of mint, sunflower seeds, and also *baranki, saiki, kalachi* [types of biscuit and fancy bread] ... Next door, exposed to the open air, are tables covered with hundreds of glasses from which you can drink your fill of hot tea boiled up in fat teapots with big-eyed flowers on them and diluted with boiling water from the gigantic samovars.[3]

With such a heavy input of nostalgia and a sense of the exotic, it is not surprising that recollections of the Russian funfairs often have a mythical flavour, and that a much subdued role is played by the unpleasant aspects of the fair, of which there were certainly some. Having a good time, as always in Russia, was linked with the consumption of large quantities of alcohol, which led to unaesthetic sights of sprawling comatose bodies and to minor injuries: 'At no other time are there so many accidents as in [Shrove] Week. Drunks crash into each other every instant, so that the climax to the occasion is usually adorned by broken and bloody heads.'[4]

At times the celebrations led to greater disasters. Russian fairs were sometimes held on the ice of frozen rivers, which had obvious dangers if a sudden thaw set in. The tipsy revellers did not last long in icy water.[5] The wooden structures of the theatres were highly inflamma-ble, and although there were regulations ensuring that fire-fighting equipment was accessible at all times and that a reasonable space was

1. The fire in Leman's *balagan*. Admiralty Square, 2 February 1836. Magazine illustration.

left between individual buildings, occasionally there were conflag-
rations. In 1836 Legat's big fairground theatre in St Petersburg
burned down with the loss of over a hundred lives.[6] The rides
themselves might be dangerous, especially the ice-hills or roller-
coasters. Crowd management was also a problem, and the good
organisation required by the presence of so many people was sometimes lacking. The fair held at Khodynka Field for the Tsar's
coronation in 1896, of which the high point was the distribution of
coronation mugs, and which ended in tragedy when thousands were
crushed to death, is a horrific example of what might happen when
organisation was slack.[7]

The fairground celebrations might represent a threat to property as
well as to person. As in any crowded place, there was always the risk
here of pickpockets, who might employ ingenious strategies to achieve
their aims. During the celebrations of the bicentenary of St Petersburg, for example, some cutpurses are said to have fomented a
stampede by yelling, 'The tigers are out!'[8] Those who returned home
with their possessions intact might well find that other thieves had
made use of the festival season in order to give their attention to
empty flats and houses.[9] There was also a risk of 'losing one's money'
in the colloquial Russian sense – that is, of wasting it. The sideshows
offered were not always very appealing. Some were badly done and
boring. Ivan Shcheglov recalled watching a dire spectacle at a village
fair in the 1890s in which two children pushed their heads through a
cardboard painted background, seaside-photographer style, and
carried on a dialogue of extraordinary ineptness.[10] Other more
cynical showmen shamelessly ripped off the public. One of the most
outrageous cheats was a very popular sideshow in which the performance of a cannibal was advertised. The cannibal, it was given out,
would first eat a hen and then a person. The spectators packed in;
when the first part of the show had ended, they waited expectantly for
the second to begin. It was announced that the cannibal would eat . . .
a volunteer from the audience. Audiences flocked back and back,
hoping someone would be foolhardy enough to agree, but in vain.[11]
Like the fleamarkets of Moscow, the fairgrounds were places run on
the principle of 'ne naduesh' – ne prodash' ('you don't trick 'em – you
don't move it'), rather than on observation of ethics.[12]

On the other hand, there is no doubt that one of the reasons for the
great popularity of the fairground was the sense of threat, the
ambivalent sensations, which visits there engendered. The fairground

rides gave their users a feeling of exhilarating danger; young bloods would spurn the safety carts provided on the ice hills in favour of a more thrilling descent on toboggans.[13] There is no doubt also that the very possibility of losing money attracted people, that there were always some willing to try their luck against impossible odds in the sideshows.[14] There was also a sense of calculated risk in a sexual sense, for, as elsewhere in Europe, the fairgrounds were – especially after dark – places of encounter. In the evenings the entertainments at Nizhnii-Novgorod became the haunt of prostitutes, as a late nine-teenth-century American observer recorded with disapproval:

> It is not until night that the amusements can be seen in full swing in the various quarters of the fair, and particularly in the Kunavino suburb, which the guide-books forbid ladies to visit. This prohibition need not be regretted by our fair readers, for in these tabooed establishments they would only hear very wretched music, see very slow and gloomy dancing, and scarcely be repaid for their trouble by the privilege of making acquaintance with the very peculiar refinements of toilet indulged in by Tatar women.[15]

Nor, it seems, was sexual activity restricted to those who could pay for it; the conception rate during the Shrovetide season was the highest in the year, and the rise was yet more marked amongst extramarital conceptions.[16]

Besides being attracted by the slight sense of threat, audiences were drawn to the fairground by the licence which prevailed there. If the fairground was a place where one might encounter noisy drunks, it was also a place where one might get noisily drunk. Commercial sharp practice was sometimes less an exploitation of the innocent than a contest between equals, a test of wits between showman and punter in which bargaining skills were displayed on both sides, and in which the emphasis might be on mental or verbal dexterity rather than on material gain. Visitors to the fairground made very much what they wanted of it; some recalled the place afterwards as a safe Arcadia, others created an equally potent mythology of an immoral underworld.

Those who attended the fairground spectacles also had the titillat-ing sensation of being close to legal prohibitions, if not beyond them, for public entertainments were hedged about with a mesh of petty regulations. Fistfights, one of the more popular entertainments, were illegal; shouting, swearing and excessive noise might all lead to trouble.[17] If things really got out of hand, noisy revellers might be charged with 'breach of the peace' or 'riotousness'.[18] For their part, the authorities were caught in ambivalent uncertainty, conscious on the one hand of the need to allow some letting of steam and on the other of the very real dangers to order which the fairground presented. The first impulse led to the organisation of grandiose celebrations in order to mark official occasions, such as coronations, the anniversary of the Emancipation of the Serfs, the opening of the Gorodskaya Duma in St Petersburg and the bicentenary of the founding of the city.[19] The coronation funfairs were especially large and opulent: for Alexander II's on 30 August 1856, 600 tables were set out on Khodynka field in Moscow, and in the middle were eight fountains, four roller-coasters, a circus, a temporary theatre, a landing-stage for a hot-air balloon and two arbours for musicians.[20] But the other impulse, the need to keep order, was equally strong, and so the funfairs were placed under the especial supervision of the police, who gave permission for them to take place and who might censor items which attracted official disapproval. Even so, disasters were not always avoided; in 1914, for example, young people at the Palm Week Fair in Moscow orchestrated what were described as 'shocking acts disruptive to public order and decorum'.[21]

Another factor in the authorities' complex of attitudes to funfairs was the great profitability of these events. The entertainments which took place at the trade fairs provided recreational facilities for economically vital occasions; the Nizhnii-Novgorod fair in particular was a lynchpin of domestic and foreign trade.[22] At the funfairs the amount of buying and selling done was relatively insignificant, since what was on offer was a selection of toys, fancy goods and jumble, but the entertainments themselves were a potential source of revenue. The larger showmen had to pay for their sites, and often the prices charged were exorbitant; they were, moreover, subject to a progressive levy on ticket prices, used to fund institutions of poor relief.[23]

In many ways the social role of the Russian carnival celebrations was similar to that of carnivals all over Europe. But the particular charm of the entertainments themselves was the mixture of native and imported elements. To the first belonged the peasants in bright festival clothes, the traditional snacks of sunflower seeds, pickled cucumber, pine-nuts and *pirozhki*. There were the stalls with wooden and clay toys, and the time-honoured amusements of Russian swings (which were made of a long plank, rather like a see-saw, hanging from a rope), ice-hills (adopted later by other countries in Europe, and known as *montagnes russes* in France, *montañas rusas* in Spain), dancing bears and, at Shrovetide, mummers in strange animal masks. From the West, on the other hand, came a ride whose name indicates its foreign origin – the *karusel'*, or roundabout, and big wheels, as well as a range of entertainments: the harlequinade, the *raek* or peepshow, the pantomime. The heterogeneous origins of the spectacles were particularly clear in the clown-shows given outside the *balagans*, or wooden theatres. The word *balagan* has come into Russian from Persian without Western European influence, but the balcony outside it was called a *raus*, from the German *draußen*, or 'outside'. On this balcony characters from the Italian *commedia dell'arte*, especially Pierrot, the *payats* (from the Italian *pagliaccio*) and the *kloun* (English clown) appeared with the nationally specific figures of the *ded* (grandad) with his false beard of flax and the *ryzhii*, red-haired clown. With them also was the *muchnik* (flour-man), who was an amalgam of Russian and foreign traditions; he was probably derived from the Italian clown Gian Farino, who had a mask of flour, but was naturalised enough to have a Russian name.[24]

The introduction of the Western elements mentioned above to the Russian carnival did not begin until around 1750; the *narodnye gulyan'ya* were already well established before this. The acts of the *skomorokhs*, or minstrel-buffoons, included dancing-bear shows, acrobatics and comic sketches, the content of which has not been recorded in detail but which was apparently often obscene.[25] The swings, ice-hills and other types of native entertainment seem also to be of ancient origin; they were certainly known in Russia before the end of the seventeenth century, for puritanical churchmen frequently condemned them. The following censorious attack of 1648 already lists many of the entertainments which were to appear on the fairground:

They put on themselves masks and clown's clothing, they decorate mares and lead them about, they tell fortunes and put on shows with dancing bears and dogs, playing *surny* [squeaky trumpets], *domry* [mandolines], *gudki* [horns], *gusli* [dulcimers], *volynki* [pipes], and all sorts of tooting satanic instruments, they put on all-night spectacles in the fields, where they listen to their blasphemous songs . . . and they fight one another in bouts of fisticuffs and they sway in circles on swings or on ropes and boards.[26]

By the early eighteenth century, the ice-hills had become a standard feature of popular Shrovetide celebrations, and dramatic entertainers would cluster round them. The famous Moscow underworld figure Van'ka Kain, bandit turned policeman turned bandit again, arranged a spectacle at this date in which a crowd of 200 were invited to beat a mock-thief for his 'crime' with birch twigs until the blood ran.[27]

Peter the Great's attempt to introduce Western carnival rituals, such as 'The Feast of Fools' to Russia, has already been mentioned (see p. 3); such ceremonies were treated by him as manifestations of personal power, and remained confined to court or state occasions; they were, in any case, grim rather than enjoyable in character.[28] The influx of Western entertainments as such came later, with the arrival of Western showmen to take advantage of the new wealth of Russian aristocrats. Circus artistes, conjurers, actors arrived in Moscow or St Petersburg to perform for noble audiences; the shortage of permanent venues led them to make appearances at the fairgrounds as well as in private houses.[29]

From the 1750s until the second third of the nineteenth century, Russian fairground entertainers were eclipsed by foreign entrepreneurs, and the fairgrounds were widely attended by members of the beau monde. An etching of the Russian fairground done by an anonymous British artist in 1806 shows a refined public; the only moujiks to be seen are those turning the pivots of the capstan wheels (see illustration 2). Then a combination of factors brought about a change. First came the Napoleonic invasion. In a fit of patriotism parallel to that in which British piano-owners sand-papered the names 'Blüthner' and 'Bechstein' off their pianos in the First World War, the Russian aristocracy dissociated itself from French entertainments.[30] The enthusiasm for 'the Russian people' led to a new tolerance for the presence of moujiks at entertainments, as the British painter Robert Johnston censoriously recorded:

Never was a scene so truly ludicrous; every one seemed to challenge the other in mirth, forwardness, and impudence. Royalty and slavery were blended together; – the common bearded Russ, in all his filthy coverings, paraded through the royal apartments, and breathed the odour of royalty! It may be proper to accustom the eye of the common people to occasional views of elegance and the effect of refined civilisation, but it does not appear to illumine his mind more than the rays of a passing meteor, which dazzles the eye for a moment, and is for ever lost.[31]

In the late 1820s and 1830s, the fairgrounds also attracted the interest of the ruling classes as an arena where national consensus might be demonstrated, and the policy of *narodnost'* (national-populism) upheld. Nicholas I made frequent visits to the fairground, one of which was recorded by the ever-sycophantic Bulgarin, writing in the

2. The St Petersburg Easter *gulyan'e* around 1800. (Engraving by Skelton after Quarenghi, c. 1806.)

reactionary journal *The Northern Bee* in 1830 (a passage already cited in the Introduction, pp. 11–12):

The Russian common people well understand that his Imperial Majesty Nicholas I entered the *balagan* precisely in order to take part in the merriment of his people and delight Russians by his presence.[32]

It is also possible that the modishness of entertainments performed by 'the common people' filled a gap left by the decline in popularity of dwarves, fools and other human pets kept in the private houses of the rich. The attachment to tame fools was customary much longer in Russia than elsewhere in Europe; as late as 1740 the Tsaritsa Anna turned the marriage of her court fool Golitsyn into a public spectacle; but by the early nineteenth century it had become an eccentricity.[33]

Whatever the reasons for the fashion, it did not last; the beau monde soon lost interest in popular entertainments. By the 1840s upper-class Russians no longer found it charming to take part in folksy pleasures. Even mumming, the delight of Tolstoy's Rostov family thirty years earlier, had lost its lustre:

The custom of going about masked from one friend's house to another at the new year and in Carnival time is no longer *bon genre*. It was some time since very fashionable to go thus disguised, and dance a polka or quadrille in these places, and then proceed to another, and so on until they were weary of the amusement. I believe the various articles missing have contributed to render the custom obsolete.[34]

The gentry also began to gravitate away from the fairground entertainments. By 1840, the public was made up predominantly of the lower orders; this can be seen in lithographs of the period. It is confirmed by the casualty list of the fire in Leman's *balagan* in 1836; even by this date, the victims were almost exclusively minor civil servants, serfs, artisans and poor students.[35] Entrepreneurs and showmen had been used to a rich, educated Russian public; they now had an impecunious, monoglot and often uneducated Russian one.

The shift in demand coincided with a new supply of Russian artistes. At about the same time, the Russian aristocratic craze for serf-theatres palled; by 1844 there were practically none left in Petersburg.[36] Cast off by their owners, the serf actors gravitated to the fairground. For the first time, the major theatres began to use Russians. In 1830 a Russian clown, one Bombov, appeared for the first time outside a *balagan*.[37] By the 1850s, the harlequinades were competing with pantomimes of Russian interest. Stirring spectacles about the Crimean War were all the rage:

In the grand theatre this last Carnival [the Russians of the lower class] have been intensely gratified with the 'glorious battle of Sinope', fought over for their amusement about twelve times a day, in which not a single Russian got wounded, although the heads of the poor Turks were rolling in all directions ... Of course the pleasant sight of so many unbelieving dogs of Mohamme-dans gave immense satisfaction to everybody, and tended much to their self-glorification, and the conviction of the Emperor's might, and so on.[38]

The imported entertainments, such as the harlequinades, began to cater for the demands of their new public; especially long-drawn-out fight scenes were included.[39] The movement was parallel to the slightly earlier change in the language, public and social emphasis on the vaudeville, as its aristocratic audience deserted it for the ballet.[40]

3. The St Petersburg Easter *gulyan'e* on Admiralty Square, *c.* 1850. (Oil and canvas, artist unknown.)

From the 1840s, though foreign artistes continued to work in the *balagans*, especially in the circus, their influence was no longer so important. The audience, too, became more and more plebeian. The subordinate classes were the fastest-growing sector of the population after 1840, and after the Emancipation of the Serfs in 1861, the increasing industrialisation of St Petersburg and Moscow brought ever larger numbers to the cities, who were drawn to the fairground as a place of cheap, accessible entertainment.[41] The upper classes remained in occasional attendance. It was traditional to take the pupils of the Smol'ny Institute for Daughters of the Nobility to the St Petersburg Shrovetide celebrations, and the town governor of Moscow is recorded as paying ceremonial visits to the seasonal fairs held in his city as late as the turn of the century.[42] But it was no longer

4. 'The 10-kopeck places in the *balagan*. Auntie Natasha gawping at the *latest sunrise effect* and losing her nuts'. Lithograph by V. Timm, 1851. From Alekseev-Yakovlev, *Russkie narodnye gulyan'ya*, Leningrad and Moscow 1948.

the tastes of the wealthy which shaped the entertainments, and by the second half of the nineteenth century even the carriage excursions, which in the past had given the upper classes a chance of admiring the funfairs from a refined distance, had been taken over by a public drawn from the merchant classes and below.[43]

The growth and industrialisation of the cities changed not only the audience, but also the character of the entertainments offered at the fairgrounds. The technological developments in factories were paralleled by the arrival of technology on the fairground. Steam roundabouts and roller-coasters appeared; in the larger theatres, the pantomimes burst into pompous flurries of sea battles with real water, battles between real cowboys and Indians, and enactments of historical pageants with casts of thousands.[44] Even the smallest and crudest of the *balagans* were invaded by new entertainments, as Bryusov's poem 'Balagany' records, with its mixture of the old and new:

> Panoramy, gramofony,
> Novyi sinematograf,
> Buddy zub i drozd uchenyi,
> Deva s rogom i udav.
>
> Za zelenoi zanaveskoi
> Otdelen'e dlya muzhchin.
> Mnogo shuma, mnogo bleska,
> Smotryat byusty iz vitrin.[45]
>
> (Panoramas, gramophones,
> The brand-new cinematograph,
> Boa-constrictor, girl with horns,
> Talking thrush and Buddha's tooth.
>
> Behind a curtain of green baize
> Is a section for the men;
> Lots of light and lots of noise,
> Busts gaze out behind the pane.)

New, factory-made fairings had appeared among the old china and wooden ones; by 1916 the old tat of the Palm Week fair (gold ribbons, china dollies and so on) had been supplemented by the new tat of exotic toys, and Nabokov recalled:

the fair in the confetti-studded slush of the Horse Guard Boulevard during Catkin [= Palm] Week, with its squeaking and popping din, its wooden toys, its loud hawking of Turkish delight and Cartesian devils called *amerikanskie zhiteli* – ('American inhabitants') – minute goblins of glass riding up and down in glass tubes filled with pink- or lilac-tinted alcohol as real Americans do (though [what] the epithet meant was 'outlandish') in the shafts of transparent skyscrapers as the office lights go out in the greenish sky.[46]

These technological innovations put paid to the old manually operated roundabouts and old-style pantomimes, but many traditional shows could not be updated, and so remained untouched. It was possible for scientific miracles to exist happily alongside shows which depended on a much more modest expenditure of resources. At the Moscow fairs around 1910, for example, the *balagans* were decorated with lurid paintings and had clowns on the balconies outside 'like those on eighteenth-century engravings', but stood alongside a cinematograph and a 'panorama' with waxworks.[47] Even some of the new 'electric theatres' or cinematographs assimilated to the character of their surroundings with a repertoire of 'the usual insane harlequinades' as well as of bloodthirsty murders.[48]

The entertainments of the fairground proved themselves to be reasonably adaptable, and it was external pressures which were more threatening. Changes in legislation in the late nineteenth century altered the seasonal character of popular entertainments; amusements were now banned from certain weeks in Lent, for example, rather than over the whole of Lent.[49] Now that it had become possible to keep shows outside the fairground open for much of the period between Shrovetide and Easter as well as being able to show during the summer, it was of considerably less interest for entrepreneurs to invest in the fairground theatres, which were limited to the old seasonal patterns. There was also the fact that considerable losses could result from showing at the fairgrounds if the weather were unfavourable. The Easter of 1890, for example, was wet and hence crowds were well down on the norm.[50]

But such financial pressures operated only in the cases of the biggest and most prestigious establishments, some of which did indeed move to permanent sites at the end of the nineteenth century.[51] A much more significant threat to the fairs in general came from official hostility. From the 1880s the authorities, particularly in St Petersburg, were increasingly concerned about the subversive potential of such large public gatherings, and began to shunt them further and further from the centre; the shows first held on the Admiralty Square and then on the Champs de Mars were moved out to a dreary suburban square, the Semenov Platz, where much diminished crowds gathered and it was no longer worth people's while to exhibit. Alexandre Benois, writing in 1921, lamented the fate of these *gulyan'ya*:

But then all this disappeared. 'The Temperance Society' . . . was successful in its campaign to have these Saturnalia removed from the centre of town. The *balagans* dragged out a dreary existence for a while on the far-off filthy Semenov Platz before they suffered the fate of all earthly things: this genuine joy of the people expired, disappeared, and with it disappeared its specific culture; customs and traditions were forgotten.[52]

This account is confirmed by a Guide to St Petersburg published in about 1910, which, however, makes it clear that the death was not so sudden as Benois suggests:

The popular amusements which previously enlivened the Champs de Mars and where the common man would go to enjoy himself are now restricted to confined spaces. In the Mikhailovsky Manège a sort of circus and variety show is put on for the common people, with jugglers, musical clowns, ventriloquists etc. The swingboats, roller-coasters and peepshow men who used to enliven the scene are now no more to be seen.[53]

Outside St Petersburg, carnival celebrations continued much as before; even in Moscow, the Devich'e Field and Tsvetnoi Boulevard celebrations at Shrovetide altered little in size and composition between 1890 and 1915, according to the newspaper reports which appeared annually.[54] In the provinces people were less sophisticated, and official restrictions less obstructive (the Nizhnii-Novgorod fair retained a huge entertainment section until well after the turn of the century).[55] The fairground showmen were in any case used to adaptation. It had always been necessary for them to find other sources of work when the fairground season in St Petersburg and Moscow ended (it lasted from Shrovetide in February to Trinity Sunday in June). As a result, many had been accustomed to decamp to the country, touring fairs in small towns and villages, or supporting themselves by a stay at the Nizhnii-Novgorod fair, which was held for two months from mid-July to mid-September.[56] Others had been accustomed to take to the streets in the big cities and earn money by busking (known in Russian as *gazirovat'*, presumably meaning 'to act under gaslight').[57] Both sources of income still remained open to them. Those who wished to remain all or part of the year in St Petersburg could perform in the leisure parks and gardens, on Stone Island for instance; be taken on by the Mikhailovsky Manège, or by the People's Palaces of the Temperance Society of which Benois writes. The summer entertainments organised for factory workers in the late nineteenth century at the Imperial Porcelain Factory and on Vasilievsky Island also had a selection of fairground rides, such as roundabouts and swings.[58]

There is no doubt, though, that the St Petersburg showmen's loss of their former niche was a setback; instead of having the monopoly of entertainments, they began to have to compete with an explosion of rival attractions, many of which were flashier and more exciting. The character of St Petersburg popular entertainment in the last years of the Russian Empire has been described by Harold Williams; he does not mention the rides and acts of the fairground:

Hundreds are attracted to the Narodny Dom, the People's Palace, with its plays and operas at extraordinarily low prices of admission. In the summer evenings, or on Sundays and holidays, there are *guliania*, 'walkings', in the public gardens, which are lamentably few and far between, and in the Petrovsky Park on the Petersburg Side. Here they walk in pairs, eating sunflower seeds, listening to the music of a military band, or else standing watching some melodrama on an open stage. And now there are scores of cheap cinematographs in all parts of the city, with scores of blood-curdling tragedies, and pictures of all the wonders of the wide world.[59]

Important here is the stress on 'extraordinarily low prices of admission'. The growth of diversity was not invariably a threat to the fairground entertainments, for some of the new, fashionable attractions were exorbitantly priced by comparison. The standard minimum charge for admission to standing-room in the *balagans* was a *grivennik*, 10 kopecks.[60] For this audience, some turn-of-the-century entertainments, such as the masquerade balls in thematically decorated hothouse settings with fountains of scent (tickets 3 roubles each), or even the mixed programmes of variety in the Moscow Manège at 80 kopecks entrance, would have been out of reach. But tickets for a horse-race at 15 kopecks, for a film or magic lantern show at 10 or 20, were much more accessible.[61] This was in turn a factor exploited by those involved in the drive for 'rational leisure' (*razumnoe i poleznoe razvlechenie*), in their efforts to dictate the direction popular pastimes should take.[62]

By 1890 the position of the fairgrounds as the main place of popular entertainment was being eroded, in St Petersburg above all; but before that, between 1840 and 1890, their importance as a public place where the urban subordinate classes could enjoy themselves was not in question.

The urban subordinate classes

What, then, were the 'urban subordinate classes' who formed the main audience for the city fairs? The word 'urban' could in no sense be properly applied to all or even most Russian towns in the nineteenth and early twentieth centuries; many of them, as Vsevolodsky-Gerngross points out, amounted to no more than a couple of streets.[63] I am using the word 'urban' quite deliberately to exclude these smaller towns, as well as the Russian villages, because the fairground entertainments with which I am concerned, such as *Petrushka*, can best be understood in the context of the conflicts and differences of the inner areas of cities, especially St Petersburg and Moscow, with their social mix of rich and poor, rather than in the context of the much simpler social relationships which pertained elsewhere.

The first possible definition of the subordinate classes of St Petersburg and Moscow is according to the official tsarist terminology of 'estates'. In this case we could say that they were drawn from the peasantry; *tsekhovye* or guilded workers; *meshchanstvo*, an untranslatable category which overlapped a good deal with the first two, since it could include, besides unguilded artisans and craftsmen, the domestic servants and small traders who might equally well be classed as 'peasants'; finally, the soldiery.[64] V. N. Vsevolodsky-Gerngross clarifies and adds to official terminology in his definition of the 'urban lower classes', *gorodskie nizy*, by classifying the workers (who might belong officially to the estate of peasantry or of *meshchanstvo*), as an autonomous group:

> By 'the urban lower classes' I mean all kinds of artisans, craftsmen, factory and other workers, technicians in various institutions, domestic servants; the 'urban lower classes' also included soldiers and small tradesmen.[65]

In classical Marxist terms this group includes *petit bourgeoisie* as well as proletariat and lumpenproletariat.

These descriptions need further clarification. There is, first of all, the matter of income. Not all individuals belonging to the 'estates', occupations or classes outlined above were poor and deprived: some extremely rich factory owners belonged, officially speaking, to the *meshchanstvo*; in the suburbs of big cities, where rents were lower, the allocation of living space might be reasonably generous, and it was possible for some to cultivate small vegetable allotments and to keep poultry or even a cow to provide extra food or income.[66] But the fact remains that most of those belonging to these classes were poor and deprived. Wages amongst all the occupations cited were low, the only exceptions being chefs in private houses. Otherwise, in the 1890s a tailor, a factory worker, an upholsterer and a baker, for example, could all expect to earn a similarly low sum of around 30 roubles a month, from which outgoings of up to 20 on rent and food had to be made; domestic servants earned around 8 roubles a month 'all found'.[67] Exploitation at work was a hazard to most; in fact, by the late nineteenth century factory workers were less likely to be exploited than apprentices in workshops, on whose behalf protective legislation had not been made.[68] Living conditions were generally appalling. In St Petersburg in 1890 nearly 50,000 people, or 5 per cent of the population, were living in basement accommodation with an average of four persons to a room, whilst 22,000 persons inhabited attics, also averaging four to a room, and 55 per cent of all available flats had windows which opened on to only an inner courtyard. In Moscow eight years earlier the situation was even worse, with 59,000 people, or 10.4 per cent of the population, in basements, and almost a quarter in habitations with four or more per room.[69] In both cities, workers at factories and workshops might be housed by their employers in overcrowded barracks with a minimum of space and air circulation.[70] Nor were barracks the worst; some workers in factories and work-shops had to sleep directly on the shop floor, whilst others, without permanent accommodation, were forced to fall back on doss-houses in which conditions were so bad that there were calls to replace them with municipal hostels in the early twentieth century.[71] The diet, though it might be better than that of the poorest peasants, was still often nutritionally inadequate and was almost always lacking in variety.[72]

The fact that socio-economic marginalisation was general did not mean that the subordinate classes were a homogeneous mass, however. Workers might be skilled or unskilled; craftsmen were divided into those who belonged to guilds and those who did not; occupations might vary. The big cities, with their stratified population and range of service industries, had a considerable variety of occupations. A survey of the population of St Petersburg carried out in 1867 is particularly detailed. Amongst the artisans and craftsmen listed are cobblers, cabbies, tailors, floor-polishers, carriage-makers, upholsterers, masons, carpenters, joiners, cooks, waiters, and *podenshchiki* or odd-job men; amonst the petty traders are pedlars, porters, shop assistants, market-stall holders. Two further categories are, first, the unemployed, and, secondly, those who would not say what they did (a number of 14,000 out of a population of 400,000).[73] This last category were presumably not tinkers or tailors, but may well have been either beggarmen or thieves. Further, the subordinate classes would have included a group not covered by any urban survey because they had no fixed abode.

But despite this impressive variety, it does not seem that difference of occupation in itself was a very significant factor in Russian towns. The sense of separateness amongst Russian crafts- and tradespeople was not supported by the elaborate guild rituals and apprentice rites of passage which had existed in medieval and early modern Europe; the *tsekh* or guild system, introduced by Peter the Great, had never taken hold as more than a system of official organisation, and a loose one at that.[74] Prints from the first half of the century indicate that some different occupations could then be distinguished by costume; some feeling of separateness amongst different occupations was also ensured by the tendency of those from a given region to gravitate towards specific occupations.[75] But these connections were quite loose: sartorial variety had more or less vanished in the big towns by the late nineteenth century, though there was still a regional element in choice of trade. Other social divisions, such as that between 'temporary' and 'permanent' guilded workers, or that between skilled and unskilled workers, caused a good deal more rancour.[76]

Other dividing factors amongst the subordinate classes included migrancy. The vast growth in numbers of these classes after 1840 had not been caused by a superhuman burst of fecundity, but by the arrival of many thousands of Russian peasants to work in the cities. By the early 1860s there was practically no part of the Empire which had not sent some residents to St Petersburg, less than a third of whose inhabitants had been born in the city.[77] After Emancipation the movement to the cities increased out of all recognition: by 1897 the proportion of the population of St Petersburg officially classified as 'peasant', that is, made up of migrants from the villages, amounted to over 57 per cent, whilst in Moscow five years later it was 67 per cent.[78]

If the figures for arrivals can be established relatively easily, it is rather more difficult to answer the question of how alien the migrant workers felt when they arrived and how alien they seemed to others. Information about attitudes either way is hard to find, and one must depend on statistics and the observations of outsiders. Statistical figures suggest that many would return home in the summer to help with the harvest, that marriage rates were low, and there was a high proportion of young men who were either unattached or had left their wives behind.[79] As we have seen, there was also a tendency for occupation to be dictated by regional origin, which extended later in the century to factory jobs; settlement and socialisation also took place according to a migrant's *zemlya*, or 'home patch'.[80] All these things suggest that ties to the village remained strong. It was also a commonplace for foreign visitors, even late in the century, to observe how closely connected with their villages the Russian workers were, though such observations tended to be based on clothing and appearance, not on the statements of informants or on a wide experience of cultural life in the popular classes.[81] The question has so far been studied in detail for only one section of the subordinate classes, the factory workers, and estimates of acculturation time range from Vsevolodsky-Gerngross' airily vague 'a very long time' to the exact, if not necessarily accurate, recent figure of five years.[82] For all migrants there was certainly a dislocation between town and country life, but whether the effects were positive or negative might vary. In some cases, as with the sweatshop workers described by Gilyarovsky who were known as 'crabs' because they were always naked, urban life can have been nothing but a nightmare; in other cases settlement no doubt seemed a preferable alternative to semi-starvation in the country.[83] The level of tension between settled town-dwellers and new arrivals is also hard to determine. Vasilich informs us that Moscow old-timers loathed the moujiks, and worker memoirs recall that 'new boys' were labelled as 'bumpkins' by scornful experienced colleagues; but on the whole such differences must have been smoothed over by the sheer numbers of arrivals on the one hand, and the association by place of birth on the other.[84]

A further factor that might lead to divisions, and exacerbate differences already present, was literacy. At all periods of the nineteenth century it was higher in towns than in villages, so lack of literacy must have increased many migrants' sense of alienation. The general rise in the literacy rate after 1860 was particularly marked in the case of young and of skilled workers.[85] Those who were additionally exposed to political radicalism and the associated drive to self-improvement often despised their uneducated and backward workmates.[86] However, the set of factors which made the divide between the literate and illiterate important was counterbalanced by a set of factors which worked the other way. The arrival of reading was not a complete break with the past, since from at least the beginning of the eighteenth century Russian town-dwellers, even if they could not read, had been part of a secondary oral culture, in contact with written and printed texts. Besides, the rise in the proportion of literate town-dwellers often reflected no more than the acquisition of very basic skills. Functional literacy was certainly far lower than literacy as officially defined, and oral transmission in the forms of reading aloud, discussion groups and lectures was still central to the culture of even the most radical, self-improving, anti-traditional workers.[87]

Of all the divisions within the subordinate classes, gender division certainly had the most clear-cut effects. First, of course, it dictated occupation. Women had a more restricted range: the occupations mentioned include laundry work, dressmaking, midwifery, domestic service, factory work.[88] Small trading and prostitution are two categories not specifically named, but which can be taken for granted. Payment for work was also much lower for women, who earned around 50 per cent of male earnings even in comparable jobs, and the literacy rate, by occupation, was also significantly lower.[89] Women members of the subordinate classes shared the oppressive living conditions of their male fellows, but their difficulties were augmented by the secondary burden of child-rearing and home management. Exploitation at work might be not only financial, but sexual; relations at home were very often bad, since domestic violence, in many cases exacerbated by alcohol, was common.[90] Contempt for women was also prevalent: 'creatures of a lower order' was a phrase in use about them.[91]

The fairground audiences

How far were the fairground audiences affected by the divisions outlined above? Difference in occupation seems, unsurprisingly, not to have been very important: there are no records of apprentice fraternities doing battle in the streets, or of mockery of one occupation by another, and the *gulyan'ya* were attended by a very wide range of those belonging to the subordinate classes; if at some of them the spectators tended to be drawn from factory workers, at others they represented 'the people in the widest sense of the word'.[92] Literacy and a wider access to tracts, newspapers and cheap books by no means always led to disillusion with orally transmitted genres; new pastimes might complement rather than diminish the appeal of the old, and there is no evidence that the literate were less likely to attend the fairgrounds than the illiterate.[93] Migrancy made a difference only in as much as the fairgrounds tended to attract the more settled workers. As Shrove and Easter, the two major carnival seasons, were also times when village celebrations took place, and times, besides, when many migrant workers chose to return to their villages, packing the trains out of the cities, it seems reasonable to suppose that this was a watershed; that those who did stay in the cities and take part in the urban celebrations were the most settled and assimilated of the subordinate classes.[94] The process of assimilation would in turn have been consolidated by exposure to the urban carnivals themselves, where visitors saw a range of spectacles very different to the seasonal rituals characteristic of village life. Again, gender was the most significant factor among fairground audiences. Young single male adults were the preponderant demographic group in the city population, and, besides, there is likely to have been a particular strength of these 'typical' inhabitants at the fairground and at street entertainments, for they had developed a taste for city life.[95] Although there were women amongst the fairground audiences, it was the interests of the men which were reflected in the entertainments and spectacles of the fairs, and it is gender division, rather than regional or educational differences, which was of importance there.

The subordinate classes in cities were marginal not only in socio-economic terms, but also in cultural terms. If the evidence on how the marginalised classes viewed themselves is sparse, there is a compensatory abundance of evidence on how the marginalising classes viewed them. Up until about 1840, they tended to be viewed with amused condescension, as a set of harmless and entertaining types. Vitengof's description of Moscow in 1842 presents them as colourful components of an ordered society where everyone knew his or her place and was happy in it, and where 'theft, drunkenness and vices' were almost unknown.[96] As the well-bred withdrew from popular life, and as the numbers of the subordinate classes increased, they began to be regarded, especially in St Petersburg, as a problem, if not a threat. The upper classes and the educated (including many intellectuals) grouped them collectively as 'the dark masses' or 'the grey [with the secondary sense ignorant] masses' or the *chernyi lyud* (proles).[97] At best they were seen as a rootless and underprivileged class, socially oppressed,

and worthy of pity; at worst as a threatening mob which might
overwhelm its controllers. Received opinion amongst the Russian
intelligentsia was that, however sordid village life might be, the
Russian peasant still preserved an intrinsic and unalienable nobility of
spirit. The squalor in which the urban underclasses lived did not
appear to have redeeming features: few were prepared to take their
part, let alone to idealise them. The split between sentimentalised
peasantry and despised urban poor is captured by Nicholas Bakhtin,
who reminisced about his own days as a liberal student as follows:

With workers we never came into contact; they seemed more remote and
unreal to us than the Ancient Greek and Egyptian slaves with whom we were
much more concerned. We imagined that we knew the peasants well. In fact
we met and mingled with them frequently and freely, had long talks about the
most important matters, personal and general, and without the slightest
feeling of superiority. On the contrary, we had an immense admiration for
their songs, their rustic wisdom, and, above all, for their colourful, racy
Russian.[98]

Access to cultural resources on the part of the subordinate classes did
not necessarily make them more acceptable. In the 1850s a university
professor poured incredulous scorn on the idea that 'lackeys' might
produce works of literary merit:

In very truth it is a mercy that the majority of lackeys are either illiterate or
that they, not being fond of writing, confine themselves to the composition of
short stories, which are easily swallowed up in the waters of Lethe. For what if
they should begin to write memoirs? In that case they would, like death itself,
destroy moral beauty, leaving in its place a rotten corpse, which is not the
same thing as a man. In any case we may take comfort. Even if there were
such memoirs, they would hardly manage to find their way into print; for who
would take it upon himself to be the publisher of such things?[99]

For other writers, the subordinate classes, a difficult subject *en masse*,
might be made more palatable by judicious selection. Some of them
were acceptable, others were not. Tolstoy, who felt that the Russian
Empire could only be redeemed by returning to a self-sufficient rural
economy, and who laid much stress on the corrupting effects of urban
life, concluded his bitter attack on the opera in *What is Art?* with the
statement that this is the sort of thing which would appeal to the worst
element in the urban lower classes:

For the educated man this is intolerably tedious; for the *genuine working man*
it is totally incomprehensible. It can only appeal (and even this is unlikely) to
corrupt apprentices who have been infected with the spirit of their masters but

who are yet unsated by the pleasures of their masters, and who wish to show off how civilised they are; and *young lackeys*.[100]

The Social Democrats, for their part, were concerned with only one section of the urban lower classes, the factory workers who would be the source of a proletarian revolution, and not with the 'lumpenproletariat' or with 'the *petit-bourgeois* peasantry, who are, inevitably, unreliable and unstable'.[101] The divisions between 'acceptable' and 'unacceptable' social inferiors rather resembles that between 'true Romanies' (clean, honest and industrious) and 'tinkers' (dirty, idle cheats) which was current at a similar period in England.[102]

That is not to say that there are no fuller accounts of life in the underclasses. There are, for example, the essays and 'sketches' of Gleb Uspensky and V. Gilyarovsky. In the latter's documentary sketch 'Khitrovka', describing a notorious low-life district in Moscow, there are vivid portraits of doss-houses, brothels, drinking-dens and slums, and of the pimps, streetwalkers, fences, thieves and the destitute who lived there. Gilyarovsky reproduces some stereotypes of low-life exploration; he stresses, for example, his bravery in venturing into the unknown by mentioning that his intelligentsia friends, brought to sight-see, found the Khitrovka slums so appalling that they refused to set foot inside. But his accounts are refreshingly free of homily; he is concerned more with the sheer vitality of Khitrovka than with the pressing need to clean it up.[103] A similar refusal to patronise can be found in two articles by G. Vasilich, written in 1910, which give a specially full account of Moscow street life, with its fleamarkets, street traders, unusually creative beggars, 'cruel romances' sung to the barrel organ, and cheap teahouses.[104]

The problems which beset a modern intellectual in trying to reconstruct the attitudes of the nineteenth-century Russian urban poor to the entertainment put before them are in direct relation to the problems already outlined. We have no immediate evidence of how the audience felt; and many surviving contemporary accounts are more concerned with the reaction of the writer to a performance than with the response of other spectators. In 1853, for example, the writer Druzhinin visited the Easter carnival, where he was both bored and offended:

The *balagan* performances go from bad to worse: surely there have never been such wretched stagings, such preposterous plays ... No sense, no effectiveness, not a glimmer of talent in the actors, not a shadow of humour in

the clown. *The Death of the Prince of Navarre* used at least to amuse me
before; this time it merely made me sad.[105]

In other cases, affronted educated watchers touched on the taste of
the audience indirectly, arguing that if they were not offended by what
they saw, they certainly should have been. In 1902 an anonymous
Social Democrat pamphleteer wrote:

> The only holiday entertainments for labourers remain the *narodnye
> gulyan'ya*, consisting of *balagans* with clowns gabbling barbarously, round-
> abouts, climbing of the greasy pole 'for prizes' and all that kind of thing.[106]

Other observers, however, do give us some idea of how the *balagan*
performances went down, albeit from the outside. External observers
were most struck by the noise made by the audience throughout; they
were not in the least cowed by the performance going on, nor, it
seems, by legal regulations forbidding spectators to 'impede the
performance'.[107] This did not mean that the crowds were unattentive
or sceptical. On the contrary, they shared in every vicissitude of the
hero's life, would shout encouragement during the play and comment
pithily and to the point when it was over.[108]

To a modern observer, the *balagan* entertainments appeal as pure
theatre; we see them through the prism of modernist stagings based on
them. To us, the dramas seem delightfully studied and unrealist, but
there is every evidence that their original audiences saw the action as
totally real. They viewed the text as the audiences of the 'school
dramas' played in Russia during the eighteenth century viewed what
they were watching:

> Everything in these old plays which we might find too primitive, or totally
> untrue to life, or cruel and unnaturalist, or even inhumane and anti-aesthetic,
> seemed to the spectators, directors and actors of that time in no way less real
> and wonderful than, for example, the psychological dramas of Chekhov or
> the theatrical system of Stanislavsky seemed to the spectators, directors and
> actors of the early twentieth century.[109]

The distinction between 'truth to life' and naturalism is a valid one;
and we must bear in mind that the result of one survey, suggesting
that 'workers like realist plays about everyday life, with which they
could identify directly', did not necessarily mean that they were
prepared to watch only plays which were overtly referential.[110] By no
means all popular dramas alluded directly to topical or social issues,
and such allusions can be misleading when they do occur. The fact

that the battles of the Crimean War appeared on stage almost as soon as they happened suggests smart reaction to external events, but in fact shows about the Turkish war were commonly included in the *balagan* repertoire well into the twentieth century, suggesting that such a topic probably appealed for other reasons than historical immediacy – perhaps, for instance, because it gave scope to plenty of good fights.[111] Dramatic convention in the fairgrounds was interpreted in line with a popular view of the world which sometimes seemed strange to the educated mind:

[The moujik's] credulity arises from his vivid imagination. If you tell him of the ordinary progress of events in Paris or London – the tubes, underground railways, telephones – he will tell you plainly that you are fooling him; but if you asserted that there were silver and gold scattered about the street he would believe every word, for he has heard many stories of the wealth of the English.[112]

Technological progress appears to have made little difference to fairground audiences' reactions; they still treated what they saw as freak shows or miracles. For example, the opening of the first Russian railway line was celebrated afterwards in a tone of naive wonder:

Ladies and gents, look inside, I'll show you a new way to ride! Here's a new kind of party for ye, a ride on the railway to Tsarkoe! What wonders of mechanics are found, steam turns the wheels round and round, in front the engine runs, dragging hundreds of tons! Carriages, rails and waggons besides, with many persons sitting inside. Less than half an hour it takes to do twenty versts to Tsarskoe gates! Wait a bit now, they'll soon have built one to Moscow.[113]

The artistes who worked in the *balagans* and the streets of cities are an even more obscure body of people than their audience. Though occasionally mentioned by name in legal prohibitions, such as in the regulation forbidding proprietors of amusement booths representation on the regulatory body of the Nizhnii-Novgorod fair, they are not recognised by official statistics as a separate estate or occupation – perhaps they belonged to the percentage of the people who would not divulge their work, or perhaps they were classified as 'odd job men' – so estimates of numbers are impossible. However, they seem to have been drawn from the subordinate classes: some were probably *meschane* (members of the *meshchanstvo*) officially speaking, others 'peasants' (see p. 34). It is not clear how many relied on performance as a main source of income, and for how many it was a seasonal or occasional occupation; in any case there were many ways in which the showman's job overlapped with others. Their exercise of manual dexterity and enforced itinerancy linked them with small craftsmen, and their need for commercial aptitude with petty traders.[114]

The fact that the showmen fell outside any classification also makes it impossible to assess how many of them were literate, though some certainly were.[115] All of them performed from memory, rather than reading from the script, but there was clearly some dependence on written and printed material. Some showmen had manuscript versions of the text they performed, which they had got by heart; others, though illiterate, were inducted by the literate by being taken through the text aloud; some seem to have depended on commonplace books or printed books for a part of the material.[116] But at the same time there was a tendency for whole families to work the circus and fairground shows, and the small children brought up to the *balagan* absorbed as much by watching and imitation as they did by direct demonstration.[117]

The lives of the showmen varied considerably according to whether they were employed in the more opulent, 'popularising' *balagans*, or in the smaller shows. In the former case they often lived well; resources were abundant, and the biggest fairground theatres in Petersburg had new repertoires not only every year, but every season (Shrove, Easter, Whitsun and the smaller festivals in between).[118] The quality of manufacture was so outstanding that the used scenery went into a repository from which it was hired by the Imperial Theatres.[119] Where such expenditure was possible, there was no need to stint payment to artistes either, and Bronislava Nijinska, whose father was a notable *maître de ballet*, recalls that her father was earning more in the travelling *balagan* theatres than he would have done as a staff member at the Imperial Theatres, and that all attempts to poach him on the part of the Mariinsky (now the Kirov Theatre) were in vain.[120]

For those in the latter category, however, life was harder. They might be as penurious as any other of the underclasses; whilst touring they might be expected to sleep in the *balagan* itself, which would be unheated for reasons of fire precautions and badly insulated to boot. During the main festival seasons they might be expected to give performances non-stop for as long as ten or twelve hours. The treatment of children was often wretched; some were sold by their parents into effective slavery with circus proprietors, were given no education, were under-fed, ill-used and regularly beaten, perhaps to death; some ten-year-olds were already alcoholics. For adults and children alike, the profession was woefully insecure, as artistes' associations were only set up at the end of the nineteenth century so rates of pay were fixed by takings, and there was no means of help for any who were too old, ill or injured to perform. Many died as paupers.[121]

It was this bottom end of the profession from which the street entertainers were drawn; the simplest acts were those which could most readily be performed impromptu. Acrobats, dancing-bear keepers, clowns, accordionists all busked in the cities. Here they were subject to police harassment on two grounds: giving illicit performances, and begging.[122] Indeed, the line between street entertainment and begging was often impossible to draw, since beggars earned better if they amused the public, and so-called performances were often little more than costumed begging. In Dostoevsky's *Crime and Punishment*, when Katerina Ivanovna Marmeladova goes mad, she takes her children out to the street and makes them perform for the public. The scene is pathetic and embarrassing, and it gives a vivid impression of what many street performances must have been like:

On the canal, not very far from the bridge and practically next door to the house where Sonya lived, a small crowd had gathered. Little boys and girls had run up in specially large numbers. As you passed the bridge, you could already hear Katerina Ivanovna's hoarse, strained voice. She kept rushing up to her children, shouting at them, pleading with them, teaching them what to do on the spot, in front of everyone, showing them how to dance and sing, hectoring them about why they had to do it, despairing when they didn't understand what to do, slapping them . . . In fact, she had tried to dress the children up like street singers. The little boy was dressed in a turban made of a scrap of red-and-white cloth, so that he should look like a Turk.[123]

A few of the street performers enjoyed a greater degree of security and stability; there was, for instance, a whole community of them established near Novinsky Boulevard in Moscow, probably because the area had been the site of a large fair before being built over.[124] But the variations in levels of prosperity amongst the showmen were quite minor; there was no divide in the street shows between the active bearers of popular culture, the players, and its passive bearers, the audience. It is not surprising, therefore, that the smaller shows were the most daring; that they, rather than the larger entertainments, manifested the spirit of carnival as 'a deeply popular movement . . . an often misunderstood and persecuted substratum of official Western

culture'.[125] It is to this pressed, stretched and aggressive type of small
show that *Petrushka* also belongs.

Petrushka

When *Petrushka* was performed on the fairgrounds, its place was
determined by custom. Like the markets and shopping-quarters of
Russian towns, the larger town fairgrounds were divided into *linii* or
ryady, rows. This was a system of commercial organisation according
to which shops or stalls were grouped together according to what they
sold; dating back to medieval times, the system had survived longer in
Russia than elsewhere in Europe; nineteenth-century Moscow still
had its 'Hunter's Row' of game-stalls, whilst London's 'Baker Street'
or 'Pudding Lane' no longer meant what they said.[126] In the fairgrounds the word 'row', however, referred as much to the size of the
operation as to its type; in the first row were placed the big expensive
luxurious theatres, in the further were ranged the small cheap ones
patronised by the poor. The *Petrushka* theatres as such were to be

5. *Petrushka* on the left of a roundabout. Shrovetide *gulyan'e*, Field of Mars, 1897.
Photograph.

found in the inferior rows, often next to the roundabouts.[127] They were considerably smaller than the biggest theatres of the first row, which held between 1,500 and 2,000 people, many standing in galleries at the back; according to Dmitriev, they were normally small *sarai* (huts) holding between 150 and 200 people, presumably standing packed together.[128] Shcheglov has described the not very grandiose outside of a standard *Petrushka* theatre:

There, at the very end [of the fairground], almost on the edge of the field beyond, stands a low white unimpressive-looking tent, with a handkerchief waving on its roof instead of a flag ... But gentlemen, approach this meagre tent with due respect, for it is the abode of Petr Ivanovich Uksusov [Petrushka]![129]

Some booths were grander – the famous puppeteer Ivan Zaitsev had an elaborate *style russe* puppet theatre in Moscow – but Shcheglov's description was probably near the norm.[130]

Besides appearing independently, Petrushka also appeared as part of mixed programmes in the smaller *balagans*. A Russian lithograph of 1862 shows him in his booth alongside a pair of acrobats, a barrel-organ and a performing dog.[131] It is doubtful whether he was shown inside the biggest *balagans*, for it would have been extremely hard to see him, but he was sometimes used as a draw on the balconies outside. The full fairground audience for the text was, therefore, considerably wider than those who went into the tents.

The history of *Petrushka* follows the general pattern of fairground entertainments; originally performed by foreigners, it was gradually taken over by Russian showmen around 1840. The information available on early performances of *Petrushka* is scanty, but we do know from the observations of a Western traveller, Daniel Clarke, that in 1813 Southern Italian puppeteers were performing in Russia; they appear to have been well established, for they toured down as far as the Don.[132] It is not clear whether the 'Italian organ-grinders, shadow-players and acrobats' whom Georgi notes as residents of Petersburg in 1794 were also puppeteers.[133] But two other accounts of the fairgrounds from much the same date as Clarke's also mention puppet theatres. In 1813 the British traveller J. T. James (of Christ Church, Oxford) saw them at the Easter Fair in St Petersburg:

A second carnival of one week succeeded this day [that is, the religious ceremonies for Easter Sunday], and afforded, though in a different way, a spectacle no less gratifying to strangers. The Isaac Platz was filled with people, drinking kvass and kislitschi, *visiting puppet shows or rope-dancers*, enjoying themselves in the tcherkeli or roundabouts, and following each other in succession, down the slopes of the summer-hills.

In 1817, P. Svin'in recorded a show which had a comic battle between husband and wife, with the jealous husband beating his spouse. The most funny thing about it, he writes, was the way that the 'German and Italian' puppeteers distorted Russian words.[134]

Unfortunately, none of the accounts records the exact texts performed by the puppets, nor do the numerous contemporary etchings of the fairgrounds show puppet booths (they would perhaps have been too small to stand out in a general view). But the information that the puppeteers came from Calabria is very important: it is likely that some brought with them the traditional Southern Italian glove-puppet text, *Pulcinella*.

Puppet shows were a favourite treat for Dostoevsky and his brother during the 1830s when they were children.[135] And we know that by the 1840s the *Pulcinella* text was being performed by Russian showmen, who hired their puppets by the day from Italians 'of the Apennine mountains'. Grigorovich's story 'The Petersburg Organ-Grinders' is the source of this information. He writes:

The main trade of the Italians is the puppet comedy. It goes without saying that the one which is played in our backyards and gives the apprentices in their striped jackets, the nannies, the children and sometimes even adults such pleasure is not at all like the one that [the Italian] has brought from his homeland. The Russianised Italian has translated it all as best he can into the language of his Russian hireling, a harum-scarum young ruffian, who has an unusual talent to spout rubbish without taking breath and to spice his rubbish with comic rhyming doggerel – and the latter has adapted it in his own way.

(Grigorovich, 13)

At the end of the story Grigorovich gives an account of such a glove-puppet performance of *Pulcinella*; it is structurally and textually similar to *Petrushka*.

At this stage the hero was called by a variant of his Italian name, 'Puchinella', and Petrushka was the name of a clown who appeared briefly at the end. This tradition persisted for some time in Petersburg: in a rough variant of his *Writer's Diary* of 1871 Dostoevsky also refers to the hero of the piece by an Italianate name, this time Pul'chinel', although in the show which he described Petrushka had increased in importance and had already developed his true aggressive and unpleasant character: 'What a scoundrel that Petrushka, Pul'chinel''s constant companion, is. How he deceives and mocks him, and Pul'chinel' doesn't even notice. He's like a Sancho Panza or a Leporello, but completely Russianised and true to folk hero tradition.' Dostoevsky's story 'Gospodin Prokharchin' also refers to the puppet character as 'Pul'chinel' '.[136] But Obol'yaninov's catalogue of children's paper games indicates that a toy theatre version of the puppet theatre was published in 1860, and that in this the hero was called 'Petrushka'.[137] So one must conclude that between 1840 and the 1870s the two names, Pulcinella and Petrushka, were alternatives. By the 1880s, at any rate, the hero's name had become fixed in its Russian version, 'Petrushka'. This is his name in the earliest *lubok* text, published in 1887. It is also his name in all later *lubok* versions, and in the later manuscript recordings of street versions. Corrupt versions of Pulcinella, 'Pushinel' ' for example, continued to be used as additional names for the street hero, whose foreign origins were also indicated by the polite address of *mus'e* (*moussier*, from 'monsieur') regularly used by other characters in the play.[138]

The difference in name between the hero of the play which Grigorovich saw and later variants does not detract from the fact that this is the earliest record we have of a *Petrushka* show. It is also the earliest record of any glove-puppet, as opposed to string-, stick-, finger- or rod-puppet, performance in Russia which has yet come to light. Grigorovich assumes that his readers will have some familiarity with the show which he describes, so it is reasonable to suppose that it had been performed for a few years at least, perhaps since the first recorded appearances of Calabrian puppeteers in Russia during the second decade of the nineteenth century.

There is, however, a long tradition of speculative or even mythologising study of *Petrushka*, which assumes, on very little evidence, that the show was first performed far earlier than the nineteenth century. In the forewords to two of the *lubok* editions, published in 1907 and 1910, which are a fair indication of received opinion, we read:

Who does not know 'Petrushka', that noisy, rowdy trickster and brawler? He has been travelling round Russia *for at least two hundred years now*, crying in his squeaky voice: 'Petrushka is here!'   (P 1910) [*my italics*]

The [Petrushka] theatre appeared in Russia *a very long time ago. About two hundred years ago* wandering *skomorokhi* [minstrel-buffoons] and *shuty* [jesters] were already giving performances of *Petrushka* to entertain people.
                                                                (P1907) [*my italics*]

In fact, the text had been in Russia for perhaps a hundred years when these passages were written, but that is long enough for a text, object or custom to become so well established that it seems to have been around for ever. The *Matreshka* dolls (Russian painted wooden dolls which fit one inside the other), for example, give the impression of having existed in Russia since time immemorial, though they were in fact invented by Malyutin and other members of the Russian Art and Craft movement in the 1890s.[139] Similar examples exist in Britain too: the fact that the Christmas tree is a Victorian import is quite well known, but fewer people might be aware that hot-cross buns have only been around since the eighteenth century.[140]

Nonetheless, conventionally (not only in the popular imagination, but in the critical imagination too) it has been accepted that *Petrushka* was performed by the *skomorokhs*. The case rests on a single piece of evidence, a description of a puppet show witnessed by the German traveller Adam Olearius in 1637. This is what Olearius says about it:

> But as [the Muscovites] are wholly given up to all licentiousness, even to sins against Nature, not only with Men, but also with Beasts, he who can tell most stories of that kind, and set them out in most gestures, is accompted the bravest Man. Their Fidlers put them into songs, and their Mountebanks make publick representations of them, and stick not to show their Breeches, and sometimes all they have to their Spectators. Those who lead Bears about, Juglers and *Puppet-players, who erect a stage in a moment, by the means of a coverlet, which, being tied about their wast, is brought over their heads, and within it show their Puppets, representing their brutalities and sodomies, make sport to the Children, who are thereby induc'd to quit all sentiments of shame and honesty.*[141]

From this description, and the accompanying engraving which Olearius made, it is clear that the show was performed by the 'skirt theatre' method – the operator had a piece of material tied round his waist and anchored above his head, above which the characters appeared as though on stage. The scene which Olearius drew had four puppet characters: a man with a tall cap, a horse, and two others, one man and one woman. The scenes formed part of an entertainment including a dancing bear and a group of musicians.

The view that the spectacle witnessed by Olearius was an early version of *Petrushka* seems to go back to D. Rovinsky's account of *Petrushka* in his book on the Russian *lubok* of 1881.[142] Rovinsky accepted without question that this was directly related to *Petrushka* and, taking their cue from him, almost all commentators have assumed a linear connection between seventeenth- and nineteenth-century traditions. Olearius' description has even prompted Russell Zguta to an assertion that *Petrushka* shows were being given by the *skomorokhs* as early as the thirteenth century.[143]

There is, however, only one concrete fact which the Olearius evidence allows us to deduce: that the *skomorokhs* did give puppet shows. Commentators who link these with *Petrushka* have made several important oversights. The first of these concerns the technique of performance. *Petrushka* was always performed using either glove puppets or marionettes – in the vast majority of cases using the former. It is not possible for a single performer to operate more than two glove or string puppets at once. The Olearius etching shows *four* puppets. Almost the only critic so far to have drawn attention to this is Vsevolodsky-Gerngross, who over-ingeniously explained two of the figures away by suggesting that they were uprights to support the sacking.[144] Perhaps he had only seen a very bad reproduction; the clearer prints of Olearius' drawing, including that in the 1656 edition which he himself oversaw, leave no doubt that all four figures are puppets. They could be stick puppets, hand-held, like the French fools' *mamottes*, or they could be finger puppets.[145] The latter seems more likely, since the distance between central and peripheral figures is too great for the span of one hand, the finger puppets could more easily have been fixed on to the sack supports whilst not taking part in the scene.

The suggestion that these were in fact finger puppets has been made yet more probable by important archaeological evidence which came to light about fifteen years ago, and was published by M. G. Rabinovich.[146] Excavations in the Zaryad'e area of Moscow brought to light, among other finds, three little pottery figurines representing comic human figures. They are legless, and have a 1.3 centimeter hollow at the base of their bodies which can be fitted on to one's finger. These figures can be dated with accuracy; they must precede the great Moscow fire of 1468. Rabinovich points out how much these puppets resemble the puppets in Olearius' etching.

Rabinovich's communication (which, oddly, has been more or less ignored by theatre historians)[147] leaves little doubt that the puppet-shows given by the *skomorokhs*, including the show seen by Olearius, were given with finger puppets. The form of these resembled the clay toys which are still manufactured in Russia, rather than the carved wooden heads used for Petrushka and the other puppets of the

Russian glove-puppet theatre.[148] According to Rabinovich's description, and Olearius' picture, these puppets were far smaller than the
glove puppets with which *Petrushka* was traditionally performed; so
small, in fact, that displays close at hand must have been necessary. The
fragility of clay would also have rendered impossible violent contact
between the figures such as occurs in almost every scene of *Petrushka*.

Besides the technical differences between *Petrushka* and these
puppet shows, there are other reasons to be suspicious of attempts to
connect the nineteenth-century tradition with the *skomorokhs*. We
have no clear evidence of what the texts of these puppet shows were
like; indeed, we have no certain evidence that they had verbal texts at
all. The verbs used by Olearius are significant: show, represent, make
sport. None indicates anything more than a pantomime.[149] Moreover,
the sack over the puppeteer's head would have muffled any dialogue,
particularly when there was music playing in the background, as
Olearius illustrates there was.

The only link which it is possible to make between this comedy and
Petrushka is that both include a scene with a horse, but there is no
evidence that the scenes were necessarily alike. In *Petrushka* a sale of
the horse takes place; from Olearius' description, in which the original
German speaks of 'obscene behaviour with horses',[150] one hesitates to
speculate for what nefarious purpose the *skomorokhs* might have
introduced *their* horse.

The likelihood that the scene which Olearius saw had a direct
connection with *Petrushka* is still further diminished by the fact that
there are no accounts of any *Petrushka* performances between 1637
and 1842. Peretts' general history of the Russian puppet theatre
includes some valuable material on puppet theatre in the eighteenth
century. He mentions various companies who performed in Moscow
and St Petersburg. Most of these were run by foreigners, but none,
apparently, by Italians.[151] The shows given fell into two types. First,
there were marionette shows on biblical subjects, or subjects of the
traditional Western European marionette repertory (*Don Juan*,
Doctor Faustus). These shows seem to have been performed largely
for wealthy audiences, and their impact on the popular tradition was
slight.[152] Secondly, there were mechanical theatre shows, often rather
elaborate and with richly decorated figures. These were even more
geared to the taste of a rich, upper-class public; they had less in
common with theatre as such than with the automatons which
eighteenth-century conjurers used to entertain the public, or even

expensive toys, the jewelled trinkets of rich people all over Europe, from tiny trees made of precious stones to miniature glitter-eyed Fabergé jasper bearkins.[153]

No scholar has produced hard evidence for *Petrushka* performances at this date. Peretts alleges that a puppet show given before the Tsarevich Paul in 1765 was 'probably *Petrushka* or *Polichinelle*', but the reference from the Tsarevich's tutor's diary which he cites says only that a puppet comedy was performed 'which was not worth watching'.[154] In the fable 'the Vixen and the Puppets' from the early eighteenth-century edition of *Aesop's Fables* in Russian the phrase *'dom kukol'nikov' '*, or puppeteers' house, is glossed as *'komedial'nyi dom'*, actors' house, and the illustration shows a vixen studying, not puppets, but a mask, with stage armour in the background.[155] This does not suggest that puppets were very familiar.

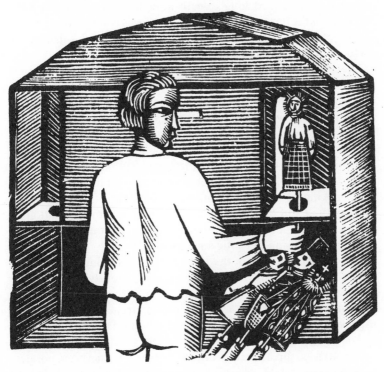

6. Operation of the *vertep*. Note the slit along which characters are slid to the front. Illustration from P. Gorbenko, *Revolyutsiinii lyal'kovii teatr*, Kiev 1924.

LORETTE WILMOT LIBRARY
NAZARETH COLLEGE

The lack of continuity in the Russian puppet tradition is also indicated by the relatively small number of puppet theatres in Russia (compared with Bohemia and Italy, where they ran into thousands),[156] and the fact that there is little resemblance, whether of technique or of subject, between *Petrushka* and other orally transmitted puppet theatres. The most important, and oldest, of these was the theatre called the *vertep* in the Ukraine and in Russia, known in Belorussia as the *betleika* and in Poland as the *szópka*. This was a portable box in the style of a Christmas crib, containing small crudely hewn wooden full-length figures operated by a system of rods running along tracks in the box's bottom surface. Records of *vertep* performances date back to the early eighteenth century, and though the surviving texts date from the second half of the nineteenth century, they indicate a stable tradition. The first half of a *vertep* performance was taken up by a short religious drama, *King Herod*, which portrayed the wicked king's death after he had commanded the massacre of the innocents. The second half was composed of various short scenes of secular mode, not connected with each other by the presence of a single character or linear narrative.

The other puppet theatres in the oral tradition, those of Toporets and the Don, were close to the secular part of the *vertep* in composition, since they were made up of unlinked short scenes; the techniques used were, respectively, rod and shadow puppetry and a type of stick puppetry where the figures were manufactured with head and hands stuck on to the three upper points of a wooden cross.[157]

I would argue, therefore, that there is no support for a view that *Petrushka* existed before the nineteenth century, or for a view that it is a re-working of existing traditions of puppetry. I think that the nineteenth-century tradition was produced by an adaptation of Italian shows; that it was, like many other fairground shows after 1840 or so, a fusion of exotic and domestic.

If the general history of the *Petrushka* show resembles that of the other fairground genres it was, however, less seriously affected by the erosion of fairground sites in the late nineteenth century. Though by the 1890s some observers were beginning to argue that the show was in irreversible decline, this appears to have been based less on attempts at exact quantification than a general feeling that traditional entertainments were threatened.[158] Loyalty to *Petrushka* never evaporated, and the show might, like other unmechanised entertainments, be performed amongst spectacular demonstrations of the triumph of the machine. In 1905, for example, several *Petrushka* theatres took their place at the Shrovetide carnivals alongside an 'electric roundabout', a 'vagodrome' for car and bike rides, and theatrical blockbusters involving casts of about a hundred people and twenty horses.[159] If forced to depart the fairgrounds, the puppeteers' great mobility and small expenditure of resources made them flexible. They were amongst the acts most familiar in the streets and courtyards of St Petersburg and other large towns.[160] They might also set up their shows at village fairs – the realist painter Solomatkin has a senti-mental, but attractive oil of such a performance – and the memoirs of an English visitor make it clear that *Petrushka* was a regular feature of Shrovetide celebrations in the country as early as the 1860s: 'There is the never-failing Punch hard upon Judy; there are swings, hobby-horses, shows and theatres, dancing bears, jugglers and monkeys.'[161] Towards the end of the century, *Petrushka* shows were also given at the *dachnye mestnosti*, surburban villages of holiday homes, and in the residential suburbs of towns.[162] And besides being engaged for shows in the new leisure parks and 'people's palaces', they were in demand for children's entertainments.[163] The frequent publication of cheap printed editions after 1890 indicates the public love of the text.

But the survival of *Petrushka* had a price – it was increasingly regarded as a text for children. Children had always been among those watching, but by the late nineteenth century it was standard practice to take Russian middle-class children to the performances. The format of some of the printed editions, with pictures of girls and boys in pinafores and boaters, speaks for itself. The change in audience led to pressure on the text; it was subject to attack not only by advocates of 'rational leisure', but also by educationalists. M. Braunschweig, writing in 1908, attacked both the clown acts and *Petrushka*: what sort of entertainment were 'the clown, waving his arms and legs in a vulgar manner' and 'the Petrushka theatre with its ugly, mangled, caricature figures, violent gestures, absurd squeaking, which can communicate nothing but crude foolery'.[164]

In provincial fairgrounds and in streets, however, the *Petrushka* show was still very much the property of the subordinate classes. Its popularity was aided by the low price of entrance. On the fairgrounds, entrance to the shows was sometimes 5 kopecks, half that of more luxurious spectacles; more often there was no entrance fee at all, and a hat was passed round afterwards.[165] On the street, where the booth was directly in the open and people might either lean out of windows

or cluster round, payment was more or less impossible to enforce, and
the show was within reach, therefore, of those who could not afford
the cheapest subsidised entertainments.

As with the other fairground genres, audience reactions to the
performance were spontaneous. When Petrushka appeared above the
booth, he was warmly greeted. Shcheglov has related how one
member of the audience at a performance which he attended greeted
Petrushka like a long-lost relative: ' "Why, hallo, Piotr Ivanovich,
how are you?" an amiable old man in a torn *zipun* [homespun coat]
calls out from the crowd and honours "Piotr Ivanovich" with a bow,
just as he would a close friend who'd stood godfather to four of his
children.'[166] The fact that Petrushka was wooden made no difference;
people would address him as they would a real person.

For many Russians the Petrushka shows were one of the most
powerful memories of childhood. For Gor'ky, Petrushka was a hero
to be ranked with Faust, for Dobuzhinsky, an attraction which
eclipsed even the edible delights of the fairground:

And, of course, there was Petrushka's guttural voice too, as he popped out
from the wings of his gaudy booth, and I couldn't take my eyes off his
convulsive movements and cheered, like everyone round me, when he
whacked the Policeman and the Devil with his club, and always came to life
again without a scratch himself.[167]

But the most eloquent tribute of all is by Benois, whose view of these
shows was soaked in the same nostalgia as his view of the fairground:

Petrushka, the Russian Guignol, no less than Harlequin, was my friend from
my very childhood. When I heard the trilling, guttural shrieks of a wandering
Petrushka man: 'Petrushka is here! Ladies and gents, come down below,
watch the Petrushka show!' my impatience to see this fascinating spectacle
made me nearly apoplectic.[168]

As with other fairground dramas, the public's affection for Petrushka did not make them unresponsive and undiscriminating. When
the *Popechitel'stvo narodnoi trezvosti* (Temperance Society) put on
puppet shows in order to proselytise at the turn of the century, various
members of the public left in disgust, saying that they could do better
than that in any backyard.[169] Puppeteers were aware of the public's
appraising eye, and would tailor their performances accordingly; one
old puppeteer, when explaining why he had ordered his version in a
particular way, replied 'The public likes it nice and tidy'.[170] But, on
the other hand, this principle of audience control, or 'preventive

censorship' as Jakobson and Bogatyrev have called it (see Introduction, p. 8), must be set against a principle which might be called 'incentive censorship', which worked in exactly the opposite manner. The audience wanted to be thrilled by the wickedness of the show, to force it beyond the bounds of what they knew, expected and accepted. The journalist V. Doroshevich watched a performance of *Petrushka* on the island of Sakhalin at which the audience yelled noisy encouragement to their own criminal Petrushka, 'the murky hero of the labour camp'; they 'shouted with laughter and yelled with excitement' (Doroshevich, a typical intellectual, for his part 'felt sick').[171]

The puppet showmen lived in much the same circumstances as other performances at the middle to bottom end of the street and fairground showmen's community. None of them made his fortune by puppetry: the amount of money the public could afford was not enough. Some, like the puppeteers described by Grigorovich, dwelt in the filthy and overcrowded attic and cellar tenements of the town:

The first object which will meet your eyes, still watery from the spiritous stink of the staircase, will be a vast Russian stove, covered with soot and hung with the rags that compose the inhabitants' wardrobe; the walls and ceiling are crawling with those charming insects which have the honour to share the name of a famous European people [i.e. cockroaches, commonly called *prusaki*, or Prussians, in Russian] . . . The walls are lined with long benches, on which the workers are lying in various extremely ungraceful attitudes. There are Russians, Germans, Italians, all of them employed by one master, a certain Signor Charlotto [*sic*] Bonissi. In the middle of the room are straw-filled boxes, in which three or four monkeys are in incessant movement, squeaking in a hideous descant; some sacks of flour and macaroni are tossed down in the corners; a slop bucket under the stove emits an especially unpleasing reek; the smoke coming from those short wooden pipes which are the inevitable accoutrement of Russian workmen fills any space left unfilled by the junk; the sounds of voices and laughter, the squeaks of the monkeys and the barking of the dogs, the wailing of the children – all does not quite mask the snoring of a few organ-grinders, who are sleeping contorted into unnatural shapes on the stove, on the bunks and on the floor.

(Grigorovich, 12)

The hardship of the puppeteers was increased by the fact that it was difficult for them to perform without someone to collect the money and provide music on a barrel-organ. So the minimal takings for the puppet show might have to be shared between operator, barrel-organ player, and 'bottler' in the English fairground jargon term (money collector), if there was one. But all the same, some puppet showmen managed to make a living. Zaitsev, for example, was part of the Novinsky boulevard community. The flat in which he lived was spacious enough to have a small separate room, which he used as a studio for making puppets. Far from being a desperate drunkard, he was an Old Believer of stern personal propriety, who refused to divorce his first wife, and always referred to the woman with whom he lived in formal style, by her name and patronymic.[172]

Like the other showmen, the puppeteers might be literate but they invariably performed without a script and had learnt their shows by demonstration, since many were from showmen's families and might well have worked as other fairground or street performers before turning to puppetry. The jobs of barrel-organ player and bottler were sometimes done by adolescents, who simply absorbed the show by being exposed to it so frequently.

This chapter has dealt with two important aspects of how *Petrushka* was culturally transmitted. The first of these is the context of its performance: not indoors and in private, but outdoors, publicly, not only at fairgrounds, but also in courtyards, streets, squares, marketplaces, amongst a crowd whose interventions were immediate and uninhibited. The second aspect is the part played historically by showmen in bringing new material across Europe, by a process which might be described as expansion diffusion: that is, 'by which information or cultural traits spread through an area while still remaining in their area of origin'. Further, the process of diffusion was at first contagious, that is, 'where direct contact is the method of dispersal'; according to Grigorovich's description, the Italian puppeteers actually demonstrated to their Russian apprentices how to perform the show; but in the later tradition was hierarchical, that is, it radiated out from urban centres to rural places.[173] The next two chapters will set out the characteristics of the result of contact, the show itself, before attempting to examine Grigorovich's assertion that, contact or no contact, there was no real resemblance between Italian and Russian glove-puppet performances.

2

The physiognomy of *Petrushka*

An entertainment by hooligans for hooligans.
(Nina Simonovich-Efimova, *Zapiski petrushechnika*, p. 18)

So far, the *Petrushka* show has been described from the outside: it was a text performed at the Russian fairground or in Russian streets from about 1840 onwards, apparently inspired by Italian puppeteers' shows. This background was very important in dictating the shape of the text, which can now be discussed using three headings for convenience. The first of these is the subjects and characters of the play. The *Kamed' o Petrushke* or *Comedy of Petrushka* as it was called ('comedy' in its old sense of 'dramatic action'), was essentially one subject existing in many variants with differences of persons introduced and of scene order. I shall outline the most commonly recurring elements, or the bare body of tradition, and show how individual puppeteers clothed it with improvisation and original adaptations; how, in the words of an old puppeteer quoted by Alferov, 'everyone uglifies Petrushka in his own way'.[1]

This first heading by no means exhausts the interest of the play; in the second section the important issues of its style and comedy must be dealt with. In his book on the Russian folk-tale V. Ya. Propp quotes a definition of this genre by A. I. Nikiforov. The definition is ill-phrased but succinct. It makes a good starting-point for a formalistic study of other popular genres, *Petrushka* among them:

The folk tale is an oral narrative current among the people, whose purpose is to entertain, the contents of which are events which are unusual in everyday life (fantastical, magical or matter-of-fact), and distinguished by its compositional–stylistic structure.[2]

The two elements of Nikiforov's analysis which will particularly concern me will be the compositional-stylistic structure of *Petrushka* and its purpose to entertain. I shall try to establish what type of humour *Petrushka* uses, both in terms of devices and of effect on the audience.

7. A *Petrushka* booth in a small *balagan*. Lithograph from the drawing by K. A. Trutovsky, 1862. From V. N. Vsevolodsky-Gerngross, *Istoriya russkogo teatra*, Leningrad and Moscow 1929, vol. ii.

Under the third heading I shall discuss *Petrushka* as a piece of theatre. Unlike the Ukrainian Christmas crib theatre, the *vertep*, the text was always performed by puppets, never by live actors. Indeed, the word '*petrushka*' is used in Russian generically to mean a glove puppet, '*teatr petrushki*' to mean the glove-puppet theatre. The use of glove puppets dictated the devices and techniques used. I shall discuss what they were, and how far they differed from the devices and techniques current in the theatre performed by live actors.

Textual variants

The reason for describing *Petrushka* as a single subject with variants is that all the texts depict the adventures of a single person, the eponymous hero, who is the text's first and most important element, its defining feature. Dal's dictionary entry for the head-word *Petrushka* mentions the puppet first, and then the theatre:

Petrushka is the nickname of a *balagan* puppet, a Russian joker and entertainer, a wit in a red caftan and red pointed cap; the name *petrushka* is also given to the whole puppet theatre ensemble.[3]

Above all, *Petrushka is* the hero, as the title suggests: not a team, Punch AND Judy, but the hero all alone.

The play always began in the same way. Petrushka, having taunted the public with offstage and off-key squeals, popped up above the booth and launched into a monologue. The *balagan* entrepreneur Alekseev-Yakovlev has recorded a particularly striking version of this monologue:

Vot ya i prishel vas pozabavit', s prazdnikom pozdravit'! golosil Petrushka, podnyavshis' nad shirmoi posle vstupitel'nogo proigrysha muyzykanta, zakanchivavshegosya obychno udarom mednykh tarelok. – Zdorovo, rebyatishki, zdorovo, parnishki! ... Bonzhur, slavnye devchushki, bystroglazye vostrushki! Bonzhur i vam, narumyanennye starushki – derzhite ushki na makushke![4]

('Here I am, come to wish you the best for the holiday and entertain you in my own way!' Petrushka screeched, popping up at the top of the booth after the musician's introductory tune, which usually ended with a clash of cymbals. 'Good day to you, boys, babies, hold your noise! Bonjour, shake your tresses, you sharp-eyed young misses! Bonjour, bonjour, flap your ears, you painted old dears!'

Then followed a scene of conversation with members of the public, which was almost entirely improvised, though, as Alekseev-Yakovlev

points out, the audience's interventions might be orchestrated by one
or two *ponukaly*, 'plants':

Petrushka's comic figure rushed to and fro on the 'beam' above the gaudy,
splotchy portable booth in expectation of replies to his greetings, which
immediately rose from the tight-packed crowd (there were always a few
'plants' there).[5]

The simplest *Petrushka* performances consisted of the appearance of
the hero and his monologue, followed by his disappearance. But even
in the more complicated versions, in which a stream of characters
went in and out, Petrushka was on stage in every scene, and remained
on stage until the end of the play. The only other permanent character
was a human being: an 'otvetchik', or 'respondent' (= feed), who was
often known as the 'Musician', because he normally turned the handle
of the barrel-organ, and who might also act as a 'bottler'. Between
scenes the Feed–Musician and Petrushka would talk to cover the
entrances and exits of the other characters, and the Feed also
suggested things for Petrushka to do, such as singing songs or
dancing, and even had the unenviable task of acting as Petrushka's
conscience, reproving him after his various murders, and trying vainly
to excite repentance.

  Petrushka's appearance was that of a clown in miniature. He was
physically deformed, with a hunch-back, distorted physiognomy (all
nose and chin with button eyes), shortened thorax, and swinging, useless legs. He carried a powerful club (known in Russian as *dubinka*),
with which he was violently active. His moral characteristics were as
unbeautiful as his physique, combining gluttony, priapism, psycho-
pathic aggression, cowardice, cupidity and overpowering egotism.
The play consisted of a brief sequence of scenes in which the hero
encountered other characters and then normally murdered them when
his *ennui* became too great. These characters were drawn from a
traditional core, and although possible combinations were infinite, in
practice the combinations were limited by the number of glove
puppets a puppeteer had in his box, and most puppeteers stuck to
about nine central characters. The other characters would come in one
at a time, and scenes began and ended with their entrances and exits.

  First among these other characters, if not in terms of verbal
contributions (she was normally silent), but in terms of the action, was
Petrushka's fiancée or wife. A variety of names indicated her lack of
definition as a figure: she was most commonly Malan'ya or Parashka,

but might also be Akulina or Matrena or a number of other names of plebeian flavour. The other most popular characters were a Gypsy horse-trader, a German, a Doctor or Apothecary, a Corporal ('Kapral'), a Policeman (usually known as 'Gorodovoi', which was the lowest rank of beat constable), the Devil, and a large fluffy dog, the 'Barbos', a name which comes from the Italian 'Barbone', meaning 'a poodle'. Each of these conventional characters was associated with a conventional scene: Petrushka would dance with his fiancée and sometimes beat her too; would buy a horse from the Gypsy and fall off when he tried to ride it; would be ministered to by the Doctor, enlisted for his rowdiness by the Corporal, called to order by the Policeman and the Devil, until finally the Barbos dragged him off-stage by the nose. The incidence of these traditional scenes has been calculated by Vsevolodsky-Gerngross. He studied twenty-three late nineteenth-century variants and on the basis of these produced the following figures:

1 the announcement by Petrushka that he wants to marry occurs in 20 out of 23 versions
2 purchase of the horse, 20 versions
3 Petrushka and his fiancée, 19 versions
4 Doctor scene, 19 versions
5 Devil or Barbos carries off Petrushka, 18 versions
6 Soldier scene, 16 versions
7 Policeman scene, 12 versions.

'The other twenty-four scenes [of which he gives no details] appear not more than six times each.'[6] This information is confirmed by the editions I have access to, with three differences: the Policeman is absent from all the complete printed versions; the Fiancée does not appear in any of the five *lubok* editions; and the evidence I have would suggest that the scene with the German appeared in a high proportion of variants (he appears in Berkov's version and in three out of five *lubok* versions).

The traditional scenes contained certain stereotyped dialogues and jokes which were used in most versions. One of these was Petrushka's description of what he wanted for a dowry: 44,000 roubles, 'with a quarter-bottle of vodka on top and four groats' worth of cabbage slop' (TP 60). Another was the scene in which the Gypsy described the horse, boasting of its virtues but making it clear that the thing was actually as clapped-out an old nag as could be imagined:

TSYGAN: Loshad' khot' kuda! Bez grivy, bez khvosta.
PETRUSHKA: [*perebivaya*]: Chto khvost i griva? odno ukrashen'e ... A golova est'?
TSYGAN: Tol'ko i est', chto golova odna ... Da i ee eshche net ... konovalu v pochinku otdana.
PETRUSHKA: A masti kakoi?
TSYGAN: Seraya.
PETRUSHKA: A dobra-to ona?
TSYGAN: Ochen' dobraya: pod goru – bezhit-skachet, a na goru polzet-plachet. A esli v gryaz' upadet – sam tashchi, kak znaesh', zato bozhit'sya gotov, chto ne traset: rys'yu ne begaet, a shagom eli-eli idet.

(Berkov 116)

(GYPSY: The highest class of horse! No tail and mane, of course ...
PETRUSHKA: [*interrupting*]: So what, no tail and mane? That's only decoration! Has she a head, at least?
GYPSY: A head's about all she *has* got ... or actually, at the moment, not! It's at the vet's repair shop.
PETRUSHKA: And what colour is she?
GYPSY: Grey.
PETRUSHKA: Is she any good, then?
GYPSY: Very: down hill she rushes and tumbles, up hill she crawls and stumbles. And if she falls in the mud, then you'd better try getting her out as best you may; I'll wager she'll not get up herself, no way. She doesn't trot either; barely puts one foot in front of the other.)

The scene with the Doctor usually contained the following absurd exchange as the Doctor tried to find out where Petrushka's pain was:

DOKTOR: Nu govori, gde bolit, pokazhi!
PETRUSHKA: Vot tut!
DOKTOR: Tut?
PETRUSHKA: Ponizhe.
DOKTOR: Tut?
PETRUSHKA: Povyshe.
DOKTOR: Tut?
PETRUSHKA: Ponizhe.
DOKTOR: Tut?
PETRUSHKA: Povyshe.
DOKTOR: To ponizhe, to povyshe! ... Vstan', vstan', da pokazhi! [*Beret ego za ukho*]

(Berkov 117–18)

(DOCTOR: Well tell me where it hurts, show me!
PETRUSHKA: Right here!
DOCTOR: Here?
PETRUSHKA: Lower.
DOCTOR: Here?

PETRUSHKA: Higher.
DOCTOR: Here?
PETRUSHKA: Lower.
DOCTOR: Here?
PETRUSHKA: Higher.
DOCTOR: One minute lower, one minute higher! Get up, idiot, show me yourself. [*Grabs hold of his ear*])

The traditional characters also had short introductory formulaic monologues, frequently in rhyme, which they would address directly to the audience. The Doctor, for example, would always introduce himself with boasts about his skill which actually made it clear that he was a dangerous incompetent:

Ya znamenityi doktor, konoval i lekar', iz-pod Kamennogo mosta aptekar'. Ya byl v Parizhe, byl i blizhe, byl v Italii, byl i dalee. Ya talantom vladeyu i lechit' umeyu, odnim slovom, kto ko mne pridet na nogakh, togo domoi povezut na drovnyakh. (P 1910)

(I'm the famous doctor and veterinary, the physician from Stone Bridge and apothecary. I've been to gay Paree and nearer to home, to Italy and further I've roamed. I have skill to cure any ill, in a word, they arrive on their feet, they go off wrapped in a sheet.)

The Gypsy's opening monologue, on the other hand, played down his sinister propensities:

Ya tsygan Mora iz tsyganskogo khora – poyu basom, zapivayu kvasom, zaedayu ananasom![7]
(I'm the Gypsy Morus from the Gypsy chorus – I sing bass, I drink kvas, I eat a pineapple slice!)

Besides the traditional, more or less permanent characters, there were several others who appeared only occasionally, and who belong to the following categories: (1) the hero's friends and relations (his Fancy Lady Mamzelle Katerina, his friend Filimoshka, his Father, his Aunt Alenka); (2) social functionaries (a 'Barin' or 'nob', a Deacon, two Nuns, a Matchmaker, a 'Dvornik' or Janitor, a Rag-and-Bone Man, a Tavern-Keeper); (3) members of non-Russian racial groups (a Jew, an Arab, a Tartar, a Chinaman); (4) relations of the latter two categories (the Corporal's Father, the Jew's Father, the German's Father, etc.); (5) fairground entertainers (a Clown, a Harlequin). In other words, nearly all the characters who appeared belonged to categories familiar to the predominantly subordinate class audience of *Petrushka*. The Devil was the main exception, and in many Russian street versions this character was replaced by the fierce Barbos, which would have been only too familiar a figure, since attacks by dogs were a noted hazard of city courtyards.[8]

Most of the subsidiary characters also had their own traditional scenes. Many of these were simple. They would come on, make some statement that indicated their roles in a crude way, and Petrushka would then dispatch them. Petrushka would offer to 'teach the Arab a Russian song', would buy food from the Jew, the Tavern-Keeper or the Porter and then pay for it in blows, would offer to 'treat his friend Filimoshka to a drink' and then kill him, and so on. The Barin's traditional scene was a little different: he would engage Petrushka as a servant and order him to put the samovar on. Petrushka would return to say that the tea was ready but the samovar had 'escaped' (TP 68, 70).

There is no one street version in which all these characters appear. The puppeteer's choice was limited not only by the size of his battery

8. Petrushka and the Doctor. Anonymous illustration from *Moskva v ee proshlom i nastoyashchem*, x (1911).

of puppets, but also by the necessary brevity of the street performance. (One commentator observes that the average performance
lasted five minutes;[9] this is an underestimate, judging by the texts we
have: from fifteen to twenty minutes would have been average). The
archive texts vary from three scenes to twenty or more; most had nine,
using the nine traditional characters.[10] Occasionally there were also
wordless *divertissements*: the most popular characters for these were
two Arabs who fought or did stick dances:

Two darkies dressed in velvet and gold would thwack each other's wooden
noddles mercilessly with sticks or throw the sticks at each other and catch
them.[11]

Another wordless *divertissement* was one in which two Nuns appeared
to bury one of Petrushka's murder victims, but were unable to fit him
into the coffin because it was too short (Berkov 120).

9.   A set of nineteenth-century *Petrushka* puppets: from left to right, Doctor, Gypsy,
      Petrushka, Corporal and Petrushka's Wife. The Dog in front.

The variants of *Petrushka*, like those of any orally transmitted text, were a product of the conflict of tradition and improvisation. The show was the result not of creation but of recreation; any individual puppeteer based a new version on a show or shows which he (or occasionally she) had seen.[12] The dynamics of the text were, on the one hand, a need not to vary a successful show too much; on the other, a need to awaken interest by originality. Re-workings of the text were never very radical: one or two new or unusual characters might be introduced, but a variant with only unusual characters would not have been possible.

But within a limited spectrum, remarkable effects were possible. The puppeteer might vary the order in which the scenes appeared, and the extent to which a logical narrative sequence was preserved. The organisation of some variants is episodic: there are several beatings which succeed each other without rhyme or reason. In others there was a whole integrated story of how Petrushka, a boy from Yaroslavl recently arrived in town, sets out to find himself a wife, a horse and a job, and how he has a series of encounters which end in disaster.

The puppeteer might also vary the ending of individual scenes. The standard outcome to all the scenes in all versions is predetermined by the hero's character: he is expected to murder, or at least chase off, his opponent. So the puppeteer might also vary the action by retarding the beating with extra dialogue, adumbrating it with allusions ('I'll just step outside for a moment', Petrushka might say, and the audience knew he would fetch his club whilst there), or occasionally dispensing with the beating altogether, leaving the audience in a state of comic disappointment.

Some commentators have attempted to suggest that certain scenes always had a certain outcome, and have contradicted each other in the process, suggesting how futile it is to try to pin down a canonical version. For example, of Petrushka's relationship with his wife, Alekseev-Yakovlev poetically states:

The only character to whom Petrushka behaved with tenderness, lyrically, was his fiancée the milkmaid Praskovya Pelageevna, also known as Parasha or Paran'ka.[13]

The anonymous contributor to the *Brockhaus-Efron Encyclopedia*, on the other hand, suggests that Petrushka and his fiancée invariably fought; and so does Yury Dmitriev.[14] The truth of the matter can only be that in some versions they did, in others they did not. Even the culminating scene, in which Petrushka encountered the Devil or the Barbos, was subject to variation: sometimes he was dragged off to hell-fire or to be eaten, but on other occasions he outwitted even this final opponent, as Gor'ky records:

Petrushka is the indefatigable hero of the folk puppet theatre, he defeats everyone and everything: the police, priests, even death and the devil, whilst himself remaining immortal.[15]

Needless to say, the series of beatings which was the core of *Petrushka* allowed for no psychological exposition or development: the characters live in the present, and their identity is limited to their function: they are there to beat or be beaten, and to represent certain social groups. The only level of sophistication is that certain victims may try to outwit Petrushka, either by tricking him, as the Gypsy and the German try to trick him, or by hectoring him (his Wife and Aunt Alenka, in some unusual variants, read him homilies about his drinking and debauchery). But the tricksters and the hectorers alike end up by getting a beating. In the scene below Petrushka takes action to silence his critical wife:

[ZHENA]: Akh, ty, p'yanitsa, p'yanitsa: ty zh moi usi khudoby propiv.
[PETRUSHKA]: A yak ty moi rukavitsy propila s kumom Regoduleyu.
[ZHENA]: Khodim do domu.
[PETRUSHKA]: Ta ne pidu.
[ZHENA]: Ty znaesh', kto ya take?
[PETRUSHKA]: Kto zhe ty take?
[ZHENA]: Ya popiv'ska dochka.
[PETRUSHKA]: Ege, shchast'e velike. A ya kvartal'nogo kuchera kuritsy kum.
[ZHENA]: Khodim do domu, a to ya tobi ochi povyderu.
[*Petrushka khvataet butylku i nachinaet eyu bit' svoyu suprugu*]
[PETRUSHKA]: A os' tobi, os'!
[ZHENA]: Ratuite, lyudi dobrye! Muzh zhinku b'e.   (TP 78)

(WIFE: Och, you drunkard, you drunkard: you've drunk all my cattle away.
PETRUSHKA: Just like ye drank my mittens away, you and your gossip Regodulya.
WIFE: Let's go home.
PETRUSHKA: I'm not going there.
WIFE: Have ye forgotten who I am?
PETRUSHKA: Well, who are ye then?
WIFE: I'm a pope's daughter.
PETRUSHKA: Eh, there's posh. And I'm the coachman on the corner's cockerel's confidante.
WIFE: Let's go home, 'fore I scratch yer eyes out.

[*Petrushka grabs the bottle and starts to beat his wife*]
PETRUSHKA: Take that, and that!
WIFE: Help, good people! Me husband's killing me!)

The hero's persona is exposed at more length, and does at least have a range of sorts (he is a rubbish-heap of *all* the vices), but no psychological motivation is allowed here either – he simply waits for an opportunity to indulge in his favourite activity, using the *dubinka* (club).

As is the general rule in orally transmitted texts, differentiation of variants was likely to occur not only at the level of motif (which in *Petrushka* would mean meetings with characters and their outcome), but also at the level of traditional comic formulae and jokes.[16] The Doctor nearly always introduced himself with the line, 'Ya doktor-lekar, iz-pod Kamennogo mosta aptekar' ('I'm the doctor and physician, the apothecary from Stone Bridge'), but after this the same idea, that he cured his patients by killing them, was expressed in different ways in different shows. There might be a mixture of different rhyming formulae, and the more talented a puppeteer was, the more formulae there would be. This version of the Doctor's speech is a virtuoso classic:

Ya doktor, s Kuznetskogo mosta pekar', lekar' i aptekar'. Kogda prikhodyat bol'nye gospoda, ya ikh lechu udachno vsegda; zhivo ikh chto delat' nauchu ... Inogda vmesto khiny mysh'yaku vsuchu ... Ko mne lyudei vedut na nogakh, a ot menya vezut na drogakh. A kakikh prinesut na nogakh, tak tekh vezut na pogost na sanyakh.   (Berkov 117)

(I'm a doctor, a baker and undertaker from Kuznetsky Most, a veterinary and apothecary. When sick gents arrive I always keep 'em alive; I show 'em what to do, instead of quinine I give 'em a grain of arsenic or two ... They bring me people on their feet, and take them away in a sheet. They come in carried, on a sledge to the graveyard they're ferried.

The better showmen would also play for laughs by alternating standard formulae, normally in rhyme, with prose asides:

Akh, doktor, ne gubi menya: pust' ot tebya ya ne poedu ni na drogakh, ni na sanyakh ... menya by v proletke otpravil i tem ot smerti izbavil.
                                                                                (Berkov 117)

(Oh Doctor, don't kill me; don't send me away on a hurdle, let me not be a sledge's burden ... send me away in a hansom, and I'll pay you a king's ransom.)

Topical or personal references might also be introduced. Many of these were probably made in Petrushka's opening monologue, so they have not been recorded, but one version gives an indication of the way puppeteers would respond to a particular audience. When Petrushka announces his marriage, he says that he is getting married to a merchant's daughter, and then names a well-known local rich man (Berkov 115).

The variations that were possible between individual scenes are best shown by direct comparison. The scene where Petrushka and the Gypsy horse-trade, which occurs in nearly all the versions, was handled with considerable freshness by street puppeteers. The two versions quoted below vary in the number and elaboration of the formulae used, in the way that rhyme and prose are alternated, and in pace of exchange:

SHUMSKY'S VERSION:

PETRUSHKA: A mnogo ona stoit?
TSYGAN: Nemnogo, ne malo – poltorasta rublei.
PETRUSHKA: Chego poltorasta? Gvozdei?
TSYGAN: Ne gvozdei, a rublei.
PETRUSHKA: Akh, ty, tsyganskaya tvoya rozha. [*B' et ego*]
TSYGAN: Kupit' ne kupil, a vlepil zdorovo.
PETRUSHKA: A chto zh tak dorogo prosish'?
TSYGAN: A skol'ko, pan, budesh' davat'?
PETRUSHKA: Vot tebe tabaku pachku, da rubl' tri grivennika s pyatakom na pridachu.
TSYGAN: Malo.
PETRUSHKA: Chtoby tebya razorvalo.
TSYGAN: Davai, pan, na pribavku.
PETRUSHKA: Vot tebe na pribavku rubl', da pirozhok s krysami.

(Tarasov 32–3)

(PETRUSHKA: Does she cost much?
GYPSY: Not too much, not too little – a hundred and fifty roubles.
PETRUSHKA: A hundred and fifty what? Poodles?
GYPSY: Not poodles, roubles.
PETRUSHKA: Eh, you, gypsy gob! [*Beats him*]
GYPSY: He may not have bought it, I think I've caught it!
PETRUSHKA: Why is she so dear?
GYPSY: How much will you give me, gaffer?
PETRUSHKA: A packet of baccy, a rouble three groats more and a fiver to keep the wolf from the door.
GYPSY: It's not enough.
PETRUSHKA: Get stuffed.

GYPSY: A little extra, gaffer.

PETRUSHKA: Here's a rouble extra, and a tart with rats inside.)

PETRUSHKA: Nu i loshadka! Ai, ai, ai! Skol'ko tebe za nee?

TSYGAN: 200 rublei.

PETRUSHKA: Dorogovato ... Poluchi palku-kucheryavku, da dubinku-gorbinku i po shee tebe i spinku.

TSYGAN: Pribav', Petrushka mus'e, detishkam na salo ...

PETRUSHKA: Tak eto tebe malo? Nu tak podozhdi; ya poidu tebe zadatok prinesu. [*Ukhodit, nemedlenno vozvrashchaetsya s palkoi. Podkhodit k Tsyganu szadi i b'et ego po golove*] Vot tebe zadatok! Vot tebe zadatok!

(Berkov 117)

(PETRUSHKA: There's a fine horse! Ooh, ooh, ooh! How much do you want for her, then?

GYPSY: 200 roubles.

PETRUSHKA: That's a bit dear ... I'll give you a lick with my big thick stick, and a rub-a-dub-dub with my club on the neck and the lug.

GYPSY: Give me some more, Petrushka moosieur, to buy the kids some bacon fat ...

PETRUSHKA: Not satisfied with that? Well, I'll bring you the down payment then. [*Goes out, brings back his club straightaway, goes up to Gypsy from behind and whacks him on the head*] There's the down payment! There's the down payment!)

Many critics of *Petrushka* have attempted to trace the development of the text historically. Vsevolodsky-Gerngross has argued that the recorded versions are a bastardisation of an original coherent and smooth narrative, on to which distorting episodes were grafted.[17] He appears undeterred by the fact that the scenes which he considers the core (those with the Barin, Filimoshka, and the Tavern-Keeper) were in fact the least usual. Anna Nekrylova takes the exactly opposite view, arguing that the tendency to sequentiality became obvious only in the late nineteenth century, and that the original structure of the puppet texts was as random as that of the cumulative tale (an international standard folklore type, of which English-language examples are 'The House that Jack Built', 'There Was an Old Woman who Swallowed a Fly', or 'And Still She Wished for Company'):

In cumulative fairy tales [*sic*] the sequencing can be motivated, but as a rule 'the art of these tales requires no logic whatsoever'. For a very long time, puppet comedy retained this particular method of joining its scenes together; only in the late 19th century performances a tendency began to emerge to provide some motivation by arranging some blocs in which the scenes seemed to continue one another, or to follow one from another.[18]

Both these views, that the primary text is more likely to be coherent than the secondary text, or vice versa, seem to me unsatisfactory a priori. Coherence is more a matter of aesthetic demands at a given historical epoch than of where that epoch comes in the series. The *commedia dell' arte* scenarios of the seventeenth century were far more elaborately plotted and structured than the Russian *intermedii* of the eighteenth century, which were based on them. Besides, as has emerged in my historical survey, it is unlikely that *Petrushka* is more than a hundred and fifty years old, and so 'historical development', whichever way, is difficult to prove. It is not possible to trace a linear development from the order of Grigorovich's texts of 1842 to the late nineteenth century. Until an exact analysis of character and scene incidence of *all* the archival texts is made, as well as the formulae in them, it makes no sense to pronounce on historical changes in *Petrushka*. The limited amount of information available so far shows that the street tradition could simultaneously support knockabout episodic farces and smoothly plotted comedies. The 1842 version quoted by Grigorovich has a relatively well-ordered plot: Petrushka is invited to do an errand for the Police Captain, agrees, the Police Captain dances with his lady friend and Petrushka is picked up for bad behaviour. On the other hand, at much the same date a school inspector in Krasnodar left the following splendidly alienated account of an episodic performance:

I was at the fair today. A circle of fiddlers, a bass, tambourines and cymbals presented themselves to my view. There was a screen of furnishing fabric with an aperture at the top. The band struck up some vulgar music, and two disreputable puppets of the male and the female gender began to dance; save that one could not see their legs, it stands to reason. After the first pair had finished, another scampered on to replace them, in quite different costumes, and so on. At the end of the dances they embraced one another. Finally a most disreputable great bulging-nosed lout [*nosatyi velikan*] appeared; at first he murdered a soldier, then a doctor, and in the end the Devil himself. At last a white dog dragged him off by the nose into the wings, and thus put an end to his debaucheries. After this we were informed that the thing had finished.[19]

As unsatisfactory as these different attempts to trace growth of coherence or incoherence is Vsevolodsky-Gerngross' theory that the ending in which Petrushka is dragged off to Hell was forced on the puppeteers by church censorship.[20] As is clear from the account

above, scenes in which Petrushka defeated the Devil were being
played quite openly in the nineteenth century, and again it was a
question of a choice between alternatives.

   The only part of the history of *Petrushka* about which there is much
evidence is the publication of the *lubok* editions at the end of the
nineteenth century. These little books indicate two trends. First, two
of them, the 1891 and the 1908 editions, indicate the growing
tendency to see *Petrushka* as a text for children. In both, his taste for
using a club is played down, particularly in the 1891 version, which
has nine scenes, in six of which the club is not used; in the other three,
murder is not committed. Instead of killing the Corporal, he offers
him a dose of 'snuff' which turns out to be pepper. The 1908 edition
has five scenes: in one Petrushka kills the Soldier, but in three others
he chases the characters off; in the fifth he does not use the club at all.
Petrushka's own character has been altered: he has become whiny and
babyish. It is hardly likely that the Doctor would have spoken to the
true street Petrushka like this with impunity:

Pered toboyu doktor-vrach, utesh'sya, milyi moi, ne plach'.   (NP 1891, 7)

(Hush, the doctor's here, don't cry, my dear.)

The street Petrushka's grandmother might well have upbraided him,
but he would not have responded by stopping his ears, as he does in
the 1908 version. There is other evidence, too, that juvenile tastes have
been accommodated: new characters have been introduced, most of
them beasties: a Crocodile in the 1908 edition, a Bear and a Woolly
Lamb in the 1891 edition. The 1908 edition also contains a Night
Watchman, Petrushka's Grandmother and Death. There are obvious
differences between the level of traditional elements in the two texts.
The earlier text reads like a street puppeteers' version done for
children: though Petrushka fails to beat the Gypsy and the Corporal,
his encounters with the Jew and the Armenian are on the traditional
pattern, including the insultingly racist manner of his address. Formulae and standard jokes are widely used, and the mixture of rhyme and
prose recalls the street versions. The 1908 version reads like a literary
adaptation which has moved quite a long way from the street text: it
retains only the scene with the Soldier, and it is written entirely in
rhyming couplets. Some standard formulae have been used, which
give it a superficial resemblance to the traditional *Petrushka*.

   The second tendency, indicated by the other three *lubok* editions (published in 1907, 1910 and 1915), is fossilisation of the plot. All three contain five scenes, with the same characters and in the same order: the Gypsy, the Doctor, the German, the Corporal, the Barbos. Superficially this might seem to confirm Nekrylova's suggestion that there was a movement towards coherence in the late nineteenth century. But it seems to me more likely that the resemblance of these texts indicates an artificial coherence imposed by printing, which was transferred from these printed books to the street. I would suggest that as literacy rose, the less inventive puppeteers turned to these editions and used them as scripts, rather than making their own version of a text learnt orally. This impression is confirmed on closer study of the texts. They preserve the character of the street version in the texts by using a mixture of formulae and improvisation, prose and rhyme. But the level of inventiveness is lower. Here are extracts from the three versions of the scene with the Gypsy. The wording is very similar in all three, although there are some original jokes, particularly in the 1915 version:

FROM THE 1907 VERSION:

TSYGAN: Zdravstvui, Petr Ivanovich, kak zhivesh'-pozhivaesh', khorosho li khvoraesh'?
PETRUSHKA: A ty kto takoi? Uzh ne doktor-li?
TSYGAN: Ya tsygan Mora, iz tsyganskogo khora, poyu tam basom, zapivayu kvasom!
PETRUSHKA: A ty yazykom-to mnogo ne boltai. Chto nado – govori, da mimo prokhodi!
TSYGAN: Mne govoril frantsuz Foma, chto tebe khoroshaya loshad' nuzhna.   (P 1907)

(GYPSY: Good day to you, Petr Ivanovich, are you feeling well, are you nice and ill?
PETRUSHKA: And who are you? Not the doctor, are you?
GYPSY: I'm the Gypsy Morus from the Gypsy chorus, I sing bass and drink kvas!
PETRUSHKA: Keep a rein on your tongue. Say your say, and get out of my way!
GYPSY: My friend the Frog Yves told me you're after a horse, I believe.)

FROM THE 1910 VERSION:

TSYGAN: Zdravstvui, mus'yu Petr Ivanovich! Kak zhivesh'-pozhivaesh', chasto li khvoraesh'?
PETRUSHKA: A tebe kakoe delo? Uzh ty ne doktor li?
TSYGAN: Ne boisya, ya ne doktor . . . Ya tsygan Mora iz khora, poyu basom, zapivayu kvasom, zaedayu ananasom!

PETRUSHKA: A ty yazykom-to ne boltai, zuby ne zagovarivai. Govori, chto nado, da mimo provalivai.

TSYGAN: Moi znakomyi frantsuz Foma, kotoryi sovsem bez uma, govorit, chto tebe khoroshaya loshad' nuzhna, chtoby prizy na skachkakh brat'.

(P 1910)

10. Petrushka and the Gypsy. Chromolithograph of about 1890.

(GYPSY: Good day to you, monseer Petr Ivanovich. Are you feeling well, are you often ill?

PETRUSHKA: What's it to do with you? Not the doctor, are you?

GYPSY: Don't worry, I'm not the doctor . . . I'm the Gypsy Morus from the chorus, I sing bass, I drink kvas, I eat a pineapple slice!

PETRUSHKA: Keep a rein on your tongue. Watch what you're saying there, say your say and get out of my hair!

GYPSY: My friend Yves the Frog, the one who's as mad as a dog, he told me you want a horse to get all the prizes at the race course.)

FROM THE 1915 VERSION:

TSYGAN: Zdravstvui, mus'yu Shishel-Myshel! Ya k tebe sam konskii zavod-chik vyshel! Kak zhivesh'-pozhivaesh'? Chasto li khvoraesh'? Ya – tsygan Mora iz tsyganskogo khora, poyu basom, zaedayu ananasom, zapivayu kvasom!

PETRUSHKA: Vot chto, chumazaya rozha, Shaltai-Baltai! Ty ponaprasnu yazykom-to ne boltai, a govori delo!

TSYGAN: Moi znakomyi anglichanin Rok, votknul sebe vily v bok, po vsei Evrope kochuet, kazhduyu noch' na Khitrovku nochuet. Shishel-Myshel, ot kogo-to slyshal, chto tebe khoroshii kon' trebuetsya?   (P 1915)

(GYPSY: Good day to you, monseer Shishel-Michel! I've come from the stud-farm to wish you well! Are you feeling all right, are you good and ill tonight? I'm the Gypsy Morus from the Gypsy chorus, I sing bass, I eat a pineapple slice and drink kvas!

PETRUSHKA: So that's who you are, grimy face! Mind what you say, not a word out of place!

GYPSY: My friend the Englishman Ride, he got a pitchfork in the side, he's been in Europe all over, every night he dosses in Khitrovka! Shishel-Michel, my friend told me you need a very fine steed?)

The *lubok* editions also give a useful boost to the information we have about topicality. In the 1915 version, the Soldier's name is changed from the Russian 'Kapral' to the German 'Feldwebel', presumably for patriotic reasons: at the height of the First World War it might not have seemed suitable to have a Russian soldier murdered by a street hooligan. This edition also contains a couple of updated jokes. Petrushka's opening speech states that he has arrived by means of a modern form of transport, an aeroplane:

Kha-kha-kha! Razlyubeznye gospoda! Vot i ya priekhal syuda, ne v tar-antase-rydvane, a pryamo na aeroplane – v dubovom yashchike!

(P 1915, 3)

(Hee hee hee! Gents and la-dies! Petrushka's arrived – not in a coach, carriage or train, but in an aeroplane – an oak box!)

Here, and in the 1910 edition, the horse which he buys from the Gypsy is said to be a racehorse:

Da, brat, ya davno khlopochu – skakovogo beguna zavesti khochu. Tol'ko khorosha li u tebya loshad'.

(Yes, brother, I've been trying for ages – want to get a horse for the races. But is your horse a good one?)   (P 1915, 5)

The collected texts of *Petrushka* display regional, as well as historical, variations in detail. As has been demonstrated, the text originated in St Petersburg, and St Petersburg was the standard setting of the text. In some versions Petrushka's address is given as 'V samom Peterburge, v Semenovskom polku, dom plesivyi, fundament solomennyi, khozyain kamennyi, nomer 9' ('In Petersburg town, in the Semenov regiment district, the house is mouldy, the foundation is grassy, the landlord is stony, number 9').[21] In others Petrushka has adopted urban ways, and expects his fiancée to be able to dance a waltz or a 'kadrel' (quadrille). He promises to buy her clothes and shoes when in town (TP 61). In the two most recently published Petersburg variants Petrushka's Bride, too, is a Petersburg resident whose preferred beverage is coffee (the drink of the Petersburg poor), and who hankers after goods from the *Gostinyi dvor*, or covered market on Nevsky Prospect (FT 286–7). As performances of the text spread outside St Petersburg, the old references stayed, but new elements crept in. The Doctor, for example, gave his formulaic opening speech, but described himself as being from *Kuznetskii Most* (a street in Moscow) not *Kamennyi Most*: Stone Bridge or 'the stone bridge' – capitalisation varies and seems to have depended on the transcriber (Berkov 117).[22] New local characters supplemented the standard core (Jews were particularly popular in the south). Incidental elements were changed: Petrushka's wife is given in some versions as a priest's daughter, rather than her Petersburg role as a merchant's daughter, working-class girl or village girl still stuck at home.[23]

It was above all in the Ukraine and in the south, as Eremin has pointed out, that *Petrushka* altered and developed (TP 77). The squabble between Petrushka and his wife quoted above is from a Chernigov variant. There is, however, one outstanding *Petrushka* variant from elsewhere: that recorded by Doroshevich in Sakhalin, in which Petrushka is transformed into a parricide as well as a murderer. When Petrushka's father requests a loan, Petrushka agrees readily, pays it (predictably) in twenty whacks, and is then carted off to prison camp. He finishes the action with a camp song:

Proshchai, Odessa,
Slavnyi karantin,
Menya otpravlyayut
Na ostrov Sakhalin![24]

(Goodbye, Odessa,
Fine quarantine!
They're sending me
To the island of Sakhalin!)

As Anna Nekrylova has demonstrated, the north Russian variants
were distinguished more by flexibility of scene arrangements than by a
range of new characters and scenes.[25] In Moscow also, the versions
played were close to the St Petersburg tradition, without significant
input of new regional material.[26] But the *lubok* editions published
there have some local references: for example, in the 1915 version the
Gypsy says that his English friend spends his nights around Khitrovka, the site of the notorious doss-houses, stews and thieves' dens
described by Gilyarovsky in his writings (see pp. 41–42). He says that
he has left his hump 'on Trubnaya square', and sings the following
Moscow song:

Vsem izvesten ya za khvata,
Khot′ poklyast′sya vam gotov –
Ot Varvarki do Arbatu,
I do Presnenskikh prudov!

(I'm known all over as a lad,
I'll stake my oath thereon –
From Varvarka to the Arbat,
Right to the Presnya ponds!)

One reason for the interdependence of variants was certainly the
cameraderie amongst puppeteers working a given area. 'There are
about ten of us working round Petersburg and we all know each
other', commented one *Petrushka* player in 1896 (TP 293). But
further information on the dynamics of regional traditions must wait
for a full study of the variants.[27]

Petrushka *and carnival culture*

The first part of the question of what *Petrushka* was has now been
answered. It was a glove-puppet text with a single subject, albeit with
many variations: the story of a country boy's misadventures in town.

The structure of the text was not, we have seen, characterised by any complexity: it was episodic, and we cannot speak of the 'morphology' of the puppet play as we can of the folk-tale. But as the action was consecutive and limited to a single scene, *Petrushka* was concentrated in setting and time-span; it observed Aristotle's three unities as rigidly as any neo-classical tragedy, and indeed its concentration on the hero makes it in some ways the mirror-image of tragedy.

Prolonged study of the plot, characterisation and structure of *Petrushka* does not reveal its most interesting elements, and analysis of them soon begins to sound heavy-footed and even self-parodistic. The story was simple; in the method of its realisation lay complexity and interest. In the Introduction (pp. 59–60) I identified the compositional–stylistic construction of *Petrushka* as an object of study. The compositional features of *Petrushka*, it has emerged, were unremarkable. I shall now proceed to a discussion of the stylistic features of *Petrushka*. It is the style of the text which brings about the comedy, above all the hero's sharp and witty comments, of which Nekrasov wrote:

Komediya ne mudraya,
Odnako i ne glupaya, –
Khozhalomu, kvartal'nomu,
Ne v brov', a pryamo v glaz ...
Shalash polnym-polnekhonek,
Narod oreshki shchelkaet,
A to dva-tri krest'yanina
Slovechkom perekinutsya,
Glyadi, yavilas' vodochka:
Posmotryat, da pop'yut!
Khokhochut, uteshayutsya
I chasto v rech' Petrushkinu
Vstavlyayut slovo metkoe,
Kakoe ne pridumaesh',
Khot' progloti pero.[28]

The comedy may not be deep,
But it's not stupid either, –
The patrolman, the policeman,
Gets it right in the eye!
The hut is full to brimming,
The public chomp their nuts,
And now and then two peasant men
Exchange a word or two.
Look, now they've got the vodka out –

They're drinking whilst they watch.
They laughing and they're having fun,
And often to Petrushka's speeches
They add an apt and witty word,
Which you'd as soon think up yourself
As swallow your quill pen.

It was Petrushka's talent as an entertainer (he has been described by one commentator as a 'konferans'e', or 'master of ceremonies')[29] which led audiences to flock to his booth and to attend performance after performance on the same day. Petrushka's character observed no principles of psychological coherence or unity: he was a cowardly sniveller one minute, an audacious murderer the next, just so long as he made people laugh. So to answer the question, 'What is Petrushka?', one must also establish how he did this.

It was partly a question of setting, of course. People went to the *gulyan'ya* to enjoy themselves: they often arrived at the entertainments mildly tipsy on mead or beer, and later in the century perhaps more starkly befuddled on vodka. Even for the non-bibulous, the atmosphere was raised and excitable, the spectacles colourful by comparison with the greyness of urban tenement life. There was a determination to have fun at all costs. People's high spirits sometimes spilled over into impromptu and unpaid side shows; Ivan Shcheglov, when visiting a country fair, saw a drunken peasant dance the trepak all by himself.[30] When shows took place in the city streets, the setting was not so sharply differentiated from everyday scenes; but here the bright colour of booth and puppets was important, as was the sense of relaxation generated in overworked lives by having enough time to stand and stare. Besides the demarcated arena and excited audience, the most important thing was the puppeteer's skill: it was vital that the performances should be brief and played at a rattling pace, and that the puppeteer should lash up enthusiasm with his high-pitched babble and stream of jokes and one-liners.

But the humour of many *Petrushka* texts survives the absence of performer, audience and original setting. The best of them are delightful: they combine lurid abuse and *double entendres* with inspired nonsense, puns and *non sequiturs*. Not surprisingly, recent criticism on *Petrushka* has applied itself to the study of the comic elements in the text. Anna Nekrylova has written that the main comic device in *Petrushka* is incongruity, and particularly oxymoron,[31] a word which she uses quite loosely, to mean 'impossible combinations of words' and not in its narrower English sense. Examples of 'oxymoron' quoted by Nekrylova include Petrushka's remark about the horse: 'She must be young, you know: there's not a tooth in her head'; 'I had 60 kopecks in my pocket, but there's a rouble left now', and the bizarre combination 'three pounds of bottle'. Such nonsensical combinations are often introduced in the form of cross-purpose dialogues, such as the following exchange between Petrushka and the Devil:

PETRUSHKA: Kuda ya s toboi poidu?
CHERT: V ad!
PETRUSHKA: V maskarad? V maskarad ya s toboi ne poidu.[32]

(PETRUSHKA: Where am I going with you?
DEVIL: To Hades!
PETRUSHKA: To a masquerade? No, I'm not going to a masquerade with you.)

Nekrylova illustrates how rhyme and prose are used alternately in the text to bring out these contrasts. Sometimes, as in the example above, rhyme links two incompatible words; in other cases prose is used unexpectedly to bring out the joke:

GORODOVOI: Teper' ya budu obuchat' tebya marshirovke.
PETRUSHKA: Khodit' po verevke?
                                        Nos razob' yu!

(POLICEMAN: Now I'm going to teach you to march.
PETRUSHKA: Do a tight-rope dance?
                                        I'll smash your face in!)

GORODOVOI: ... budu obuchat' tebya marshirovat'.
PETRUSHKA: Uchit' vorovat'?
                                        Mozhesh' sam![33]

(POLICEMAN: I'll teach you how to pick your feet up.
PETRUSHKA: Lift some stuff?
                                        You can do that yourself!)

  Later in her essay, Nekrylova argues that the source of the humour in *Petrushka* is these incongruous combinations. Neither component of the 'oxymoron' is funny in itself; it is the unexpected association of them which brings about the humour.[34] Fair enough; although there is nothing intrinsically funny about absurd incongruity (in Shakespeare's *Romeo and Juliet* the oxymoron expresses confusion and tragic ambivalence); the idea that comedy rests on contrast is a banality of theories of comedy.[35]

But in order to explain why *Petrushka* was so popular with its audiences, it is necessary to go deeper than this, to look more closely at the components of the contrast. The point is that in *Petrushka*, as in other comic fairground texts, the apparently innocuous absurdity of the comic oxymoron often conceals far from harmless references. A standard comic monologue spoken by the carnival barkers in Russia told an anecdote about working as a barber which on the face of it was nonsensical:

Byl ya tsyrul'nikom na bol'shoi Moskovskoi doroge. Kogo pobrit', usy popravit', molodtsom postavit', a net, tak i sovsem bez golovy ostavit'. Kogo ya ne brival, tot doma nikogda ne byval. Etu tsyrul'nyu mne zapretili.

(Berkov 132)

(I was a barber on the main Moscow highway. I shaved some, gave their whiskers a comb; made them look fine feathers, else I took their heads off altogether. I shaved some that never went home. In the end that barbering was forbidden me.)

The Moscow audience would fall about when they heard this, because it was obvious to them that the clown was referring to barbering in the honest tradition of Sweeney Todd: this 'barber' was in fact a highway robber. Many examples of oxymoron quoted by Nekrylova likewise turn out on analysis to be less absurd than they seem. Petrushka's enthusiastic exclamation: 'The horse must be young, there's not a tooth in her head' reveals to the audience that he is being cheated by the Gypsy; they understand that what appears to Petrushka to be a sign of youth is in fact an indication of extreme decrepitude. Likewise, the seemingly crazy statement, 'I had sixty kopecks, and now there's a rouble left' may contain a subtextual reference to thieving, the only way in which Petrushka can be supposed to have increased his supply of money. The rhyming word-plays which Nekrylova quotes also have sinister elements. In the passage quoted above, the verb *marshirovat'* (literally: 'to march': translated as 'pick your feet up') could have been made to rhyme with any of the very large number of Russian verbs with the suffix *-ovat'*: *vorovat'* (literally 'to thieve'; translated as 'lift some stuff') is selected.

The humour of *Petrushka* exists at more than one level: the childish humour of feeble puns and nonsense masks references to social and sometimes also sexual taboos. It is allied to the techniques of

Aesopian narrative: to a knowledgeable watcher it conveys social comment, whilst deceiving the eye of the censor or outsider.[36] Pleasure comes not only from the distorted analogies, but from the sense that these are mischievous, that they touch on forbidden subjects.

This humour is *Witz*, as defined by Freud. By *Witz* (which means 'wit' in both senses, abstract and concrete, and also 'joke',) Freud meant a type of humour which shares the structural devices of other kinds of humour, such as incongruity, *double entendre* or deliberate misunderstanding, but which is distinguished from these other kinds of humour by its motivation – it is a lowering, aggressive genre, anything other than harmless in its intention:

> Wit can either be *hostile* (it serves the end of aggression, satire, or resistance), or *obscene* (which serves the end of exposure).[37]

The texts of *Petrushka* manifest a high degree of social and sexual aggression. Petrushka's class origins are stressed: in one variant the Musician refuses to do any of the things Petrushka commands him to, because Petrushka's plebeian status does not require it:

PETRUSHKA: [*vazhno*]: Nu, tak segodnya loshad' privedi!
MUZYKANT: I sam ne barin, skhodish' i privedesh'.
PETRUSHKA: Tak ne poidesh'?   (Berkov 116)

(PETRUSHKA: [*grandly*]: Well, bring me the horse today then!
MUSICIAN: You're no gent yourself, *you* go and get it.
PETRUSHKA: So you won't fetch it?)

Many of Petrushka's victims in the play are his class enemies, and in certain scenes, such as his rebellion against military service, his actions attack the political fabric of society.

His sexual aggression is mainly manifested towards his fiancée. When she first emerges, he describes her charms to the Musician as if admiring a horse:

MUZYKANT: Khorosha-to khorosha ... da kurnosa.
PETRUSHKA: Ai vresh', muzykant! Da ty posmotri, chto za glazki, chto za rotik! Ruchki!! Gubki!! Sheika!!   (Berkov 116)

(MUSICIAN: Well, she's pretty enough ... but snub-nosed.
PETRUSHKA: Musician, you're lying! Just look at her button eyes! Her rosebud mouth! What hands!! What lips!! What a neck!!)

The published versions of *Petrushka* have gone through a triple censorship process. Puppeteers were reluctant to give unvarnished variants to the educated philologists who went round collecting texts; philologists were reluctant to record outright smut; and there has been hesitation about publishing such crudities as have survived the first two stages of repression. But from eyewitness accounts it is clear that in some versions of the text an extra scene, of which no variants exists, was played as a coda to the comedy. In this scene, known as 'Petrushkina svad'ba' (Petrushka's Wedding), Petrushka's priapism towards his fiancée was such that he was unwilling to wait as long as his wedding night, and eventually persuaded her to give herself up in advance.[38] Descriptions of unpublished variants in archives suggest that they, too, contain 'uncensored' items: Eremin reveals that Petrushka's demand for a dowry usually alluded to 'unmentionable' objects (TP 61).

The effect of *Petrushka* on its audience was similar to that of wit. Unlike comedy (which requires two people only – mocker and butt), wit posits a complex triangular relation between the originator, the object and the audience. It is a dramatic genre *par excellence*. In *Petrushka* the hero, subsidiary characters and audience exactly correspond to the anecdote-teller, anecdote subject and listener of Freud's text. Moreover, like wit, the comedy of *Petrushka* demands that the audience not only has detailed knowledge of the political and cultural background in order to understand the jokes, but that they also share the sexual and ideological standpoint of the wit him- or herself, in order not to be offended by the jokes, as Prince Dolgoruky was by a puppet show he saw in the early nineteenth century:

I have always found it strange that at such spectacles a monk is shown and is made an object of mockery. There is no puppet comedy that has not a cassock in it. I find this most improper, and am astounded that it is allowed. In time the common people will have got so used to seeing a wooden monk with a hussy in Komaritskaya that they will not be able to look at a real one without thoughts of that kind coming into their heads.[39]

Petrushka has not been compared before with Freud's theory of wit, but the political aggression of the text has been recognised. In the Soviet Union it has often been seen as a straight political satire. Berkov's anthology of folk texts classes *Petrushka* as a 'satire'. Gor'ky wrote of him:

He is the crude and naive image in which working people embodied themselves and their belief that in the end they themselves would have victory over everyone and everything.[40]

In support of this view, it has been alleged that the authorities, both ecclesiastical and temporal, persecuted the puppeteers. One Soviet critic speaks of 'merciless hounding' of showmen by the police.[41] This is an exaggeration of the truth. As has been shown in the previous chapter, the lives led by some puppeteers were certainly uncomfortable. The ruling classes did regard their shows with suspicion and hauteur. Archbishop Ierimy, who visited Arzamas in the early nineteenth century, left a disapproving account of a puppet show he saw there:

Outside the town cathedral a puppet show had been set up, which paid heed neither to time nor to the decency demanded by the virtue of children and young girls.[42]

But it is incorrect to present the situation as heroic puppeteers versus blind state. As Vsevolodsky-Gerngross writes, Petrushka's conflict is anarchic.[43] His attacks on others are unprincipled: it is clear why he should kill the Policeman, for example, but not why he should murder his friend Filimoshka or drive his fiancée from the stage when she bores him. The authorities, moreover, were frequently willing to turn a blind eye to Petrushka's antics, as the puppeteer Zaitsev relates:

The police forbade our performances, but the ban was often only observed on paper, and when they felt like it, they would enjoy watching our shows themselves.

Zaitsev relates how he once realised in mid-performance that he was playing right outside the local police station, but all was well: the police lined up at the windows to watch, rocking with laughter, and at the end 'our strict guardians made generous donations'.[44]

The label 'satire' is unsatisfactory not simply because it implies a coherent political standpoint, but because it suggests that *Petrushka* makes direct reference to reality. There are certainly some ways in which the shows do coincide with available documentation of subordinate class life. The murder, violence and institutionalised oppression which are represented correspond with the written records of domestic brutality, drunken quarrels between man and wife which might occasionally end in murder, and holiday fist-fights, a favourite pastime amongst the urban poor; and the scenes with the Doctor and Policeman are a fair reflection of the contemptuous treatment meted out to these people by authority. Even Vitengof, in his generally roseate view of Moscow life, admits that Moscow quacks were often filthy, badly dressed and offensively mannered, and that their professional incompetence was matched only by their greed.[45] The show may reflect besides the experiences of the subordinate classes more subtly; some devices in it correspond to classic manifestations of urban alienation as defined by Marx. Reification, for example, is found when the horse is presented as a broken object which can be 'repaired' (the phrase used in Russian, *na pochinku otdana*, would more commonly be used of boots, watches or buckets with holes in them); the social relations portrayed are characterised by atomisation and mutual incomprehension.[46] Yet the image of reality presented is selective and generalised. Petrushka is never presented as a factory worker, nor even as a craftsman or a navvy. His conflicts with the authorities, likewise, are of hyperbolic character, without the down-to-earth and downbeat detail of those represented in other urban popular-cultural genres, such as the factory lament. In the following stanza, for example, the misery of shop-floor life is represented directly:

A, fabrichnye devchonki,
Pochemu vy bledny?
Potomu my khudy, bledny
Chto zhivem my bedno
Poutru rano vstaem,
Pozdno spat' lozhimsya,
U nas mashinushki khudye,
Shpindelya krivye.[47]

(Ah, lasses from the factory,
Wherefore are you so pale?
We are thin and we are pale,
Since we live so poorly.
Early we are forced to rise,
We must work till late,
Our machines do not work well,
They have crooked shuttles.)

Realising that the term 'social satire' is not adequate to describe *Petrushka*, recent critics have turned instead to seeing the play as directly derived from fertility cults. Anna Nekrylova has traced the many murders in the play to the beatings and killings of agricultural festivals, the straw figures burned 'for the sake of their future revival'; she has conjectured that Petrushka stands for the 'symbol of world conflagration', as in Ancient Greek rite, and has suggested that the play goes back to an *Urdrama*, the characters of which, she suggests, were 'a warrior, a woman, a cook, a doctor, a shaman etc.'.[48]

Nekrylova's analysis, reducing the meaning of *Petrushka* to an obscure reflection of agricultural ritual, is as unsatisfactory as the analyses which reduce the text to a political manifesto. There are some elements of *Petrushka*, certainly, which cannot be explained on practical or technical grounds. Like all the fairground genres, it was performed, as noted earlier, on religious festivals such as Easter and Shrovetide, though not exclusively on these days. The respect for tradition in the texts sometimes reached the level of ritual: many puppeteers would include formulae which were garbled and incomprehensible because they had heard them used elsewhere – the formula for Petrushka's salary, for example, which went:

Na pervyi mesyats – pud myakiny,
na vtoroi mesyats – chetvert' gniloi ryabiny,
na tretii – pis'mo ot Kateriny.[49]

(The first month's – a quart or two of steam,
The second month's – a ton of rotten beans,
The third – a letter from Katerina.)

The red colour with which Petrushka is associated clearly does have symbolic associations. But Nekrylova's attempt to trace every element of *Petrushka* to its assumed historical origins strains credulity. For example, she writes:

The compositional principle of pairing [is] clearly in evidence in the comedy, reflecting the ancient dualistic system of thinking.[50]

At least as important a reason for pairing in *Petrushka* was the fact that a single-operator glove-puppet text demands that there be two puppets on stage in most scenes – the operator has two hands, and on each of them is a puppet.

A more serious criticism of Nekrylova's ethnographical approach is that it misrepresents the character of the *Petrushka* text as played in the nineteenth century. There is no proof that Russian nineteenth-century audiences and showmen felt that the show had any connection with agricultural rite, a fact admitted by Olga Freidenberg, an earlier advocate of similar views to Nekrylova's:

At the fair and in the fairground booth [*balagan*], in those sacred places of archaic times, they play a leading role to this day ... showing the puppet theatre and the former temple chest, the holy of holies of the god – the peep-show; in the courtyards, to the music of the barrel-organ, they do their acrobatics to this day, *not knowing that* their ancestors were Icarus, Dedalus, Phaeton and other sun people, the acrobats who rose from death into the sky.[51]

Petrushka is little concerned even with the family rituals which were part of the urban scene. The recruitment of a soldier, an important occasion accompanied by traditional family ceremonies, is here stripped of ritual significance and becomes an occasion of rebellion.[52] Any connection of the wedding ceremony with fertility ritual is subsumed, in Petrushka's case, to the more pressing issue of erotic gratification.

Of still less significance are the agrarian rituals, such as the sacrifice of straw dolls mentioned by Nekrylova. I have shown in chapter I how the urban lower classes, the audience of *Petrushka*, were in the process of becoming alienated from their original village life. The entertainments they patronised reflected this shift. In Russian villages, important events of the agrarian year were commemorated by dramatised rituals. Players and audience were as one, sharing in a joint celebration, but the genders were separated: the spring festival of *Kostroma*, for example, was a women's festival, the Christmas mummers' plays were performed only by men.[53] In the towns, these were eroded by spectacles in which men and women performed together, but in which the audience and players were separated. The dramatised rituals of the village were functional; the dramas of the towns were entertaining. The differences between *Petrushka* and the rural drama parallel the differences between toys in towns and villages. In the villages they had served to educate children in their social roles; in the towns they were used primarily for entertainment:

In the town children spent more time playing than in the village. The peasant child took an active part in working life from an early age; for town children the process of socialisation by play took much longer. They became involved in working life much later, were cared for by adults to a greater extent, and they grew up more isolated from nature. Therefore they needed another, more extensive medium of objects and games, which would cater for their extended period of childhood. For this reason, the demand for entertaining toys which would occupy a child's attention one way or another increased greatly. These toys had to possess certain qualities essential to the dynamics of the game – they had to be capable of motion and sound, be made of an attractive variety of materials, in short they had to be spectacular, to be actively theatricalised.[54]

In the context of a nineteenth-century Russian town, the remote ritual origins of *Petrushka* were of considerably less importance than its capacity to entertain. Laughter in Russian villages had connections with fertility cults; it was ritually linked with the act of conception.[55] In Russian towns, laughter was connected with a desire to let off steam, pure and simple. This vital shift in emphasis has been obscured by the tendency in recent Russian criticism to use the word *smekh* (laughter) to mean 'humour' as well.[56] The capacity for laughter is a universal human capacity which may be unconnected with amusement: it can express high spirits, or high emotion. The *yurodivye*, or 'holy fools', of medieval Russia used laughter in their performances, but woe betide anyone who dared to find the spectacle entertaining.[57]

Freud has argued that humour, as opposed to laughter, is an escapist device, caused by the desire to return to lost childhood:

The euphoria which we attempt to reach in these ways is in fact the mood belonging to a time in our lives in which we used to carry out our psychological work with only a small expenditure of energy, the mood of our childhood, when we were ignorant of comedy, incapable of wit and had no need of humour in order to feel happy.[58]

I introduce this analogy not to suggest that Russian villagers were somehow more childlike or less evolved than the urban subordinate classes, or that they were incapable of humour, but to suggest that the shift of focus brought by the social movement to towns made ritual laughter redundant, and humour as escape more important.[59] One Soviet critic has observed with disgust the 'degeneration' of the traditional ritual drama *Tsar' Maksimilian* which occurred from the beginning of this century, a degeneration manifested above all in the comic travesty of originally magnificent characters.[60] Where village-dwellers' interest in printed literature was dictated above all by whether it was useful and improving, town-dwellers were more likely to demand excitement and interest from the printed books which they read.[61]

Petrushka springs from this shift in world-view. It expresses a fragmented sense of morality. The hero commits murder, and gets away with it; in some versions he even eludes the Devil, in others his punishment is brief and carries little weight. The story does not manifest the rough but tenacious notions of justice to be found in some comic folk-tales of rural origin; *Ivan-durak* (Ivan the Fool's) foolish behaviour illustrates that those around him are greater fools; the joker figure thieves from and cheats people whose greed and selfishness makes them deserving victims.[62] But on the other hand, moral boundaries are not erased completely in *Petrushka*, as they are in the rites involving straw dolls; when Petrushka dispatches a victim it is murder, not ritual killing. The text is ambivalent in that it blurs or shifts moral boundaries. A. Nekrylova describes the attitude as 'pre-ethical',[63] but in fact a better description is 'anti-ethical'. The hero is well aware of the moral laws which he transgresses: he has the Musician as a conscience:

PETRUSHKA: Ya teper' nikogo ne boyus'.
MUZYKANT: A ky boisya.
PETRUSHKA: Kogo?
MUZYKANT: Pridet chernyi barbos, otkusit tvoi dlinnyi nos, ili zhe domovoi, za tvoei golovoi ...
PETRUSHKA: Ne boyus'! U menya est' ruzh'e pokoinogo dyaden'ki ... Ya ego zastrelyu.   (Tarasov 37)

(PETRUSHKA: Now I'm not afraid of anyone.
MUSICIAN: Well, you'd better be, then.
PETRUSHKA: Who of?
MUSICIAN: The big black Barbos'll bite off your long nose, or else the House Spirit'll grab your head and go off with it ...
PETRUSHKA: I'm not afraid! I've got a rifle ... belonged to my uncle who died ... I'll shoot him.)

Sometimes (though rarely) the hero even feels a brief stab of repentance himself. One of the funniest moments in Doroshevich's Sakhalin version of the text is when Petrushka begins to wail his head off, realising he actually has murdered his father:

– A ved' i vpryam' ubil! – reshaet, nakonets, Petrushka i vdrug nachinaet *vyt' v golos* kak v derevnyakh baby voyut po pokoinikam. 'Rodimyi moi batyushka-a-a! Na kogo ty menya poki-i-nul! Ostalsya ya odin-odineshene-e-k, gor'kim slovom siroti-i-nushkoi![64]

('So I really have killed him!' – Petrushka decides at last and begins to *keen*, as peasant women do over the dead. 'My dear fa-a-ather! Why have you le-e-eft me? Now I'm all alo-o-one, now they call me by the bitter word o-o-orphan!')

The ethics of *Petrushka* are not smooth and coherent in the manner of a properly constructed satire; but, unlike ritual drama, it does not stand outside ethics. It is too stylistically complex for a satirical drama, and also too ideologically simplistic. On the other hand, presenting it as an ethnographical eccentricity has significant dangers. There is, first, conceptual confusion in an approach which can simultaneously insist that popular texts have meanings which are only accessible to the educated observer, and yet argue that popular culture is irreconcilably separate, in its unreconstructed 'primitivism', from the educated world-view. Secondly, there is incoherence in an approach which draws heavily on biological models of evolution, and which can yet insist on a biological impossibility, the phenomenon which transcends time and environment. Thirdly, treating these texts as ethnography is a method which defuses them, tones them down for decent lecture-hall consumption, and ignores the fact that the violence of the play is disturbing, and that it does have real-life parallels. Both the ethnographical and the satirical description fall down also because they turn the humour of the piece, its most outstanding characteristic, into an irrelevance.

A satisfying account of the humour of *Petrushka* must take account of the effects of the jokes as well as their construction. Freud's theory of *Witz* made a good starting-point, but (for all his citations of Galician Jewish jokes) his book is too concerned with high culture and the function of wit in educated bourgeois society to be relevant. His only reference to folk humour is the supercilious observation that obscene jokes are especially popular amongst 'the common people', and that few formal demands are made: the mention of taboo subjects is enough.[65] The popularity of obscenity in the fairground genres is incontrovertible; but formal elements were in fact extremely important for 'the common people', as Nekrylova's structural studies make clear. Also, whilst Freud's study gives a good indication of how the humour of *Petrushka* is received, it cannot be used to explain some of the imagery in the texts which does not allude to taboo subjects: the constant use of food and drink references, for example.

For an outline of the humour characterising *Petrushka* which does not confine itself to structural features and which puts the political–moral stance into perspective, one must turn to M. M. Bakhtin's definition of the carnival text in *Rabelais and His World*. In it Bakhtin described how Rabelais' humour, his 'exceptional freedom and pitiless gaiety', was the product of the social and also linguistic upheaval of the Renaissance, its 'intense re-orientation and mutual clarification of languages'.[66] It was urban in origin: 'Rabelais' humour belongs to the city marketplace, to the town fair and carnival square of the late Middle Ages and of the Renaissance'.[67] Whilst taking account of high literature and entering into debate with it, this humour was anti-literary: 'part of the stream of folk culture, which at all stages of its development has opposed the official culture of the ruling classes and evolved its own conception of the world, its own forms and imagery'.[68]

Petrushka, too, was an urban text, and although it originated later, the time of its emergence was characterised by similar social and linguistic upheaval, as its performers adapted themselves to life in towns and fought to establish their right to a place beside foreign showmen. It is not surprising, given the similar background, that Bakhtin's description of carnival humour in the Rabelais book should also fit *Petrushka*.

Like carnival humour, the humour of *Petrushka* is centred on the body; and the image of the body given is not classically smooth and perfect, but grotesque. As Bakhtin writes:

The stress is laid on those parts of the body which are open to the outside world . . . or through which the body itself goes out to meet the world . . . the open mouth, the genital organs, the breasts, the phallus, the potbelly, the nose . . . The body discloses its essence as a principle of growth which exceeds its own limits only in copulation, pregnancy, childbirth, the throes of death, or defecation.[69]

From the moment of Petrushka's arrival onstage the physical character of the comedy is apparent. His face and body are exaggerated to carnival proportions: the nose and mouth are huge, the eyes small and beady, and his limbs in comparison shrink to nothing. The physical references then continue in the next scene. When Petrushka announces his marriage, his praise of his fiancée lays emphasis on just these carnival parts of the body: her mouth, her lips, her fingers. Moreover, the physique displayed by Petrushka and the other characters manifests reversal: the lower parts of the body change places with the higher parts. Petrushka's club, his nose and his hump are all direct references to his phallus.

The carnival body in *Petrushka* is usually seen engaged in carnival activities. These are, of course, the copulation and defecation mentioned above; but at least as important are eating and drinking, of which Bakhtin writes, 'Eating and drinking are the most significant manifestations of the carnival body.'[70] There were several traditional scenes in which food played a part: notably those in which Petrushka obtained refreshment from the Porter or the Tavern-Keeper and then refused to pay. In many versions Petrushka asks for his dowry in food; in Elena Mitcoff's English version there is an additional scene in which Petrushka breathlessly describes the eating and drinking at his wedding banquet:

And what a wedding feast! Never before did the guests eat so. Barley soup
made with the best of barley, two kernels to a plate. Noodles to put you in a
spasm. Fried chitterlings, and the remarkable thing is, they were all gobbled
up. As much salad as you could down without choking. Macaroni, the sort
crows build their nests with. And when dessert was passed round, it was all
they could do to keep from choking.   (Mitcoff 296)

Petrushka was no mean drinker, either: in his opening speech he
would sometimes boast, 'Bez mery vino p'yu', 'I drink wine without
measure', and one of the parody folk-songs which he often sang was
associated with toping:

Chizhik-pyzhik, gde ty byl?
Za goroyu vodku pil.
Vypil ryumku, vypil dve,
Zashumelo v golove.   (Berkov 119)

(Little birdy, where've you been?
Drinking vodka on the green.
I had one glass, I had two,
Head began to ache right through.)

The other characters were expected to share his interest. Occasionally
the Gypsy, too, was paid partly in food: he received 'a tart with rats
inside', as in Tarasov's version quoted above (see pp. 71–72), or
'polovinu dengami da pirog s gribami' ('half in money and a mushroom pie') (NP 1891, 6). Petrushka sometimes attempted to bribe his
way out of conscription by offering the corporal tea and tobacco (NP
1891).

Petrushka's traditional surnames underlined his link with food:
they were Uksusov, from *uksus*, vinegar, and Samovarov, from
samovar. In the south he was often known as Van'ka-ratatui. It is
normally suggested that this comes from the warning cry 'Ratatui',
''Ware thief!' But Elizabeth Warner has ingeniously suggested that it
might be connected with the dish of ratatouille, vegetable stew.[71] This
charming idea began to seem more likely when I discovered a
reference in Vertinsky's memoirs to a favourite salad of Chaliapin's
called *ratatui*, which was apparently a Volga dish.[72]

That Petrushka came from Yaroslavl was also not a neutral piece
of information; Gilyarovsky informs us that the *yaroslavskie vodok-
hleby* (Yaroslavl water-slurpers) were traditionally employed as
waiters, in Moscow at least.[73]

The attitude of the carnival to the body is ambivalent. Whilst hyperbolically celebrating its size and power, it simultaneously stresses sickness, dismemberment and weakness. The body 'destroys and generates, swallows and is swallowed'.[74] *Petrushka* manifests this too. The hero himself is hunch-backed and his legs are useless. His wife is hideously ugly, and often blind (for example, in Tarasov's version). His horse is by no means a prize specimen, as is emphasised in the following extract by the ironic pun, *tselykh tri* (three *whole* ones):

PETRUSHKA: A kakaya u tebya loshad'?
TSYGAN: Tselykh tri: est' chalyi, kotoryi golovoi ne kachaet, est' pegii, kotoryi nikogda s dvora ne begal, est' tretii – grivochka gusta, golova pusta, kak spotyknetsya – cherez golovu vody nal'etsya, kogda bezhit, to vsya drozhit, a kogda lyazhet, to i sovsem ne vstanet.   (Tarasov 32)

(PETRUSHKA: What's your horse like?
GYPSY: I've got three whole ones: a roan that never nods, a piebald that's never run out of the yard, and a third – thick mane, empty brain, when it stumbles on the road you hear water rumble in its head, when it trots I believe it trembles like a leaf, and if it lies down – then, it'll never get up again)

The hyperbolic size and appetites of the characters are a source of abuse as well as praise. In one version Petrushka abuses an Armenian for having a large nose, though he has one himself and is proud of it (NP 1891, 12). Petrushka's commonest terms of abuse refer to the bodies of his enemies: 'Gypsy gob', 'filthy chops'.

The body is under constant threat: physicality is expressed not only in eating, but also in fighting and murder. In every scene Petrushka is ready to attack or kill; at the end of the play the stage is more littered with dead bodies than at the end of a Jacobean tragedy.

The sick humour of this is softened by the characters' capacity to dismember and reconstitute themselves at will. Petrushka is at liberty to separate himself from his hump, as he reveals in his dialogue with the Soldier:

KAPRAL: Vot ya tebya v soldaty voz'mu.
PETRUSHKA: Ya ne gozhus'.
KAPRAL: Pochemu?
PETRUSHKA: U menya gorb.
KAPRAL: A gde on u tebya?
PETRUSHKA: On tam, khata na gore, tak on ostalsya v trube.
                                                          (Berkov 121)

(CORPORAL: Right, I'm going to enlist you as a soldier.
PETRUSHKA: I'm no good.

CORPORAL: Why not?
PETRUSHKA: I've got a hump.
CORPORAL: Where is it, then?
PETRUSHKA: It's there, stuck up the spout, like a hut on the mount.)

The sick horse's troubles are also curable: as well as reification, resurrection and renewal are implied by its head being sent 'to the vet's repair shop' (*konovalu v pochinku otdana*) (Berkov 116). And at the end of the play, Petrushka's own death is softened; the Clown announces that he will soon return:

Konchilos' delo. Petrushku sobaku s''ela. Odno konchaetsya – drugoe nachinaetsya. Pozhaluite, zakhodite, Petrushku posmotrite. (Berkov 123)

(That's it for now. Petrushka's been eaten by a bow-wow. One thing ends – another begins. Please come in, *Petrushka* will soon begin.)

Nichego, ne goryuite!
Petrushka zhiv vstanet,
Opyat' s vami shutit' stanet!   (Tarasov 39)

(Never mind, don't be sad!
Petrushka will rise again,
He'll come out and joke with you, ladies and gentlemen!)

The most important indication of carnival ambivalence in the texts is the pun. Occasionally Petrushka makes harmless puns which have no relation to carnival subjects:

KAPRAL: Ty chto chepukhu poresh'? Vot ya tebya priemam uchit' budu. Budesh' chelovek kazennyi.
PETRUSHKA: Budesh' chelovek skazhonnyi?   (Berkov 121)

(CORPORAL: What's this rot you're blethering? I'll teach you what's what. You'll be an army man.
PETRUSHKA: What do you mean, I'll be a barmy man?)

But more often the misunderstandings and mishearings shift the dialogue from neutral subjects on to the central subjects of the carnival: the body, death, food or sex. Petrushka addresses the Corporal as *vashe skovorod'e* (your frying-pan-hour), not *vashe vysokorod'e* (your honour), and interprets his commands as food words:

KAPRAL: Komandu slushai!
PETRUSHKA: Spasibo, poidu pokushayu!   (Tarasov 36)

(CORPORAL: Ten-Shun!
PETRUSHKA: Thank you, I'll be off for a bun!)

When he meets the German, on the other hand, he misunderstands his greetings as statements of aggression:

NEMETS: Gut morgen!
PETRUSHKA: Za chto po morde?[75]

(GERMAN: Grüss Gott!
PETRUSHKA: Why a whack on the nut?)

A more complex sort of carnival pun is that in which the obsessional concerns of the text are intertwined: food is associated with death, for example. In the following dialogue with the Musician, Petrushka links his murder of the Doctor with cooking:

MUZYKANT: Ty zhe ego ubil.
PETRUSHKA: Kupil.
MUZYKANT: Ne kupil – ubil ... On pomer ...
PETRUSHKA: Chto? Povar? ...
MUZYKANT: Nado khoronit'.
PETRUSHKA: Chto svarit'?   (Tarasov 35)

(MUSICIAN: He's bought it.
PETRUSHKA: I've bought him.
MUSICIAN: No – he's bought it. He's copped it.
PETRUSHKA: He's cooked it?
MUSICIAN: You must inter him.
PETRUSHKA: Stir him?)

Petrushka passes off the bodies of his dead victims as food: as he carries round the German he calls out 'Buy my potatoes! My sucking pigs!' (Berkov 114). There is even a version in which Petrushka sees his death in a food form: 'It's digging potatoes at the allotment beyond the city boundary' (P 1915, 10).

Food is sometimes linked with sex in the plays. Typically, Petrushka's desire for his wife is expressed in terms of food: he praises his wife's 'sugary lips' in two St Petersburg versions (FT 287, 289); and she is 'white and sweet as enriched dough' ('bela i mila kak svodnoe testo') (NP 1891, 3). When Petrushka himself is dragged off by the dog, his phallic-symbol nose is the first bit to be eaten in all the plays in which this scene appears.

The obsession with the body and its functions is the focus of the plays, and the body is their only topography. The setting does not vary, and the images of the outer world are crazy and distorted. Misdirections are a frequent source of humour. When the Musician is asked by the Soldier to say where Petrushka is, he replies: 'Poshel nalevo, a mozhet byt, svernul napravo' ('He went left, but he may have turned off to the right') (P 1915, 18). The only clarity in the directions is a reference to some carnival subject. When Petrushka asks for the Gypsy in one version, he is told he is in the tavern:

PETRUSHKA: Gde on zhivet?
MUZYKANT: Nalevo, napravo, na levoi storone, v traktire vodku p'et.

(Tarasov 32)

(PETRUSHKA: Where is the Gypsy?
MUSICIAN: On the left, on the right, on the left-hand side, in the tavern getting tipsy.)

For Petrushka, the Caucasus is not an exotic place with mountains, but a larder for new types of food: he will ride to it on his horse and drink 'kakhetskii kvas' (P 1910, 10).

The focus on the body in *Petrushka* dominates the structure too. The progress of events is dictated by the need to use carnival standards, not by proto-logical processes of pairing and contrast, nor by any kind of sequentiality. Petrushka introduces his wife with more or less overt sexual innuendoes, and then she disappears; he is taken on for work with his master, negotiates his salary in comestibles, but never starts work; he indulges in unmotivated bouts of drinking; and so on. Equally, the binary and trinary structures on which popular-cultural texts are often held to depend are eroded in these texts: the scenes of available variants do not resolve themselves into neat sets of three or two.[76]

The political stance of *Petrushka* is much more easily understood if seen in conjunction with the ambivalence and curious topography of the carnival text. 'From the wearing of clothes turned inside out and trousers slipped over the head to the election of mock kings and popes the same topographical logic is put to work.'[77] Petrushka, the hero and the fool, is given absolute power for a while, overturning the status quo, but his rule lasts only until the end of the carnival. Moreover, his power offers no real alternative to the power which it replaces, since it is based on the same despotism and bullying as that of his predecessors. Petrushka's only law is that might is right, and he torments outsiders who do not belong to his social group: women, the aged, members of different races. The *Petrushka* show reinforced its audience's sense of power not only by showing the downfall of the oppressors of the urban lower classes, but by suggesting that a member of a specific race and gender group – the Russian young male worker – should be allowed absolute domination over the other members of the urban subordinate classes. Women and ethnic minorities are alike characterised as passive in the face of violence and handicapped in linguistic terms: they are silent (in the case of women), speak in a fractured, distorted language (in the case of ethnic minorities), or provoke terrible revenge when they open their mouths (in the case of both groups). This, for example, is an Armenian from one of the *lubok* editions:

ARMYANIN: Izdravstvui, barin! S Teplis tébe poklon i dénga myl'en. Zlykyl ya na storona, chto ty khochesh' sébe zhina?
PETRUSHKA: Iskal da ne nashel. A ty syuda zachem prishel? Kto ty za chelovek: bolgarin ili grek?
ARMYANIN: Ya armyanin, Budagov-shakh, rodilsya na Kapkaz-gorakh.
PETRUSHKA: Chto tebe nuzhno, govori, mne nedosuzhno?
ARMYANIN: Pokupa u méne beshmet, kakoi u tébe nét.
PETRUSHKA: Govori russkim yazykom, ya s tvoim ne znakom.

(P 1891, 11)

(ARMENIAN: [in an Armenian accent]: Good day to 'e, sir! From Teeflis I you greet, may you be never in need. I 'eard I belief that you wanted a wif?
PETRUSHKA: I looked, had no success. Is it any of your business? What kind of man are you, a Greek, a Bulgar or who?
ARMENIAN: I'm an Armenian, o Great Shah, from the Caucasus mountains afar.
PETRUSHKA: Get on with it, say your say, I haven't got all day.
ARMENIAN: Buy a fine beshmet from me, the best you'll ever see.
PETRUSHKA: Speak Russian will you, I don't know your filthy lingo.)

It is noticeable that even in the variants where Petrushka's Bride escapes beating (FT 286–7, 296–7) she is excluded from active participation in the carnival: sexual initiative comes entirely from Petrushka's side, and the Bride denies that she is a spirits-drinker.

It has been argued that the abuse directed at marginal social groups was contained by the process of 'abjection displacement' – that is, each marginal group would derive comfort from the scorn poured on others.[78] But this does not get round the fact that the central and dominant group had to make no such adjustment or accommodation. Nor does it explain a further aspect of this male proletarian self-assertion: the way that puppeteers belonging to marginalised groups

would play scenes directed against these very groups. Jewish puppeteers, for example, played shows in which not only the Jew
appeared, but also an unusual character called Rabbi Moishe.[79]

Though subversive in some of its orientations, the carnival text was
aggressively conservative in others. It was unruly and truly ambivalent: two-faced but in no kind of equilibrium. In asserting this I
would go still further than Bakhtin, who has argued, too idealistically
I feel, that 'the popular tradition is in no way hostile to women and
does not approach her negatively'.[80] I believe that such hostility is, on
the contrary, clear, making Petrushka's club, in the Russian prover-
bial phrase, 'a stick with two ends', a double-edged sword.

Staging

The most important technical feature of the glove-puppet theatre is
the construction of the puppets themselves. Each one must be tailored
to the hand of the puppeteer, and, whilst it must be large enough to be
visible, it must not be so large that it is unwieldy.[81] (The puppets used
for the television show *Spitting Image*, which are so large they require
two operators, and which severely limit 'take' time, would not be of
any use on a fairground).[82] The material used must be strong enough
to be whacked repeatedly without cracking or showing signs of
fatigue. In Russia, wood was the traditional material, as it was also
for toys. The carving had to be effective rather than attractive. Many
marionettes are beautiful objects off-stage; glove puppets rarely so.
The general standard of carving was crude, and by no means all
Petrushkas seem to have been as sophisticated as Zaitsev's wonderful
head, which appears to change expression if seen from different
angles.[83] The lesser puppets had even less aesthetic appeal.

The body of the puppet, the 'glove' itself, was of cloth. Only
Petrushka, and occasionally his wife, had legs: these might have steel
rods inside to aid operation. Petrushka would impudently hang his
legs over the side of the booth to emphasise his familiar attitude to the
audience, and his wife's could be seen when she danced.

The puppets were usually manufactured by the puppeteers. The
costumes, on the other hand, seem to have been the responsibility of
women: the puppeteer's wife, perhaps, or another female relative.[84]
They were made of any available scraps of cloth, and, like all
costumes in the popular theatre, they were rudimentary, suggesting
character by a few key attributes. Petrushka himself was always in

11. Petrushka Russian style (left) and Italian style (right). The left a *balagan* puppet, the right made for E. Demmeni's theatre in the 1920s.

red, and there were two possible versions. He might either be in a traditional clown's striped suit with little bells on it (as he is in a lithograph of the *balagan* dating from the 1860s, and in the Leningrad TYuZ, Theatre of Young Viewers, version), or he might wear Russian national dress of a red *rubashka* (peasant shirt), wide trousers and shiny leather knee-boots (as in Zaitsev's version). Parashka or Malan'ya was usually in the latest fashion, and, as Eremin puts it, 'all the Fiancée's "modish" furbelows were grotesquely exaggerated, it stands to reason' (TP 58). She might also occasionally wear peasant costume: Putintsev describes her as wearing a pink blouse and a green skirt, with a red scarf and a scrap of muslin veiling on her head (VLB 7). Filimoshka was an urban dandy, the male counterpart of the Fiancée (TP 59). Other costumes gave a symbolic indication of social roles or of nationality: the Doctor was always in black and wore glasses; the Corporal and the Policeman wore uniforms; the Gypsy wore black and carried a whip, and so on. Putintsev has some interesting descriptions of the appearance of the non-human characters. The Devil was black all over and had red eyes; the Barbos (a separate character here) was a dog made of rags with wooden jaws. He also gives the only extant description of the horse sold by the Gypsy to Petrushka: this was not a specially made puppet, but a 'bazaar toy made of papier mâché' (VLB 8). The illustrations in the *lubok* editions also give vivid, if rather fanciful, impressions of how the show must have looked.

The puppeteer imitated the voices of all the puppets, providing as much variety as possible. Petrushka's voice was distinguished from the voice of the other puppets by the employment of a *govorok*, *gnusavka* or *pishchik*, a piece of tape sandwiched with metal, which produced a raucous squeak when held in the right position in the mouth. It required skill to use this squeaker device, for which the technical English term is 'swazzle', correctly, as Rozenberg, the amateur philologist who was recording Lashchenko's *Petrushka* text discovered:

It is very hard to speak wearing this contraption. It takes quite some skill to produce a single sound out of it. At any rate, not a squeak came out when I tried. My every attempt provoked convulsions of the throat and even made me want to vomit.
(Berkov 329)

The Petrushka booth was often rudimentary: it might be a piece of cloth, head-high, stretched between two poles knocked into the ground; but the standard Russian word, *shirmy*, means 'screen', and the classic booth was indeed a three- or four-sided canvas or plywood folding screen. The decoration was flowered cotton print (for the cloth type) or crude *lubok*-type paintings (for the wooden screens). The booth was also used indoors (whether inside a *balagan* or in a room, for a children's party), and in this case the three-sided type must have been used for balance's sake.

It is easy to sum up the technical features of *Petrushka*, but rather less easy to discuss their meaning. The effect of the use of puppets, and how far the puppet theatre is different from the live theatre, are matters of debate. Some attention has been given to the 'semiotics of the puppet theatre' in two articles by P. G. Bogatyrev and Inna Solomonik.[85]

Bogatyrev's article, despite its title, 'On the interrelation of two similar semiotic systems: live theatre and puppet theatre', makes few concrete statements about the puppet theatre, apart from declaring that puppets are not necessarily comic. Solomonik's article is much more detailed. She states that the distinguishing feature of the folk puppet theatre is that visual elements are more important than aural elements:

> The word comes into the foreground by and large only in dramatic spectacles which copy the repertoire of the dramatic theatre and attempt to imitate it in different ways, or which make wide use of narrative, not translating the plot into dramatic form ... In most cases the folk puppet theatre attempted to transfer the centre of equilibrium to non-verbal means, which were more accessible for it and which were more organically connected with sculpture.[86]

Solomonik's distinction on the basis of primacy or non-primacy of words will not work. It is certainly true that visual elements are important in the street glove-puppet theatre, to which the high-theatre tradition of a 'reading room for intellectuals', with dozing public, in Meyerhold's description, is utterly alien.[87] This is evident in *Petrushka* too: pantomime scenes without words appear in most versions. But the fact that entire puppet shows can be given without words does not make the absence of words a distinguishing feature of the puppet theatre. On the Russian fairground, wordless pantomimes and theatricalised acrobatics were performed by live actors. In *Petrushka* the word is very much more important that it is in the live Russian folk theatre, or indeed in the so-called 'school plays', where gesture, costume, and the use of long silences are of great significance.[88]

Besides, the different types of puppet theatre cannot be lumped
together. The visual appeal of the glove-puppet theatre is limited: the
puppets are capable of a very restricted range of actions. Words
therefore take on a great significance. In the marionette show, on the
other hand, a wide range of actions is possible, and much more
interesting pantomimes can be shown. This distinction was clear in the
Russian fairground theatre, in which marionettes were kept almost
exclusively for circus acts and pantomimes, glove puppets for verbal
texts.

Like many branches of the popular theatre, *Petrushka* made
simultaneous use of resources which the modern Western high theatre
has traditionally separated. It was simultaneously drama, pageant
and musical. The *Petrushka* show was preceded by music on a
barrel-organ, and cymbals were used to mark the hero's entrance and
other dramatic moments. During the play the hero would talk against
the barrel-organ music, and this meant that although the dialogue was
spoken, it observed the musical rhythm patterns – that is, it sounded
like dub poetry or rap.[89] The hero himself often broke off to sing a
quick song:

PETRUSHKA: Muzykant, kuda nemets ubezhal?
MUZYKANT: On seichas vernetsya. Za shampanskim poshel, tebya, dolzhno
byt', ugostit' budet!
PETRUSHKA: Ladno! Podozhdu da pesenku spoyu!

>   Po ulitse mostovoi
>   Shla devitsa za vodoi
>   Za nei paren' molodoi
>   Krichit: devitsa, postoi!   (P 1907, 8)

(PETRUSHKA: Musician, where's the German run off to?
MUSICIAN: He'll be back soon. He's gone off for some champagne, I
expect he's going to treat you!
PETRUSHKA: Fine! Whilst I'm waiting I'll sing a song!

>   Down a street in town
>   Went a girl for water.
>   A young lad cried after:
>   Hey, sweetheart, hang on!)

Other characters (such as the Jew or the Arab) who have no
introductory monologues often come on singing little songs. The
following anti-Semitic ditty is sung by a Jew in one of the *lubok*
editions:

EVREI:
Ya zidotsik tsesnyi
Kazhdomu izvestnyi,
Zoloto lyublyu,
Zoloto koplyu.
Vshe, chto v zyzni svyato
Geto zlyato, zlyato ...
S zolotom v adu
Mozno zit' zidu.   (NP 1891, 12)

(JEW [in a Jewish accent]:
I'm an honest little Jew
Known well unto you,
How I love gold,
To have and to hold.
All I hold dear
Is gold, gold, you hear.
With gold, even in Hell
Jews can live very well.)

Unfortunately, the importance of music in *Petrushka* was not recognised by most collectors, so the tunes have not been recorded. Some
verses were sung to the tunes of popular songs (they were often
parodies of them, in fact, as with 'Down a street in town', above). The
only original melody which survives is the Arab's song, quoted by
Eremin (TP 68).

Another argument sometimes used to distinguish the puppet
theatre from that of live actors is that the puppet theatre is more
self-conscious, more 'theatrical', because the puppets cannot directly
mimic human beings.[90] There is a resemblance between the puppet
theatre and certain types of theatricalised toy; not for nothing were
fairground and clown toys extremely popular during the nineteenth
century.[91] But analysis of *Petrushka*'s audience has revealed that
spectators accepted Petrushka as an equal, did not question his
existence, and gave him exactly the same status as the human actor,
the Musician. Puppeteers have always been conscious of the uncanny
aliveness of their puppets; Czech puppeteers in the nineteenth century
were so attached to them that they did not want them called 'puppets'
at all, but 'actors'.[92] Russian, like other Slavonic languages, takes
account of the eerie half-human quality of puppets by assigning the
word for them, *kukla*, to the class of animate nouns (along with
people and animals).

The argument of *uslovnost'*, conventionality, like that of visual elements, is better used to distinguish different types of puppet theatre from each other than to make a distinction between the puppet and live theatre. The marionette theatre has traditionally aped the human theatre; the glove-puppet theatre has not. What is more, the marionette theatre is the theatre of indoors, even of drawing-rooms, whilst the glove-puppet theatre is associated with the street and the marketplace. All over Europe, the glove-puppet heroes are rude and rough, hard-hitting with wood and coarsely witty in word. The glove-puppet heroes are the carnival clown *par excellence*. Their own bodies are grotesque caricatures of the human body, and at the same time they distort the body of the puppeteer, turning his hands into swollen horrors covered in monstrous carbuncles, so that the only view of the puppeteer seen by the audience is a collection of excrescences.

There has been much argument also over the swazzle or squeaker with which the voice of the hero is produced. Its practical function is limited: in the hands of a less skilled puppeteer, it can make Petrushka's speeches almost incomprehensible. Remote ritual origins have been posited for it: Nekrylova sees it as representing Petrushka's 'other-worldly' origins.[93] It may well have some connection with the occult qualities of an unnaturally high-pitched voice: the shamans in their trances often spoke in falsetto.[94] The whistle toy, or *svistul'ka*, widespread in Russia, has origins in early pagan cults.[95] But since Petrushka in his nineteenth-century incarnation is not a shamanesque figure, but a representative of the subordinate classes, the squeaker, too, is best seen as a contribution to the carnival humour of the text. There is an exaggerated carnival contradiction between the phallocratic aggression with which Petrushka behaves, and the squeaky eunuch-like voice which comes out of his mouth.

The formal and structural simplicity of *Petrushka* makes it apparently innocuous, but the text cannot in fact be easily assimilated by the intellectual tradition. It presents important problems at two levels. The first level is the way in which it was perceived by audiences from the subordinate classes in streets and fairgrounds; the second the way in which it appears viewed from the 'ethnographic present' of the educated observer.[96] I believe that we should recognise these problems, and beware of any critical reading which seems to make the text simpler than it is. Though any appreciation we have of the first level can only amount to a reconstruction, it must be in three dimensions; it is essential to recognise that *Petrushka* was not simply a set of logical relations, not simply a satire, and not simply a rehearsal of religious or quasi-religious beliefs, however well it may fit into each of these models. The references to food, for example, are used in several ways simultaneously: as equivalences in oppositions or paradoxes, as allusions to the semi-starvation in which many of the subordinate classes actually lived, as indications of a ritual pattern of feasting alternated with fasting, and as an expression of the vitality of the carnival body, of its need to fuse with the outside world. It is essential to recognise, too, that this was a *theatrical* text: in other words, one in which the audience were invited to collude with the action, to show it open approval.

The complexities of this reconstruction multiply when we look at the text at the second level, recognising ourselves as outsiders. It is important to decide why the text is interesting at the moment, and to be aware of the difficulties that the attempts to use it as a source of 'traditional values', or even as an index of subordinate class values, may place in the way of the user.[97] I am not pretending to rise above these problems myself; I am a feminist who finds the text funny, which must necessarily mean accommodating to the male point of view; and my decision to use *Petrushka* strategically, in order to attack the exclusivity and marginalising devices of high culture, has obvious flaws and incoherences.

3

Petrushka, Punch and Pulcinella

The Italian hero Pulcinella began life as one of the characters of the *commedia dell'arte*, played by a live actor. He originated in Acerra, enjoyed tremendous popularity in Naples, and was as firmly associated with the south as the Bergamese Harlequin was with the north. Like Harlequin he was a trickster, although he had fewer redeeming features; his capers were more frequently the result of malice:

Being self-centred and bestial, Pulcinella had no scruples whatever, and because the moral suffering from his physical deformity reacted upon his brain at the expense of his heart, he was exceedingly cruel ... Pulcinella was not endowed with the gay and lively imagination for vulgarity which saved Harlequin from obscenity. For all his cleverness, Pulcinella was sadly lacking in delicacy, and he was epicurean only in the most popular sense of the word.[1]

Like all the *commedia dell'arte* characters, Pulcinella was masked, and his mask showed a hideous beak-nosed face, as befitted his name, derived from the word *pullus*, or chicken.[2] His body was contorted and hunch-backed; traditionally he had two humps. It has been suggested that Pulcinella is descended from Maccus, the hero of the Atellan farces, another hunch-backed, hook-nosed figure. But there are no records of appearance by Pulcinella until the late sixteenth century, and in his present form he is undoubtedly a Renaissance figure, as his costume shows.[3]

In his human incarnation, Pulcinella had a less central place in the popular imagination outside his home region than had his fellow masks Harlequin, Columbina and Pedrolino or Pierrot. But like many other *commedia dell'arte* figures he also had a non-human existence: as a marionette or glove puppet. It was in the latter shape that he took Europe by storm. From the early seventeenth century, Italian puppeteers travelled over most of Western Europe, taking their show to the north of Italy, to France, England, Germany, Austria, Belgium, Holland and Spain.[4] In many places Pulcinella visited, he was adopted by the popular tradition and naturalised: in England he became Punchinello or Punch, in France Polichinelle, in Catalonia Pulxinellis, in Spain Don Cristóbal Pulchinela. In Germany, Austria and Bohemia Pulcinella left rather fewer traces, probably because there was a well-established folk-puppet tradition; his name seems never to have been adopted, but nonetheless individual scenes seem to have made their way into these traditions too.[5] In Holland and Belgium the puppet heroes soon acquired local names, but here again many of the scenes played seem to come from Italian tradition.[6]

The first wave of Pulcinella's influence in the seventeenth century appears to have passed Russia by. But in the early nineteenth century there was an upsurge of enthusiasm for the circus and street theatre, and a second wave of Italian puppeteers travelled Europe. In England, Italian puppeteers brought about a revival of the *Punch* tradition.[7] It was this second wave which brought the Western European glove-puppet tradition to Russia.

All over Europe, as in Russia, the glove-puppet theatre was in essence a working-class entertainment, 'the rub-a-dub that quickens the pulses of the infant poor'.[8] The puppeteers belonged to the same class as their audience; they often went hungry, and even the most skilful ran the risk of a pauper's death. Bertelli, one of the most famous puppeteers in Italy during the nineteenth century, died a pauper.[9] The puppeteers suffered harassment from the authorities everywhere, and the ruling classes regarded them with hauteur. In

12.   'A School of Pulcinellas'. Drawing from an Italian collection of *commedia dell'arte* scenarios. Reproduced from K. M. Lea, *Italian Popular Comedy*, Oxford 1934.

Spain, they excited the disapproval of the Inquisition for their 'evil-sounding interpretations, which offended in particular against the ordained regulation of the Holy Sabbath'; and Cervantes described them as 'a tribe of vagabonds, who portrayed divine matters with indecency'.[10] But does the resemblance between Russian and Western European tradition go beyond the generic similarities which one would expect in subordinate-class entertainment, beyond the law that 'analogous conditions produce analogous phenomena', as Vsevolodsky-Gerngross put it?[11] How far do the *Petrushka* texts depend on the Italian puppet theatre, and how far are their characteristics unique to Russia?

This important question has attracted little critical attention so far. Too often commentators have substituted prejudice for analysis. Russell Zguta, for example, writes with a significant choice of words: 'Petrushka *remained untainted* by the [foreign *invasion*].'[12] The two studies which give the matter more space, Alferov's article on the European puppet theatre and Tsekhnovitser's chapter in TP concentrate on the alleged pre-history of puppet comedy (the Atellan farces and the Sanskrit hero Vindusaka) and give little account of the later European puppet theatre.[13] Both base their sketchy remarks on two early nineteenth-century sources, Charles Magnin's book *Le Théâtre des Marionnettes* and John Payne Collier's introduction to his edition of *The Tragical Comedy of Punch and Judy*. Neither seems to be aware of the controversy surrounding Collier's work: there is substantial evidence that he polished up the text of *Punch and Judy* which he published, and invented parts of his historical study.[14] The only detailed study of the relationship between the Russian puppet theatre and any other European tradition is Bogatyrev's comparative analysis of the Czech and Russian theatres, which deals with formal similarities and not with historical or contextual connections.[15]

There are good reasons why many critics have steered clear of the subject. There is, first, a methodological problem with distinguishing historical and generic connections. Some motifs in *Petrushka* resemble motifs in Stith Thompson's international motif index of folklore, even though this does not deal with dramatic genres. For example, the scene in which Petrushka is thrown by the horse may be related to 'youth trusts self to horse over which has no control'. Equally, *Petrushka* provides examples of 'humour directed at other social classes' or 'other races and nations'.[16] It is arguable that a historical approach is not best suited to material like *Petrushka*: it may give a false sense of national specificity and a notion of unity may be more helpful. I feel, however, that attempts to search for such unity outside the specific historical context and outside evidence of immediate connections have occasionally led commentators towards the Scylla and Charybdis of biological determinism and of religio-mysticism.[17] As chapter I makes clear, I prefer with Peter Burke to emphasise that there is evidence for the historical role of the travelling showmen in disseminating popular cultural material:

> In Central Europe, in particular, they were no respecters of frontiers, and it is to men like this – as much as to archaic Indo-European traditions – that European popular culture owed its unity.[18]

Secondly, if a historical approach is used, I think it must depend on the presence of *some* evidence. No well-founded case has yet been made that there were puppeteers from anywhere except Western Europe who could have brought a text like *Petrushka*. There is, equally, some intrinsic textual evidence that seems to indicate how the Italian tradition was subject to a process of acculturation in Russia, that is, to the dynamic of 'the increased similarity of cultures consequent upon diffusion in one or both directions', how it was filtered through 'linguistic, religious, political and psychological barriers', and could only pass through them by undergoing certain transformations.[19] Some material was added, some adapted, and the final product owed much to domestic popular traditions. The value of a comparative approach lies as much in the comparison which it facilitates between *Petrushka* and other orally transmitted traditions in Russia as in the comparison which it facilitates between Russian and Western European practice. The peculiarity of the way in which the material passed through the barriers can also aid appreciation of the text's simultaneously referential and anti-referential character.

Besides problems with methodology, there are also certain problems with material in a comparative study. The difficulty of dealing with Western European texts is not so much lack of material as lack of a system in collecting and classifying it. No critical editions of French, Italian, German, Austrian or Spanish texts are available; one must rely on quotations in printed books and on the late nineteenth-century printed editions.[20] The English *Punch and Judy* texts are rather better served, though there is no single representative collection even of these.[21] But enough texts can be assembled to answer the central questions: which characters and episodes can be traced to Western

European tradition, and which cannot? Can the characters who do not appear in Western European plays be traced to the Russian folk tradition?

A rare firm statement on the subject comes from Eremin:

> The masks of the Fiancée, the Doctor, the Devil, and perhaps the Arab and Turk in all probability go back to the unknown variant of the German puppet comedy played by the wandering *Spielmänner* [strolling players] which was adopted by our *skomorokhs* and was the basis of the Russian comedy of Petrushka ... Other [masks] go back the masks of the *vertep* (the Jew), *lubok* literature (Filimoshka), and the folk dramatised games (the Gypsy, the Barin).   (TP 59)

The clarity of Eremin's statement is to be welcomed, but it is unfortunate that he provides no evidence. It is vital to establish that the characters of *Petrushka* either do, or do not, coincide with characters in other European traditions, and this can only be done by direct comparison.

Eremin's mention of a single variant on which *Petrushka* is based is misleading. There is no such thing as the canonical text of the Pulcinella drama, or that of any other puppet hero. In the Italian *commedia dell'arte* tradition Pulcinella was a character with fixed attributes of costume but rather fluid personality who appeared in many scenarios with differing degrees of prominence. In one scenario he might be a servant who aided his master's intrigues; in another, he might appear as a lover scheming to sate his own lust.[22] His traits of personality were almost always low and anti-heroic, but within this general orientation there were contradictions. 'He is faithful, revengeful, shy, sentimental, lazy, a scandal-monger and full of malice in turn', writes K. M. Lea.[23] In the Italian puppet theatre he retained his versatility, appearing in many hundreds of scenarios, some of which were derived from traditional *commedia dell'arte* plots, some from folk-tales, and some from works of printed literature.[24] Even after 1900, when the Italian puppet tradition had declined, its repertoire remained vast. Orest Tsekhnovitser recounts that a Russian acquaintance of his toured Italy with a *burattini* player in the 1920s; this man, who was by no means unusual, had a repertoire of about 250 distinct plays (TP 29). In France and Spain the naturalised Pulcinella's repertoire was smaller; nonetheless, there was a large number of basic plots, many of them based on fairy-tales and on adaptations of high-literary plays.[25] The puppet heroes of Northern Europe and Bohemia also manifest a remarkably rich repertoire.[26] Each scenario might introduce several new characters drawn from fairy-tale or from literature. But besides these characters who appeared only in one scenario, there was also a central core of traditional characters, who like the hero, appeared again and again in different plots.

In England and Russia, on the other hand, the repertoire of the glove-puppet theatre is extremely limited. In both countries the hero appears in only one play, *The Tragical Comedy of Punch and Judy* in England, *The Comedy of Petrushka* in Russia. Where many Italian puppet plays, even glove-puppet plays, had quite sophisticated and finished plots,[27] both these plays have a series of episodes, and the episodes are not necessarily ordered in any particular way. The entire action consists of the hero encountering a number of other characters, most of whom he kills. What is more, several of the traditional characters in *Petrushka* are also found in *Punch and Judy*: the hero's wife, a Policeman (also called a 'Beadle'), a Black Man (also called a 'Nigger'), a Doctor, a Horse.

Can this be traced back to direct contact between the English and Russian puppet theatres? The answer is an almost certain no. There is no record of English puppeteers in Russia in the early nineteenth century (though circus, especially equestrian, artistes made frequent visits).[28] Nor is there any record of Russian puppeteers in England. It seems likely that the similarity between English and Russian tradition goes back to the fact that the texts of *Punch* and *Petrushka* played in the nineteenth and twentieth centuries were introduced in England and Russia at a similar date – early in the nineteenth century, and in a similar way – by Italian puppeteers.

This conjecture is supported by textual evidence. The scene in which Petrushka mounts and attempts to ride the Horse does not appear in most versions of *Punch and Judy*. But an almost identical scene can be found in an early nineteenth-century version, created by an Italian puppeteer, Piccini: Punch produces his horse, which 'prances about, and seems very unruly':

PUNCH: Wo, ho, my fine fellow! Wo ho! Hector. Stand still, can't you, and let me get my foot up to the stirrup.

When Punch does succeed in mounting, the horse 'soon quickens its pace', then 'sets off at full pace, jerking Punch at every stride with great violence'. Finally Punch is thrown on to the platform. As in many Russian versions, this scene is immediately followed by the scene between the hero and the Doctor. Equally, Grigorovich's

account of *Pulcinella* contains the figure of the Devil, unusual in the
Russian tradition, but commonly found in England; here, too, the
Dog attacks the hero not at the end, as in later versions, but in the
middle, as in the English tradition.[29]

Many characters which the two national traditions have in
common are found elsewhere in Europe. They resemble the traditional central characters of the Italian *Pulcinella* scenarios, which
Michael Byrom has listed as follows:

1 Pulcinella
2 his wife (sometimes called Zeza)
3 the baby, known as a *pulcinelluzo*
4 Columbina
5 a Blind Man
6 Death
7 an Old Woman
8 a Young Woman
9 an Arab
10 a Friar
11 a Brigand
12 a Turk
13 a Servant Girl
14 a Gypsy Girl
15 a Soldier or Policeman
16 a Jew

Besides these, the similarities between the European puppet plays
suggest that the early nineteenth-century Italian *Pulcinella* scenarios
included:

17 a Devil
18 a Hangman
19 a Dog or Cat

all of which can be found in Dutch and German as well as French and
English puppet plays; and

20 a Horse, which appears in *Punch and Judy*.[30]

Many of these figures have equivalents in the Russian tradition:
Pulcinella and his wife, of course; the Jew, the Arab, the Friar (as the
Deacon), the Soldier and the Policeman, the Dog (whose name in
Russian, 'Barbos', is of Italian origin, as was mentioned in chapter 2,
p. 63), the Horse, the Devil. This leaves about nine Italian characters

unaccounted for. The Old and Young Women may be related to the occasional characters of *Petrushka*, such as the hero's Aunt, but without more information it is impossible to be sure. The Gypsy Girl and the Brigand are specifically Italian characters who are found in none of the other European puppet plays. Death appears in a *lubok* edition of *Petrushka* (P 1908), and may also have been included in certain street texts. Columbina does not appear in most *Petrushka* texts, but the similarity of name makes it possible that the Mamzelle Katerina recorded in Grigorovich's version of the text may be a version of her, who, like Punch's girlfriend Polly, rapidly disappeared from the text.[31]

The most interesting absences in the Russian texts are the Hangman and the Baby. In the first case we see evidence of political filtering. By the time *Petrushka* became established, capital punishment was no longer an issue in Russia, and so the hanging scene which figures in several other European traditions, where the hero hangs the Hangman, is absent. (The clergyman, on the other hand, went

13.   A set of nineteenth-century German puppets purchased by George Speaight in the Portobello Road, 1986: from left to right: Kasperl, his wife, a Priest, the Devil.

through a religious filter: he was a popular figure in the Mediterranean and – illicitly – in Russia,[32] but was not significant in England, presumably because the English working classes had little reason for anti-clerical feelings.) The Baby's absence highlights a striking instance of psychological filtering: Petrushka, unlike the heroes of other European puppet plays, but like the 'typical' member of the subordinate classes in Russian cities, is usually unmarried.

The social standing of the puppet heroes in the different traditions went through a more elaborate filtering process. In most of Europe they belonged, like their main audience, to the urban subordinate classes. Only Spain was an exception: Don Cristóbal Pulchinela, as his name suggests, was an *hidalgo*, a Spanish noble. The definition of the hero's status in detail varied. Often he was a servant; this was frequently the case with the German Kasperl, the Czech Kasparek and Guignol of Lyons. But all three might equally well appear as artisans: Guignol was originally conceived as a Lyonnais silk-weaver. In this matter, as in others, the English and the Russian puppet plays depart from European tradition, though in different ways. Punch's social position is ill-defined, and it would be hard to guess his occupation. The Russian texts, on the other hand, define their hero's social standing with unusual exactitude. The presentation of Petrushka as a provincial boy recently arrived in the city, turning to violence and drinking, takes up a theme found in other popular genres, such as the 'Tale of Misery and Misfortune', a Russian version of the story of the Prodigal Son.[33] It is a standard motif of the 'cruel romance' (sentimental urban popular song). Petrushka himself sings such a 'romance' in a version quoted by Eremin:

Ne uezzhai, golubchik moi,
Ne pokidai polya rodnye,
Tebya ustretyat lyudi zlye,
Ne dadut serdtsu tvoemu poloi.   (TP 71)

(O my love, don't leave me please,
Stay in the fields where you were born;
There are wicked people there in town,
They will give your heart no ease.)

The perniciousness of life in the big town was also a favourite subject of the penny-dreadful novels.[34] On the other hand, Petrushka's lady-love, Parashka or Malan'ya or whatever she is called, has been through no such filtering process, and strongly resembles the wife of

14.   'Opportunity makes the Thief – Spectacle for Honest Husbands.' Polichinelle with
         a victim and the Cat. Lithograph by Langlumé, about 1820.

European puppet play tradition: she is hideously ugly, if she speaks at all it is to nag, and she is frequently engaged in physical battles with her partner.

There is one other instance of psychological filtering in the battery of characters: the figure of the Ghost, a popular puppet in England and Holland, was too alien to folk perceptions of the supernatural to take root in Russia.[35] It appears in only one street variant (FT 312). There is also one instance of linguistic filtering. The character of Death, when present (it is relatively rare in Russia, and more often Petrushka's death arrives in the matter-of-fact shape of the hairy Barbos,) takes the customary form of a skeleton with scythe and shroud, but is female, as always in Russian popular tradition, a fact dictated by the feminine gender of the noun *smert'*, 'death' (P 1908).[36]

The printed *lubok* editions seem to have gone through a second stage of influence from outside: the crocodile, which only appears in these, is likely to have come from German children's-book versions of Kasperl. It is not found in the Italian puppet theatre, and appeared in the English puppet theatre only in the second half of the nineteenth century.[37]

Besides these general processes of filtering, *Petrushka* reveals the effects of more mechanical procedures: motif and formula variation, adaptation and combination are all manifest. Certain scenes between Petrushka and those characters which were accepted in Russian tradition closely resemble those between the hero and subsidiary characters in other European texts. For example, this is the encounter between Punch and Dog Toby:

PUNCH: There's a beautiful dog! I knew he'd come to help his master; he's so fond of me. Poor little fellow! Toby, ain't you fond of your master?

[*Toby snaps*]

PUNCH: Oh, my nose![38]

And this between Petrushka and the Barbos:

PETRUSHKA: [*laskaet sobaku*] Shavochka, kudlashka, kakaya ty zama-rashka, uzh ne iz derevni-li? [*Sobaka khvataet Petrushku za rubashku*] Stoi, pes ty etakii, razorvesh' rubakhu! Bol'no! . . . Oi, ruku, ruku! . . . Mukhtarka, Mukhtarochka! [*Sobaka khvataet ego za nos*] Golubchiki, batyushki, za nos skhvatila!   (P 1907, 28)

(PETRUSHKA: [*stroking the dog*] Here, Roverkins, how now, dear little bow-wow, from the village, are you, eh? [*The dog grabs Petrushka's shirt*] Hey, stop that, you dratted hound, you'll tear my shirt! It hurts! Hoy, me arm!

Fluff! Fluffikins! [*The dog grabs him by the nose*] Oh, my goodness, my godfathers, he's got hold of my nose!)

The various foreigners are given speeches which are alike: not only are they in nonsense, but they are in similar-sounding nonsense: the Chinaman in one *Petrushka* variant uses almost the same nonsense word as 'The Native of Other Lands' in a *Punch and Judy* text:

KITAETS: Shikham-balai.
PETRUSHKA: Chto, davai, govori po-russki.[39]

(CHINAMAN: Shikham-balai.
PETRUSHKA: What's this, speak Russian will you.)

THE NATIVE OF OTHER LANDS: Shallabala!
PUNCH: Why don't you speak English?[40]

The German hero Kasperl's encounter with the Recruiting Sergeant is very close to Petrushka's:

KASPERL: [*kommt gesungen*] Radi ridi rulala, rulala – radi ridi rulala, ru – [*er rennt an den Werber*] Au weh, da bin i' an 'n Stock gestossen und hab' mir meine ganze Nasen verkrumpt!
DER WERBER: Nein, Du bist an mich gestossen, und ich bin ein keiserlicher Werber!
KASPERL: Schau, schau, das hätt' ich nicht geglaubt, dass Du a Gerber bist!
. . .
DER WERBER: Du muss jetzt exerzieren!
KASPERL: Wart' ich will dich vexieren!
DER WERBER: Da hast Du eine Flinte, damit musst Du schiessen!
KASPERL: So? Da giess' ich wohl a Wasser 'nein und zünd's danach an?
DER WERBER: Nein, du dummer Kerl, da kommt Pulver und Blei hinein, und wenn ich kommandier': 'schlagt an', so gibst Du Feuer. Also pass' auf: 'schlagt an' [*Kasperl schlägt ihn mit der Flinte auf den Kopf*] Au weh, au weh![41]

(KASPERL: [*comes in singing*]: Radi, ridi, etc. [*he runs into the Recruiting Sergeant*] Ooh, ouch, I've gorn an' run into a post and I've bent me nose all up!
R. SERGEANT: No, you ran into me, and I'm an Imperial Recruiting Sergeant!
KASPERL: Fancy now, I'd never 'ave thought you was a merchant!
R. SERGEANT: Now you must do these exercises!
KASPERL: Just you wait, I'll vexercise you!
R. SERGEANT: There's a rifle for you, you must shoot with it!
KASPERL: Yes? Put water in this, do I, and then set light to it?
R. SERGEANT: No, you daft pillock, you put powder and shot in, and when I

tells you, 'fire away' then you pulls the trigger. Right, ready: 'Fire away'.
[*Kasperl whacks him on the head with the rifle*] Ow yow yow!)

KAPRAL: Slushai voennuyu komandu … Molchat′ … Vot tebe ruzh′e.
PETRUSHKA: Eto – palka.
KAPRAL: Pervyi raz durakov obuchayut palkoi, potom ruzh′em. Beri.
PETRUSHKA: Davai!
KAPRAL: Komandu slushai!
PETRUSHKA: Spasibo, potom pokushayu …
KAPRAL: Nalevo, v krug!
PETRUSHKA: [*b′et kaprala palkoi po golove*] – Po zatylku vdrug!
KAPRAL: Ty chto, negodyai, sdelal?
PETRUSHKA: Vinovat … Shel da spotyknulsya …
KAPRAL: Smeesh′ ty spotykat′sya …
PETRUSHKA: Sleduyushchii raz budu starat′sya.
KAPRAL: Pali!
PETRUSHKA: Derzhis′! [*ubivaet kaprala palkoi*]   (Tarasov 37)

(CORPORAL: Fall in … Silence … Here's a rifle for you.
PETRUSHKA: This is a stick.
CORPORAL: We teach idiots with a stick first, then a rifle. Here.
PETRUSHKA: Give it!
CORPORAL: Ten-shun!
PETRUSHKA: Thanks, I would like a bun.
CORPORAL: Left turn about!
PETRUSHKA: [*hits Corporal on the head*]: Quick whack on the nut!
CORPORAL: What do you think you're doing, cretin?
PETRUSHKA: 'Scuse me … I slipped.
CORPORAL: You try that just once more …
PETRUSHKA: I'll do my best, I'm sure.
CORPORAL: Fire!
PETRUSHKA: On guard! [*kills the Corporal with the stick*])

There are also formulae from the European tradition which do not
appear in *Petrushka*. There is no equivalent of the most famous *Punch
and Judy* phrase – 'That's the way to do it', nor of the following
standard routine between Punch and the Doctor:

DOCTOR: Now Punch, *are* you dead? No reply! [*Thrashing him*] Physic!
Physic! Physic! [*The mixture as before is repeated each time*]
PUNCH: [*reviving under the influence of the dose*]: What sort of physic do you
call that, Doctor?
DOCTOR: Stick-liquorice! stick-liquorice! stick-liquorice![42]

Although the European tradition is arguably the source of the
Petrushka play, and although many scenes seem to come from it, it

does not account for all the characters. Some of the minor ones, such as the Doctor's Father, were added by individual puppeteers. But that still leaves the Gypsy, the German, the Barin and Filimoshka with no parallel elsewhere in Europe.

The Gypsy and the Barin were two very important characters in Russian folk drama. They are found in the mummers' plays performed at Christmas, in the Ukrainian *vertep* plays, and in the Cossack puppet plays.[43] But the presentation of these characters in the rural tradition has not much in common with their presentation in *Petrushka*. The Gypsy in Vinogradov's Russian *vertep* text is not a horse-dealer or a national stereotype but an undifferentiated thug who insults and beats several puppet Jews.[44] A more likely immediate source from which these characters could have been absorbed into the *Petrushka* text was the *intermedii*, 'interludes', performed in the popular theatre of the eighteenth century. The *intermedii* were an urban genre, performed by the lower orders; in other words, they belonged to the same milieu as *Petrushka*. They remained in the repertoire of servants' amateur theatrical groups well into the nineteenth century.[45] The Gypsy was a particularly popular character in *intermedii*. A wily rogue, he was associated (as in *Petrushka*) with horse-dealing and sharp practice:

Skazhu vam: vivat, mnogo leta, dolgo zhiti,
Albo skolko komu khochettsya.
Byv zhe ya, panove, v Egipte, khoroshi tsygan,
A nad baryshnikami pervyi ataman,
Nad kon'mi miloserdy getman.
Da shchok kazhut ni rodis' ni khorosh, ni prigozh,
Rodisya zhe schastliv.[46]

(I say to you: vivat, many happy returns, long may ye live,
As long as ye all may wish, withal.
For I, my lords, was in Egypt a fine Gypsy,
Of the horse-traders I was the first ataman,
Of the horse-breeders the gentle hetman.
As you see, better to be born not good, not fair of face,
But to be born lucky.)

The absurd language in which the Gypsy speaks in some *Petrushka* versions also goes back to the *intermediya*:

Yako, dyako, romalo,
Yako, yako, chuvalo,
Ya segodnya minchu iikhav ...   (Tarasov 32)

(Yako, dyako, romalo,
Yako, yako, chuvalo,
I today minchu avegorn …)

although the *intermediya* versions are longer and more flowery:

Goi, goi, goi!
Edu, edu na Chigasy,
Tochit' lyasy,
Bolendryasy, mindryasy,
Findryasy,
Naditsy, vitsy,
Nadverovitsy,
Kartashi, ellashi,
Kastylinki, mogilinki,
Mylniki, shilniki.[47]

(Hoi, hoi, hoi!
I'm going, I'm going to Chigasy,
To sing tra-la-lasy,
Bolendrasy, mindrasy,
Findrasy,
Visors, vices,
Doorwaywises,
Pataters, ellaters,
Shavicles, gravicles,
Awlicles, ballicles.)

The Barin, always represented as a fully-fledged idiot, was usually engaged in some tussle with his servants, who tricked him and stole from him as Petrushka did from his master.[48]

Filimoshka is not found in the *intermedii*: but he was apparently a popular clown figure from the *lubki*, allied with Foma, Erema, Farnos and others.[49]

The mystery character is the German, who certainly does not come from the Western European tradition, and is also without precedent in the Russian tradition; he is not found in the *intermedii*, nor in the rural folk plays. It is possible that he was introduced to replace some comic foreigner in the Italian puppet plays. One of the *commedia dell'arte* masks is a braggart Spaniard, who would have made no impact on the Russian audience.[50]

The finished *Petrushka* text had gone through a much more complicated process than a tidy side-by-side arrangement of foreign and Russian characters. Characters were adapted and fused from both traditions. The foreign characters were given the formulaic opening speeches of *intermediya* characters: the Doctor in *Petrushka* spoke in words which had belonged to the Gypsy–Apothecary, who says in one *intermediya*:

Oi, sterezhisya, beregisya!
Poprav'! edet dobry lekar',
Svinoi obtekar'.
U kogo trudna bolna lezhit,
Tekh gotov lechit'.[51]

(Take care everywhere!
Get well quick! It's the good physician,
The swinish obstetrician,
All people suffering and unwell,
I am prepared to heal.)

The Jew in *Petrushka* has been adapted to the social context: he is a small-time *makler* (fixer) in the Eastern European style, a seller of tin tacks and sandpaper, rather than a Shylock:

PETRUSHKA: Chto u tebya est', chtoby pokushat'?
EVREI: Vus' u menya est' vse, chto zavgodno.
PETRUSHKA: Nu, a zharkoe est'?
EVREI: Vus' zharkoe – zharkoe net.
PETRUSHKA: Govori skorei, chto u tebya est'?
EVREI: U menya est' kerosin, degot', mylo, svechi, melkie gvozdi, sol', bebul'naya bumaga ...[52]

(PETRUSHKA: What've you got to eat then?
JEW: [*in a Jewish accent*]: Anyting you like, shir.
PETRUSHKA: Well, got any roast meat then?
JEW: No shir, shorry shir.
PETRUSHKA: What have you got then, no mucking about?
JEW: I've got kerosene, tar, soap, candles, tintacks, salt, sandpaper ...)

The Jew is one of the few characters for whom the source appears to be the *vertep* plays. In Vinogradov's recording several of them appear together, and sing the following chorus about how they are food traders:

Kaby nam, panushkam, gel'd sobrat'
My stali by vnov' torgovat'
Mekhom, lekhom, sholemekhom.[53]

(If we, the toff's brats, are to have *geld*
We must again start to buy and to sell
Wax and lachs and Shalomtacks.)

The hiring scene in Grigorovich's version, in which Puchinella is invited to carry a note to Mamzelle Katerina, is like a simplified version of the scenes in which servants are used to carry out love intrigues, a standard of the Italian scenarios:

KAPIRAN-ISPRAVNIK: U menya, bratets, zhalovan'e ochen' khoroshee, kushan'e otlichnoe, pud myakiny da polchetverika gniloi ryabiny, a esli skhodish' k mamzel' Katerine i otnesesh' ei zapisku, to poluchish' 25 rublei nagrazhdeniya.

(Grigorovich, 25)

(THE CAPTAIN OF POLICE: I'll pay you a good salary, my fine fellow, and feed you well, two quarts of steam and half a ton of rotten beans and if you go to Mademoiselle Katerina and take her this note, I'll give you 25 roubles' reward.)

This is Brighella offering his services to his lovesick master Florindo in an Italian scenario:

FLORINDO: Ah, yes, love is the cause of my troubles.
BRIGHELLA: And with Brighella to help, what lover could despair?
FLORINDO: And what can you do to help me?
BRIGHELLA: Tell me your trouble. Tell me the name of the girl, and then I will know what to do.[54]

In later Russian versions the hiring scene had been replaced by an *intermediya*-style comic confrontation between Petrushka and the Barin, but a garbled reference to the scene Grigorovich saw remains when Petrushka describes his salary: the third month's pay was always said to be 'a letter from Katerina' (see chapter 2, p. 88).

Episodes, too, have been altered and adapted. The scene of Western European origin in which the hero falls off a horse is fused with the purely Russian scene of a horse sale, going back to the mummers' plays.[55]

As we have noted in the study of the *Petrushka* variants, an alternative method by which the puppeteer might build up an original version was by varying the outcome of the scenes. Comparison of the European versions indicates to what flexibility this method could lead. Alternative interpretations were made in particular of the scenes with the wife or fiancée (who was generally spared being murdered in Russia, not so in England or Holland). In the concluding scene there was also variation. The hero might be dragged off to Hell, losing his final battle with the Devil (or in Russia, the Barbos), or he might win his fight and emerge triumphant. The necessity to get the puppet off-stage and definitively end the show vied with the demands of incentive censorship, that the hero be allowed to get away with it. Petrushka, like the other puppet heroes, might sometimes be spared; there was no consistent moralising in Russian popular culture of this type like that in Russian popularising literature where, as Jeffrey Brooks has pointed out, the bandit or law-breaker figure invariably ended up by being brought into line, or coming to a terrible end. Like the bandits in other orally transmitted genres such as the ballad, Petrushka did sometimes evade retribution.[56]

The name for the Russian hero in later variants also illustrates how Russian and domestic elements were absorbed and adapted. Having been 'Puchinella', he became 'Petrushka'. This change follows a pattern which can be observed elsewhere. In many European countries, in the early nineteenth-century local, corrupt pronunciations of the Italian Pulcinella – Punch in England, Polichinelle in France, Pulchinela in Spain – disappeared, to be replaced by a traditional clown's name, which in Northern Europe was usually a form of John or Jacques: Jan Klaasen in Holland, Hanneschen in Cologne, Jack Pudding in England, Mester Jakel in Denmark, and Jacques Leuflé of Rontaix, who was created by a Belgian puppeteer who settled there in the 1870s.[57]

It is tempting to suggest that the name 'Petrushka' came from the cognate name of one of the *commedia dell'arte* masks, Pedrolino, known as Pierrot in France. Pulcinella and Pedrolino in Italy, Polichinelle and Pierrot in France, frequently appear together. Though it is usual for Pedrolino–Pierrot to be the dupe and Pulcinella–Polichinelle the aggressor, occasionally the two roles were reversed.[58] The idea that Petrushka was linked with Pedrolino–Pierrot gained currency amongst the Russian Symbolists.[59] More recently, it has been put forward by the Italian scholar A. M. Ripellino.[60]

Attractive as the idea is, there is one important link missing. In order for 'Petrushka' to be traced to the Italian, it is necessary to find a corrupt Russian version of the name Pedrolino or Pierrot. Neither name is recorded in any text, nor does either name appear elsewhere in the Russian popular tradition; neither can, for example, be found in Dal's dictionary. On the other hand, there is much evidence for the fact that the name Petrushka was in general use in the eighteenth century, well before the arrival of the glove-puppet texts. A name as common as Jack, it was one of the several names used generically for a servant. It appears in this usage in an *intermediya*, where a character bearing this name behaves towards a nobleman with a particularly bare-faced lack of respect:

SHLYAKHTA: Odnakozh poklichu: Sluga!
Akh, ek ane, kanalii, zanyalis',
A sobaki-to vse razbrelis'
Net, da ya khot' imenem-ta nazovu:
Petrushka!
SLUGA: Koi chert vorchit, kak v lesu lyagushka? ...
SHLYAKHTA: Kanal'i, al' vy oglokhli?
SLUGA: Da uzh my s golodu izglokhli.[61]

15. 'Conversation of the Clown Farnos and his Wife Pegas'ya with Ermak the
Tavern-Keeper.' Eighteenth-century *lubok*, reproduced from D. Rovinsky, *Russkie
narodnye kartinki*, 2nd edn, St Petersburg 1800, ii, p. 278.

(NOBLEMAN: But let me call; Sirrah!
Ah, alack, the villains have disappeared;
They are hard at work, the curs, I fear.
No, I'll try calling by name:
Petrushka, you dog!
SERVANT: Who's that croaking like a sick frog?
NOBLEMAN: You villains, have you gone deaf?
SERVANT: Of course not, we've all starved to death.)

The name remained in use during the nineteenth century. In Gogol's novel *Dead Souls* Chichikov's servant is called Petrushka:

Petrushka was wearing a slightly too roomy brown overcoat, a cast-off of his master's, and, as is customary in people of his station, *had a large nose and mouth*.[62]

Gogol's description suggests that this servant is not only uncouth, but clownish too, and indeed the name was already established as that of a clown. In the *lubok* a hero of this name is shown riding on a pig, and the text uncoyly details his many disgusting habits.[63] According to some authorities, the name Petrushka developed from Pedrila, the familiar name by which Empress Anna's Italian court jester was known.[64] It must also have been irresistibly linked in the popular memory with the idea of a famous Petrushka, Peter I, who insisted on being known by the nickname of the 'Skipper', whose manners were as unpredictable as those of his puppet counterpart, and whose liking for sadistic games and practical jokes kept his court on a knife-edge:

All of [the courtiers] had constantly to bear in mind that any of them might at any moment be given a sound beating by the 'Skipper' with his club [the same word, *dubinka*, is used as in *Petrushka* texts] or executed.[65]

Petrushka's patronymic, however, was Ivanovich, not Alekseevich, and there is no record that he was ever referred to as 'the Skipper'.

The puppet Petrushka is linked with the eighteenth-century tradition by another appellation. He is known as *Petrushka-farnos, krasnyi nos* (Farnose the red-nose). The character Farnos was one of a pair of *lubok* clowns, the other of which was called Gonos. The word *farnosyi* is given by Dal' simply as 'snub-nosed', but Carla Solivetti thinks it can be traced to the Italian clown Gian Farino, so called because of his mask of *farino*, flour.[66] The similarity between Petrushka and these characters, however, ends at the name. They were greedy, anally obsessed boobies who lacked Petrushka's capacity for malice:

Both of them are full of 'inner powder', which is 'quick on the draw' but its
bullets 'never make anyone sore', and behind they have the fool's 'symbol-
crow, to keep off the mos-qui-toes'.[67]

The hunch backs and hook noses of these characters do not indicate a
hereditary line to Petrushka: they come from the general tradition of
carnival comedy. The similarity of name is incidental. The nineteenth-
century puppet tradition could quite happily accommodate the fact
that the northern glove-puppet hero was called Petrushka, whilst his
exact counterpart in the south was called Van'ka. There is the same
situation here as in the *shut* (joker) and *durak* (fool) stories, in which
the same character in different stories may have no name at all, being
called simply 'the soldier' or the 'moujik', or may go by a variety of
different names: Klimka, Kanyga-prolyga, Naum, Anton, Vlas,
Matrokha, Senka, Fomka-shut are some of the 'joker' names; Luto-
nyushka, Foma, Erema some of the 'fool' names. The name 'Iva-
nushka-durachok' is used for both 'fools' and 'jokers'.[68] Similarly, in
Italy the name 'Pulcinella' was used for two diametrically opposed
characters, a virulent and viperous trickster and an empty-headed,
greedy and garrulous buffoon, the 'second zanni' and 'first zanni' as
they were called in the *commedia dell'arte*.

  The various different names by which Petrushka was known were
brought out ceremoniously by the puppeteers, and in the same variant
he might be known as 'Petrushka', 'Petrushka-mus'yu / mus'e' 'Petr
Ivanovich', 'Petrushka-ratatui', 'Petrukha-razrukha' (Peter the
Beater), and his surname Uksusov or Samovarov. This naming of
names seems to have given the audience particular delight. It resembles the comic device by which the names of objects or activities are
repeated. The following excellent example is quoted by Eremin:

BARIN: Chto tebe nuzhno?
PETRUSHKA: Vot chto nuzhno!
BARIN: Da chto tebe nuzhno?
PETRUSHKA: Nuzhno.
BARIN: Tak skazhi, chto tebe nuzhno.
PETRUSHKA: Da vot chto nuzhno ...   (TP 74)

(BARIN: What do you need?
PETRUSHKA: That's what I need!
BARIN: But what do you need?
PETRUSHKA: Need.
BARIN: Just say what you need.
PETRUSHKA: But that's what I need.)

What technical features can be traced to direct influence of other European theatres on *Petrushka*, rather than to the generic similarities of the carnival tradition? The screen, or *shirmy*, in which *Petrushka* was performed, appears to have been imported. The native forms of Russian puppet theatre, including the show Olearius saw, were all performed in theatres improvised from blankets or other pieces of material, a tradition which is also found in Turkey and Central Asia.[69] The *Petrushka* screen is a simplified version of the canvas or wooden booths used in Germany, France, Holland and England.[70] Though elsewhere in Europe the puppet theatres were usually hard-sided and topped by a rococo proscenium arch, and might even have miniature painted backdrops, this difference can probably be traced to practical grounds. The simplicity of the Russian practice made it possible to assemble and dismantle the structure quickly, important in a country in which puppet performances were subject to restriction. The open-topped canvas structure did not give the puppets and puppeteers much protection if it rained or snowed, but this was not a matter of moment for performances in the *balagans*, where the canvas booth was protected inside solid walls and a roof.

The musical accompaniment which *Petrushka* always had can be traced back to the puppet shows of the *skomorokhs*, but the barrel-organ used in nineteenth-century performances was an import from Western Europe; the early examples were owned by Germans and Italians, and hired by the day to Russians, as Grigorovich's story tells us.

The construction of the puppets used for *Petrushka*, with the operator's first finger in the head, and the thumb and second finger in the arms, is similar to the construction of glove puppets everywhere in Western Europe, with the exception of Catalonia.[71] The speaking-device used by the operator, *govorok* or *pishchik* in Russian, also appears to have come from Europe. It is not used in Turkey, nor in Central Asia.[72] But it is found all over Europe, where it has various names: *pivetta* in Italian, *pito* or *cerbetana* in Spanish, swazzle in English. In most of Europe, as in Russia, it was used just by the hero. (In the Catalan theatre, however, all the characters spoke with it.)[73]

The details on the costumes of *Petrushka* are so scanty that it is hard to speculate on their origin. There is no record that the hero ever had a costume like the Italian Pulcinella (a white baggy suit with floppy collar and a black half-mask). Even the Italianate version of his costume did not resemble this. But the Pulcinella costume was in fact not found in any other European theatre: the similarly named, Punch, Polichinelle and Don Cristóbal Pulchinela do not wear it. The puppet heroes everywhere were clad like miniature clowns in red cotton suits, usually striped white, with pointed clowns' hats; or in a version of local plebeian clothing, frequently preserving only the red colour, and in some cases the dunce's cap, from the clown's outfit. The hero's wife or fancy lady tended to wear a female version of her husband's clothing, whether this was generic clown's attire or local costume. The costumes of some of the characters were general, found in all European countries, others national. The Doctor looked much the same from Sicily to Siberia: he always had glasses and a conventionalised version of medical clothing. Foreigners, such as Turks and Chinamen, also had costumes which resembled each other in most European countries. The local characters had local costumes, as one would expect.

A technical feature found in many European countries was the trick puppets, such as Langhals (Long Neck) in Holland and the Grand Turk in England, which had expanding necks, and Dame Gigogne in France, from beneath whose skirts a whole family of diminutive children would appear.[74] Such trick puppets were not a usual feature of the Russian glove-puppet theatre. Zaitsev had a couple in his battery of puppets, but they appear to have been marionettes.[75] As does the trick 'bush turning into a shack' mentioned by an observer of a puppet show in 1843:

The whole comedy, its entire plot consists of Polichinelle coming in and out. Then a Spaniard comes in and goes out; then a Russian peasant woman comes in and goes out again; then a dwarf turns into a giant; then a bush tries to turn into a shack and . . . that's it! Just look what kind of entertainments are put before our poor children![76]

The fluidity of national traditions within different countries makes it hard to trace a neat linear progression between texts in the way of a high-literary influence study, the more so if one is discussing the character of style and comedy rather than plots and masks. But it is necessary to examine this problem in passing, in order to dispel some more of the myths about Petrushka. There has been a tendency to condemn the Russian hero as less funny than his European counterparts:

When he reached Russian soil, Petrushka became irrevocably adapted to the tastes of the common people and became a far less witty and biting humorist than, for example, the French Polichinelle or the English Punch ... With us, as in Germany too, he did not rise to play the role of a voice of public opinion, because in the milieu with which he was associated, there is not yet any conception of such a role.[77]

This opinion is yet another example of the intellectual tendency to find popular culture acceptable only if it is far enough away. In fact, Petrushka and the other European texts are linked by the tradition of carnival humour, which we have defined with Bakhtin as universal and anti-literary, 'that peculiar folk humour which always existed and was never merged with the official culture of the ruling classes'.[78]

The physical humour which we have identified in *Petrushka* exists in abundant measure in the *Pulcinella* texts, and in the other glove-puppet texts. It can also be found in texts which belong to quite other eras and regions: the satyr plays of Greece with their hairy, goatish satyrs and crude humour, their lowering of authority; the Atellan farces; the Sanskrit ritual dramas; the Turkish and Greek shadow-puppet plays whose hero is Karagöz or Karaghiozi. Naturally it existed in Russia before the foreign glove-puppet plays ever got there. The entertainments presented to Olearius are excellent examples of the crudest type of carnival humour. In later periods, there are plenty of examples of the carnival humour tradition in entertainments which had nothing to do with the fairground. In a bawdy rhymed verse, 'Skomoroshina o chernetse', sex and eating are associated:

> Khodit chernets po monastyryu,
> Prosit chernets milostinu.
> Daite, chernitse,
> Daite, chernichne,
> Cherntsovi milostinu.
>
> . . .
>
> Vynesli emu yagodnykh slastei,
> A on prosit u nikh mezhnozhnykh strastei
> Daite, chernitse,
> Daite, sestritse,
> Cherntsovi milostinu.[79]

(The monk pays a call on the nuns,
The monk's come to ask for alms;
Dear nun, give,
Sweet nun, give,
Alms unto the monk.

They bring him out berries red,
But the food he wants is between their legs,

Dear nun, give,
Sweet nun, give,
Alms unto the monk.)

But the carnival tradition, united by imagery, puns and anti-authoritarian stance, nonetheless was divided by different emphasis at different stages of history and in different regions. As Bakhtin writes: 'Even in its narrow sense carnival is far from being a simple phenomenon with only one meaning.'[80] The complexity of the carnival affected *Petrushka* too: it was divided from the Western European puppet theatre by regional origin, from Russian rural folk humour by belonging to a different era and different political context.

The imagery of carnival humour varies from country to country: in different areas different aspects are predominant. Certain genres are more popular in some countries than others: in Russia the clowns' monologues and the peepshows were more prominent than elsewhere, the puppet theatre and the dramatic genres were less developed than in Italy or Germany. The nature of the jokes also varies. Some nations laugh more at anal jokes, others at bad taste, for example illness and mock funerals, some at sexual farce, etc. The Russian specialities are sick jokes linking food and death, physicality in the sense of roughness, and emphasis on distortion and disablement. Jokes about excretion are rare. In the German theatres, on the other hand, excretery comedy played a larger role than almost anywhere else, as Goethe's version of the traditional Hanswurst plays makes clear.[81] Like *Petrushka*, *Punch and Judy* had a penchant for sick comedy and was relatively innocent in a sexual sense. In Turkey there were jokes about homosexuality (rare elsewhere, and despite Olearius' suggestion that 'vile sodomies' were a feature of the early Russian puppet theatre, unheard of in *Petrushka*), and opium-smokers.[82] The Western European theatre revelled in comic drunks, but was without this social type.

Though every carnival genre manifested ambivalent humour, in which death and suffering were mocked, the nature of the death and suffering was not always the same. Italian jokes were particularly outspoken and heartless: references to illness, especially skin disease, insanity, impotence, enemas and circumcisions abounded. In the following scene from an Italian puppet-play scenario Pulcinella abuses an old woman whom Brighella has substituted for the lovely Diana, his promised bride:

PULCINELLA: Go and get chopped! [*he slaps her*]
OLD WOMAN: Don't touch this bad arm.
PULCINELLA: What's the matter with your arm?
OLD WOMAN: A boil, but the doctor says it will heal.
PULCINELLA: It can burst and explode if it likes; it doesn't matter to me.

. . .

PULCINELLA: And how was I to know you were an old crock?
OLD WOMAN: So you say! Apart from the maladies I have told you about and a little ring-worm on my head which the doctor says will soon heal, I am very healthy and envied by the most beautiful of women.[83]

Most other European theatres are more reticent. In Russia the sick humour is limited to jokes on the subject of Petrushka's hump, mockery of dead bodies and occasional comic funeral scenes. Physicality in the sense of rough stuff, however, was particularly favoured in Russia, as I noted (chapter 1, pp. 19, 28), in the case of the harlequinades. Petrushka's final list of murder victims in the most extreme variants is longer than any other puppet hero's: no other European hero starts going through the victims' families when he runs out of victims.

Not only the type but the construction of the jokes varies from place to place. In some countries, such as Italy, the jokes might be developed and elaborate. The standard food and putrefaction link is ornately embroidered in the following speech of Pulcinella's from a *commedia dell' arte* commonplace book:

The fish of promises hidden in the grotto of deceit look fresh but they stink; the fruits of love are wormy; the lard of her whiteness looks fresh but will melt.[84]

In Russian carnival genres, jokes of a more pithy and abbreviated character were valued. They differed also, not only from Italian genres, but from other Western European countries, in their metrical variety. In the typical Russian fairground dramatic piece, the bulk of the text was composed in prose, but rhyme was used to point the witticisms, and especially the central carnival images. In other European countries this was unusual. Occasionally the more pretentious marionette plays were composed entirely in rhyming verse; in the rough street glove-puppet theatre, rhyme was little used.

The particular character of *Petrushka*'s carnival comedy, with its emphasis on violence and lowness, links it with other Russian genres. Indeed, *Petrushka* is mild by comparison with the explicit sexual and scatological references of many Russian popular texts.[85] Mockery of the dead and even necrophilia are common topics of the obscene *chastushka*.[86] Among the comic tales of the fools and jokers is one in which the fool uses his mother's dead body to obtain money by extortion.[87] The comic tales also abound in terrifying violence, in which people are torn to pieces. The fusion between physique and food is found in many of the obscene proverbs, sometimes pointed by punning rhymes. For example, among the proverbs and sayings which Dal' declined to publish we find:

Kak etot spirt nazyvaetsya, chto iz zhopy dobivaetsya?

(What do you call the alcohol that comes out your arsehole?)

Kashei khuya ne nakormish'.

(You'll never sate a prick on porridge.)

Kolbasa da para yaits.[88]

(A sausage and a pair of eggs.)

But *Petrushka*, like the European glove-puppet texts, is an urban nineteenth-century tradition, and this distinguishes it from the rural traditions of humour, as does its bond with the fairground. The urban carnival or fair was in many ways remote from Russian village life. It was seen as disturbing and potentially intrusive, a haunt of wickedness. The fairground is not used as a setting for the folk-tale, and in the *narodnye anekdoty* (funny stories) it appears as a place where simple village people are under threat:

A stupid village woman goes to the fair to buy an icon of the *Vremennaya Pyatnitsa* (Occasional Friday). She goes into the *balagan* and says to the peddlar, 'Grandad, would you ever show me an icon of the *Vremennaya Pyatnitsa*?' Instead he shows her an icon of Saint George the Brave. 'Grandad!' she says, 'What's she doing on a horse, Our Lady I mean?' 'Get on, woman, you're a dim one! What do you think she's called *Vremennaya* for? It's because occasionally she rides a horse, occasionally she walks. Look, that's why the horse is waving his big feet about like that.'[89]

In the *volshebnye skazki* (magic tales) it is unthinkable that the existence of the supernatural should be questioned. But in the comic stories, literal belief in agrarian rituals, magic and the existence of spirits is parodied. In one of the stories in which Lyutonyushka appears, his mother is deceived by a con-man who poses as a traditional manifestation of spring, *Vesna krasna* or Beautiful Spring. He pretends that he has come for a traditional offering of food, and makes off with a whole hunk of meat given to him by the credulous woman.[90] Traditional ideas of time and space are also mocked. In another 'joker' story the hero deceives a whole crowd of feeble-minded villagers by pretending to hang himself first on one tree, then on another further on. Their perceptions of the universe are so simple they fail to realise that he has simply moved from the first place to the second.[91]

The comic folk-tales are an interesting genre, in which the comedy often comes from the tension between ideas taken for granted in the magic tales, and their impossibility in the matter-of-fact village world. In the urban genres these ritual perceptions were so remote that they were not parodied (they were already extinct).

The rural genres contain comic material which is not found in *Petrushka*; conversely, the most characteristic comic device of the puppet play, the ambivalent pun, is a rarity in rural folklore.[92] But more important than this is the difference in the effect of the carnival humour. The reversals of hierarchy in the village dramas are softened by the fact that the events and characters portrayed are remote from reality: the character of the Tsar in *Tsar' Maksimilian*, for example, stands for authority only in the most general sense, unlike the Policeman in *Petrushka*.

The village dramas, it has been observed, were not performed by professional actors. The relationship between actors and audience was without the commercial pressure found in the fairground. The appeals to the audience for money, which appear as formulae in all the carnival texts, are absent from the village dramas. The mummers' shows usually ended with a request to the persons watching for rewards, but these were given in the form of food. If an offering of money was made, it was a small amount: a token coin or two. The significance of these payments was ritual, not commercial, as the following extract from Berkov's anthology makes clear:

BARIN: Skol'ko za nee khochesh'?
OTKUPSHCHIK: Sto rublei den'gami
Sorok sorokushek
Solenykh ...
Sorok anbarov
Morozhenykh tarakanov,
Arshin masla

Kislogo moloka tri pasma
Mikhaila Tamintsyna nos,
Nashei Kozharikhi khvost.   (Berkov 47–8)

(BARIN: How much do you want for the mare?
MONOPOLY OWNER: A hundred roubles,
Forty times forty
Salted [*obscenity omitted by Berkov*]
Forty barns full
Of frozen black beetles,
Of butter, half an ell,
Three lees of sour milk:
The nose off Tamintsyns' Mikhail,
And the tail off Bonebag the cow.)

In *Petrushka*, on the other hand, the need to make money was always
blatant. The spectators were invited in with a formulaic speech which
stressed the value of the text:

Pozhaluite, zakhodite, Petrushku postmotrite. A deneg, esli khotite, tak khot'
i ne nesite. I tak pustim posmotret'. Ne otdadite v kasse, otdadite v balagane
... Kak-nibud' pomirimsya s vami! Gospoda, gospoda! Pozhaluite syuda!
Pyat' kopeek den'gi nebol'shie, a udovol'stviya – tri koroba! (Berkov 123)

(Please come in, *Petrushka* will soon begin. You needn't pay right away if you
prefer it that way ... we'll let you come in anyhow. If you don't buy a ticket
outside you can pay inside ... We'll make it quits later! Ladies and gents,
come here now, watch our show! Five kopecks isn't much for three tons of
fun!)

Often the action would be interrupted half-way through, so that the
audience could be asked to 'pay for the German's funeral', the idea
being that the show might not go on if they were stingy (Berkov
120).[93]

The *Petrushka* texts themselves were full of references to money.
The hero purchased a horse, and in one text also bought clothes from
an Armenian (NP 1891). Not only objects, but services are purchas-
able. In some plays the hero is hired for work; in most the Doctor's
medical attention is bargained for. In the village rituals the Doctor
had a fertility function: he was a life-restorer, who brought fallen
heroes back to life. In *Petrushka* he is one of the characters who
sponges off the poor, a class enemy and representative of exploitation:

DOKTOR: Pozvol'te za vizit.
PETRUSHKA: Seichas ... [*izchezaet*]
DOKTOR: Muzykant, a on ne obmanet?
MUZYKANT: Net, net!

DOKTOR: Poskorei by denezhki poluchit'. Loshadi zhe stoyat, nado otsyuda
uekhat'.   (Tarasov 24)

(DOCTOR: My fee, if you please.
PETRUSHKA: One moment ... [*vanishes*]
DOCTOR: Musician, he's not going to cheat me, is he?
MUSICIAN: No, no!
DOCTOR: Hope he hurries up with that money ... The horses are waiting, it's
time to go.)

Petrushka's attitude to his fiancée also has commercial elements: he is
greedy over her dowry. In some plays the commercial atmosphere in
which he lives works against him, however: he tries to engage a
Matchmaker, but when she finds out how little he is worth she loses
interest (NP 1891).

In all the texts money is closely associated with violence. Whenever
Petrushka is asked for money, he brings out his club. Often the
connection is pointed by money euphemisms for beating, most
notably when the Sakhalin Petrushka promises his father twenty
roubles and gives him twenty whacks. The sick jokes often involve
puns on death and money: it is a commonplace for Petrushka to
mishear the Musician's rebuke 'ty ego ubil' (he's bought it, lit. you've
killed him) for 'ty ego kupil' (you've bought him). In the Sakhalin
version Petrushka even protests over the dead body of his own father:
'zachem kupil, on svoi, domoroshchennyi' (Why 'bought' him – he's
our dad, he's home-grown!).[94]

The earlier urban genres, the *intermedii* and the comic printed
povesti (tales) are, not surprisingly, much closer to the puppet plays in
style than the rural genres. They share not only the obscenity and
violence, but also the commercial hard-headedness of the nineteenth-
century carnival texts. In 'The Tale of Frol Skobeev' the hero adopts
women's dress to contrive the rape of a merchant's daughter, a virgin,
in order that he can force her into marriage and collect her dowry.[95]
Harlequin or Gaer, the hero of many an *intermediya*, is utterly
cynical: he is corruptible in the sense that he accepts money for
undertaking to do immoral things, but not corruptible in the sense
that he then does what he has undertaken. He offers, for a consideration, to conceal a faithless wife's affair from her husband; for
another consideration, he betrays her to her husband.[96] He sells a
pregnant female friend of his to a stupid Polish nobleman and
persuades him that a birth two months after the wedding can only be a
sign of exceptional virility.[97]

The plots of the *intermedii* and *povesti* are more complicated than those of *Petrushka*. They involve motifs of cross-dressing and mistaken identity, larger numbers of characters are introduced and the characters are developed to a greater extent. But these differences can

16. 'Then the adulteresses did berate him / With a mallet one did chase him / With water th' other inundate him, / For his part he cried 'oh!' and run / As fast as he could go.' An *intermediya* in performance, c. 1725. From N. Tikhonravov, *Russkie dramaticheskie proizvendeniya 1672–1725*, ii, St Petersburg 1874.

be explained by the demands of the glove-puppet theatre, in which changes of clothes and mistaken identity are impossible, and which is not suited to character development. The type of humour and the clowns which appear in these stories are part of the same tradition as *Petrushka*. The puppet plays, arriving in Russia in the early nineteenth century represented the second wave of Western European literary influence in Russia, and grafted itself on to the existing popular tradition, which already showed signs of the first wave of influence. Pulcinella–Petrushka himself was readily appreciated by an audience used to heroes Gerlikin and Gaer, based on the *commedia dell' arte*.

Out of its twin roots, the Russian and the foreign tradition, *Petrushka* developed into an independent genre, absorbing formulae and motifs from other genres, but never totally parasitic on them. Variations in the national traditions happened along the same lines as the variations in the local traditions: different selections of motifs were made, sequences of episodes were varied, the episodes differently resolved, and idiosyncratic formulae used. Sometimes the changes reflected various types of external filters: political, religious or psychological, as when certain characters were excluded or added (the rag-seller in Russia, the hangman in Western Europe, the priest in Spain are specific instances). Sometimes, on the other hand, they did not, and formulae would remain in use which were redundant in a social or political sense; often the incomprehensible would be resolved in the terms of a carnival opposition (as was the case with the Mamzelle Katerina formula quoted above). The hero himself underwent a process of naturalisation which was just as specific: from a character who was exotic because of his Italian name, he became a character exotic because he was associated with the abnormal events of the carnival, outside everyday limits.

Chapters 4 and 5 will analyse what happened when this living, mobile tradition was appropriated by the literary tradition, which tried at once to transform its unstable, unpredictable material into a canonical version, a seamless whole, and to reduce it to an aesthetical or political parable.

4

Petrushka and *Petrouchka*: fairground and carnival in high literature

Literary treatments of the fairground

The street and fairground entertainments in all the big cities in Europe during the nineteenth century resembled each other very closely, because the rides and acts were similar (or even identical: by the late nineteenth century many steam roundabouts and other rides were imported from Germany or America),[1] and because everywhere they were the main source of entertainment for the urban lower classes. The difference between Russia and other countries was the greater contempt with which these entertainments were regarded by the educated classes. Fairground historians in other countries can draw on museums of fairground architecture, and on many literary and artistic accounts. In Italy the ceremonies of the carnival and the acts of the *commedia dell'arte* are very richly documented, as can be seen in the studies by Duchartre, Oreglia, Lea and Bragaglia.[2] In Britain also, the big fairs attracted enthusiastic memoirists and painters.[3]

This goes not only for factual accounts. In Western European high literary tradition, there are many instances of scenes or sometimes whole works inspired by the fairground tradition: Ben Jonson's *Bartholomew Fair*, Goethe's *Jahrmarktsfest zu Plundersweilen* and *Hanswursts Hochzeit*, to say nothing of his *Faust*, and scenes in Cervantes' *Don Quixote*. During the Romantic period, the life of wandering actors and showmen took on a particular significance for poets and writers as a metaphor for the lives of all creative artists, and the significance was expressed, for example, in Goethe's *Wilhelm Meisters Lehrjahre*, Mörike's *Maler Nolten* and Browning's *Fifine at the Fair*. But besides its use as a motif in this specific context, the fairground was at all periods valued as an arena of carnival discourse in a general sense: as a place where licence, hedonism and hostility to officialdom might safely be given rein, where puritanism was put to rout and safe domestic virtues were ignored for the while.[4] The Russian fairground, on the other hand, suffered from relative neglect on the part of both memoirists and *littérateurs*. Moreover, on the rare occasions when it made appearances in the high cultural tradition, it was as often portrayed from the point of view of the puritans as from that of the revellers. For many writers it was not a place which offered respite from authoritarianism, but a crying example of how authoritarianism exploited and hoodwinked the masses; it represented a threat to civilised society rather than an alternative to it.

During most of the nineteenth century, Russian high literature ignored the fairs. The life of wandering actors and showmen inspired no Romantic poets, as it had done in France, Germany and England. The only exception is Baratynsky's *The Gypsy* (also known as *The Concubine*), a narrative poem which describes how a rich young man tires of his gypsy mistress when he falls in love with a well-bred young girl. The action opens at a funfair on the boulevard:

Tam tselyi den' razgul'nyi pir;
Tam razdayutsya zvuki trubny,
Zvenyat, gremyat litavry, bubny,
Payasy s zybkikh galerei
Zovut, manyat k sebe gostei
Tam kleper znaet chët i néchet;
Nozhi provornye ventsom
Krugom sebya indeets mechet
I biser nizhet yazykom.
Gordyas' likhimi sedokami,
Tam odnokolki, zastuchav,
S poteshnykh gor letyat stremglav.
Svoimi dlinnymi shestami
Kacheli krashenye tam
Lyudei unosyat k nebesam.[5]

(All day the unbridled feast goes on:
Sounds of the noisy trump sing out,
Drums big and little ring and boom,
Clowns call from rocking galleries,
Shouting to guests to tempt them in;
A clapper counts even, uneven numbers,
And round himself a quick Red Indian throws
Knives in the air like a wreath, whilst he
Threads beads on a string with his tongue;
Proud of their load of valiant riders,
The one-railed gigs run clattering down,
Fly headlong from the pleasure mountains.
And on their elongated beams
The swing-boats, each one brightly painted,
Carry the revellers heavenwards.)

The fairground scene is not simply a set-piece; it represents the marginal demi-monde to which the gypsies belong, and from which the heroine's temporary, and fragile, rise in social status has removed her.

Apart from Baratynsky's narrative poem (written 1829–31, and revised in 1842), the fairground theme did not surface in Russian literature until the 1860s, when some of the so-called *shestidesyatniki* (eighteen-sixty-ites, that is, radical realists) produced documentary sketches of the fairs and fairgoers. Among them were Pomyalovsky, Levitov and Sleptsov.[6] Gleb Uspensky, and at a later date Gor'ky and Grigorovich, wrote studies of the *byt* of the performers themselves.

These descriptions of the fairground life are hostile in tone. There is much emphasis on the dirt and degradation in which the performers lived, on the petty thieving and drunkenness which prevailed and on the wretchedness of the performances. In Gleb Uspensky's gloomy story 'V balagane' ('In the Balagan'), one of the actors remains behind to die in the damp and cold of the Big Top; another announces his intention of making a living as a thief. The company and *balagan* itself come to a wretched end:

After the balagan had been taken down, somebody, no one knows who, took it away; the only piece of property which had stayed in the *balagan* when the boy left, a boot which the sick man had been wearing, was appropriated by a conscript policeman and immediately bartered for drink.

The hurdy-gurdy player wandered round the town, playing a polka called 'The Kazbek' again and again at full blast; stray dogs danced to it; he was accompanied by a tall man in a nankeen coat and torn trousers stuck into a pair of top-boots and with a cap turned up at the back of his neck. He held a drum in one hand which he thrummed with the thumb of his other hand, gathering a big crowd of spectators round him, frightening the dogs to death and making them howl.[7]

The one exception to the general rule was Nikolay Uspensky, who, after paranoic suspicions that he was being cheated by Nekrasov had overcome him and driven him from Petersburg, became destitute and adopted the life of a wandering showman himself, as Korney Chukovsky describes:

Uspensky's begging was of a unique variety. He was not at all inclined to simply ask for alms. He was a beggar with the temperament of a street showman, with much bravura and spirit, of the eccentric sort. When he was begging, he was on stage; before he collected his coppers, he felt obliged to put on a show. He clearly had no small talent for this beggars' cabaret. He would entertain the passers-by with tunes on the guitar or the fiddle; he would sing couplets and little verses (*chastushki*); he would act out whole scenes with a little model crocodile which he dragged round everywhere with him, and, tugging at the string round its neck, he would speak monologues for it: 'My best wishes to you, honoured ladies and gentleman crocodiles!' he would call out to the crowd in the character of the crocodile.

And at the end of the act the writer would spread out a mat on the pavement, and his daughter, dressed as a boy, would start to dance to his harmonica, and then she would do the rounds of the crowd with her father's battered old cap.[8]

Uspensky ended his life showman-fashion too, as a pauper in a ditch.

The fairgrounds and carnivals of Russia were marginalised in another way too; the traditions of street theatre were ignored by most dramatists working in the high theatre. Pushkin may have written that the fairground was the home of all drama,[9] but he turned to high literary models, Shakespeare and Schiller among them, when writing his own dramas. Gogol's two plays reveal signs of street-theatre influence – direct relations with the audience, stock clown figures, carnival humour references to food, abundant use of physical humour – but it was an influence which he soaked up willy-nilly, like a sponge, and which he denied at a conscious level.[10]

One of the major reasons for the apartheid of high theatre and low theatre was the organisation of the Imperial Theatres. Not only the academic traditions practised here, but a range of other factors emphasised difference and elevation. Where the fairground theatres often operated at subsistence level, these were cocooned from the crudities of the marketplace by large subsidies, and housed in buildings whose superb neo-classical architecture emphasised their substance, permanence and respectability. Unlike the theatres and companies of Shakespeare's London, they were quite apart from common life, from 'the circulation of social energy'.[11] They were, moreover, separated in bureaucratic terms by the operation of the 'theatrical monopoly'. This was the rule that only the Imperial Theatres might hold theatrical performances open to the public in St Petersburg and Moscow. Ostensibly a measure to protect the Imperial Theatres from competition by guaranteeing their income, it was, of course, a covert censorship regulation. It meant that between 1827 (when regulation of theatre life in the capitals was first entrusted to the Imperial Theatres) and 1882 (when the monopoly was suspended), new plays which were not accepted by the Imperial Theatres reading committee had to be given in private theatres, or, after these were banned in 1857, in private readings or amateur performances. By no means all members of the subordinate classes could afford the ticket prices of the Imperial Theatres, and they had no access to the private performances.[12] Educated writers, on the other hand, were unlikely to be involved in the *balagan* performances; even had any been interested, the acts in the big *balagans* were limited to almost wordless pantomimes until the 1860s, and entrepreneurs had trouble putting on full-length dramatic texts even after that.[13]

The radical literary lobby had long campaigned for the suspension of the theatrical monopoly. On achieving what they wanted, the literary progressives were suddenly given the opportunity of communicating with a mass audience. The *Narodnyi teatr*, or People's Theatre movement, came into existence, and there were many anxious heart-searchings about what repertoire should be offered the lower classes: adaptations of the classics, or new plays of informative and educational content?[14] But whatever the differences in shades of opinion, the activists were united by their failure to recognise that the masses already had their own theatre, as the theatrical historian Boris Varneke sarcastically pointed out.[15] If they did recognise the existence of such a theatre, they were suspicious of it, considering it insufficiently educational. The aims of the movement were summed up by A. N. Kremlev, who presented a project for an *obshchestvennyi teatr* (public theatre), to the Gorodskaya duma (town council) of St Petersburg in 1896:

The public or popular theatre must not pander to all; it must be *accessible* to all.[16]

This sternly didactic attitude even reached the *balagans*, where Alekseev-Yakovlev's theatre Razvlechenie i pol'za (Entertainment and Benefit) started to present programmes in the *balagan* manner, but based on adaptations of high literary works and socially conscious fables.[17]

At the end of the nineteenth century, critics and writers began to be interested in the fairground theatre because of a general feeling that the old entertainments were under serious threat.[18] Even at that stage, however, it was given less attention than other forms of popular culture; fewer recordings were made of the puppet shows and the texts that accompanied the peepshows than of folk songs, street songs, and folk epics. No systematic attempt was made to take down the repertoire of the *balagans*, or even to record the texts of individual plays. A very rare verbatim account of a *balagan* programme, complete with spelling and grammatical mistakes, can be found in Chekhov's short story 'Yarmarka'.[19]

It was not until the turn of the century that the importance of fairground literature achieved recognition, in the works of the Symbolist movement. The Symbolists were responsive to the fairground for two reasons: they had an insatiable appetite for urban low life, especially its entertainments (*café-chantants*, cheap restaurants, suburban resorts, red-light districts); and they were, superficially at least, culturally eclectic, reassessing Western European high cultural tradition, or turning away from it to, for example, oriental culture, the art of the Mayan Indians, Japanese painting. The memoirs of many Symbolists record their attraction to the art of the fairground. Blok, who was a keen circus-goer, recalled the circus spectacles on offer in 1910 in the preface to his narrative poem 'Vozmezdie' ('Retribution'):

The zenith of French wrestling in the Petersburg circus is inextricably linked with all this for me. The crowd of thousands was interested in this alone; there were real artists among the wrestlers; I shall never forget the fight between a hideously lumpish Russian heavyweight and a Dutchman whose outstandingly beautiful muscular system had the perfection of a musical instrument.[20]

Meyerhold's brief 'Biographical facts' of 1921 recall the '*balagans* of the fairground, and secret sneaked visits to evening performances at the circus, invariably to seats in the gallery in the company of grooms, cooks or workmen' as outstanding impressions of childhood.[21] Other Symbolist recollections of the fairground, besides, of course, the two arch enthusiasts Benois and Dobuzhinsky, are Bryusov's charming lyric 'Balagany' (quoted in chapter 1, p. 30), and Annensky's monologue of a fairground balloon-seller.[22]

But the Symbolists' view of the fairground was contradictory; it had patronising and supercilious elements. Their appropriation of popular culture by no means always implied whole-hearted approval of the phenomena it purported to imitate. This is obvious in the fragmentations and paradoxes of their views on drama. When the Symbolists wished to reach a wider audience with their lyrics, they turned, as Symbolists in France and Belgium had, to lyric drama. They saw drama as a collective medium, as a means of communicating with the people. Vyacheslav Ivanov wrote in 'The Aesthetic Norm of the Theatre':

The theatre of heroes who have been removed by fantasy from the spheres of mutual external and internal communication with the broad mass of the people is false; there is no place for solitude in the holy places of the orgiastic god (that is, the god who reveals himself in collective fusion); but the theatre of the opposite type, with a weakened heroic principle, that is, the theatre which depends wholly on the social principle, is aesthetically acceptable.[23]

Despite the Symbolists' democratic posturing, and their interest in popular dramatic forms in a passive sense, they tended to ignore the genres which had collective appeal in contemporary Russia. Vyacheslav Ivanov and Annensky turned to classical drama, particularly Attic tragedy, written in a high-style mode.[24] Bryusov's essays on the theatre gave undivided attention to high literature (Greek and Latin tragedy, Shakespeare, Symbolist drama). Although he was hostile to Stanislavsky's stagings, his hostility did not cause him to turn to the folk theatre; and in his own plays he adapted the traditions of the Greek stage.[25]

The Symbolist failure to take account of the manifestations of popular culture around them in their theorising was acidly noted by Bely in his essay 'The Theatre and Modern Drama':

But the popular theatre – the *balagan*, where the story of the robber Churkin has been shown from time immemorial, and the cinematograph – are coming more and more to adopt the role which is ascribed to the future democratic theatre. After all, there *is* mythopoeia in the cinematograph: a man – O edifying victim of the fatal struggle! – sneezes fit to burst. What is more: there is all this talk about collective creativity, and yet it exists already. Isn't a round dance in any Russian village the same thing as the orchestra of Greek drama? Poor Russia, they're threatening to cover her from end to end with orchestras, when she's covered with them already. Take a walk any evening in a village: there you'll find not only the choric principle, but also the choric creativity . . . of filthy language.[26]

Some Symbolists did turn to the folk theatre, in a movement towards what Ellis disapprovingly described as 'nastoyashchee balaganstvo i eksperimental'noe khlestakovstvo' (The genuine spirit of messing about in *balagans* and of experiments in the vein of Khlestakov [the boastful hero of Gogol's *The Goverment Inspector*]).[27] But their theory was fragmented, their practice inconsistent, and theory and practice were rarely, in any case, co-ordinated. Sologub praised the *balagan* traditions in his essay 'Theatre of One Will', but his tone is patronising, and although he speaks for a mixture of tragedy and farce, he allows the first place in it to tragedy:

Behind the rotting vizors and the scarlet-cheeked mug of the fairground *skomorokh*, and the pale mask of the tragic actor glows a single Countenance ... And not only beneath the frightful mask of the tragic hero, but also beneath the comic persona of the joker, the butt of the comedy, and in the person of the fairground clown who contorts himself to amuse the people in the cheap seats in the gallery in his gaudy garb of multi-coloured rags – under all these coverings the watcher must recognise Me.[28]

Later in the essay Sologub makes it clear that the value which he places on fairground drama comes from a desire to *épater la bourgeoisie*: it is a type of theatre disliked by complacent bourgeois theatre-goers:

And if the bourgeois himself trembles before the intolerable banality [of these stereotyped devices], then that is all to the good. That will be a reassuring indication that he too is approaching comprehension of the single Countenance which hides itself beneath various vizors, which is wounded, but not killed by the banality of earthly utterances. This is the unerring justification of light comedy and farce and *even* the buffoonery of the *balagan*. And even of pornography.[29]

By juxtaposing the fairground theatre and pornography, Sologub makes it clear how provisional is his view that the *balagan* is the equal of tragedy.

Many writers associated with Symbolism who praised the vitality of the folk theatre ignored the native Russian tradition and turned instead to Italian or French street performers (the *commedia dell'arte*, or the medieval Passion Plays). Meyerhold's essay 'Balagan', despite using the Russian word for its title, is devoted exclusively to the Western European theatre:

Surely the point of scenic art is to cast off the vestments of one's surrounding environment, to choose a mask with skill, to select a decorative costume and to show off one's brilliant technique to the public – as a dancer, *as a scheming character at a masked ball, as a simple-minded figure from the Italian comedy*, as a juggler.

To study the crumbling pages of the collections of scenarios, *say those of Flaminio Scala (1611)*, is to sense the magic power of the mask.[30]

In their romanticisation of distant forms of popular culture and blindness to the near, the Symbolists rather resembled Chekhov's cynical Dr Dorn, who was charmed by the crowds of Genoa as he would never have been by crowds at home.[31]

Those Symbolists who were interested in the folk theatre mostly oriented themselves to the drama as performed by peasants in villages, not by the proletariat in towns. Some of the plays, such as Remizov's *Tsar' Maksimilian*, were based on subjects taken directly from the folk dramatic repertoire. Others, for example the same author's *The Dance of Herodias*, were freely adapted from traditional plays; in this case the King Herod action of the traditional *vertep* is combined with a modernist-decadent standard: the story of Salome.[32] Many Symbolist plays, however, were based on songs or on prose narratives: these included Sologub's *Van'ka the Chatelain*, Kuzmin's plays, and some of Remizov's – *The Devil's Action*, and his *Judas* plays.[33] In all of them, language and convention are modelled on the rural folk theatre, not on the urban fairground acts.

Where the Russian fairground was used in Symbolist *belles-lettres*, it as often became a symbol of degradation as of the colourful lost years of childhood. This divided attitude to carnival celebrations had been anticipated by Frazer's *The Golden Bough*, where popular celebrations evoke both regret for the passing of the simple life, and a sense of the universal tragedy of human existence:

We may feel some natural regret at the disappearance of quaint customs and picturesque ceremonies, which have preserved to an age often deemed dull and prosaic something of the flavour and freshness of the olden time, some breath of the springtime of the world; yet our regret will be lessened when we remember that these pretty pageants, these now innocent diversions, had their origin in ignorance and superstition; that if they are a record of human endeavour, they are also a monument of fruitless ingenuity, of wasted labour, and of blighted hopes; and that for all their gay trappings – their flowers, their ribbons and their music – they partake far more of tragedy than of farce.[34]

In the lyrics and dramas of the Symbolists the comedies and celebrations of circus and fairground are used, however, with individual rather than general cultural significance. The 'flowers, ribbons and music' recall the youth of poets and artists; the tragedy and degradation are not those of human life in general, or the waning of a particular culture, but stand for the public misunderstanding and abuse to which the poet is subject. Identification of the trades of poet and circus artiste was a Symbolist poetical *topos*. In Blok's 'Balagan' a bedraggled troupe of travelling actors are identified with the poet by the words '*my* faded *balagan*' in the first stanza. In the following stanzas the actors' attempts to perform amidst dirt and squalor parallel the poet's power to create from the murk of his interior world:

Tashchites', traurnye klyachi!
Aktery, prav'te remeslo,
Chtoby ot istiny khodyachei
Vsem stalo bol'no i svetlo!

V tainik dushi pronikla plesen',
No nado plakat', pet', idti,
Chtob v rai moikh nezemnykh pesen
Otkrylis' tornye puti.[35]

(Pull away, sad nags!
Actors, see to your craft,
So that your travelling truth
Makes your watchers feel pain and joy.

Mould has crept deep into your souls
But you must weep and sing and walk;
To the heaven of my outlandish songs
You must lay smooth paths.)

The same connection is made by Khodasevich in two poems from *By the Way of the Grain*: implicitly in 'In Petrovskii Park', which describes the death-defying routine of a trapeze artiste; and explicitly in 'Acrobat', in which the calm artistry of the acrobat is contrasted with the vulgar expectation of the 'false populace' that he will fall off the rope:

Ot kryshi do kryshi protyanut kanat.
Legko i spokoino idet akrobat.

V rukakh ego – palka, on ves' – kak vesy,
A zriteli snizu zadrali nosy.

Tolkayutsya, shepchut: Seichas upadet!
I kazhdyi chego-to vzvolnovanno zhdet.

Napravo – starushka glyadit iz okna,
Nalevo – gulyaka s bokalom vina.

No nebo prozrachno, i prochen kanat,
Legko i spokoino idet akrobat.

A esli, sorvavshis', figlyar upadet,
I okhnuv, zakrestitsya lzhivyi narod –

Poet, prokhodi s bezuchastnym litsom:
Ty sam ne takim li zhivesh' remeslom?[36]

(The high-wire's extended from roof to roof.
Along it the acrobat is walking aloof.

He is holding a stick: he hangs like a balance.
Below him, with noses stuck up, are the audience.

They're talking, they whisper: 'He's certain to fall!'
And this expectation's exciting them all.

On the right an old woman looks out of a window,
On the left is a reveller with his goblet of vino.

But the sky is transparent, the high-wire is taut,
Calmly, aloofly, the acrobat walks.

And if the daredevil mountebank slips and falls off,
And the false public sighs, makes the sign of the cross –

Then poet, go past with expressionless face,
For do not you also live by this trade?)

The image of the pathetic clown was particularly popular. Voloshin's poem 'The Circus' describes a tragic Pierrot performing to a vulgar and indifferent audience:

Kloun v ogenennom kol'tse . . .
Khokhot merzkii, kak prokaza.
I na gipsovom litse
Dve goryashchikh bol'yu glaza.

Lyazg orkestra: svist i stuk.
Tochno kazhdyi ozabochen
Zaglushit' pozornyi zvuk
Mokro khleshchushchikh poshchechin.

Kak ogon' podvizhnyi krug . . .
Lyudi – zveri, lyudi – gady,
Kak stoglazyi, zloi pauk,
Zaletayut v kol'tsa vzglyady.[37]

(The clown is in a ring of fire . . .
Nasty laughter, like a challenge,
Out of his face – it's white as plaster,
Two eyes look out and burn with anguish.

The band thrashes, whistles and pounds,
As though they all were anxiously
Drowning out the shameful sounds
Of those palms clapping sweatily.

The encircling ring is like a fire,
Public of beasts, public of vipers,
From all about come round-eyed stares
Like a hundred-eyed, evil spider.)

The figure of Pierrot appears in almost the only important Symbolist dramatic action which is based on the performances given at the Russian fairground, Blok's play *The Little Balagan*.[38] In this the traditional harlequinade is adapted as a tragic drama of the poet's own life. No texts of the harlequinades as played in the *balagans* have survived, but Benois gave a detailed description of one he saw as a child in his memoirs.[39] In this piece Harlequin and Pierrot quarrelled, and Pierrot murdered and dismembered Harlequin. Harlequin was then magically reconstructed and restored to life by the fairy Cassandra, who granted him the hand of her daughter Columbine. He then returned to his master's house, so that he could torment Pierrot and his master. Harlequin and Columbine elude pursuit, and eventually lead their captors to Hell. Then they are spirited off to Heaven, whilst their pursuers find that their heads have been turned to the heads of animals. In Benois' words, 'their gestures express extreme embarrassment', as well they might.[40]

In *The Little Balagan*, the relationship between Harlequin, Pierrot and Columbine has become a tragic love triangle: the faithful but unhappy Pierrot is cuckolded by the glittering and heartless Harlequin. This relationship is only one element in the dense symbolic structure of the play; Pierrot and Columbine are among several couples who re-create the motifs of Blok's love poetry. The others include the Knight and his illusory Lady, and the Stranger and her duped Admirer. Columbine herself takes on many of the features of the female archetype of Blok's lyrics; she has elements of the Eternal Feminine and of Death. Both Pierrot and Harlequin speak in the language of Blok's lyric poetry, representing each a separate facet of his lyric hero. The weight of the language in the play is very different from the weight of the language in the *balagan* pantomimes, where language was always subordinated to action. In fact, Blok has taken a fairground genre in which the text was of little importance, and adapted it as a play in which the text is of primary importance. The visual effects of *balagan* pantomime, with its transformations achieved by lighting, stage mechanics and explosions of powder, its *lazzi*, or comic gestures and nimble acrobatics, are of no significance to this text.

As T. M. Rodina has pointed out, *The Little Balagan* is related to the *balagan* tradition only by orientation. She sees the most important inheritances in the facts that the action is manifestly non-referential and the characters, like the masks of pantomime, are universal, that is, they cannot be associated with the actors who play them, yet at the

17. A design for the costume of Pavlova as Columbina by K. Somoff.

same time they are individual: each character has his or her own distinct features, coming from theatrical tradition. She also argues that Blok has adopted from the popular theatre its calculated naivety, the device of interpreting metaphor literally.[41] On the first two points I would agree with her, but on the third I would argue that the relationship with carnival tradition is less simple than she suggests. In the carnival naivety and literal metaphors were two devices for making the audience laugh. For example, clowns would interpret the phrase 'high-ups', meaning those in positions of social dominance, quite literally, to mean those who worked on a higher physical level, such as firemen ('Who is above all?' 'I don't know.' 'The fireman, when he's in the watch tower.') In *The Little Balagan*, which could not be described as a humorous play, such metaphors are tragic. The fact that Columbina is a shallow and vapid character is expressed in a metaphor: she is 'cardboard'; when at the end of the play she turns out actually to be made of cardboard, we are not dealing with a joke but with a tragic expression of futile love.[42] A similar radical adaptation of carnival tradition is shown in Blok's use of the ambivalent link between food and death. In the most striking line of the play, the Clown calls out: 'I am bleeding to death with cranberry juice!'.[43] Contextually, though, as in Blok's short lyric 'The Little Balagan', in which the line was also used, the carnival humour of the line is transformed into a tragic metaphor. The characters of this 'Little Balagan' are trapped and doomed in cruel humiliation:

> Vdrug payats peregnulsya za rampu
> I krichit: 'Pomogite!'
> Istekayu ya klyukvennym sokom!
> Zabintovan tryapitsei!
> Na golove moei – kartonnyi shlem!
> A v ruke – derevyannyi mech!
>
> Zaplakali devochka i mal'chik,
> I zakrylsya veselyi balaganchik.[44]

> (Suddenly the clown leans over the booth
> And shouts, 'Help!'
> I am bleeding to death with cranberry juice!
> I am bound with a rag!
> On my head is a cardboard helmet,
> In my hand is a wooden sword!
>
> The little girl and boy burst into tears,
> And the merry little balagan closed its doors.)

After the Revolution, the entertainments presented at the Russian fair attracted the attention of the new Soviet arts establishment. They were used in heavily adapted forms, at demonstrations and for propaganda purposes, especially during the literacy drive.[45] But, apart from the agitprop movement, literary appropriations of the fairground genres were scarce. In the mid-1920s, Evgeny Zamyatin adapted Leskov's story, 'The Left-Hander' as *The Flea*, a play purportedly in the manner of fairground drama. A *raeshnik*, or peepshow operator, figures in it, and it is partly set at a fair. The play, however, is long-winded and literary in manner; its comedy creaks, the exchanges between characters are verbose, and the diction is irritatingly pseudo-folksy. This supposedly fairground text would have stood a good chance of being booed out of any self-respecting *balagan*. The following passage, in which one of the characters goes through a peepshow routine, gives an idea of its style:

CHEMIST-MECHANIC: [*winching round a church*]: And this, if you please, is the very fine St Peter and Paul Cathedral, all covered in silver and gold and other stuff most fine to behold, and on a foundation of real marble.
LEFT-HANDER: [*hissing through his teeth*): On ma-arble eh! A likely story! Well, mate, we've got a St Nick-on-the-Raindrops in Moscow and a St Nick-on-the-Chambers and a St Nick-on-the-Chicken-Legs and a St Nick-on-the-Cabbage-Stalks. So well then. But this one now – On-the Ma-arble?
MASTER: On-the-Cabbage-Stalks? Coo! And it stands up, does it?[46]

How pallid and feeble this seems beside the quick-fire repartee of real fairground dialogue, and how insulting to the intelligence of the fairground audiences: their supposed inarticulacy is made the butt of the bourgeoisie. Here, for contrast's sake, is a dialogue recorded on the fairground:

KHOZYAIN: Chem vy torguete?
PAYATS: Tovarom.
KHOZYAIN: Kakim?
PAYATS: Sapozhnym varom: zimoi v'yugoi, a letom – vetrom.
KHOZYAIN: A gde vasha lavka?
PAYATS: A vot s kraya ne moya, a v seredine chuzhaya, a svoyu sovsem ne znayu; v moyu lavku zaidesh', da von poidesh'.
KHOZYAIN: Durak! Eto nuzhnik.[47]

(BOSS: What do you deal in?
CLOWN: A good deal.
BOSS: What exactly?
CLOWN: Boot seal; in winter – wind, in summer – in breezes I deal.
BOSS: And where's your stall?

CLOWN: That one on the corner's not mine, and in the middle not either;
mine is another; you go in, then you come out again.
BOSS: Idiot! That's the privy.)

With the exception of Zamyatin's play, treatments of the fairground and circus theme are uncommon in Soviet high literature.
Depictions of the life of fairground and circus artistes are even more
rare in Russian literature of the twentieth century than of the
nineteenth. In Leonov's novel *The Thief* the story of the trapeze
artiste Tanya is a subplot to the main story of the thieves' underworld.
Her accidental death when undertaking her extremely dangerous
routine counterpoints, by a presentation of an artiste who risks all in
performance, the presentation of an artist who risks nothing, and
whose art parasites itself on the objects which it depicts: the story of
the writer Firsov.[48] Vsevolod Ivanov's three-volume novel *The Adventures of a Fakir*, a largely autobiographical work, draws in volumes 2
and 3 on the author's own experiences as a uniquely talentless circus
artiste travelling the eastern reaches of the Russian Empire in the
company of a sad nag named Nubia just before the Revolution.[49]
Apart from this, there is no other material of note.

Two of M. Zoshchenko's stories are concerned with the world of
fairs and circuses from the punters' point of view. 'The Roundabout'
relates the disastrous consequences when rides on a roundabout are
allowed free of charge: one rider overindulges himself to the point of
collapse.[50] 'A Theatre of One's Own' relates how the *kul' torgy*
(cultural administrators) of a provincial town are desperate to better
their ludicrous audience numbers in the municipal theatre. Serious
drama and operetta attract a maximum of ten, so they decide to
engage a really 'democratic' show – the circus. Thirty people attend.
But when the circus parade reaches the station the entire town is out
to watch it leave, and the *kul' torg* frantically suggests an impromptu
performance:

'Hem, couldn't you,' he says, 'put together a little circus programme with
three or four "numbers", for free, here out of doors, in the fresh air, right here
on the platform?'
But unfortunately, just at that moment the last warning bell went.
Shrugging sadly, the circusites went to their seats, and the train took them off.
And so no one ever found out the whys and wherefores for the most
democratic art form making a loss too.[51]

The most remarkable tribute to the post-revolutionary fairground,
however, is a poetic one. Esenin's lyric 'Pervoe maya' describes a

demonstration for the First of May which has some of the Dionysiac jollity of the old *gulyan'ya*. For once the tone is naive, rather than sentimental, to borrow the terms of Schiller's famous dichotomy; the events are taking place in the present, rather than in the lost world of the past, the observer is able to take part wholeheartedly, and no attempt is made to persuade the reader that some sacrifice of human dignity is at stake, or that the decline of civilisation is imminent.

Est' muzyka, stikhi i tantsy,
Est' lozh' i lest' ...
Puskai menya branyat za 'Stansy'
V nikh pravda est'.

Ya videl prazdnik, prazdnik maya –
I porazhen.
Gotov byl sgibnut', obnimaya
Vsekh dev i zhen.

Kuda poidesh', komu rasskazhesh'
Na ch'e-to 'khny',
Chto v solnechnoi kupalis' pryazhe
Balakhany?

Nu kak tut v serdtse gimn ne vysech'
Ne vpast' kak v drozh'?
Gulyali, peli sorok tysyach
I pili tozh.

Stikhi! stikhi! Ne ochen' lefte!
Prostei! prostei!
My pili za zdorov'e nefti
I za gostei.

I, pervyi moi bokal vzdymaya,
Odnim kivkom,
Ya vypil v etot pradznik maya
Za Sovnarkom.

Vtoroi bokal, chtob tak, ne ochen',
Vdrezinu lech',
Ya gordo vypil za rabochikh
Pod ch'yu-to rech'.

I tretii moi bokal ya vypil,
Kak nekii khan,
Za to, chtob ne sgibalas' v khripe
Sud'ba krest'yan.

Pei serdtse! Tol'ko ne v upor ty
Chtob zhizn' gubya ...
Vot potomu ya pil chetvertyi
Lish' za sebya.[52]

(There's music, there's verses and dances,
Flattery and lies ...
Don't give a toss if they knock my stanzas,
I've said right, in my eyes.

I've seen the festival, the May one,
And I was struck.
I wanted to grab the girls and ladies
Hug 'em fit to bust.

Where shall I go, who shall I tell it,
So they won't make fun,
How the people's tatters were all swimming
In a skein of sun?

My heart just had to sing a hymn there
And trembling too.
I saw forty thousand walk and sing there
And drink, look you.

Verses, verses! But not too left-wing!
Simple is best!
We drank to the future of the oil-rigs
And to our guests.

And, raising my first glass I
Drank it down in one;
And on that festival I toasted
The Sovnarkom.

With the second glass – taking care not to
Get really slewed –
I toasted the workers as the speaker wanted
And felt right proud.

I downed a third – that one I drank to
– Just like a khan –
That the peasants' fate shouldn't get bogged down
Like a stagnant pond.

Drink, heart! I know that you don't want me
To wreck my life ...
That's why I drank my fourth shot quickly
Just to myself.)

The paucity of post-revolutionary high literature based on the fairground genres is balanced by the enthusiasm with which activists in theatre and film turned to fairground techniques in the early 1920s. The inauthenticity of Zamyatin's *The Flea* as a text was compensated for by the acting and direction – as Annenkov wrote in his memoirs, 'The play was performed as some imaginary actors from the folk theatre in Tula would have performed it' – and by Kustodiev's vivid and utterly *balagan*-like designs.[53] As a child, the film director S. Yutkevich was fascinated by the performances given in Cinizelli's circus in St Petersburg.[54] The circus was also an important influence in Sergey Eisenstein's childhood:

More than anything he liked the circus. Aping the *bon ton* which reigned amongst the circle of people in Riga to which his father, too, aspired to belong, he would always maintain that he liked the circus horses best, the dressage horses which Cinizelli brought with him from Petersburg, with the ringmaster in tails and holding an ivory-handled whip. But the boy liked the red-haired clowns.[55]

The official proclamation of the doctrines of Socialist Realism in 1932 meant that fairground drama, which was overtly anti-realist, fragmentary, and of dubious political commitment (since it engaged with *any* authoritarian system, whether that of the tsars or of Stalin) was no longer considered suitable material for adaptation by Soviet writers – a shift which was contemporaneous with the suppression of the fairground (to be described in chapter 5). Faced with the disappearance of their raw material, and with ideological pressure, high literary attempts to imitate fairground drama ceased. Vsevolod Ivanov was criticised in the late 1930s for the fairground elements in *Adventures of a Fakir*, which were thought to be unsuitable material.[56] The institutionalisation of the circus and fairground robbed them of romance, since it gave their artistes civil servant status. The last oblique Soviet treatment of the carnival was Eisenstein's film *Ivan the Terrible*; central scenes show the performances of the *skomorokhi*, drawing on the vanished tradition of problematic and disturbing carnival entertainment in Russia; and, as we know, this film did not have an easy passage.[57]

The circus and fairground theme does not seem to have resurfaced in recent Soviet literature. But the circus theme does come up very occasionally in *émigré* literature. Vertinsky records in his memoirs that France in the 1920s and 1930s was home to numerous Russian *émigré* circus artistes.[58] The lives of these people were also commemorated in a peculiar collection of stories by an *émigré* author which came out in the 1960s, and which abound with heaving bosoms under spangles, brave efforts on the trapeze by young orphans, and the sad tear-filled brown eyes of sealions.[59] Of considerably more interest are two lyrics by Alla Golovina, written in 1930, in which the Symbolist commonplace of nostalgia for the fairground as a lost paradise of childhood is broadened: the *balagans* and spectacles of fairground and circus entertainments witnessed in emigration are painful reminders of the divide between 'there' and 'here':

> A v balagane l'vitsa-kaleka,
> Tesno svernuvshis' pod voi myateli
> Snova uvidela sad Gagenbeka
> I kupola na dvortsakh Chinizeli.[60]

> (And in the Big Top the lioness cripple
> Curling up tight to the moan of the storm,
> Dreams once again of the Gagenbeck garden,
> Dreams once again of Cinizelli's dome.)

Petrushka *in high literature*

In Western Europe, the puppet theatres were no less favoured than other fairground genres by artists and reminiscers. Punch, described by the nineteenth-century journalist Blanchard Jerrold as 'the very merriest fellow – the truest benefactor – that has ever paced the streets of London'[61] appears in dozens of paintings and prints, as well as in memoirs from Samuel Pepys onwards.[62] Pulcinella and the German heroes Kasperl and Hanswurst are equally well documented, as are the French Pierrot, Guignol and Polichinelle, and the Czech hero Kasparek.[63]

The puppet theatres of Europe also inspired many adaptations and imitations. The German fairground puppet play *Dr Faustus* was one of the sources of inspiration for Goethe's *Faust*. In France, the Polichinelle plays were charmingly adapted by the poet L. E. E. Duranty in a version 'pour les esprits naïfs et savants'. Later, Alfred Jarry was to use Guignol in the preface to *Ubu sur la Butte*, and Ubu himself has taken many characteristics of the Lyons puppet-play hero. In Spain, Federico García Lorca wrote two plays based on the adventures of the Spanish puppet hero Don Cristóbal Pulchinela.[64] The authors of these plays might take issue with the commercial aspirations of the fairground, as Jarry and Lorca did in their plays, separating 'the spirit of the fairground' from its vulgar intent to make money, and attributing commercial concerns to hostile and philistine entrepreneurial figures.[65] But the heroes of their adaptations, and of Duranty's too, preserved their traditional fairground characteristics: they are greedy, priapic, given to foul language and vile actions. The plays are genuinely funny: rich in absurd incident, full of textual comedy. Puns and carnival humour abound. The high literary reworking has not changed the nature of the humour, but has tellingly juxtaposed the language of the street with parodies of high-literary texts (*Macbeth* in *Ubu-roi*, Lorca's own early romantic comedies in *Don Cristóbal*, and the Romantic tradition of the misanthrope in Duranty's 'Polichinelle retiré du monde').[66]

Against this background, the literary recollections of *Petrushka* and literary reworkings of it seem scanty both in quantity and quality. The tendency, as with other fairground genres, was to despise or distort. For Sleptsov, *Petrushka* was one of the entertainments which diverted the eyes of the poor from their real condition, a means by which the ruling classes pulled the wool over their eyes. The narrator catches sight of a drunkard uplifted by Petrushka's victory over his enemies, and launches into a sarcastic apostrophe to the reader:

Now it seems to him that he has killed the policeman, and killed the doctor and killed the gypsy and that no one will dare to touch him. He is very pleased with his lot. Try to be like that too, dear children! For only he is genuinely happy, who is pleased with his lot.[67]

The minor radical writer V. A. Kurochkin produced two or three puppet plays in the 1870s, but based them on translations from the French.[68] Gumilev's puppet play *The Child of Allah* has an oriental or pseudo-oriental subject.[69] Where *littérateurs* did use *Petrushka*, they adapted the text, like other fairground texts, as a political satire or as a late Romantic myth of the doomed artist.

With some of the radicals, Petrushka achieved a certain currency as a representative of popular rebellion. In *Those in Russia who Live in Clover*, Nekrasov praised the wit and vigour of the show. Nonetheless, he looked forward to a time when the Russian peasantry would desert it and other traditional entertainments, such as the *lubok* books, for the love of high literature:

> Ekh! ekh! pridet li vremechko,
> Kogda (pridi, zhelannoe!)
> Dadut ponyat' krest'yaninu,

Chto roz' portret portretiku,
Chto kniga knige roz'?
Kogda muzhik ne Blyukhera
I ne milorda glupogo –
Belinskogo i Gogolya
S bazara poneset?[70]

(Eh! eh! will there come the time
When (roll on, oh long awaited),
The peasants can be got to see
That pictures are not all the same,
That there are different kinds of books?
When a man stops taking Blücher
And the stupid Milord stories home –
When he carries back Belinsky,
And Gogol' from the bazaar?)

The poet G. N. Zhulev, who wrote for *Iskra*, the satirical journal published in St Petersburg between 1859 and 1873, wrote a lyric in 1864 on the Petrushka show. In it he takes silent issue with the public's reading of the demise of the puppet hero:

Zapishchal Petrushka ... 'Ne yuli vpered!'
Vot tebe nauka!' – poreshil narod.
Ya b skazal slovechko za Petrushku, no
Mnogikh ved', pozhalui, razdrazhit ono.[71]

(Petrushka's loudly squealing ... 'Don't step out of line!
That must be the message!' – folk are of one mind.
I'd say a word in his defence, weren't it that I fear,
Quite a lot of people'd find it annoying to hear.)

In 1905 one number of a satirical journal called *Petrushka* came out; it was one of the many short-lived political journals to emerge after the relaxation of censorship in that year, and its contributors included the poet Petr Potemkin, who was on the fringes of Symbolism. Only one item was devoted to the puppet hero, however: a short lyric by one V. Zhukov, and in it Petrushka appears not in his own right, but as a metaphor for the bewildering and disingenuous promises of political freedom made after the Revolution by the government. There, words, like Petrushka's, are nonsense, stories for babies:

Ne raz v mladenchestve moem,
V podrugi nyanyu vzyav starushku
Ya s neyu shestvoval vdvoem

Poslushat' milogo 'Petrushku'.
Dlya detskikh radostnykh ochei
'Petrushka' byl veselym raem,
No tainyi smysl ego rechei
Byl dlya menya ne dosyagaem!
Proshli tyazhelye goda ...
Blesnulo solnyshko svobody ...
Zhizn' zaburlila, kak voda
Pod vikhrem letnei nepogody!
Sulila mnogoe molva,
No, pri nalich'e groznoi pushki,
Mne i svobodnye slova
Slovami kazhutsya 'Petrushki'.[72]

(More than once in my youth
With my old nurse as guide
I went hand-in-hand
To hear my beloved Petrushka.
To my childish joyful eyes
Petrushka was a happy Eden,
But the secret meaning of his words
Was far beyond my ken!
Years of hardship passed ...
All at once the sun of freedom shone
Life boiled and bubbled like a puddle
Stirred by a summer storm!
Rumour promised much,
But in the fearful cannon's face
To me these words of 'freedom' seem
To mean no more than Petrushka's.)

The most full-blooded nineteenth-century tribute to *Petrushka* comes from Dostoevsky, who described it as 'this immortal folk comedy'.[73] He, too, appropriated the text for political purposes: with an artist friend of his he dreamed up a jokey adaptation, with discussions between Pul'chinel' and Petrushka at cross-purposes about a train crash and a bank crash in Moscow:

PUL'CHINEL':   Tak vse 117 ubity?
PETRUSHKA: Net, vsego tol'ko dvoe ubity, a pyat'desyat odin raneny, a ostal'nye shest'desyat shest' tol'ko sgoreli.
PUL'CHINEL':   Tol'ko sgoreli? a ne ubity?[74]

(PUL'CHINEL':   And so all 117 were killed?
PETRUSHKA: No, only two were killed, and fifty-one injured, and the other sixty-six only went up in smoke.
PUL'CHINEL':   Only went up in smoke? But they weren't killed?)

It is possible that Dostoevsky's enthusiasm was caught from Dickens, who himself was a great admirer of *Punch and Judy*.[75]

Dostoevsky aside, *Petrushka*, like other fairground entertainments, had to wait for the Symbolist period before being universally appreciated. At that stage, the increasing tendency to regard him as an entertainment for middle-class children meant that most of the Symbolists encountered him in childhood. Apart from Benois and Dobuzhinsky, his fans included the theatre director N. Evreinov (though not Evreinov's parents!):

And then *Petrushka* . . . Good heavens, the excitement which the appearance of this street hero aroused in me! I nagged and nagged my parents until they gave me one of the sets of all the *Petrushka* puppets which were so popular at the time, a little book with the text and a mesh 'squeaker' for my mouth, so I could squeal like 'Petrushka himself'. What a tip the house looked! For whole days on end, the silken screen from my mother's boudoir was used to conceal the *Petrushka* player, until in the end it disintegrated; my brother, as the organ-grinder, incessantly turned the handle of the *Ariston* [wind-up gramophone] until my enraged father fell on him foaming at the mouth; and our guests, under threat of tearful scenes, had to watch the same thing a dozen times on end, applauding every time the Devil took Petrushka off to Hell. My poor parents! Our poor guests! Happy childhood! Magic puppets![76]

But probably the most vivid evocation of *Petrushka* – certainly of the sounds of a street performance – is the short chapter 'Payats-Petrushka' (Petrushka the clown) from Bely's *Kotik Letaev*:

Kurii krik –
          – Krr-kr!
                    – kazernik: ras-
treshchalsya treshchotkoi; on – grudgorbaya,
zlaya, pestraya, polosataya fintiflyushka-
petrushka: v redkostyakh, v edkostyakh, v shu-
strostyakh, v yurostyakh, vostren'kim, mert-
ven'kim, dokhlen'kim nosikom, kolpachish-
koi i shchetkoyu v ruke-raskoryake kolotit-
sya, chto est' mochi bez tolku i proku na
balagannom uglu –
          – krr-krr-kr! –
                    - vysoko![77]

(Cockerel cry –
          – krr-kr!
                    cheeky crackle
like cracker; crook-backed,
cross, coloured, splashy-flashy flibbertigibbet puppet:

with witty ditties, rascal-king of the castle,
with nozzle shrunken drunken sunken, with cap and
shock of hair like mop, hand-held he whacks and smacks
for all he's worth – for why? who'll say – on
the *balagan* corner –

                                                    – krr-krr-kr! –
– Catch if you can!)

A number of the Symbolists wrote theoretical pieces on *Petrushka*. They ignored the subversive, disturbing, and violent elements in the text, as well as its carnival nature. Petrushka was seen as a mythical archetype, with roots in Indian cult, which represents the suffering and degradation of humanity. In Zigfrid (Siegfried) Ashkenazi's essay 'The Immortal Petrushka', for example, the 'universal' phenomenon of Petrushka is carefully separated from proletarian culture: 'he may be considered the child not only of the common people'.[78] Petrushka's lewd and wisecracking Austrian counterpart Kasperl is turned by Ashkenazi into a brooding and introspective German Romantic:

In the north, Petrushka is a *raisonneur* with a tinge of melancholy, a deep-thinking joker with a refined Shakespearean sense of humour. 'Where am I? Who am I? What am I? What do I mean? What am I for?' asks the German Petrushka, who has tasted of the Tree of Knowledge of German philosophy.[79]

Petrushka's vulgar jokes are seen to be the result of a Romantic attempt to escape from reality, and his cynicism parallels the suffering of Christ and Prometheus:

Petrushka solves the tragedy of life, everything that cramps the human soul and is felt by it, as he sunders the heavy bonds of earth, with his dreadful fool's laughter, which does not liberate, but which destroys and poisons only. He, too, is an unbinder, this red-faced myth of the marionette theatre, this ugly 'monkey of God', and at the opposite pole he is oddly similar to another Unbinder, who solved the tragedy of life in tragic pathos.[80]

This reading of *Petrushka* as a tragic myth, and the coincidence of name, led the Symbolists to identify Petrushka with the sad white-faced clown Pierrot; without historical evidence, as we have seen (chapter 3, p. 125). This was similar to the process which had overtaken the traditional French fairground figure of Pierrot in the nineteenth century. Pierrot derives ultimately from the *zanni* Pedrolino, who was Pulcinella's opposite, being 'a young, personable, and trustworthy individual who can be a charming lover when necessary

... when Pedrolino is induced by Harlequin to play tricks on Pantaloon or the Doctor he is inevitably the only one ever caught and punished'.[81] The French nineteenth-century incarnation of Pierrot was largely based on the mime performances of Pierrot-Deburau, whose appearance and characterisation was only tenuously connected with the *commedia dell'arte* mask; this was the figure which later inspired such literary adaptations as Albert Giraud's *Pierrot Lunaire*.[82]

Where Petrushka appears in Russian Symbolist literary works, he bears little resemblance to the Russian fairground character. In a poem by Sologub, 'He Wears a Ragged Caftan', which is used by Ashkenazi as an epigraph to his article, Petrushka is an obscure and sinister figure who haunts the poet's imagination:

> Na nem iznoshennyi kaftan
> I shapka kolpakom,
> No ves' on zybkii, kak tuman,
> I net litsa na nem.
>
> Ne slyshno golosa ego,
> Ne vidno ruk i nog,
> I on stupit' ni u kogo
> Ne smeet na porog.
>
> Ne podoidet i ne proidet
> Otkryto vperedi, –
> On za uglom v potemkakh zhdet
> Bezhit on pozadi.
>
> Ego nikak ne otognat',
> Ni slovom, ni rukoi,
> On budet prygat' da plyasat'
> Bezzvuchno za spinoi.[83]

> (He wears a tattered coat of rags,
> He wears a pointed hat,
> But he's elusive as the fog,
> And he has no face.
>
> You'll never hear him speak a word,
> You'll never see his limbs,
> You'll never see him dare to cross
> A threshold anywhere.
>
> He comes not in, he goes not past,
> He's open to the wind –
> He waits on corners in the dusk,
> And always runs behind.

18.   The hero of Benois' *Petrouchka*.

You cannot make him go away
With words or with your hands,
For he will always dance or play
In silence at your back.)

The collaboration between Stravinsky, Benois and Fokine, the ballet *Petrouchka* (first performed in 1911), is another reworking of *Petrushka* in the style of the Pierrot myth. This is by far the most famous Symbolist adaptation of *Petrushka*; indeed, it is without question the most famous adaptation done at any period, and, what is more, an outstanding work of art in its own right. It was this production more than any other which established the style of the Ballets Russes. It brought about a revolution in the history of ballet. The choreography was innovatory, discarding classical notions of leg extension and limited movement in the upper body: 'Instead of the customary light, fluttering movements, the spectator was presented with angular, doll-like, *terre-à-terre* dancing, full of rhythmic accent.'[84] Moreover, the production took ballet out of its previous circumscribed existence as expensive, refined entertainment for the aristocracy and *haute bourgeoisie*; as one observer of the first performances, Peter Lieven, put it, 'hearing and seeing *Petrouchka*, it was unthinkable to mention *"divertissement"*, "entertainment", "soothing music" or "pretty women"'.[85] The production drew people to the ballet who had not been there before; it was a theatrical event which defied attempts to pigeon-hole or patronise it; for Lieven it represented a sort of balletic *Gesamtkunst*: 'I had never had the good fortune to see on a stage before such a unified, such an integrated spectacle, satisfying simultaneously eye, ear and mind in one great artistic expression.'[86]

The power and effectiveness of *Petrouchka*, whether as music or choreography, are so great that the question of whether or not the scenario is like the fairground text is finally of little importance. But, since the centre of our attention here is *Petrushka*, not *Petrouchka*, and since the ballet has dictated and distorted Western European impressions of the popular text, and since there is no study so far which outlines the problem, I shall devote a little space to it here. It is commonly enough stated that the ballet is very like *Petrushka*. Simon Karlinsky has described Stravinsky's *œuvre* as 'a compendium of the theatrical genres of old Russia', and contrasted it with the music of earlier Russian composers, in which Russian folklore was adapted according to Western models.[87] Various memoirists have even erroneously adjusted their childhood memories of the street text to conform with the ballet *Petrouchka*. Lieven writes that the fairground show was done with marionettes; Bronislava Nijinska recalls the 'sad Petrushka' whom she loved as a child.[88]

If one compares the two texts it is obvious how misleading these comments are. The hero of Benois' adaptation, with his sad white face and his subjection to ill-treatment, is the mirror-image of the vigorous street original. His scream, at the end of the drama, is the cry of suffering humanity, not the falsetto voice of the tyrannical puppet. Throughout the play he is mocked and spat on by his owner, by the Moor and by Columbina.[89]

In Benois' version, the Moor is no closer in character to the traditional street prototype than the hero is. In fact, the relationship is exactly opposite to that in the fairground *Petrushka*. In some traditional variants of *Petrushka* the hero torments and beats a Moor, offering to teach him 'a Russian dance', encouraging him to sing and then mocking him. The Moor is portrayed as a fool, who can sing only in nonsense language. At the end of the scene, Petrushka kills the Moor. In *Petrouchka*, on the other hand, the Moor competes successfully with Petrouchka for the affections of the Doll, and in the end murders his pathetic rival.

The vapid but attractive Columbine of the ballet is also unrelated to the puppet Petrushka's monstrously ugly fiancée. The central action of the ballet, with its tragic love triangle and Petrouchka's reappearance as a ghost above the puppet booth in order to revenge himself on the sadistic Showman, like Akaky Akakevich in Gogol's story 'The Greatcoat', was invented by Benois. Romance is absent from *Petrushka*: the very idea is absurd. Thwarted and languishing lovers who are outwitted by their rivals and by the parents of the beloved are standard in the *commedia dell'arte*; in *Petrouchka* Benois has imported such a plot into the background of the Russian puppet play, and has turned it from a comedy into a tragedy. The figure of the Showman-Charlatan underlines this change: unlike the traditional puppet showman, a man who shared his audience's outlook and class, this Showman is a sinister other-worldly magician who fits well into the mythic character of the play.

By presenting *Petrouchka* as a silent spectacle, Benois has also ignored the language of the puppet play, the area of its greatest comic inventiveness. In fact, his adaptation of *Petrushka* is the mirror-image of Blok's adaptation of the fairground pantomime in *Balaganchik* –

where Blok has turned a mime into a spoken play, Benois has turned a spoken play into a mime.

Benois' reshaping of the *Petrushka* text was not, of course, caused by his ignorance of street tradition; as we have seen, he knew well the text as played in Petersburg. It was brought about by his Symbolist reading of the myth of Petrushka. In the chapter in his memoirs devoted to the ballet, he, like Ashkenazi, sees Petrushka as Pierrot-like, the representative of suffering intellectual humanity, and the opposite of the unthinking and ruthless Harlequin-Moor:

If Petrushka was an embodiment of all human inspiration and suffering, or to put it another way, of the poetic principle, if his lady, Columbina the ballerina, emerged as the personification *des ewig Weiblichen* [of the Eternal Feminine], then the 'luxurious' Moor became the embodiment of the principle of unthinking enslavement, powerful masculinity and undeserved triumph.[90]

That Benois preferred the puppet play to other fairground genres is rooted in Symbolist contempt for the human actor. All the Symbolists were violently opposed to the traditions of 'star acting', as displayed in the Imperial Theatres and elsewhere. They were heavily influenced by Gordon Craig's concept of the actor as *Über-Marionette*. Craig's views drew on Romantic notions of the puppet as especially adequate representative of frail humanity on the one hand, on post-ethnographical notions of the puppet as fetish, or residence of the divinity, on the other. He argued that the Super-Marionette would 'aim to clothe itself with a death-like beauty while exhaling a living spirit', and related it to the religious images of the Hindus.[91] Many of the Symbolists stated these ideas in almost identical words. Sologub, for example, wrote:

And why, after all, should the actor not be like a marionette? This idea is not at all offensive to human dignity. The unshakeable law of performance the world over is that man should be like a divinely constructed marionette. He cannot escape this, he must not forget it.

The appointed hour will come for each and every one of us, and before the eyes of all we will be transformed into an immobile and unbreathing puppet, no longer capable of taking any role.[92]

This did not mean that the Symbolists were actually interested in puppets as such, that they learnt about the techniques of manipulating glove puppets (for Petrushka) or string puppets (for the harlequinades). Like Gordon Craig, they believed that carnival shows degraded the majesty of the puppet:

19.   Petrouchka by S. Soudeikine.

All puppets are now but low comedians. They imitate the comedians of the larger and fuller blooded stage. They enter only to fall on their back. They drink only to reel, and make love only to raise a laugh . . . They are cocksure in their wooden wisdom.[93]

The only puppetry with which the Symbolists were associated directly was that created by Yuliya Slonimskaya, who gave some performances in 1916. Her productions were elegant, intellectual and archaising. The first play chosen was a seventeenth-century French text, *Les Forces de l'amour et de la magie*; the puppets were beautifully carved in the manner of French or Italian marionettes by N. Kalmakov.[94]

Just after the performances took place, Slonimskaya published a long article, 'Marionetka', in *Apollon*, the Symbolist journal. She gives no details at all about the technique of her production, but her comments about the puppet theatre and the live stage illuminate the Symbolist attitude to puppetry. She, too, makes a link between the helplessness of the puppet and the helplessness of the human being: 'man is a tragic marionette, the toy of Fate'.[95]

For the Symbolists, the fairground puppet theatre represented the degradation of humanity in two different ways: as human and as artist. The puppet hero stands for the poet. He is deceived in love, duped, degraded, but must still, like the clown, perform for the amusement of an indifferent or hostile public. He is both sub- and super-human. The content of the actual texts and techniques used by puppeteers entertaining a subordinate class public were ignored by the Symbolists, for whom puppets were simply the best available vehicles for their mythical dramas.

The second point made by Slonimskaya is that puppet theatre is the purest form of theatre, since it does not represent human actions directly, but symbolically: 'The marionette gives the theatrical formula without fleshly expression.'[96] Benois, too, was attempting to break away from the representational theatre by using the techniques of the puppet theatre: though he never used puppets. In *Petrouchka*, after an intermediate stage of having his actors actually dressed as glove puppets, he decided it would be more satisfactory to direct them to move and gesticulate like puppets:

About a year previously we had made an attempt at a sort of 'Petrushka with live actors' in the Artists' Club, and although Dobuzhinsky had invested this production with all his usual acumen, all the same the result was rather laughable and, moreover, simply tedious. Real people, large as life, wearing masks, carried out some kind of actions above the edge of a curtain, over

which they had tossed wooden legs which were attached to their costumes . . .
But as soon as the screen was taken away, they had of course to be replaced
on the stage by a theatre, a booth. The puppets of this booth had to come to
life, but at the same time remaining true to their puppet nature.[97]

Benois and Stravinsky were less interested in recreating *Petrushka*
the puppet show than in the new theatrical possibilities of the visual
and musical effects of the fairground. Benois recalls in his memoirs
that he was less attracted by Petrushka in particular than by the
Russian Shrovetide celebrations in general:

But I was even more tempted by the idea of representing the Butter Week on
stage – the dear *balagans*, that great delight of my childhood, which had been
the delight of my father too. And because these *balagans* had been unused for
around a decade, the temptation to commemorate them became overwhelming.[98]

Stravinsky's score, which Prokof'ev called 'this assemblage of musical
trash [*trukha*]', likewise recreates the staggering effect of fairground
racket: the barrel-organ accompanying the puppet show itself mingles
with the sounds of dancing and revelry from other parts of the
fairground. Indeed, Stravinsky's contribution was more authentic, in
that his inspiration was contemporary street music, whilst Benois had
gone back to the lithographs and etchings of the 1840s for his
inspiration, basing his hero on the stripey-suited Italianate Petrushka,
and Italianising the wife and Moor too.[99] Benois' fairground panora-
mas in the opening and penultimate scenes of *Petrouchka*, despite the
terre-à-terre dancing, the street shows, and the masked mummers, is
more graceful than the late nineteenth-century reality, possibly than
the reality at any period; in spirit, if not in actual props, it could be a
dramatisation of Baratynsky's piece from *The Gypsy*.

After the Revolution, a more realistic image of *Petrushka* found its
way into high literature. Again, the interest of *littérateurs* was less
conspicuous than that of theatrical activists. The famous film director
Grigory Kozintsev began his career with a puppet theatre, which he
organised jointly with Sergei Yutkevich, later to be an equally famous
film director. Kozintsev wrote:

Our old friend the guttural-voiced Petrushka leapt up from the booth with its
crude *balagan* print roses and took us into his power. We made some puppets
and put on Pushkin's *Tale of the Priest and his Servant Balda*. We began
touring clubs and schools . . . For it was just these things – the petrushkas, the
Ukrainian clay toys, the good-hearted monsters with their kind green-and-

brown muzzles and fuzzy manes, the *lubok* pictures with processions of mice dragging the cat to his funeral on a sledge, or the tipsy merchant leaping out of a chimney-pot with a top-hat in his hand – which were the friends of our childhood; it was in their company that I visited the merry land of folk fantasy, which everyone must visit who has dreams of art.[100]

There is a wonderful photograph of Yutkevich taken in the 1920s, in which he is holding the magnificent Petrushka of the Leningrad TYuZ (Theatre of Young Viewers).[101] Much later in his career, he returned to the puppet theatre for some interesting experiments in filming puppets which, however, had nothing to do with the traditional *Petrushka*.[102]

Two rare examples of writers who were inspired by *Petrushka* after the Revolution were Osip Mandelstam and Anna Akhmatova. In his writings on the theatre, Mandelstam praised the popular theatre without condescension, taking unfeigned pleasure in it, as no Symbolist writer had.[103] In his 'Radio Talk on Goethe' he described Goethe's youthful visits to 'the fair, which is open to all', and pointed out that the puppet theatre was the source of Faust:

Don't knock the puppet theatre. Remember how much pleasure it's given you. All his life Goethe remembered the leaps and gestures of all those Moors and Mooresses, shepherds and shepherdesses, dwarfs and dwarfesses and the dreadful deed of Doctor Faust, who sold his soul to the devil.[104]

In his memoir of Komissarzhevskaya Mandelstam suggested that the fairground theatre of *Petrushka* was more important than the high theatre:

The life of the theatre always has been and always will be the human voice. Petrushka presses a curl of copper to his palette in order to change his voice. Better Petrushka than Carmen and Aida, better he than the pig's snout of declamation.[105]

It seems that Mandelstam's enthusiasm did not prompt him to adapt *Petrushka* for the theatre, or even to devote any lyric poems to the subject, however.

In Akhmatova's *Poem Without a Hero* Petrushka makes a brief appearance in a manifestation which is half-way between his traditional role and his Symbolist one. Like the street hero, he is dragged off to Hell; but the wording of the passage, with its reference to a *mask*, suggests that it may refer to the hero of *Petrouchka*:

> Do smeshnogo blizka razvyazka,
> Iz-za shirm Petrushkina maska,

Vokrug kostrov kucherskaya plyaska,
Nad dvortsom cherno-zheltyi styag ...[106]

(The denouement is ludicruously close,
Petrushka's mask above the booth,
The coachmen's dance around the bonfires,
The black and yellow flag above the palace ...)

Akhmatova's reference to Petrushka is interesting in that it comme-
morates him at a period (the 1940s) when he had disappeared, and all
the forms of alternative, non-realist theatre had been under attack for
a decade (see chapter 5). Her portrait seems to be the last in Soviet
literature, with the exception of the children's book *Petrushka – the
Soul of the Skomorokhs*, published in 1974, the eponymous hero of
which is a *skomorokh* so remarkable that the puppet hero is later
named after him.[107]

The coda to my survey of fairground appropriations is an interesting late adaptation of the *Petrushka* text, which appeared in the
émigré press not long ago. This was 'Petrushka', a verse text by Ivan
Elagin.[108] Elagin's *Petrushka* is not a play, whether performed by
puppets or otherwise, but it is dramatic: most of it is a monologue in
four-line stanzas of *raek* (doggerel) verse, spoken by Petrushka
himself. The accompanying illustration by Sergey Gollerbakh shows a
humanised Petrushka whose costume distantly resembles the traditional hero's: he has a peaked fool's cap, baggy trousers and shirt,
rather like an eighteenth-century *lubok* clown. The hero exchanges
words with, and then beats, three of the characters from the traditional puppet play: the Gypsy, the Doctor and the German. Their
appearances are not plotted; they appear as *divertissements* in his
monologue.

Unlike Petrouchka, Elagin's hero is no white-faced sad Pierrot. He
retains all the unpleasantness and rough comic skill of his folk-theatre
ancestor. He shows a carnival obsession with food and drink:

Mne – tarelku kashi grechnevoi,
Mne – govyadinu tushenuyu!
U menya – butylka vermuta
Zapivat' moi vareniki!   (Elagin 33)

(I've got a plate of buckwheat kasha
I've got plenty of braised beef!
I've got a bottle here of vermouth
To drink down my cheese dumplings with!)

He launches unprovoked attacks on the Gypsy, the Doctor and the German, and he boasts of his great skill with the weapons of a street hooligan, beer-mugs and paving-stones:

> Nazyvayus' ya Petrushkoyu,
> Prozyvayus' sharomyzhnikom,
> Ya derus' pivnoyu kruzhkoyu,
> A kidayus' ya bulyzhnikom! (Elagin 33)

> (By the way, the name's Petrushka,
> I'm quite a lad, I'm often told!
> I have a lot of fights with beer-mugs,
> Or sometimes I throw cobble-stones.)

Petrushka's immorality, though, has a new note. He is not *with* his audience, but *above* them. He vaunts his possession of material goods which they do not have, and he contrasts his enjoyment of rich food with their penury. Petrushka, in fact, has become a petit-bourgeois *poshlyak* (vulgarian):

> Na stole moem – pirozhnye,
> I ya kofe p'yu so slivkami,
> A u vas stoly porozhnye,
> Vam i khleb dayut uryvkami.

> U menya matrats pruzhinistyi!
> A za vash tyufyak solomennyi –
> Na tolkuchku esli vynesti –
> Ne dadut i grosh polomennyi. (Elagin 33)

> (Got cakes and pastries on my table,
> I drink my coffee full of cream,
> *Your* tables ain't got nothing on them,
> You only get bread now and then.

> My mattress has got springs inside!
> You've got a pallet full of straw,
> – Try flogging it down the flea-market,
> You'd get a broken groat, no more.)

The language of Elagin's poem is colloquial, and the pace fast, as in the puppet play. The linguistic comedy resembles that of *Petrushka*. Puns and *non sequiturs* are frequent. In the sixth stanza Petrushka puns on the word *vyskochka*, 'upstart', relating this to his action in leaping out of the *yashchik s kuklami*, or box where the puppets are kept:

Velichayut lyudi vyskochkoi, –
Ya iz yashchika vyskakivayu!   (Elagin 33)

(Some people get the name of 'upstarts' –
Just watch me start up from my box!)

In a refrain repeated several times in the poem, Petrushka draws
attention to the natural surroundings, the crows flying above gardens
and vegetable patches, a meaningless comment which is then illogi-
cally discarded:

Vo sadu li, v ogorode,
Galki tuchei nosyatsya!
Eto k nashei teme vrode
Vovse ne otnosyatsya.   (Elagin 34, 35, 36)

(In the garden, in the cabbage-patch,
Flies a crowd of crows!
Got nothing to do with the theme of this story,
Has it, I don't suppose!)

But as the narrative progresses these comic devices take on a sinister
significance. Petrushka's pun on the word *yashchik* appears again at
the end of the poem, where it is transformed as the idiomatic phrase
sygrat' v yashchik, literally 'to play into the box', idiomatically
translated, 'to end up in one's box':

K udivlen'yu vyashchemu
Zritelei vopyashchikh,
Tut po-nastoyashchemu
Ya sygrayu v yashchik.   (Elagin 40)

(Then the squealing public
Will get their biggest shock,
At that moment, in all earnest,
I'll end up in my box!)

In the following stanza the refrain reappears, but this time the image
of the circling rooks is ominous; they seem to be about to descend on
the cadaver:

Vo sadu li, vo ogorode
Galki tuchei nosyatsya.
Eto k nashei teme vrode
Pryamikom otnosyatsya.   (Elagin 40)

(In the garden, in the cabbage patch,
Flies a crowd of crows –
Got nothing to do with the theme of this story?
Oh yes it has, you know!)

Elagin gives his Petrushka an explicitly contemporary setting from the opening lines. The hero introduces himself not simply to 'the honoured public', but to his 'dear contemporaries':

> A, pochtenneishaya publika!
> Dorogie sovremenniki!   (Elagin 33)

> (Eh, my greetings, honoured public!
> My dear contemporaries!)

References to modern objects are scattered in the poem: Petrushka has 'patent-leather shoes', and the wretched nag of the traditional play is advertised by the Gypsy as a race horse. Petrushka's taunts to the German can now be read as oblique references to the Second World War:

> I za mnoi eshche vchera
> S avtomatom begali,
> I evreitor-nemchura
> I svoi aptekari.   (Elagin 39)[109]

> (Only yesterday the Kraut
> Jefreiter was haring after me
> With his automatic out,
> And all his apothecaries.)

Elagin's Petrushka has retained his traditional strength and wickedness, but has lost his moral ambivalence. He is no longer the audience's friend and the mouthpiece of their anti-authoritarian, anti-ethical desires. He is greedy, philistine, and threatening; he is now a negative symbol, standing for the worst elements in the character of the Russian, and specifically Soviet, 'grey masses': their chauvinism, opportunism, callous and unprovoked violence. He is the Soviet *petit bourgeois* seen from the perspective of a shocked liberal intellectual. The avant-garde appropriations of *Petrushka* might as well never have existed; we have returned to a nineteenth-century polarisation of urban lower classes and educated opinion.

Despite the diversity of fairground and circus appropriations in Russian high literature, two general tendencies can be observed. The first is the writing out of the subordinate classes. In fiction or semi-fiction by writers of a radical tendency they are seen as victims. Mostly the audiences and showmen of the fairgrounds do not enjoy themselves; here, as in the English 'industrial novel', 'rarely do … characters exhibit any feeling of spontaneous joy or happiness'.[110] Where they are admitted to enjoy themselves, the reader is reminded that this enjoyment is either specious or positively pernicious. In Symbolist and much of later writing they either do not appear at all, or they stand for cloddish and constricting philistine taste, an unknowledgeable public that, however, knows what it likes. The first way of seeing the carnival, then, is as an arena for the assertion of intellectual authority. The second way of seeing it is as an arena where another kind of authority can be asserted: that of the author. The fairground is systematically dissociated from carnival discourse, that is, where 'the structure of the author emerges as anonymity that creates and sees itself created as self and other, as man and mask'.[111] The clown mask adopted by Symbolist poets does not bring them into the collective; it emphasises that they are removed from it, that they have the magic powers of the shaman or magician, from whom, in Frazer's reading, modern clowns had 'degenerated'.[112]

In the discussion of *Petrushka*'s place in the carnival tradition, I quoted M. Bakhtin's comment that the tradition of folk humour was always subversive and hostile to high culture (p. 92). The same attitude holds in reverse: high culture is implacably hostile to folk humour. Before the Revolution, Petrushka was used as a vehicle for political satire or, more often, for an idealist view of the artist as doomed social outcast. After the Revolution, the fairground genres surfaced briefly, before carnival humour dried up – or, to put it more accurately, before the tap was turned off. Outside the Soviet Union, the politically subversive and morally ambivalent nature of the street puppet theatre is denied by an interpretation which makes Petrushka the proponent and lackey of authoritarianism, not its violent enemy.

5

Sanitary Petrushka and sanitised *Petrushka*

The modern Petrushka has become a cultured actor.
(G. Tarasov, *Petrushka v shkole i v pionerotryade*, p. 39)

Street theatre after the Revolution

Throughout the nineteenth century, Petrushka had proved his resilience and his ability to survive the pressures of politics, cultural didacticism, economic hardship and changing fashions in entertainment. But it might have been expected that the Revolution would have finally killed him off. Indeed, it has been stated that it did. In his authoritative book *Punch and Judy* George Speaight wrote that the *Petrushka* show vanished with the old order.[1] As one would expect, the Revolution, the famines of the early 1920s and the Civil War were a quiet period for *Petrushka* and the other Russian carnival and street entertainments, but they survived even these. In 1919 Nina Simonovich-Efimova and her husband managed to find enough showmen working in the traditional manner to revive the old Moscow *gulyan'-ya* at Sokol'niki; the event was repeated in 1923.[2] And later even than this, in 1925, she recorded that in the back streets off the Novinskii Boulevard in Moscow still resided a thriving community of street showmen, as they had since the 1850s, offering each other help, support and artistic co-operation.[3] Vsevolodsky-Gerngross notes that dancing bears still performed in Leningrad and in many other places well into the 1920s, although their appearances were spasmodic.[4] Moreover, the traditional audience for these entertainments had survived. In 1927 Sergey Obraztsov wrote: 'A puppeteer or organ-grinder has only to appear in our courtyard and every proletarian in the place practically falls out of the seventh-floor windows for joy.'[5]

There were plenty of puppeteers surviving outside Moscow too, even after the Civil War. Their traditional sites, the trade fairs, had declined in importance, but they were still held regularly. It was in Voronezh, a town in the provinces a few hundred miles south-east of

Moscow, that the local historian and philologist A.M. Putintsev encountered, in 1923, two puppeteers performing a traditional *Petrushka* show, *Van'ka* (VLB 5–6). He took down fascinating details of their life, which followed very much the traditional pattern. The leader, M.A. Plotkin, had worked in the *balagans* since the age of nine, and was a demobbed soldier, as were his companion, N.D. Zakharov, and the accordion-player V.P. Kolesnikov, who had been taken on for the performances in Voronezh (the first two were touring in the region). Though they were literate, the skill was clearly not very important, since, as Putintsev put it, 'they occasionally read newspapers' (VLB 6). The three made little money – a few roubles per performance – but appeared to lead thoroughly enjoyable lives. Any profit was spent by them on 'spiritous beverages'.

Putintsev recorded the play performed by this itinerant troupe, and the result was an outstanding text, preserving many features of the old tradition, yet rich in improvisation and topical reference. Putintsev's recording is immensely valuable because it is a southern version of the text (the hero is called Van'ka, as was usual there), and because it is a phonetic rendition, preserving the regionalisms and pronunciation of south Russian dialect – features which are only partly transmitted in the printed version to which I had access, and which, alas, it is not possible to convey in translation at all. The text is mostly in prose, but the lack of rhyming aphorisms is compensated for by unusually plentiful evidence of carnival humour.

The play has the lack of plot typical of the fairground genres; it is a series of more or less unlinked scenes. Many old motifs are present: Van'ka decides to marry, buys a horse, fights with and kills a series of adversaries before being dragged off by the Barbos. Some of the traditional scenes are slightly altered: Van'ka / Petrushka's encounter with the Doctor happens when the Doctor arrives to examine the dead Gypsy. But the Doctor's traditional formula of introduction is present in a witty variant, and his examination of the Gypsy follows the same pattern as his examination of Petrushka:

OTVETCHIK: Eta, Vanya, dokhtar; on lichit' prishel.
DOKTOR: Ya dokhtar, lekar', nemetskii aptekar'. Zuby vstavlyayu i vyryvayu, lyudei na tot svet atpravlyayu. [*nachinaet osmatrivat' i oslushivat' tsygana*] Tuta?   (VLB 12)

(FEED: Vanya, 'ere's the dog-ter come to cure ye.
DOCTOR: I'm the doctor, physician, German obstetrician. I knocks in teeth, I

knocks out teeth, I send my patients to their death. [*Begins to examine the Gypsy and listen to his chest*] Here?)

The characters have been preserved in their traditional forms – indeed, Putintsev's descriptions are the only record we have of how the Devil and the Dog looked (see chapter 2, p. 102). Van'ka's appearance resembles that of the traditional Petrushka, with a clown's hat, a hump and a hooked nose. His character is also little changed: he displays a horrible mixture of priapism and sentimentality towards his fiancée. One stage direction reads: '*From time to time they stop dancing, embrace, and give each other juicy-sounding kisses*' (VLB 10). The following hilarious exchange takes place with the Feed. No translation is adequate to the revolting stickiness of the terms of endearment used:

VAN'KA: [*obnimaet i tseluet nevestu*]: Kharoshaya, prigozhaya! Galubachka!
OTVETCHIK: Simpampon'chik.
VAN'KA: Simpamposhichka.   (VLB 10)

(VAN'KA: [*embraces and kisses his wife*]: My beauty, my comely lass! Ducky!
FEED: Sweetie-pie!
VAN'KA: Sweetie-weetie-pie!)

Van'ka loves violence just as much as usual. He commits four murders in less than six pages of text. He remains quite unrepentant when rebuked by the Feed for his bad behaviour; when no one is left to bury the corpses, he is unperturbed:

OTVETCHIK: Vanya! Ty iisho ubil chilaveka?
VAN'KA: [*burchit*]: I etava skharanyu.
OTVETCHIK: A s kem ty budish' kharanit', vit' ya ni budu.
VAN'KA: S kem? Khot's chortam.   (VLB 14)

(FEED: Vanya! Have you killed another person?
VAN'KA: [*mutters*]: I'll bury this one too, won't I.
FEED: Who are you going to bury 'im with, I'm not going to, you know.
VAN'KA: Who? Why, the devil, for all I care.)

Van'ka remains equally unperturbed when the Devil takes him at his word.

Van'ka also displays the traditional obsession with drinking and eating. As usual, he demands his dowry in food and drink. He offers to bribe the Feed with alcohol for information about a horse:

OTVETCHIK: A znaiish, Vanya, ya znayu, u kavo loshad' kupit'.
VAN'KA: U kavo?
OTVETCHIK: Dash na chai, tada skazhu.
VAN'KA: Dam tibe na butylku samagonu, skazhi tol'ka.   (VLB 11)

(FEED: Hey Vanya, I know who you can buy a horse off.
VAN'KA: Who?
FEED: Buy me a cuppa tea, I'll tell you.
VAN'KA: I'll buy you a whole bottle of vodka if you'll only tell me.)

Perhaps the most outstanding reworking of a traditional motif is the mistaken identity/food–death link, which is developed here with macabre fantasy. When Van'ka kills the Gypsy, the following exchange takes place:

OTVETCHIK: Zachem ty, Vanya, cheloveka pabil. On pomir.
VAN'KA: On povar?
OTVETCHIK: Net, ni povar, a pomir: povar na kukhni kartoshku zharit'.

(VLB 11)

(FEED: Why've ye killed the man, Vanya. He's copped it.
VAN'KA: He's cooked it?
FEED: Not cooked it, copped it; cooked it is what ye do to spuds in the kitchen.)

When Van'ka returns from burying the Gypsy and the Doctor, he announces that they have been put to use for food:

VAN'KA: Atpravili na kolbasu.   (VLB 13)

(VAN'KA: They've bin turned into sausage.)

The punishment enacted by the traditional Barbos has been made even more vicious than before: Van'ka's nose is bitten off before he is dragged away to Hell.

The politically subversive nature of the text is evident everywhere. This incarnation of Petrushka has retained his old rebellious spirit. He announces as he arrives:

Pozdravlyayu vsekh vas s praz'nikom, s savetskim, a ni kadetskim.

(VLB 9)

(Best wishes for the 'oliday, the Sov-iét 'oliday, not the Cadet 'oliday!)

But his actions in the play do not express much sympathy with the *savetskii prazdnik* (Soviet holiday). His traditional enemies, the Soldier and the Policeman, here appear in Soviet guise as the Krasnoarmeets (Red Army Soldier) and the Militsioner (Soviet Policeman). When the Red Army Soldier appears and pompously enquires how the Doctor and the Gypsy died, Van'ka bribes the Feed to say: 'Eti sami umirli' ('They just went and died by themselves');

then, when he is warned that he will be sent to trial, he takes justice into his own hands:

OTVETCHIK: Sichas' tibe, Vanya, mil'tsianer sudit' budit'.
VANYA: Ya iivo rassuzhu pa svoimu. [*Otpravlyaetsya za shirmy, vozvrash-chaetsya s dubinkoi i razmakhnuvshis' ubivaet militsionera*] Vot i fsimu sudu kanets.   (VLB 13)

(FEED: Now the p'liceman'll judge you, Vanya.
VAN'KA: I'll give him judge. [*Goes off-stage, comes in with his club, whacks the policeman on the head and kills him*] There's an end to all judgements.)

Shortly after liberating himself from the Policeman's attentions, Van'ka is taken for a deserter by the Red Army Soldier, and is made to take part in impromptu military training. This has predictable results:

KRASNOARMEETS [*pokazyvaya na Van'ku*]:   Khto eto takoi? Dizirter? [*Van'ke*] Nu-ka stanovis' va khrunt pat ruzh'e.
VAN'KA: Ni khachu i ni khachu! [*mashet golovoi i rukami*]
KRASNOARMEETS: Biri, gavaryat' tibe, ruzh'e f ruki. Ni to f tribunal zabirem. [*Van'ka beret ruzh'e v ruki*]
VAN'KA: Ya ni umeyu!
KRASNOARMEETS: Budish umet'. Slushai moei komandi.
VAN'KA: Ruzh'e u mine, kaby ni tak. Tiperich ya tibe ni bayus'. Adnim mentam zakalyu. [*Zakalyvaet na smert' krasnoarmeitsa*]   (VLB 13–14)

(RED ARMY SOLDIER [*pointing at Van'ka*]:   'Oo's that then? A deserter, eh? [*To Vanya*] Right, cop 'old of this then.
VAN'KA: Don't want to! Won't!
RED ARMY SOLDIER: I'm telling you to take this rifle, or we'll have you up in front of the tribunal. [*Van'ka takes the rifle*]
VAN'KA: Can't!
RED ARMY SOLDIER: No can'ts. Now do as I say.
VAN'KA: I've got the rifle, ain't that so. Now I'm not scared of you. I'll stab you this minute. [*Bayonets the Red Army Soldier to death*])

Van'ka's cynicism is so consummate that at the end of the play, when he is seized by the Barbos, he is even prepared to call religion to his aid; and at this point, the Feed reveals that (incredibly) Van'ka has held the position of Church Elder in the parish:

VAN'KA: Atpustitya dushu na pakayaniya.
OTVETCHIK: Eta ni pa modi, Vanyusha, kaiitsa. A tibe vprot'chim nada; ty, vit', f zhivetskai tserkvi titaram sastaish.   (VLB 14)

(VAN'KA: Release my soul that I may repent.
FEED: Tain't the fashion, Vanyusha, repentance isn't. But maybe you ought, though; after all, you're the Parish Church Elder, aren't you?)

The neologisms in *Van'ka* add to the comedy. Van'ka has been in Germany, a new touch, but has returned home for a conventional reason, to find a suitable bride – a *papova doch'* (pope's daughter). Twice when he attempts to bribe the Musician he offers payments of a newfangled sort: 'Ya tibe veksil' vyshlyu pa radii' (I'll send you a cheque over the radio) and 10 roubles 'pa zalatomu kursu' (on the gold rate) (VLB 10, 12).

The text of *Van'ka* reveals how the subversive tradition of street theatre was continued. Quite logically, the hated pre-revolutionary bearers of authority were replaced by their Soviet equivalents, who aroused no greater love than their predecessors. As in the pre-revolutionary tradition, the subversion was short-lived and only skin-deep. None of the showmen Putintsev describes was anti-Soviet – all three had served in the Red Army. What we have is a marvellous carnival text, in which the social order is stood on its head, not stabbed in the back.

But it was not long before the disquiet of the Soviet state was roused at such attacks on its fabric. The cultural hierarchy of the Soviet state, divided by opposing views on whether there was to be a new proletarian art, and what form this should take if there were to be, was united by its mistrustful attitudes to popular culture, which it shared with the pre-revolutionary progressive intelligentsia. Some Soviet cultural observers believed that, like pre-revolutionary bourgeois art, pre-revolutionary popular art would be redundant in new social conditions; L. Sosnovsky, for example, condemned 'mangled *balagan* language and vulgarity'.[6] Others believed that the new literature must be based on the achievements of pre-revolutionary high art. Trotsky, for example, wrote:

They who refuse to master technique will come to look 'unnatural', imitative and buffoon-like. It would be monstrous to conclude from this that the technique of bourgeois art is not necessary to the workers. Yet there are many who fall into this error. 'Give us,' they say, 'something pock-marked, but our own.' This is false and untrue. A pock-marked art is no art and is therefore not necessary to the working masses.[7]

The high-art models chosen might be less traditional than Trotsky's quotation suggests; for the theorists of Proletkul't drama they were

German Expressionism and the Symbolist theories of Vyacheslav Ivanov.[8] But they were all remote from the street theatrical tradition. The few commentators who did think there was some place for street theatre were presented with considerable problems. Its popularity could not be denied, but it had unseemly commercial elements and was unduly committed to entertainment, not education. A. Lunacharsky's article on the circus reflects the distaste which many Bolsheviks felt for popular literary modes:

No communist ought ever to wave a hand in contempt at any genuinely popular phenomenon, understandable as it is when so-called refined intellects, confronted by popular songs (*chastushki* and *zhestokie romansy*), pulp novels and lurid adventure films, wrinkle their noses as if there was a bad smell ... Naturally there are many undesirable elements in all these forms of art; elements, moreover, which do not contribute to the enjoyment of the masses, but which are merely a routine and unnecessary addition.

What I have said above is partly applicable to the circus too. As I have already said, its great popularity should be enough in itself to necessitate serious discussion and to introduce enquiries about how to purify and perhaps adapt the circus, whilst at the same time preserving its essential qualities.[9]

The necessary changes in the character of popular entertainment were not to be allowed to happen of themselves; they were to be directed from above. The *narodnye gulyan' ya* were to be purged of undesirable elements and fitted for communist reality:

It cannot be expected that, if left to themselves, the masses will produce anything more than noisy merry-making and thronging crowds of people dressed up in their holiday best.

Like everything else with a capacity to inspire elevated aesthetic enjoyment, a genuine holiday must be organised ...

A festival organised without the help (but also without the hindrance) of Dionysus would perhaps be rather greyer than before, but it would certainly also be infinitely more decent.[10]

One of the first acts of the new cultural administration was to turn the main auditorium in the Narodnyi dom (People's Palace) in St Petersburg, which until then had been a sort of music-hall, into a theatre for the performance of realist drama.[11]

The bureaucrats were as disgusted with the carnival genres as their tsarist predecessors had been, and they expressed their disgust infinitely more effectively. As with every instance of Soviet censorship, direct evidence is hard to find, but there is, fortunately, one published document which shows how the showmen were attacked in their most vulnerable place – they were deprived of their livelihood. Sergey Obraztsov, the Soviet puppeteer, then a young man with his heart in the right place, published an article in *Pravda* in 1927 criticising a recent order banning street performances in Moscow, which he quotes as follows:

> The administrative department of *Mossovet* [the Moscow local government body] has directed all organs of the *militsiya* not to allow performances on the streets, squares and boulevards of Moscow by organ-grinders, violin-players, performing bears etc., which cause crowds of gawpers to assemble and obstruct the traffic. Offenders will be subject to the processes of justice according to administrative regulations.[12]

The position of traditional entertainers was further eroded by the abolition of the trade fairs in the early 1930s, and by the changes to the Civil Code of the RSFSR in 1936 which banned the keeping of roundabouts by private individuals.[13] The first measure was, of course, part of the process of economic centralisation, and not primarily intended to suppress the puppeteers and other fairground players, but it came as a blow nonetheless; the second was a direct attack.

The next step was to bring all the fairground artistes under state control. In the case of the circus, the immediate post-revolutionary regulation according to which private circuses existed alongside state ones under the directive of the Circus Section of TEO, the Theatre Department of Narkompros, the People's Commissariat of Education, ended in 1922, when TsUGTs (the Central Directive of State Circuses) was set up. More and more circuses joined this, and it was replaced in 1931 by an all-Soviet association GOMETS (The State Union of Music Halls, Variety Theatres and Circus Enterprises), and in 1936 by the Chief Directive of Circuses. After this there was no room for private circuses.[14]

Private fairgrounds were also replaced in the late 1920s and 1930s by the new network of Parks of Culture and Rest. There were the new 'folk festivals' of the mass demonstrations, organised by the authorities in the manner of the nineteenth-century *gulyan'ya*, of which Kuznetsov wrote:

> In the context of Stalinist five-year plans and in the conditions of the classless Socialist society our funfairs have taken the form of funfair-carnivals celebrated by the whole people, the most significant of which have taken place in the A.M. Gor'ky Central Park of Culture and Rest, Moscow, in the S.M. Kirov Central Park of Culture and Rest on the Islands in Leningrad, and, finally, in

the many parks of culture and rest which form a more and more important part of the life and experience of the Socialist town in the era of Stalin.[15]

The puppet theatre, too, was centralised and 'professionalised', under organisers who often had little sympathy with the traditional street theatre. One or two showmen were invited to join the new state puppet theatres, but only in an advisory capacity. Zaitsev, for example, gave occasional performances of his show at the Central State Puppet Theatre in Moscow, but there was no interaction between his shows and those of the theatre itself.[16]

By the end of the 1930s the process of organisation and adaptation had gone so far that most types of popular entertainment bore little resemblance to those on offer before the Revolution. The old itinerant entertainers had disappeared; fairgrounds were now permanent and mechanised. The circus acts were engaged in seriously ideological work, as Eugene Lyons wrote:

The circus, of course, is as completely ideological as the library. Every act under the big top has its proletarian moral. Uncle Durov's animals, and a remarkable lot they are, illustrate current slogans, satirise current political villains, and generally show signs of having been trained in the editorial room of *Pravda*.[17]

Outside its artificial reservations, the street tradition became extinct. By 1940 the puppeteers had disappeared from city courtyards.[18] Their one form of continuing existence during the 1930s seems to have been as children's party entertainers, and there are no records that they were active in this way after 1940.[19] If there were any performances after this, they are, with one exception, not recorded. The exception is a very curious account by Vero Roberti, an Italian journalist who visited the Soviet Union in the 1960s, of an 'underground' performance of *Petrushka* which he saw at the Moscow bird-market.[20] The details he gives are circumstantial, but not all of them recall the traditional performance. Petrushka had a red shirt, but instead of his pointed cap wore 'a black skull-cap with a green ribbon hanging down over his shoulders'. The show was given, not in a booth, but in a skirt-theatre arrangement recalling Olearius' description of the performances of the *skomorokhs*. In the little play Petrushka 'told of his adventures on the moon': he had found some plans for a flying machine belonging to a group of conspirators executed by Alexander III, and flown to the moon on it. After describing his adventures, and 'beating the stupid puppet who had provoked him', Petrushka went off-stage, only to return with the words, 'Naturally when I went to the moon I did not leave my *avos'ka* behind!' (An *avos'ka*, literally 'a perhaps', is the string bag which is often carried in the Soviet Union in case something enticing might perhaps – *avos'* – turn out to be on sale.)

This peculiar story is the only written account of a *Petrushka* performance in the street after the early 1930s. The idea that Petrushka has carried on his existence underground is certainly attractive, but there are some elements in Roberti's account which make me wonder how accurate it is. The play he describes was an hour long – too long for a glove-puppet performance – and most of it consisted of one speech by Petrushka himself. The skirt theatre which he described was never used in the *Petrushka* show. It is possible that Roberti consciously or unconsciously embroidered the details of the show he saw in order to turn it into something historic and significant, something that would prove his contention that 'Petrushka is Russia's Punch and not the Soviet Union's, because the Soviets, being Communists, have no imagination and do not know how to laugh'.[21]

That tendentious comment is best passed over in silence. It is doubtful, in any case, whether performers of carnival genres could operate successfully given the considerable restrictions to ensure public order which obtain in the Soviet Union; like their counterparts before the Revolution, they would risk contravening laws on obscenity as well as mendicancy.[22] The situation in the Soviet Union today is that certain showcase forms of entertainment, the circus in particular, enjoy a high level of support and work to universally recognised high standards. The performers receive years of training, respectable salaries, and state pensions: all this must be the envy of their colleagues in the West. But, in the Russian Federation at least, the traditional, deregulated, subversive street entertainments have disappeared. Their absence here stands out against the situation in other countries. In Britain, for example, the *Punch and Judy* tradition is still very much alive: over twenty showmen work the beach sites, many more give performances at fairs, children's parties, and so on; recently the surviving showmen's families (where the current performer may be the fourth generation to show) have been joined by enthusiastic converts, such as the Major Mustard group, who have initiated a revival.[23] In the late 1960s there were more than two hundred fairs a week during the season, some of which were still steam-operated.[24] In May 1987, Covent Garden Piazza in London was the site of a celebration of the 355th birthday of Mr Punch. About ninety active Professors (i.e. showmen) took part, with their Punches, Judies and Crocodiles, and there were about twenty booths giving shows more or less continuously for two days. Visitors from abroad included a French booth, a German booth, and a marvellous *Pulcinella* show from Italy.

Nor is this situation limited to Western capitalist countries. In China the recent establishment of heavily subsidised state puppet theatres has not yet killed off street puppet shows.[25] In East Germany the puppet hero Kasperl, who was under a cloud in the 1950s, has recently been revived in his traditional form.[26] At Covent Garden in 1987, there were performers from Hungary with their *Vitez Laszlo* show, and a Czech troupe who did a version of *Petrushka*, alas rather overlong and flaccid in pace, and projected through loudspeakers.

In the introduction I mentioned the fact that Bakhtin denied the importance of the carnival tradition in Russia (p. 3). His denial is unlikely to have been a result of ignorance. He was born in Orel in 1895, so it would be surprising if he had never seen any Russian funfairs. The reason for his denial becomes clear, though, if one remembers that *Rabelais and His World* was begun in 1934. His remarks on the character of the Russian carnival are not incidental; they must be placed in the context of the manipulation of popular-cultural forms which had been going on since the Revolution. At the same time when the book was written, the native Russian carnival forms were beginning to be a taboo subject, and could be mentioned only obliquely. Read like this, Bakhtin's book on Rabelais, which apparently ignores the Russian carnival, is in fact a monument to it that was constructed at the moment when the fairground tradition was about to vanish.

The agitprop puppet theatre

In the first section of this chapter I examined the unofficial street tradition of *Petrushka* after the Revolution. *Petrushka* as text also continued its existence in another form: as one of the weapons used by the new Soviet State for agitprop, 'agitation and propaganda'. The new *Petrushka* was part of the exciting artistic upheaval in the Soviet Union during the 1920s that stretched from the two-dimensional rhyming posters of the ROSTA windows designed by Mayakovsky to the massed spectacles on Red Square involving thousands of people,

20. Alekseev-Yakovlev's 'agit-van', Petrograd 1918. From Alekseev-Yakovlev, *Russkie narodnye gulvan'ya.*

and that went from the cultural hierarchy to the smallest village culture clubs.

Krystyna Pomorska remarks in her foreword to the English-language edition of *Rabelais and His World*: 'The official prohibition of certain kinds of laughter, irony and satire was imposed upon the writers of Russia after the Revolution.'[27] In fact the prohibition was not immediate; it had two phases. Immediately after the Revolution, the entertainments of the Russian carnival were seized on, since they seemed ideal for the purposes of agitation and propaganda. In the May Day carnivals in St Petersburg in 1918 and 1919 circus acts and puppet shows were revived, and new, Socialist elements were added; there were processions of decorated agit-vans and even agit-trams; the squares were embellished, not now with the traditional fir-branches, but with red banners and caricatures; vast Enemy of the People dolls were incinerated on public bonfires.[28] During and after the Civil War, popular-theatrical forms were adopted by travelling troupes of actors who worked to keep up morale among the soldiery during the war, and after it to propagate literacy and hygiene. Some of these groups used live actors, and based their work on the traditional folk theatre repertoire for live actors, and on the conventions used in the folk theatre. The largest and most important group was the Sinyaya bluza (Blue Blouse) movement; its shows mixed circus acts and acrobatics with literary forms, such as *raeshnik* (comic doggerel) and *igrishche* (a comic sketch or short scene). The actors' habit of indicating the function of characters by pinning key details to the outside of their uniform blue blouses was probably derived from the folk tradition; plays of the folk repertoire, such as *Tsar' Maksimilian*, were often performed by soldiers who would pin foil stars and other emblems to their army-issue greatcoats.[29] Perhaps the closest of all these groups to the pre-revolutionary popular theatre was Sergey Radlov's Narod-naya komediya (Popular Comedy) in Petrograd, in the People's Palace on the Petrograd side. This place was unusual in that the productions were played on a projecting stage, almost 'in the round', and in true *balagan* tradition:

As on the town square, the public in the auditorium of the people's palace kept on their outer clothing and gnawed away at sunflower seeds. They clapped excitedly at the antics of Jimmy the Monkey (played by Aleksandrov-Serzh) . . . No less excitement was aroused by the topical jokes which filled the production . . . The political satire was expressed with the naive directness and crudity of a *balagan* performance.[30]

The repertoire of the Narodnaya komediya gives a fair indication of the repertoire of most agitprop spectacles:

The Monkey's Trainer would turn to him. 'Jimmy, show us how the White Army arrived in Petersburg!' Aleksandrov would 'put on an arrogant, bow-legged walk, moving his legs like a bear'. 'And how did they leave?' Then he would 'skulk off comically to hide somewhere, clutching his sore backside'. In another sketch the Monkey was asked how to avoid getting spotted fever. He rushed up to his master, studied his hat and frenziedly squashed an imaginary louse.[31]

The agitprop theatres were distinguished from the theatres and spectacles (discussed in the first part of this chapter) because their organisers and participants did not usually have the backgrounds of traditional showmen. They were members of the intelligentsia, often students or young people, who had preserved an enthusiasm for fairground, street and circus spectacles since childhood. This was true, for example, of Sergey Radlov, the director of the Narodnaya komediya; he was an amateur of the popular theatre, but his own experience was exclusively in the high theatre: he had worked with Meyerhold before the Revolution.[32] It was true also, of course, of Mayakovsky, who had not worked in the fairground tradition until composing his immediately post-revolutionary spectacle *Mystery-bouffe*.

On the other hand, the agitprop spectacles were distinguished from high-literary appropriations of the fairground and street theatre (discussed in chapter 4) by the involvement of street and fairground artistes, if only in an advisory capacity. Mayakovsky drew on the advice and knowledge of the ex-entrepreneur of the *balagans*, Alekseev-Yakovlev, for the staging of *Mystery-bouffe*, and later worked on circus scenarios with the famous clown Vitaly Lazarenko.[33] They were distinguished also from high literature by the fact that they addressed themselves primarily to a proletarian or peasant audience; the puppet theatre activist Tarasov was disgusted when he found that the group of pioneers he was expected to show to in one village whilst touring a rural area was composed largely of the children of small tradesmen and artisans (Tarasov 11).

Many of the mobile agitprop groups preferred puppets, above all glove puppets, to live actors. *Petrushka* was selected by Lunacharsky himself as a particularly suitable vehicle for agitprop in his essay with the hortatory title 'We will laugh':

Surely the figure of a Russian Petrushka will appear on our fairgrounds as a favourite, to figure as the herald of public opinion who would be capable of exploiting the inexhaustible resources of Russian fairground jingles [*pri-bautki*], the Russian and Ukrainian languages with their genuinely heroic humorous force? Surely the tuneful Russian song with its disjunctive rhythm which is so good for dancing will be heard again, surely all this will be infused with the astringent humour of the radical Revolution?[34]

There were also practical reasons for the popularity of puppets. The canvas booths, puppets and other equipment used for shows were portable, they could be easily stored, rapidly dismantled and reassembled; an adequate show could be put on by only one operator, using two puppets simultaneously, and perhaps also a musician to provide accompaniment. A puppet theatre was also ideally suited to performances on the back of floats, from the back of vans or even the window of a bus or train.

Throughout the 1920s, active puppet collectives travelled round European Russia staging shows which were based on the adventures of the glove-puppet hero of the Russian fairground, Petrushka. The most important groups were the Red Petrushka collective, begun in 1927 under S. Malinovskaya, the Red Army Petrushka Group begun in 1928, the Special Automobile and Chemical Factory Petrushka, which played in factory clubs, and the Sanitary Petrushka, which 'carried out idiosyncratic and extremely useful educational work in schools, clubs and pioneer camps'.[35]

From the first years of Soviet power, the puppet theatre had a central place in official theatre policy. In 1918 the TEO of the Narkompros organised a Puppet Theatre Studio in Moscow.[36] After the Civil War the puppet theatres became an integral part of the agitprop campaign in Soviet villages; puppet groups were founded by Glavpolitprosvet (Chief Political Education Directive) in many places. The expansion of the agitprop puppet theatre was encouraged by the publication of texts of original plays in the journals *Ranenyi krasnoarmeets* (The Wounded Red Army Soldier) and *Doloi negramotnost'* (Away with Illiteracy), as well as in separate editions. Numerous manuals and technical articles were produced which advised club organisers in villages how to manufacture their own puppets and booths.[37] For the less enterprising *kul'torg* (culture administrator), sets of puppets were available from central clubs.[38] Many of the new Petrushka plays became popular; N. Smirnova states that in one Soviet town audience reactions to performances of the puppet group were so lively that people would bring their complaints to Petrushka and ask him to settle them.[39]

As the second phase of carnival prohibition came into force in the late 1920s and early 1930s, the politically committed and socially critical agitprop theatre met the same fate as the traditional street and fairground theatre. Its socially critical function was seen as a threat, and there were now much more effective ways of, say, persuading peasants of the benefits of collectivisation than of showing them the antics of monkeys converted to Socialism. In fact, there seems to have been active repression as well as neglect and restriction. One by one, the groups were disbanded. Sinyaya bluza was forced to close down in 1932.[40] Yuzhanin, the leader of the movement, was sent to a camp, where for a while at least Sinyaya bluza continued its existence, in bizarre parallel to the convict theatres of the tsarist labour camps described by Doroshevich and Dostoevsky.[41]

The various Red Petrushka groups lasted only slightly longer. Red Petrushka itself 'ended its existence, according to the natural order of things', as Smirnova euphemistically puts it, in the mid-1930s.[42] Petrushka's subversive character did not suit the new atmosphere of the 1930s, as the famous Soviet puppeteer Sergey Obraztsov makes clear:

Before the Revolution Petrushka would hit people whom it was not only forbidden to hit, but whom one might not even criticise. He embodied, so to speak, the dream of the common people which could not possibly be realised in tsarist times. He restored the spirit of justice missing from the world around.

With the coming of Soviet power, though, justice was established, and Soviet law began to do battle with anti-social elements – embezzlers, swindlers, idlers. The services of anarchic boot-boys were no longer required. The more the legal system gained in strength, the more senseless and even harmful Petrushka's arbitrary quarrelsomeness began to seem; it perverted all conceptions of law, of human moral norms, and of right social behaviour. And so the attempt to revive Petrushka, the positive–negative hero, could not succeed.

The reasons for these failures are obvious. In the modern theatre it is quite in order to perform a classic pre-revolutionary comedy, but it would be quite wrong to use the hero of such a play as the hero of a modern work.[43]

This information could not come more directly from the horse's mouth. In 1931, when the Central State Puppet Theatre was set up in Moscow, Sergey Obraztsov was appointed artistic director. He has remained in this position ever since, and has not unnaturally lost the radical views which he expressed in his *Pravda* article in 1927. Since the 1930s, the Soviet puppet theatre has followed two main lines: productions catering for children, mostly *skazki* (folk-tales) or original plays with a cast-list of small furry creatures; and productions aimed at adults, with performances of Russian and foreign classics adapted for the puppet theatre, and original plays, such as Obraztsov's *The Extraordinary Concert*. Any social criticism is directed at the capitalist West or at pre-revolutionary Russia, or falls into the category which Lev Losev named 'The Produce Section's Imperfections', that is, criticism of trifles for show.[44] Artistic standards are high, but there is no element of riotousness and little to disturb the audience, whether adult or child.

I do not intend here to discuss the final stage, where the established traditions of *Petrushka* have no relevance, but the intermediate stage, in which the old carnival genres were appropriated as agitprop. The agitprop puppet plays provide interesting evidence on how the carnival tradition, potentially dangerous to any authoritarian discourse as has been shown in the study of *Van'ka*, was defused. To be fair, *Petrushka* was not only more widely but also more directly imitated than other types of carnival text. The post-revolutionary *raeshniki* (comic doggerel verses) published in such collections as *Krasnoarmeiiskii fol'klor* bear little resemblance to fairground comedy – a typical title is 'Stalin is Our Golden Sun'.[45] The standards of the little plays were often also quite high – they were written by authors who were aware of the length of line necessary in the glove-puppet theatre, and who had a certain sense of the dramatic. But they do also manifest Soviet puppeteers' distrust of what was being presented in the folk tradition, which can be found in most of the manuals and writings of the period. 'The Petrushka showmen are accomplished masters in portraying what is commonly known as indecency', Simonovich-Efimova writes.[46] Alongside prurience, there was hauteur on supposedly aesthetic grounds too: as Tarasov put it: 'We do not need the old *Petrushka* comedy; it is pointless and senseless' (Tarasov 42). 'In the old days, when Petr Ivanovich Uksusov wandered the fairs and village streets, he had to be content with the wailing music of the barrel-organ; the musician would turn the handle of his clapped-out "machine", and its ridiculous racket would draw a crowd of gawpers' (ibid. 125).

Besides, there were difficulties on political grounds. The pre-revolutionary texts analysed in the earlier chapters of this book, and the street text *Van'ka*, have given abundant evidence that, in the words of Vsevolodsky-Gerngross already referred to, Petrushka is not an enlightened political campaigner, but an anarchist: 'Petrushka's rebellion has no definite purpose; it is an anarchic rebellion.'[47]

How then was Petrushka to be appropriated by the agitprop theatre? It certainly did not lack a definite political purpose, and in it, as Tarasov put it, Petrushka's function was to be a mouthpiece of enlightened ideas:

> Instead of showing the 'physician and apothecary, obstetrician and veterinary from the Kamennyi Most', Petrushka must be shown doing battle with kulaks and layabouts, assailing saboteurs, telling stories about the way things are going in housing cooperatives, collective farms and political cells. Who can doubt that such a Petrushka will bring immense benefits not only as a merciless critic but as an energetic agitator on every front of the construction of Socialism? (Tarasov 46)

There was, however, a problem with this: Petrushka could only adopt such a role if his traditional character was denied: he was not well suited to being on the side of the angels. Obraztsov sums up the problem:

> A sort of 'scissor-effect' came into play. If Petrushka was depicted as a drunkard and a skiver, his charming comic personality would still inspire the spectators' sympathy, and this went against the meaning of the play and its educational purpose. If the author and the producer tried to safeguard their educational purpose by stripping Petrushka of all his attractive qualities, and the spectators were forced to disapprove of his behaviour, then Petrushka would lose his essential characteristic – his role as the public's favourite, whose every action, every word inspired approval and amusement – in other words, he would no longer be what he was in the folk puppet theatre.[48]

Tarasov, a man whose capacity for self-deception was breathtaking, got round this little difficulty by alleging that Petrushka's character was so fluid that he was capable of representing any type (Tarasov 42). He was certainly traditionally capable of the contradictory qualities of cowardice and aggression, but his ungenteel appetites and anti-authoritarian character were well-defined. The only vice which the old Petrushka recognised in his audiences was a failure to line the pockets of the showman. It is preposterous to think of him castigating audiences, as Tarasov wanted him to be, for 'disruption of the disciplinary order of the Pioneers', 'smoking, trouble-making or swearing', 'liking for makeup and fashionable clothes – in girls' (is one to assume this liking was to be encouraged in boys?) and 'slacking in school-work' (Tarasov 93).

In order to illustrate what was done with the puppet hero, I have chosen the three agitprop puppet plays published by Eremin and meant to encourage village culture administrators in their own

Petrushka performances. The plays are *Crack on the Nut* (*Khlop v lob*) by Leo Miryanin, *Witch-Doctory is the Depths of Ignorance* (*Znakharstvo – debri t'my*) by M.D. Utenkov, and *An Amateur Performance* (*Predstavlenie lyubitel'skoe* – the full title stretches three lines) by M. Vol'pin (TP 144–74). All three plays are rather longer than the average street theatre performance: they would probably take about half an hour to play. The simplest and closest to the prototype is *Crack on the Nut*, in which Petrushka introduces himself, hits a variety of undesirables over the head with his club (including Denikin, Vrangel' and a Bourgeois), and is saved by a Teacher and a Red Army Officer from falling into the jaws of the traditional Barbos, here in a new incarnation as the Barbos-Negramotnost' (Cur of Illiteracy). In the second play Petrushka falls into the hands of several charlatans and quacks before being cured of his illness instantly by a Soviet Doctor. In Vol'pin's play Petrushka is peripheral to the action, on which he gives a running commentary. The play depicts the attempt by an unscrupulous merchant to bring the local co-operative into disrepute; whilst the co-operative member in charge of the shop is canoodling with the merchant's daughter, the merchant himself is busy sabotaging all the goods in the place.

The authors of all three plays have aimed to make them authentic. Some old characters, such as the Gypsy, the Doctor and the Barbos, appear; some of the new characters, such as the Merchant in Vol'pin's play, are modelled on old ones. Many of the traditional formulae appear. Miryanin's Petrushka, for example, introduces himself in the traditional manner (though his expressed intention of 'educating' is a novelty):

Ya Petrukha
po prozvishchu Farnos –
krasnyi nos.
V kamed' igrayu,
Vsekh zabavlyayu,
shutki shuchu,
a koli zakhochu –
prouchu.   (TP 144)

(I'm Petrukha,
my nickname's Farnose – the red-nose.
I'll show you my comedy,
And make you all happy.
My jokes'll amuse you

And if I choose to,
I'll teach you a thing or two too.)

Utenkov's Gypsy and Doctor also use traditional formulae of introduction:

Ya tsygan Mora
iz tsyganskogo khora,
poyu basom ...   (TP 155)

(I am the Gypsy Morus
From the Gypsy chorus
I sing bass ...)

Ya znamenityi doktor-lekar,
iz za kamennogo mosta aptekar',
akusher i konoval,
znaet menya ves' Zatsepskii val.   (TP 158)

(I'm the famous doctor-physician,
the apothecary from Stone Bridge,
veterinary and obstetrician,
known all along the Zatsep ditch.)

Traditional comic devices are used in all three plays. Foreigners'
strange accents are mocked in Miryanin's play (English and French
voices rather than the traditional German). There is a comic song to
an old tune ('Sten'ka Razin') in Vol'pin's play:

Vse propalo, vse propalo,
Akh, prikazchik, sukin syn,
Vmesto myla budet salo,
Vmesto sala – kerosin.
Zadadut tebe, brat, strakhu!
Kooperatsiya, proshchai!
On podsypaet soli v sakhar,
On podsypaet perets v chai.   (TP 170)

(Everything has gone to pot,
Through that bastard salesman's fault.
There'll be lard instead of soap flakes,
Paraffin instead of lard.
Brother, will our life be hard!
Our co-op is bound to die.
He has mixed the salt and sugar,
And put pepper in the tea.)

The imitation of popular tradition is superficial, however. None of the writers was very skilled in mixing prose and verse in the manner of the traditional *Petrushka* showmen. Miryanin's is almost entirely in prose, apart from short verse passages which stand out from the basic texts; the other two are entirely in doggerel, the effect of which is monotonous. What is more, most of the carnival elements have been excised.

The curious and distorted physique of the traditional Petrushka has been modified. In the picture reproduced by Eremin he is humpless and, though his nose is large, his expression is kindly rather than frenziedly malevolent. The other puppets in the collection have much less emphasis on mouth, nose and cheekbones than the traditional figures of the *Petrushka* stage (TP 188ff).[49]

The physicality of the text is played down. Petrushka has no wife, so there is no sexual horseplay. His aggression is also tempered: in Vol'pin's play he loses his *dubinka*, and becomes a passive commentator; in the other two plays he is allowed to keep the club, but commits no murders, and hits out less often than before. The witty euphemisms

21.   Petrushka as village dandy. From V. Stepanov, *Derevenskii krasnyi Petrushka*, Moscow 1926.

of the street Petrushka have gone too. Miryanin's hero hits out each time with an inane cry of 'Khlop v lob' (Whack on the nut). The motivation for Utenkov's Petrushka's attacks on the charlatan doctors who visit him is fairly convincing, but only once does he precede his blows by innuendo in the traditional style:

Oi, lomaet, oi, korezhit,
Razve eta dryan' pomozhet?
Pogodi zh ty u menya,
Zagovorchik znayu ya.   (TP 157)

(Oh! I'm aching, oh I'm writhing,
That rubbish does no good at all.
Just you wait here at my bedside,
I know some good spells as well.)

There are fewer references to physical elements and bodily functions in these plays than in the traditional text. The prologue to Miryanin's play is self-consciously and embarrassingly vulgar, but it is not representative of the tone of the rest of the play:

Tak seichas narod sobiraetsya, molodoi da staryi, osoblivo rebyatishki, pridut, kruzhkom stanut, ushi navostryat, burkaly vystavyat – smotryat, smotryat, i izo rta slyunki, burkaly vystavyat – smotryat, smotryat, i izo rta slyunki ot radosti tekut ... Kto kushak poteryal, kogo mat' so slezami ishchet, *u kogo stanishki, izvinite, mokrye* ...   (TP 145: my emphasis)

(I can see them rolling up from here, old and young, especially the children, they come here and stand round me, ears pricked, eyes out on stalks – watching and watching, dribbling with delight ... Someone's lost her sash, someone's mother's lost him and is bawling her eyes out, *and someone else (excuse me for saying so) has just wet his pants.*)

The old Petrushka would never have apologised for such an innocent remark; for the new one it is an isolated lapse from propriety.

In the new plays only the negative characters dance and kiss in the manner of Petrushka and his girl-friend. In Vol'pin's play Petrushka presents the activities of Nyurka and the Salesman to the public with evident disapproval:

Ya skvoz' zanaves vizhu p'esku,
Nedarom ya – Petrushka rasskazchik;
Vot k lavke podkhodit prikazchik,
A Nyurka zhdet ne dozhdetsya,
s nogi na nogu mnetsya.
Tselovat'sya polez. Shchekochet usami,
Ne verite? Pozhaluista, smotrite sami.   (TP 169)

(I can see it through the curtain,
I'm not the narrator for nothing, that's certain:
The salesman's coming to the shop,
Nyurka's so excited she can't wait,
From leg to leg she jumps hip-hop.
He's creeping in to kiss her. His whiskers he twirls.
You don't believe me? Just look, boys and girls.)

In Miryanin's *Crack on the Nut*, Petrushka's desire to *flirtanut'* (flirt) with a Frenchwoman in the White Russian entourage is used to point up the ridiculous snobbery of the White Russian supporters, not to contribute to the characterisation of him. The only other characters in this play who attempt physical contact are also negative: Aunt Sabotage and Uncle Famine, who announce their intention of 'caressing Petrushka.

Eating and drinking are also confined to the negative characters in the three plays. In *Crack on the Nut*, Denikin is portrayed as a secret tippler; in *Witch-Doctory* the Gypsy introduces himself (as in the street text) with a reference to his favourite foods:

Poyu basom,
Zaedayu ananasom,
Zapivayu kvasom ...   (TP 156)

(I sing bass
Eat pineapple slices
And drink kvas ...)

He also invites Petrushka to contribute to his household expenses with a traditional formula:

Pribavlyai rebyatishkam
Na molochishko ...   (TP 156)

(Add a quid
For milk for the kids.)

In *Amateur Performance* the Merchant compares his greedy and giddy daughter to a rat on the prowl:

Kak krysa k salu, tak ty k pudram.   (TP 167)

(You go for face-powder like a rat
For bacon-fat.)

The only other role played by food in *Amateur Performance* is that food substances are among the goods belonging to the co-operative which Nyurka's father sabotages; but they are not differentiated in value from the other goods, and little comic play is made of them.

In summary: the only carnival elements in the three plays are insignificant, and their presence is incidental. Moreover, there is a new spirit of puritanism. In *Amateur Performance* physical attraction is punished by a prison sentence:

Sud nynche strog:
kuptsa v ostrog,
Nyurku v ostrog.
(Ne udalos' sukhim iz voditsy vylezti.)
Da i prikazchiku ne bylo milosti:
za veseloe vremyaprovozhdenie,
za lyubovnoe pokhozhdenie,
kak sleduet vletelo:
baba – baboi, a delo – delom.   (TP 173)

(The law's arm is long:
Nyurka gets sent down,
the Merchant gets sent down.
(So they didn't get away with it.)
The Salesman too was hit where it hurts:
for his flirtations
and time-wastations,
he got his deserts:
no use mixing up women and work.)

In *Witch-Doctory* the audience are urged to heed the physical, not in a hedonistic sense, but in the sense of washing behind their ears and taking regular exercise:

Koli khotite sovsem byt' na lyudei pokhozhi, –
Nauchites' skoree gramote
Da pochashche moite rozhi,
Ne zabyvaite i tela, –
I togda v shapke budet delo.   (TP 163)

(If you want to be much better,
just make sure you learn your letters;
wash your faces every day,
and your bodies, by the way, –
then you'll make a fine display.)

The political ambivalence of the carnival text has also disappeared. Petrushka has become the mouthpiece of authority, rather than its scourge; in Miryanin's play he even joins forces with a Teacher and a Red Army Officer.

The only significant element which the new *Petrushka* has in common with the street prototype is the presentation of female characters. Here, as in the shows of itinerant puppeteers, women are passive; they are the subject of physical attacks, are manipulated by other characters, and have restricted access to language. Moreover, an incidental element in the street shows – that Petrushka's bride is a merchant's or a priest's daughter – is now central. The women in the new puppet shows are almost always class outsiders, and represent 'backward' attitudes. The struggle to advance is directed by heroic men, whilst the women cling despicably to their three 'Cs': comfort, clothes, the church. In *Witch-Doctory* the Soviet doctor is male, but two of the four benighted healers are women. The seduction of the merchant's daughter Nyurka in *Amateur Performance* is achieved by a gift of cosmetics:

PRIKAZCHIK: Vy, vy – boginya.
NYURKA: Akh, ostav'te svoi komplimenty.
PRIKAZCHIK: Chto vy, chto vy, Nyurochka. Ento ... To-est', eto, za temnotu prostite nas, ne kumpliment, a fakticheskaya istina-s.
NYURKA: Slushaite, davaite luchshe 'na ty'.
PRIKAZCHIK [*obnimaet*]:   Dushka moya, apel'sinchik, chervonchik, odekolon, mompasechka, limonchik ... [*Kazhdoe slovo soprovozhdaet potseluem*] I chtob byl potselui eshche bolee zharok, [*napravlyaetsya k kooperativu. Poyavlyaetsya s bankoi krema 'Metamorfoza', kotoruyu podaet Nyurke*] razreshite predpodnesti podarok.
[*Nyurka rassmatrivaet banku*]
NYURKA [*s vostorgom krichit*]:   Nu gde eshche takikh naidesh' dushek.
　　Me-ta-mor-foza! Krem ot vesnushek!　　　　　　　　　(TP 171)

(STOREKEEPER: You're – you're a goddess.
NYURKA: Ooh, enough of your compliments.
STOREKEEPER: Nyurochka, what are you saying. It ain't ... Ooh whoops scuse me, mean to say isn't, a coompliment, it's plain to see.
NYURKA: No need to be so formal with me.
STOREKEEPER [*embracing her*]:   My lovey, little orange, my goldilocks, my eau-de-cologne, my lap-dog, my lemon ... [*Kissing her with every word*]
　　Actions speak louder than words, I'm told,
[*Goes into the co-op and emerges with a jar of 'Metamorphosis' cream, which he gives to Nyurka*]
　　So I've brought you a pressie, if I may be so bold.
[*Nyurka looks at the jar*]
NYURKA [*screams with delight*]:

> Lord love a duck, some men are a dream,
> He's brought me a big jar of vanishing cream!)

The stereotype of woman as lackey of reaction is repeated in *Crack on the Nut* in the figure of the French Mamzelle; her understandable failure to respond to Petrushka's advances is ridiculed, and her linguistic incompetence is also a source of humour – she has a comic French accent:

MAMZEL′:   Mon d′e, mon d′e. Kakoi uzhasnyi kavaler.
PETRUSHKA: Pardone, mamzel′-strekozel′. [*Khochet obnyat′ ee*]
MAMZEL′:   Akh, ostav′te, kto vy?
PETRUSHKA: Ne uznala, kak budto. Ya tutoshnii . . .
        Ya Petrukha, syn Farnos,
        Mirovoi ya est′ kolos.
MAMZEL′:   No u vas est′ krasnyi nos.
PETRUSHKA: Nos kak nos, nu kak chto zh. [*Khochet obnyat′*] Nu-ka, frantsuzhinka, dozvol′te flirtanut′.
MAMZEL′:   Ekh, ostav′te, moveton.   (TP 150)

(MAMZELLE: Mon dieu, mon dieu. What an 'orrible cavalier.
PETRUSHKA: Pardonnay-mooa, dingdongbelle-mamzelle. [*Tries to embrace her*]
MAMZELLE: 'Ands off! 'Oo are you?
PETRUSHKA: I'm Petrushka, Farnos' son,
        World Colossus number one.
MAMZELLE: Eek! Your nose! Red like ze sun!
PETRUSHKA: Handsome is as handsome's done. [*Tries to embrace her*] Come on, Frog lady; let's flirt.
MAMZELLE: Eee! Hands off, canaille!)

The agitprop puppet plays were written as part of a movement which had a paternalist attitude towards the masses; in the texts themselves this level of paternalism is supported by a secondary level: the domination of women by men is advocated. The militaristic overtones of the propaganda movement, the emphasis on 'class war', reduced women to their traditional role in wars: that of support. When allowed a place in the movement forward their task was to be useful; when, as in these puppet plays, they supported the forces of reaction, they were likewise perceived as accessories or tools.[50]

Paternalism was also manifest in a second type of puppet-play adaptation – that done for children, rather than adults. Here, too, there was a tendency to tone down the carnival qualities of the text, though for slightly different reasons. The violence of the text was the most perturbing element for Simonovich-Efimova:

Petrushka kills the Doctor with blows of his stick. The Musician assures him that now he'll be sent to gaol. But Petrushka slings the Doctor over his shoulder and shouts: 'Who'll buy my potatoes? My fine potatoes?' Then Petrushka kills the Policeman with a well-aimed blow on the forehead, then he kills the Musician by banging him several times on the nape of the neck.

Of course, all this is scenically impressive and even classically simple (I'm not joking), but I cannot force my hand or my tongue to perform this sort of thing in front of children.[51]

The fact that children might actually *like* smut and unpleasantness is something which Simonovich-Efimova does not recognise; she adopts an attitude of protection. But, at another level, her scruples are understandable. In the context of the street, carnival violence is fluid; it may even be frivolous; in its ambivalence any 'message' is cancelled out. If, however, the text is integrated into a new context, where it is seen as having pedagogical uses and moral messages, the violence takes on new meaning. The text must then be seen as not only condoning but advocating physical force. The changes advocated by Simonovich-Efimova were further-reaching than those made in the agitprop plays for adults, but her promptings were more humane.

In fact, her puppet plays, and other Soviet versions made for children, bowdlerised the texts much in the manner of certain of the printed editions of *Petrushka* at the turn of the century. The traditional scenes, where used, have been transformed and made more genteel. The following scene between Petrushka and the Gypsy comes from a play by Yu. Gaush, *Petrushka's Name Day (Imeniny Petrushki)*. It is a good piece of writing for the puppet theatre: the lines are short and punchy, and there are several good jokes. The Gypsy's description of his wretched horse is a particularly good version in the traditional mould:

TSYGAN: Kupi loshadku.
          Ne budet zhalko.
          Glaza – vkos',
          Ushi – vroz,
          Khvost – truboi,
          Nogi – dugoi.
PETRUSHKA: Eto po chasti krasoty.
          A kak naschet bystroty?   (Tarasov 99)

(GYPSY: Buy my fine pony,
          You'll have no cause for moaning.
          Eyes – squint,
          Ears – lop,

> Legs – bent,
> Tail – flop.
> PETRUSHKA: Right, she's a looker, it's true.
> But can she run too?)

But the sting has been taken out of the scene. The humour, attractive as it is, would pass the most stringent tests of decency, and carnival elements of physicality and violence have been removed. At the end of the scene, the traditional murder of the Gypsy has been replaced by a rather feeble joke about the horse, which turns out to be a donkey, and a babyish fight over whose it is:

> PETRUSHKA: Khoroshii kon', krasivyi ... A zachem on pokhozh na osla?
> TSYGAN: Nu chto-zh!
>   Na osla pokhozh
>   I ty, i ya!
> OSEL: I-a! I-a!
> PETRUSHKA: Loshadka moya!
> TSYGAN: Net, moya!
> OSEL: I-a! I-a!   (Tarasov 100)

> (PETRUSHKA: A very pretty pony! But looks like a donkey!
> GYPSY: Like a donkey?
>   Why, so do we,
>   You and me!
> DONKEY: Ee-yore-ee!
> PETRUSHKA: Give her to me!
> GYPSY: No, me!
> DONKEY: Ee-yore-ee!)

The Gypsy's lies about the horse's speed have been turned into moral advice about food:

> TSYGAN: Ezda –
>   Khot' kuda.
>   Vse delo –
>   Eda!
>   Ovsa ne dash' ei, –
>   Bezhit rys'yu cherepash'ei;
>   Bol'she davai –
>   Bezhit, kak tramvai;
>   A korm obil'nyi –
>   Khod avtomobil'nyi.   (Tarasov 100)

> (GYPSY: She can run
>   Like a bullet from a gun.
>   If you want her fleet,

Give her enough to eat!
If she gets no corn,
She'll crawl like a worm;
Give her some more,
Like a tram she'll roar,
More than that again,
She'll go faster than a train.)

In two plays written by Simonovich-Efimova, *Merry Petrushka* (*Veselyi Petrushka*) and *Petrushka is Ill* (*Bol'noi Petrushka*), and in Marshak's play for children, *Petrushka the Foreigner* (*Petrushka-inostranets*), the emphasis is different. In all three, Petrushka retains a shadow of his old antisocial spirit. Efimova's hero is greedy, cowardly and lazy; at the end of the play he celebrates his various successes with a song in praise of eating:

Vot ya i ozhil!
I chut' do bedy ne dozhil.
Tram-tram-trushki,
El vatrushki,
Tram-tram-trom,
S tvorogom![52]

(So I got away!
Nearly my unlucky day!
Tram-tram-try!
I ate a pie!
Tram-tram-tried!
With cheese inside!)

There is a comic scene in which Petrushka is visited by the doctor and, on being asked the source of his pain, mentions an archetypally carnivalesque part of his body – the belly. As in Utenkov's play, though, he displays uncharacteristic reticence, saying 'Excuse me if my language is coarse.'

Efimova's plays, and Marshak's version, have considerable charm as texts for small children. But all of them trivialise Petrushka's antisocial tendencies; he not only loses his spouse and his *dubinka*, but is transformed from a dangerously uncooperative adult into a naughty but finally tractable child. In Marshak's version the quintessence of Petrushka's rebellion is his refusal to go to school:

Sumku shkol'nuyu svoyu
Ya nadenu na svin'yu.[53]

(My school-bag is much too big,
I will hang it on a pig.)

An interesting oddity in the history of *Petrushka* for children was the puppet theatre organised by a Frenchwoman, Henriette Pascar, in Moscow in the 1920s. She says of her Petrushka:

Perhaps he was less cynical, less of a fighter, but he showed more verve and *esprit* in the speeches which his new function of Prologue assigned to him.[54]

In fact, the passages quoted by Pascar indicate that Petrushka had developed a poetic turn of phrase and that little humour remained, let alone carnival humour, save for a few tiresome eccentricities, such as a dialogue between a hick from the sticks and a St Petersburg bourgeois – 'Is Rostov a big town? – Don't know, never measured it', and on and on in the same vein.[55]

The assault on rural folklore after the Revolution in some ways parallels the assault on *Petrushka*, above all in the exploitation of traditions of violence and conflict to new ends.[56] But there are interesting differences, as well as similarities. Despite a declaration of intent to use it for propaganda purposes made by Lenin in 1918, rural folklore was much less popular with the agitprop supporters of the 1920s; perturbation was caused by suspicions that it reflected the ideology of the ruling classes. In the 1930s, on the other hand, as the agitprop theatre groups were disbanded, village folklore acquired a new importance. Its active bearers were now considered 'moulders of the minds ... who had to propagate those ideas believed to have special significance during certain periods'.[57] The genres encouraged were, with the exception of the *chastushka*, all heroic: the *skaz*, *bylina*, *novina*; and in them technological progress and notable events of Soviet history were hymned.[58] Besides acting as a repository of the right sort of oral history, these genres had a secondary function: to make it clear that the new village of collectivised agriculture, the *kolkhoz*, was part of Russian tradition, that there was no discontinuity between it and age-old village custom. Since the 1930s the status of rural folklore has remained high; the artefacts of a fantasy Russian village past, the lacqueur spoons, carved bears, print shawls and painted boxes are reproduced in hundreds, whilst song and dance troupes dressed in pastel peasant costume give polished performances to traditional material. No such encouragement is given to 'low' rural genres, offensive to moral and aesthetic criteria alike.[59]

The transformation of popular entertainment in the Soviet Union was analogous to the development of propaganda described by Peter Kenez: like the latter process, it worked by a relegation of opposition to certain demarcated areas; the control and orchestration of opposition then acted as a precondition for the development of a far harsher set of restrictive practices. Like the development of propaganda, the transformation of popular culture was based on 'an unwillingness to believe that the people want what they profess to want'.[60] As with propaganda, too, there is a danger that a condemnation of this process will fall into the same paternalist attitudes as the process itself, and will fail to recognise that members of the subordinate classes do not always treasure the past in the way that enlightened intellectuals feel that they ought.[61] I believe that I have avoided this danger here, however, for my regret that the true text of *Petrushka* has vanished is anti-conservative rather than protectionist: it is a regret for the anti-conservatism of the text. The carnival, we have seen, opposes itself to the authoritarian rule of high literature, and the attempts to make Petrushka into an exemplar of the Romantic artist seem incongruous and on occasion actually comic. But the carnival is equally opposed to political authoritarianism. The Soviet critic Smirnova describes a revolting-sounding *Petrushka* of 1918, in which Petrushka was a lackey of the White Russians. She is rightly contemptuous.[62] But Petrushka the ward orderly, Petrushka the Pioneer leader are almost as contemptible, and equally as preposterous. Like the literary adaptations discussed in chapter 4, the agitprop plays failed to recognise that, as Dana Polan puts it, 'Popular culture, as Bakhtin invokes it and as it operates today, is a complex form that is accessible to logocentrism and monologism only at the cost of critical reduction.'[63] Where the high literary adaptations reduced the ambivalent, many-layered action of *Petrushka* to a ritual drama of private suffering, the political plays reduced it to a crude representational satire.

I am not arguing in general against adapting *Petrushka*. Any enthusiast of the show would rather have it used as it was in the 1920s than inviolate in the sense that it is not performed at all, which is the situation at present. Also, there are elements in the traditional show which will not bear performance today: its racism and sexism would be offensive. But any such modernisation must work from within. In the Soviet Union during the 1920s, by contrast, the changes were imposed from outside, by educated authors who had little experience of or respect for the orally transmitted puppet theatre, except as a vehicle for a political message alien to it. In Britain, France and Italy much more successful innovations have been made by those who have come to the traditional glove-puppet theatre from inside, as operators and improvisors. They have heeded one guideline: the subsidiary characters and the puppet hero's adversaries may be modernised, but the protagonist must remain unchanged, or the text becomes unrecognisable.

The second essential of modernisation is that the carnival elements should be recognised and respected. The carnival tradition is naturally aggressive and subversive; it is drama for independent adults, who are treated as equals with the puppeteer, not patronised and hectored. It is drama which engages with authoritarian political or literary discourse. The Russian agitprop puppet theatre, unlike its street counterpart, and unlike, for example, Gary Friedman's *Puns en Doedie* shows in South Africa today,[64] used *Petrushka* not to disturb, but to teach, as a herald of the new Reformation. Ignoring the aggressively subversive aspects of the text, such as its hostility to authority, it imitated instead its aggressively conservative qualities; the hero's power is unchallenged, and women and certain ethnic groups are subject to at least as much oppression in these plays as in the street tradition. There is no agitprop adaptation in which Petrushka's traditional victims give as good as they get, in the manner of Percy Press' *Judy Femme Fatale: or The Boot on the Other Foot*, in which Judy has the better of Punch; or of Lorca's *Don Cristóbal*, in which the priapic hero's wife has quintuplets by different lovers and causes him to burst with apoplectic rage.[65]

The disappearance of *Petrushka* in its street form illustrates some of the deep divisions and paradoxes underlying Soviet official culture. The instrumental view of culture held by Lenin and other Bolsheviks, according to which it was 'the opposite of backwardness, a combination of a certain economic well-being, industrial and technical accomplishments, modern attitudes to the problems of existence, and certain very basic intellectual accomplishments',[66] was unaccommodating to popular culture; 'backward' genres were eradicated. The fate of *Petrushka* is now to appear, if at all, in occasional museum-style performances, 'ethnographic concerts', as Obraztsov put it. The street theatre is no more; to quote Obraztsov again, speaking prophetically in 1927:

That art has vanished, the art serving a sector of the population for whom its disappearance meant the disappearance of *all* art, since they knew no other.[67]

Yet despite this, popular culture retained a central, symbolic place in the official tradition, which 'does not want to lose its hegemony over the popular classes and which to exercise this hegemony better, accommodates part of proletarian ideology'.[68] The merry reversals of the carnival, the comic violence of the street shows, were adapted by Stalinism, as Bakhtin hints, into the grotesqueries of the Terror; though such extremes are past, references to the popular tradition have often been used, and are sometimes still used, to legitimate the darker phenomena of Soviet society: misogyny, racism and political violence.[69]

Conclusion

With the final sightings of the authentic street *Petrushka* in the mid-1930s this study comes to an end. I have traced *Petrushka*'s path from its origins, showing how the puppet comedy, arriving from Italy between 1810 and 1840, quickly became naturalised, so that by 1870 it was accepted everywhere as the voice of the urban subordinate classes, and by 1880 people no longer believed in its foreign origin. Like Gaer, the *commedia dell'arte* character of the eighteenth century, Petrushka was well suited to express the frustrations of the rapidly changing life in Russian towns, but, unlike him, he was firmly rooted in the nineteenth century. In *Petrushka* we see how the elements of carnival, as defined by Bakhtin, altered and adapted themselves in the conditions of industrialising Russia, and how they reflected the developing capitalist system there. But at the same time *Petrushka*, partly because of its association with the temporary, unusual conditions of the carnivals and feasts, was never reducible to a picture of reality; it was a complex and many-layered phenomenon, defiant of attempts to give it a final classification.

Imitating many Russian migrant workers, Petrushka went from the town into the villages, where he showed off what he had learned in St Petersburg ('Peter'), and where he was adopted by fairground showmen living in the country. Occasionally the urban *Petrushka* shows, too, were affected by this migration, and absorbed elements from the rural shows, such as the *vertep*, though this seems to have been rarer. But wherever he was, whether called Petrushka or Van'ka, the hero of the Russian glove-puppet theatre remained a carnival figure: lumpy-bodied and never at a loss for crude joke. Throughout the nineteenth century, his clowning broke taboos, poked fun at figures of authority, ridiculed morality and decency, and was tolerated by officialdom only because it was understood that the reversals were temporary, that the rebellion would end with the carnival. Opposition came not only from repressive paternalism, but from enlightened paternalism as well; it was increasingly felt that shows like *Petrushka* threatened the commitment to education and the edifying ideals of high culture which were shared by observers on all sides of the political spectrum.[1]

After the Revolution, the street Petrushka's anti-authoritarian spirit continued as before: the disruptive attacks were now made on representatives of Soviet authority: the traditional Soldier was replaced by the Red Army Soldier, the Policeman by the Soviet Militsioner. But the official attitude to *Petrushka* changed. There was now a much more effective drive towards education, and the show, like other popular genres, was tolerated as long as it appeared to be an effective instrument in this. When repressive paternalism surfaced, it, too, took a more effective form; Soviet power could not tolerate even temporary and symbolic opposition from the subordinate classes, whose support was its basic legitimisation. The rising intolerance to *Petrushka* paralleled events after the French Revolution, when the street hero Polichinelle was solemnly executed on the guillotine:

The puppet theatre now came into conflict with the new leaders. This conflict is extremely characteristic, for it reveals the class antagonism existing between the victorious bourgeoisie and the broad masses of the people. Previously the revolutionary bourgeoisie had been Polichinelle's supporters.   (TP 34)

So wrote Orest Tsekhnovitser in 1927, in words that are heavy with irony for today's reader, for they describe just as accurately how, after the Soviet Revolution, *Petrushka* was first castrated, then suppressed altogether.

The fate of *Petrushka* illustrates that it is not only high culture which was subject to restructuring according to Socialist Realist tenets in the 1930s. Popular culture, too, was re-shaped, its prickly anti-authoritarianism smoothed out. The genres unsuitable for the voicing of carefully orchestrated and permissible protest vanished. Subversive cultural activities vanished indoors, to the clandestine sing-songs of obscene *chastushki* at weddings or the swapping of political anecdotes at home. Mass entertainment was made safe and respectable, and, as it was now organised for, rather than by, the masses, popular creativity was now confined to the level of interpretation. It was possible for the watchers, as with nineteenth-century mass spectacles, to deliberately misunderstand what was put before them; but such misunderstandings and misreadings had to be kept private, and so one can only speculate about them.

There were changes in academic disciplines connected with popular culture too. After the Revolution there was, at first, a great deal of freedom to collect material; under Stalin both collection and commentary were subject to restraint. The attentions of collectors and scholars began to be focused on ritual genres (for example, the proto-dramatic rites of villages) which reflected the aspirations of the state to secure itself by ritual;[2] if carnival genres were discussed, they were presented as political satires redundant in a new society where conflicts had been resolved and consensus achieved. Though the first stage of de-Stalinisation led to modifications, these meant that de-politicised folklore studies were now possible, not that there was a re-examination of the political principles to which folklorists had formerly been forced to conform. *Petrushka* was now taken out of any specific historical or social context, and transformed into material for academic investigation. Righteous horror of 'vulgar sociologism', the crude class-based analysis which meant that according to one account rooms containing French Impressionist and post-Impressionist paintings were signposted 'the taste of the industrial bourgeoisie' (Monet and Cezanne) 'the taste of the small bourgeoisie' (Van Gogh)[3], has led to an avoidance of class-based analysis of any cultural material. Nor has a self-conscious attitude to popular culture been developed. The collecting of folkloric and ethnographic material is still carried out by large groups of outsiders who descend on bemused villagers with notebooks, and who neither make attempts to blend in, nor to analyse what disruption their presence might cause.[4]

The process by which *Petrushka* was neutered reflects more than Stalinist and post-Stalinist cultural manipulation, however. The ideals propagated by the early Soviet cultural hierarchy, education and high culture for everyone, go deep. Popular culture seems threatening, and is widely mistrusted: a mistrust which undercuts the conventional polarisation of 'official' and 'unofficial' Soviet literature. The proponent of Soviet official culture, the puppeteer Obraztsov, and the *émigré* Elagin alike saw the street Petrushka as a sinister hooligan, 'an anarchic boot-boy', though one read him as a danger to Soviet propriety, the other as a symbol of all that is worst in Soviet life.[5]

The fetishisation of high culture extends even to counter-cultural genres, at any rate those intended for public performance. The Soviet rock-song expresses its protest in the devices and language of high culture, and adopts a viewpoint above the crowd and the marketplace:

Kak legko reshit', chto ty slab,
Chtoby mir izmenit',
Opustit' nad krepost'yu flag
I vorota otkryt'.
Pust' tolpa voidet v gorod tvoi,
Pust' tsvety oborvet,
I tebya v sumatokhe lyudskoi
Tam nikto ne naidet.[6]

(It's easy to think you're too weak
To alter the world,
To lower your flag at the castle peak
And fling the gates wide.
Let the mob come into your town,
Let them tear up the flowers
In the fuss and din of the crowd,
You'll never be found.)

It is doubtful whether *glasnost'* can bring back the *glas* (voice) of Petrushka; he is too remote from current Soviet life. If the pedestrian-isation of central urban areas such as the Arbat in Moscow, the relaxation of administrative regulations, and the new tolerance of freelance economic activities, do bring back professional street per-

22.   Buskers in Moscow, December 1988. Photographed by Ian Thompson.

formers to European Russia, they are more likely to be inspired by the street spectacles of Western Europe than by the nearly forgotten shows of the first third of this century.[7] Even given the social and political changes, there would remain cultural obstacles to a revival of subversive popular entertainment. There is still widespread lack of understanding and contempt for such phenomena amongst many intellectuals, whatever their political standpoint. A Soviet journalist has described London buskers as beggars who practise extortion accompanied by threatening behaviour.[8] The liberalisation of fiction and the arts has so far led simply to a revival of nineteenth-century stereotypes of 'social exploration', the subordinate classes as Dostoevskian 'poor people' observed by an external narrative voice, rather than to a recognition of cultural autonomy.[9] It remains to be seen whether the recent, and continuing, cultural reforms can counter one of the more dubious side-effects accompanying the building of the glossy, monolithic edifice of Soviet culture: the fact that cultural protest, in the dominant Russian-speaking milieu, has, for all the populist dress of some of its forms, become an intellectual occupation; not the shout of the crowd or collective, but the voice crying in the wilderness.[10]

Appendix A

Petrushka, alias *Van'ka-Ratatui*: text in translation

The following is a complete translation of the text in Berkov's anthology, pp. 113–23. It was collected by the schoolteacher L. K. Rozenberg on 19 April 1902 from the *meshchanin* (member of a Russian estate including traders, craftsmen, workers) Aleksey Pavlovich Lashchenko, of Maikop. My translation below is, so far as I know, the first translation of an authentic street version of Petrushka into English. The Russian *mus'e* (a corruption of the French 'monsieur') has, following the original, been translated in several different ways to accommodate rhymes.

Scene I

Off-stage, from somewhere down below, a loud, jangling cry can be heard: 'A-o-o-o-o-u! Ha-ha-ha!' Then Petrushka emerges, dressed in a red peasant shirt, velveteen trousers and knee-high patent boots. He is wearing a dunce's cap.

PETRUSHKA [*bowing to the public*]: Good day to you, ladies and gents! It's me here . . . Petrushka-mooseer, come to amuse you all: young and old, small and tall!
[*Sings*]:

> I'm Petrushka, I am,
> What a merry lad I am!
> I drink wine without measure,
> I'm always singing and ready for pleasure,
> Tra-la-la! Tra-la-la-la-la!
> Ha-ha-ha! Ha-ha-ha!

So you see what sort of Petrushka I am! Eh! [*smiting his forehead*] I've gorn an' forgotten. Petrushka, yes, Petrushka, but what's my nickname? Ra-ta-tui? you hear? Ra-ta-tui! [*Laughs. He sits down on the edge of the booth and thumps it with his hand*] Here, Musician!

217

Scene 2

MUSICIAN: What's this, Petrushka?

PETRUSHKA: I've got some news for you.

MUSICIAN: What?

PETRUSHKA: I've decided to get married, mate. A bachelor's life is no life for me! No-one gives me a bit of respect . . . But when I get married and get my hands on the dowry . . . oh, then I'll live the life of Riley!

MUSICIAN: Who are you marrying then, Petrushka?

PETRUSHKA: A merchant's daughter. [*He says the name of the richest merchant or landowner thereabouts*]

MUSICIAN: Getting a big dowry, are you?

PETRUSHKA: Ee-ee-ee! Worth more than I am!

MUSICIAN: Petrushka, you're lying. She won't marry you, no way, she'll only lead you astray. You'll spend your last groat and more, and they'll tan your hide raw. Chuck it!

PETRUSHKA: No mate, *you're* lying! She'll fall in love with me for sure, since I'm so handsome! [*preens himself*]

MUSICIAN: Well, show me your bride then.

PETRUSHKA: I can manage that, it's not hard. I'll go get her now and show her to you. [*Goes off-stage and brings out another puppet*] Have a look, Musician, pretty, isn't she?

MUSICIAN: Well she's pretty enough . . . but snub-nosed.

PETRUSHKA: Musician, you're lying! Just look at her button eyes! Her rosebud mouth! What hands! What lips! What a neck! You'll not find her equal, I bet! And just wait till you see her dance! Play a bit of a tune now, will you! [*The Musician plays a* Kamarinskaya *(Russian dance). Petrushka and his bride dance*]

MUSICIAN: Well, that's all fine and dandy, but it'll cost you a pretty penny. A rich toffee-nosed bride who'll never walk when she can ride . . . You must buy a horse, mate . . .

PETRUSHKA [*anxiously*]:   And where do you get one of those?

MUSICIAN: Off the gypsies, of course.

PETRUSHKA [*grandly*]:   Well, bring me the horse today, then!

MUSICIAN: You're no gent yourself, *you* go and get it.

PETRUSHKA: So you won't fetch it?

Scene 3 [*The same and the Gypsy, a puppet dressed in Gypsy costume with a whip in his belt*]

GYPSY [*bowing*]:   Good day to you, Petrushka monseer!

PETRUSHKA: Good day yourself, Pharoah's by-blow! Get on with it, say your say and get out, 'fore I give you a clout!

GYPSY: Petrushka monseer, they say you need a horse.

PETRUSHKA: A horse, eh? Yes, yes, yes! Got a good one, have you?

GYPSY: The highest class of horse! No tail or mane, of course . . .

PETRUSHKA [*interrupting*]:   So what, no tail or mane? that's only decoration! It's got a head, I suppose?

GYPSY: A head's about all she *has* got – or actually, at the moment, not! It's at the vet's repair shop.

PETRUSHKA: And what colour is she?

GYPSY: Grey.

PETRUSHKA: And is she good-tempered?

GYPSY: Very: downhill she rushes and tumbles, uphill she crawls and stumbles. And if she falls in the mud, then you'd better try getting her out yourself as best you may: she'll not get up herself, no way. She dosen't trot either; barely puts one foot in front of the other.

PETRUSHKA: Ha-ha-ha! That's my horse! Just right for me and my bride! The ladies are so timid, and if the horse has no head, she'll be all the quieter for that! [*To the Gypsy*] Well, go and get her, then.
[*Gypsy goes off-stage*]

PETRUSHKA: Eh, Musician!

MUSICIAN: What?

PETRUSHKA: How much should I give him for the horse?

MUSICIAN: Hum – fifteen roubles or so.

PETRUSHKA: That's too dear. I'll beat him down, just you see.

Scene 4

[*Gypsy enters, leading the horse*]

PETRUSHKA: There's a fine horse! Ooh-ooh-ooh! How much do you want for her, then?

GYPSY: Two hundred roubles.

PETRUSHKA: That's a bit dear . . . I'll give you a lick with my big thick stick, and a rub-a-dub-dub with my club on the neck and the lug.

GYPSY: Give me some more, Petrushka moosieur, to buy the kids some bacon fat.

PETRUSHKA: Not satisfied with that? Well, I'll bring you a down payment, then. [*Goes out, brings back his club straightway, goes up to the Gypsy from behind and whacks him on the head*] Here's the down payment! Here's the down payment! [*The Gypsy runs off, leaving the horse behind*]

Scene 5 [*The same, minus the Gypsy*]

PETRUSHKA: Listen, Musician, nice horse, eh?

MUSICIAN: Nice enough, just long in the tooth.

PETRUSHKA: You're lying! Hang on, hang on, whilst I work out how to get the saddle on. [*Mounts the horse. It bucks. Petrushka lets out a yell*] Whoah! Whoah! Who-oah! Who-oah there! ... [*He falls off*] Fetch me a doctor! I've killed meself!

Scene 6 [*The same. Doctor enters, dressed all in black and with an enormous pair of glasses*]

DOCTOR [*to audience*]:   I'm the doctor, the baker and undertaker from Kuznetsky Most, the veterinary and apothecary. When sick gents arrive I always keep them alive; I show 'em what to do, instead of quinine I give them a grain of arsenic or two ... They bring me people on their feet, and drag 'em away in a sheet. They come in carried, on a sledge to the graveyard they're ferried ...

PETRUSHKA: Oh Doctor, don't kill me; don't sent me away on a hurdle, let me not be a sledge's burden ... send me away in a hansom, I'll pay you a king's ransom.

DOCTOR: Well then, tell me where it hurts, show me!

PETRUSHKA: Just here.

DOCTOR: Here?

PETRUSHKA: Lower.

DOCTOR: Here?

PETRUSHKA: Higher.

DOCTOR: Here?

PETRUSHKA: Lower.

DOCTOR: Here?

PETRUSHKA: Higher.

DOCTOR: One minute lower, one minute higher! Get up, idiot, and show me yourself! [*Takes him by the ear*]

PETRUSHKA [*jumps up*]:   Ah! Um! Most grateful ... Feel better already!

DOCTOR: Well, now you can pay me for curing your ailment!

PETRUSHKA: My compliments too ... but why?

DOCTOR: You know perfectly well: because I cured you!

PETRUSHKA: All right then. A moment or two, I'll bring you your due. [*Goes out and brings in his stick*] You won't get off scot-free either from *me*, Doctor, I'll give you your pay in my own special way. [*Hits him over the head. Doctor runs. Petrushka goes after him. Doctor runs off-stage, and Petrushka follows him*]

Scene 7

[*Musician plays a waltz. The German comes on and dances. Petrushka enters.*]

PETRUSHKA: Musician, what kind of creature is this?

MUSICIAN: It's a Frog, Petrushka monseer.

PETRUSHKA: What does he want here?

MUSICIAN: No idea. Ask him yourself.

PETRUSHKA: What should I say to him?

MUSICIAN: Say: Bon jour!

PETRUSHKA: [*to the German*] Bon jour!

GERMAN: [*gives him a silent bow*]

PETRUSHKA: Why isn't he saying anything?

MUSICIAN: He's a German.

PETRUSHKA: A German? Deutch, eh, are you, damn you! Well, how did you get here?

GERMAN: Ei, ei, ei!

PETRUSHKA: Yes, you're I and I'm I too, that makes two of us! Will you stop gobbling like a gander and talk like a Yaroslav man, eh?

GERMAN: Wa-a-as?

PETRUSHKA: Kvas? There's no kvas here. Get away will you, we don't want to know you. [*Shoves German away*] Musician! Has the German gone off to drink some kvas?

MUSICIAN: No, Petrushka monsewer, he said 'I'll just bring you back some liqueur'.

PETRUSHKA: Well, that's all right. I'll just sit down here for the moment and sing a song. [*He sits down and, whacking his hands on the top of the booth, sings*]:

> Little birdy, where've you been?
> Drinking vodka on the green.
> I had one glass, I had two,
> Head began to ache right through.

[*The German comes in and whacks Petrushka with a stick. Petrushka grabs hold of his head. 'Ow-yow-yow! What's all this?'*]

MUSICIAN: It's only a gnat bite.

PETRUSHKA: What the hell do you mean, a gnat bite, don't be daft, it was more like a whack from a shaft!

MUSICIAN: Pay no attention, Petrushka, sing your song.

PETRUSHKA:

> Little birdy, where've you been?
> Drinking vodka on the green.
> I had one glass, I had two,
> Head began to ache right through.

[*The German comes in and hits him on the head again. Petrushka turns round in a flash and flings himself on the German. A fight starts, and Petrushka gets the better of it. He throws the German down on the top of the booth and makes the man run his finger across his own throat, yelling, 'I'll slit your gullet!' Then he twists his face round and whacks his head on the barrier, repeating, 'I'll knock your teeth out ... knock your teeth out ... knock your teeth out !' Then he sits astride him and bounces up and down. The German doesn't stir. Petrushka lays his ear to the German's chest a few times and finally decides that he has had it.*]

PETRUSHKA: Musician, the German's drunk.

MUSICIAN: What do you mean, drunk? He's bought it.

PETRUSHKA: Who bought him? He came here all by himself.

MUSICIAN: He's bought it, I told you.

PETRUSHKA: You've killed him? Well, get rid of him, then.

MUSICIAN: No, no! *You* killed him, *you* get rid of him.

PETRUSHKA: There's nothing for it, I'll have to go and get the nuns. [*To the Musician*] Play a Kamarinskaya, will you. We're burying the German! [*Goes off*]

Scene 8

[*Two Nuns come in. They pick up the body of the dead German and wrap it in a shroud. Then they bow to the public and go off to fetch a coffin*]

Scene 9

[*Petrushka comes in*]

MUSICIAN: Why are you so sad, Petrushka?

PETRUSHKA: Oh, Musician, there's no money to bury the German.

MUSICIAN: Ask the ladies and gents, then. Maybe they'll give you something for the funeral.

PETRUSHKA: Ooh yes, that's true! Here, take this plate, and do the rounds.

[*Musician takes the plate and goes round collecting from the public*]

PETRUSHKA [*bowing and scraping*]: Ladies and gentlemen! Give us

your pennies to bury the German! He happened to run across
Petrushka from Yaroslavl and bit off more than he could chew and . . .
choked to death!
[*Musician gives what he has collected to Petrushka*]
PETRUSHKA: Oho! That'll do for the wake as well as the funeral!
[*The Nuns bring in the coffin. They pick up the German and start to
measure him. The coffin turns out to be too short and too wide. They
measure three times and pause to consider. Then they grab the German,
bend him up and fold him in three, and stuff him in the coffin. One of the
Nuns bends down low to check whether the deceased is lying comfort-
ably. The other is distracted and doesn't notice; banging down the lid of
the coffin, she catches her friend's head in it. The first Nun screams at
the top of her voice and struggles for all she is worth to get free. When
at length she succeeds, she attacks her careless friend. Finally they carry
out the coffin to the sounds of the* Kamarinskaya.]

Scene 10

PETRUSHKA [*runs in bending and kicking his legs and clapping his hands
in time to the music and yells*]: Musician! Musician! I've buried that
Schweinhund of a German . . . Cost three roubles . . . Has anyone
been looking for me here?
MUSICIAN: An officer was here looking for you.
PETRUSHKA: What did he want with me?
MUSICIAN: He said he was going to take you off to the army 'cause of
you killing the German.
PETRUSHKA [*in tears*]: O-o-o-oh! Tell him Petrushka's not here.
Musician, say he's gone off to Moscow to learn some more songs.

Scene 11

[*The Corporal comes in and whacks Petrushka over the head*
PETRUSHKA [*grabbing his head*]: Help, help!
CORPORAL: What are you yelling and bawling for, not letting decent
folks have a moment's peace? [*Hits him*]
PETRUSHKA: Help!!! Police!!! Musician, why aren't you helping me?
MUSICIAN: Petrushka monseer, it's that Corporal I was telling you
about.
PETRUSHKA: To hell with him! What does he want?
MUSICIAN: He's going to teach you to be a soldier.
PETRUSHKA: Ow-yow-yow! What do you want?

MUSICIAN: I'm taking you off to the army.

PETRUSHKA: I'm no use.

CORPORAL: Why not?

PETRUSHKA: I've got a hump.

CORPORAL: Where is it, then?

PETRUSHKA: It's there, up the spout, like a hut on the mount.

CORPORAL: What's this rot you're blethering? I'll teach you what to do. You'll be an army man.

PETRUSHKA: What do you mean, I'll be a barmy man?

CORPORAL: Trying to be funny, are you? [*hits him*]

PETRUSHKA [*seizing his head*]:   Ow-yow-yow! What shall I do now? I've gone to pot with my head and my hat and my tassel and all! Musician, go instead of me!

MUSICIAN: How much will you give me?

PETRUSHKA: A couple of kopecks, and a whack on the neck!

MUSICIAN: Well, you're no gent yourself, you'll do your stint!

CORPORAL: Do as I say! Say – One!

PETRUSHKA: Say – One!

CORPORAL [*beating him*]:   Don't repeat it! Say – One!

PETRUSHKA: One!

CORPORAL: Two!

PETRUSHKA: Two!

CORPORAL: Three!

PETRUSHKA: How much?

CORPORAL: This much! [*hits him*]

PETRUSHKA: Go to hell, you and your lesson!

CORPORAL: Say – One!

PETRUSHKA: One!

CORPORAL: Two!

PETRUSHKA: Two!

CORPORAL: Three!

PETRUSHKA: Four!

CORPORAL: One! Two! Three! [*hitting him each time*] Take this gun!

PETRUSHKA: This ain't no gun, is it? It's a club!

CORPORAL: Belt up, animal! Ri-ight turn!

[*Petrushka takes a swipe with the rifle and hits the Corporal*]

CORPORAL: What do you think you're doing? [*hits him*]

PETRUSHKA: I tripped.

CORPORAL: I'll give you tripped! ... Listen! Right, left, march!

PETRUSHKA [*takes the rifle in both hands, and hits the Corporal, repeating*]:   And ri-ight, and le-eft! And ri-ight, and le-eft! Take that!

[*The Corporal runs out, Petrushka goes after him*]

Scene 12

PETRUSHKA: So, Musician, I've put paid to the Corporal and been to his funeral! Now I'm a free man! Ha-ha-ha! That's my Petrushka! Found a nice wife, ended the German's life, bought a fine mare and seen the Corporal to his bier! Now I'll sing a song.
MUSICIAN: Go on, Petrushka, sing!
PETRUSHKA:

> A dog was walking in the cabbage patch,
> It curled its tail into an *o*
> And made a dash ...
> I'll sing this song one more straight through ...

Good song eh, Musician?
MUSICIAN: Yes, it's a good song.
[*Petrushka sings the same song again. At that moment a Dog of impressive dimensions appears and seizes Petrushka's sleeve*]
PETRUSHKA [*yells*]:   Shoo! Shoo! I'm scared ... Shoo! Shoo!
[*The Dog goes off*]
PETRUSHKA: Hang on Musician, I'm going to get the stick.
[*Runs off and comes back with the stick*] Right, now we'll see! [*calls*] Here, Rover, Rover, Rover! Come here, Rover dear, woof woof woof! Rover ... grr, grr!
[*The Dog runs back on and leaps at Petrushka. Petrushka hits it on the head, but the Dog disarms him by taking away his stick. The Dog runs away.*]
PETRUSHKA: Rover, Rover, Rover, here!
[*The Dog appears*]
PETRUSHKA: Musician, will it bite me?
MUSICIAN: No, it's quite tame.
PETRUSHKA: [*goes up to the Dog gingerly and tries to stroke it*] Rover, Rover, Roverkins! Dog, Doggie, doggiekins! Bitchie, bitchie, bitchie, [*coming closer and closer*]
[*At that moment the Dog grabs Petrushka's head and starts to maul him. Petrushka gives despairing shrieks. The Dog drags him off-stage. Another person (a puppet dressed as a clown) rushes on and yells to the public*]:
CLOWN: That's all for now. Petrushka's been eaten by a bow-wow. One thing ends and another begins. Please come in, Petrushka will soon begin. You needn't pay right away if you prefer it that way ... We'll let you come in anyhow. If you don't buy a ticket outside you can pay inside ... We'll make it quits later! Ladies and gents, come in and watch our show! Five kopecks isn't much for three tons of fun! Come on in, come on in!

Appendix B
Legal regulation of popular entertainment

I: THE RUSSIAN EMPIRE*

(a) Legislation directly concerning popular entertainments

From the Statute on the Prevention and Curtailment of Crime, Section Three, Articles 128 ff [vol. xiv]

128. The police must keep vigilant surveillance that no disorders occur during public gatherings, processions, festivals and assemblies in public places and to this purpose, in necessary cases, the co-operation of the military is to be requested.
(from 8 April 1782)

129. The police is to ensure that on those ceremonial occasions when it is deemed proper to admit the decoration of public buildings by flags, only the Russian flag should be used....

(from 28 April 1833)
[omitted 130–134: on private entertainments]

135. It is forbidden, without the consent of the police, to organise, whether in towns or outside them, public games, amusements and theatrical performances.
(from 8 April 1782)

136. Abusive words or gestures disruptive to decency or which might cause harm to any person are not to be included in any public games, amusements, theatrical performances or songs.
(from 8 April 1782)

137. Boxing matches are forbidden.
(from 20 October 1684)

138. In any case where permission to organise games dependent on the use of force and physical daring and a specific level of skill, also amusements or theatrical performances, is requested, and if nothing is found contrary to law and to general or private interest, then the police shall give permission and shall specify the day and time for the event to begin.

---

* [*source: Svod zakonov Rossiiskoi Imperii*, edited by I. D. Mordukhay-Boltovsky, 21 vols., in 6 with index (St Petersburg 1912)]

(from 8 April 1782)

138(1) (acc. to Cont. of 1906) The Directorate of the Imperial Theatres in Petersburg and Moscow is granted an especial and exclusive right to print posters advertising plays, concerts, masquerades and every kind of performances, and likewise public entertainments and spectacles, with the exception of announcements, printed at the consent of the Town Governor of St Petersburg, relating to performances during Shrove and Easter Weeks.

(from 4 December 1873)

139. [On duty of amusement clubs to have a fund-raising event for charity once a year]

Supplement to Statute 139 (acc. to Cont. of 1906)

1. The Directorate of the Board of Institutions of the Empress Mariya is granted the exclusive right of exacting a supplementary revenue from spectacles and entertainments in all parts of the Empire excepting the *guberniyas* of the Warsaw General Governorship and of the Grand Duchy of Finland.

(from 5 May 1892)

2. Public spectacles and entertainments of all kinds where financial remuneration is demanded from the spectators (performances, concerts, balls and masquerades in all theatres, not excepting the Imperial Theatres, in circuses, clubs, gardens and other public places, trotting and flat races, etc.) shall be subject to payment of the above-mentioned revenue (para. 1 of this suppl.)

. . .

The revenue is exacted from entrance tickets to spectacles and entertainments and is paid by visitors to them, in supplement to the price of the tickets.

. . .

4. The sum of the revenue is to be defined as follows: for tickets costing less than 50 kopecks – not more than 2 kopecks, for tickets from 50 kopecks to 1 rouble – not more than 5 kopecks and for tickets of one rouble and more – not more than 10 kopecks per ticket. From tickets which give the right of entry to several persons (for boxes) or to several performances (by subscription), the revenue will be exacted according to the sums given above, according to the number of persons or number of performances respectively.

As above, para 4

140. The price of seats shall be determined with police permission. No one may demand entry without payment; and the performances shall begin at the stated hour without attending anyone.

(from 8 April 1782)

141. At public games and amusements the police shall ensure (1) that the place selected should be suitable [*prilichno*], and should not be the cause of danger or harm to anyone; (2) that all constructions should be stable, and that, should the games, amusements or theatrical performances take place within them, lanterns with candles or some other illumination be placed in the

boxes, gangways, on the stairs and at the entrance and exit doorways, and the doors be made to open outwards and not inwards; (3) that public swings should be of strong manufacture and none of them should be defective; and that ice-hills and roller-coasters should be enclosed by railings and should be safe.

(from 8 February 1752)

142. At public games, amusements and entertainments no-one must make noise, shout, speak loudly, interrupt the performance or hinder its execution, whether at the spot where the performance is taking place or up to a distance of 100 *sazhen* (216.9 m) away.

(from 8 April 1782)

143. At the place of performance or up to 100 *sazhen* away it is not permitted to engage in quarrels, rows or fights, to cause anyone offence or insult, to withdraw a dagger from its sheath, to use any firearm, to cast a stone or to fling powder or anything else which might cause injury, harm, loss or danger.

(from 8 April 1782)

144. The prevention of noise and any indecency at public spectacles and masquerades, whether these should take place in a theatre, or, with police permission, be given by a private individual for a certain sum of money in a dwelling-house, is entrusted to the surveillance of the police.

(from 22 December 1796)

145. (acc. to Cont. of 1906) All public amusements and entertainments, including theatrical performances, concerts, masquerades and other spectacles are forbidden: on Christmas Eve and Christmas Day, on the days preceding the Twelve Festivals and the Feast of the Beheading of St John the Baptist; during the first and fourth weeks of Lent and Holy Week, and also on the first day (Sunday) of the second week (Orthodoxy Week) and the Saturday of the third week of Lent, on Palm Sunday, on the first day of the Holy Feast of Easter and the feast days of the Elevation of the Lord's Crucifix and the Beheading of St John Baptist.

Statute on General Regulation of the Guberniyas, article 314 [vol. II]

(a) One of the most important duties of the Governors is to ensure, by every means at their disposal, the preservation of moral standards amongst the inhabitants of the *guberniyas* entrusted to them, supervising through the local authorities [*nachal'stva*] subject to them the full execution of the acting regulations for the prevention and curtailment not only of crimes but of profligacy, depravity, forbidden games and anything which might incite vicious tendencies and habits or encourage them amongst the people. (b) For this purpose, amongst other things, the governors are to instruct the local and district police that they should keep constant and vigilant watch on the preservation of order during public gatherings, celebrations, meetings at fairs, markets and other places of trade and at public entertainments, theatrical and other spectacles, finally also in taverns, drinking places and other institutions of this kind, and are to demand that every breach of this order, the more so all rowdiness and offensiveness should be brought to an end immediately by police and that those guilty should not escape the due processes of law. But, recalling to the subordinate police boards their duties in this and making where necessary special arrangements to increase surveillance by them, the Governors must on the other hand explain to them within what boundaries their surveillance lies, and in general the action of the police must be so constituted as to avoid measures excessively restrictive to the inhabitants and detrimental to the preservation of order (from 3 June 1837)

[*The Building Statute*, article 163 specified that 'temporary wooden theatres and circuses' might be up to 20 *sazhen* [42.68 m] in width and length, and that *balagans* 'for spectacles' might be up to 25 *sazhen* (53.35 m) in length and 8 *sazhen* (17.07 m) in length, measured inside the building; the gap between two *balagans* must be at least 10 *sazhen* (21.34 m)]

[vol. XII, part 1]

(b) miscellaneous pieces of legislation relevant to fairground and street theatre

[The Trade Statute, supplement to article 665 point 1 laid down that the Nizhnii-Novgorod fair might last no longer than 15 July to 10 September, if wares held out (14 July 1864); point 8 (2) states that those not entitled to vote for members or to be members of the organising board of the fair included proprietors of public entertainments and eateries.] [vol. XI, section 2]

The Statute on the Prevention and Curtailment of Crime, Section 3, Chapter 5: On Begging

159. It is strictly forbidden to beg or to live a life of vagrancy in towns or settlements [*posady* and *poselen'ya*], at fairs, high roads and trade routes for the purpose of extorting alms.
(from 30 November 1891)
159(1) (acc. to Suppl. of 1906) Gypsies are strictly forbidden to lead a nomadic existence whether in their registered place of residence or in other parts of the Empire, and they are also forbidden to dwell in camps in any place or to construct temporary dwellings in the form of pavillions or tents. Any Gypsies found to be in breach of this regulation will be deported under the supervision of the police to the place of their registration and will be subject to a two-year ban on movement and all temporary dwellings constructed by them and materials from which they are constructed will be destroyed under the supervision of the police.
(from 3 June 1894)
[The Statute on Punishments, art. 50, stated that the penalties for begging 'because of sloth and idleness' were up to one month's imprisonment in simple cases, up to three months' in cases where insulting behaviour had been used.
[vol. XV]]

II: THE SOVIET UNION

It is impossible to give more than an approximate account of legal measures under Soviet power; Soviet legal codices are much less full than their pre-revolutionary counterparts, exclude certain classified information, and give no historical overview of previous legislation resembling that to be found, for example, in Mordukhay-Boltovsky's code above. The following extracts can only give an outline of certain relevant legislation.

(a) various public order regulations

The Criminal Codex of the RSFSR, art. 79, 'Mass disorders' states that: 'The orgainisation of mass disorders accompanied by riots [*pogromy*], wanton damage, arson and other such acts, and also the actual execution of such acts by the participants in the above-mentioned crimes or armed insurrection against the authorities is punishable by a deprivation of liberty over a period of two to fifteen years.'

Art. 206 states that 'hooliganism' is punishable by up to a year's imprisonment or corrective labour; where it is aggravated, that is, 'distinguished in content by exceptional cynicism or especial offensiveness [*derzost'*]' the punishment rises to up to five years; if a weapon is used to from three to seven years.

[*Svod zakonov RSFSR*, VIII, pp. 576–7]

The code of the RSFSR on Breaches of Administrative Regulations; art. 158 'Minor hooliganism' states that 'minor hooliganism, that is the use of uncensored abuse in public places, insulting behaviour towards citizens and other such actions disruptive to public order and the peace and quiet of citizens' is punishable by a fine of 10–15 roubles, or corrective labour of 1–2 months with 20% of pay docked, or in special cases by 'administrative arrest' of up to fifteen days.

[*Svod zakonov RSRSR*, VIII, pp. 439]

'On the basic duties and rights of the Soviet Militia as regards public order and the struggle with crime' Article 1 States that: 'The Soviet Police is called upon to ensure the preservation of public order nationwide, and also of socialist property, the rights and legal interests of citizens, enterprises and organisations, from criminal encroachments and other anti-social activities'.

[*Svod zakonov USSR*, x, p. 230]

On the basic duties and rights of the Voluntary People's Druzhinas as regards the preservation of public order. Article 4 states that: 'The Voluntary People's Druzhinas carry out the following basic duties:

(a) they take part in the preservation of public order in streets, squares, parks, transport routes, stations, harbours, airports and other public places, and also in the protection of public order during various mass enterprises;

(b) co-operate with the organs of Internal Affairs, the Procuracy, Ministry

of Justice and the courts in their activities to underpin public order and in
their struggle with breaches of regulations;
(c) participate in the struggle with hooliganism, drunkenness, illegal distilling
of spirits, misappropriation of state and social property, and also of the
personal property of citizens, with breaches of the regulations relating to
trade, with speculation and other infringements of law [*pravonarusheniya*].'
[*Svod zakonov SSSR*, x p. 248]

(b) Laws applying to prohibited economic activities

The Codex of the RSFSR on Breaches of Administrative Regulations, art.
150 states that 'street trading in unauthorised places' is punishable by a
warning or a fine of up to 10 roubles.
Art. 156 states that 'breach of the regulations applying to the carrying-out of
small craft industries and other kinds of individual work activity' is punishable by a fine of 50–100 roubles and that products, apparatus for producing
them and raw materials may be confiscated.
[*Svod zakonov RSFSR*, viii, p. 438]
The Criminal Code of the RSFSR, art. 209 states that, 'Vagrancy, begging or
the leading of some other parasitic way of life': 'Those occupying themselves
by vagrancy, begging or the leading of some other parasitic way of life will be
punished by a deprivation of freedom of between one or two years or by the
same period of corrective labour'. If there is a previous conviction the
sentence rises to between one and three years.
[*Svod zakonov RSFSR*, viii, p. 577]
The Civil Codex of the USSR, art. 54, Section 4, states that 'Extract from the
rules of the NKF of the USSR on the registration of craft industries, conf. by
the SPK of the USSR of 26 March 1936', point 3: 'The following trades are
forbidden and so is the issuing of permits for them: . . . (m) the keeping of inns,
roundabouts, bathing-places [*kupal'ny*], scales at bazaars, *shooting-ranges and
the organisation of various games*. [My emphasis]
[*Grazhdanskii kodeks RSFSR*, p. 150.]

NOTES

For anon., see bibliographic entries under title

INTRODUCTION

1 Yu. A. Dmitriev, 'Na starom moskovskom gulyanii', in *Teatral'nyi almanakh VTO*, vi (Moscow 1947), p. 350; Ivan Shcheglov, *Narod i teatr* (St Petersburg 1911), p. 117.

2 James Clifford, *The Predicament of Culture: Twentieth-Century Literature, Ethnography and Art* (Cambridge Mass. and London 1988), p. 93.

3 See *Muzei teatral'nykh kukol: katalog* (Moscow *c.* 1982).

4 A. F. Nekrylova, *Russkie narodnye gorodskie prazdniki, uveseleniya i zrelishcha* (Leningrad 1984); Jeffrey Brooks, *When Russia Learned to Read: Literacy and Popular Literature, 1861–1917* (Princeton 1985). The title of the exhibition is 'The narodnye gulyan'ya and popular entertainments of Petersburg'. According to a member of the museum staff, it had more visitors than any other exhibition ever organised there.

5 The figure for literacy in the Russian Empire given in the First General Census of 1897 was 21 per cent: there were, however, significant variations according to gender, creed, place of residence and occupation. Literacy was higher in males than females, in town-dwellers than village-dwellers, amongst Jews and Muslims than amongst Orthodox Christians. Skilled workers and recruits to the army also had a high literacy rate: see *Novyi entsiklopedicheskii slovar' Brokgauza i Efrona* ed. K. Arsen'ev, 29 vols. (St Petersburg 1911–16), xiv, headword *Gramotnost'*, p. 713; Brooks, *When Russia Learned to Read*, p. 4. There was probably also some difference between the specified *gramotnost'* rate and functional literacy. In St Petersburg, where the rate of literacy was 65 per cent in 1890, over 38 per cent had received only elementary education, *Entsiklopedicheskii slovar' Brokgauza i Efrona*, ed. I. Andreevsky, 42 vols. and 4 supp. vols. (St Petersburg 1890–1907), xxviii, headword *Sankt-Peterburg*, p. 311. The circulation rate for the most popular weeklies containing fiction is some indication also of the popularity of the fairs: *Niva* was recorded at 78,000 in 1884, see the journal *Bibliograf* (1885), 11; at the same time the audience for just one of the big fairground theatres during the fairground season was over 60,000; there were five of this size in Petersburg, as well as several dozen sideshows and small theatres: A. Ya. Alekseev-Yakovlev, *Russkie narodnye gulyan'ya* (Leningrad and Moscow 1948), p. 50. In towns and villages where the illiterate population was larger, the comparison would have produced yet more striking results. The censorship of

printed works intended for a popular market was particularly repressive, see *Sbornik postanovlenii i rasporyazhenii po tsenzure s 1720 po 1862 g.* (St Petersburg 1863), pp. 279, 283, 293, 297, 305, although there have been doubts raised about how effective it was, see Brooks, *When Russia Learned to Read*, pp. 302–3.

6 Alekseev-Yakovlev, *Russkie narodnye gulyan'ya*, pp. 11–12.

7 Simon Karlinsky, *Russian Drama from its Beginnings to the Age of Pushkin* (Berkeley, Los Angeles and London 1984).

8 See my unpublished D.Phil thesis, 'Innokentij Annenskij and the Classical Ideal', Oxford 1985, chapters 4 and 5.

9 Vyacheslav Ivanov, 'O deistvii i deistve', 'O sushchestve tragedii', 'Esteti-cheskaya norma teatra', in *Sobranie sochinenii* (Brussels 1974), II, pp. 156–71, 190–203, 205–15; Vsevolod Meyerhold, 'Balagan' (1912), in *Stat'i, pis'ma, rechi, besedy,* (Moscow 1968), I, pp. 207–29; A. M. Remizov, *Tsar' Maksimilian* (Petersburg 1920); *Plyas Irodiady* (Berlin, nd); *Rusal'nye deistva* (Munich 1971). See also chapter 4 above.

10 M. M. Bakhtin, *François Rabelais and His World*, trans. Hélène Iswolsky (Bloomington 1984), pp. 218–19.

11 The anti-Stalinist subtext of Bakhtin's *Rabelais* is discussed in chapter 5. *Rabelais* was published in Russian in 1965.

12 Clifford, *Predicament of Culture*, p. 332.

13 The examples are taken from V.Yu. Krupyanskaya and N. S. Polishchuk, *Kul'tura i byt rabochikh gornozavodskogo Urala* (Moscow 1971); they occur together on p. 7.

14 V. N. Vsevolodsky-Gerngross, *Istoriya russkogo teatra*, 2 vols. (Lenin-grad and Moscow, 1929), II, pp. 369–70. An example of the tendency in certain Russian Soviet commentators to combine ignorance with dogma-tism in their statements about non-Russian cultures is Konstantin Rud-nitsky's assertion, in *Russian Soviet Theatre* (London 1988), p. 116, that there was no theatre in the Islamic parts of the Russian Empire before Soviet rule, and, further, that this is explained by Islamic disapproval of the theatre. He seems to be unaware that many Islamic countries (among them Turkey and Indonesia) have a thriving theatrical tradition of considerable antiquity: see Metin And, *Karagöz: Turkish Shadow Theatre* (Istanbul 1980), and that pre-Soviet theatrical traditions in Central Asia are documented in Soviet sources, see, for example, N. I. Smirnova's *Sovetskii teatr kukol 1918–1932* (Moscow 1963), p. 162.

15 Krupyanskaya and Polishchuk, *Kul'tura*, pp. 125–6. My emphasis.

16 Iurii M. Lotman, Lidiia Ia. Ginsburg and Boris A. Uspenskii, *The Semiotics of Russian Cultural History*, ed. A. D. and A. S. Nakhimovsky (Ithaca, New York and London 1985). In his introduction Boris Gasparov writes pertinently: 'The binary model is in fact not so much a metatext – a description or interpretation – as it is *a text* of Russian culture; it does not interpret or explain so much as it spontaneously reflects the deep structure of the Russian cultural consciousness' (p. 28).

17 Carlo Ginzburg, *The Cheese and the Worms*, trans. J. and A. Tedeschi (London 1980), p. xiv.

18 Peter Burke's *Popular Culture in Early Modern Europe* (London 1978) is an excellent introduction to the subject. Other studies which I found particularly helpful include, besides Carlo Ginzburg's *Cheese and Worms*, Keith Thomas, *Religion and the Decline of Magic: Studies in Belief in Sixteenth- and Seventeenth-Century England* (Harmondsworth 1978) and *Man and the Natural World: Changing Attitudes in England 1500–1800* (Harmondsworth 1984); Robert Darnton, *The Great Cat Massacre and Other Episodes in French Cultural History* (Harmondsworth 1985); Christiane Klapisch-Zuber, *Women, Family and Ritual in Renaissance Italy*, trans. L. D. Cochrane (Chicago 1985); Natalie Zemon Davis, *Fiction in the Archives: Pardon Tales and their Tellers in Sixteenth-Century France* (Oxford 1988).

19 Charles A. Moser, 'Jeffrey Brooks: *When Russia Learned to Read*', review, *Slavic and East European Journal*, 30:4 (1986), 568–9.

20 Rose L. Glickman, *Russian Factory Women: Workplace and Society 1880–1914* (Berkeley, Los Angeles and London 1984), p. 16. Victoria E. Bonnell (ed.), *Life and Labour under the Tsarist Regime* (Berkeley, Los Angeles and London 1983), p. 26, records a range of 'frivolous pastimes' which is a little wider: visits to taverns, card games and social dances.

21 For example, Diane Koenker, *Moscow Workers and the 1917 Revolution* (Princeton 1981) sees worker *oblik* (self-image) entirely in terms of such statistically assessable factors as age, gender, occupation, wages (p. 27). Despite my admiration for the range of materials included in Brooks' *When Russia Learned to Read*, and its intellectual scope, I am doubtful of the relevance of all the numerical tables; it seems odd to index by title and subject rather than motif, and to suggest trends on the basis of such tiny numbers of publications. I am still more uneasy about the tendency on occasion to assume a direct correlation between reading-matter and reception, see p. 160 on Verbitskaya: 'It was ... the combination of emancipation and submission that appealed to her readers'; to rely on statements by outsiders about which people read which material (is the fact that contemporary critics thought of books as 'shop-girl romances' – p. 160 – a reliable indication that shop girls actually read them?); and to assume 'literary merit' as a self-evident quality in Gor'ky's writings (p. 284). Richard Stites' interesting article, 'Iconoclastic Currents in the Russian Revolution: Destroying and Preserving the Past', studies popular culture only where it impinges on political upheaval: see Abbott Gleason, Peter Kenez and Richard Stites, *Bolshevik Culture: Experiment and Order in the Russian Revolution* (Bloomington 1985), pp. 1–24.

22 C. Ginzburg, *Cheese and Worms*, p. xv.

23 Ivan Shcheglov, *Narodnyi teatr* (St Petersburg 1898), p. 109.

24 N. Ya. Simonovich-Efimova, *Zapiski petrushechnika* (Leningrad 1981), p. 119. My emphasis.

25 Elizabeth Warner, *The Russian Folk Theatre* (The Hague and Paris 1977), pp. 109–19; Russell Zguta, *Russian Minstrels: A History of the Skomorokhi* (Oxford 1978), pp. 112–19.

26 See TP; A. F. Nekrylova, 'Genezis odnoi iz stsen Petrushki', *Sovetskaya etnografiya*, 4 (1972), 126–31; 'Severnorusskie varianty Petrushki' in *Fol'klor i etnografiya russkogo severa* (Leningrad 1973), pp. 242–9; 'Zakon kontrasta v poetike russkogo narodnogo kukol'nogo teatra Petrushka', *Russkii fol'klor* XIV (1974), pp. 210–18; 'Stsenicheskie osobennosti narodnogo kukol'nogo teatra Petrushka', *Narodnyi teatr* (Leningrad 1974), 121–40; 'Iz istorii formirovaniya russkoi narodnoi kukol'noi komedii Petrushka', *V professional'noi shkole kukol'nikov* (Leningrad 1979), 137–47; 'The Traditional Archetectonics of Folk Puppet Street Comedy' (in English) *Proceedings of the UNIMA Symposium* (Moscow 1983), pp. 26–40. For Smirnova see note 14 above.

27 Burke, *Popular Culture*, pp. 25ff.

28 Dan Ben-Amos, 'Toward a Definition of Folklore in Context', in A. Paredes and R. Bauman (eds.), *Toward New Perspectives in Folklore* (Austin and London 1972), p. 15.

29 R. Jakobson and P. G. Bogatyrev, 'Die Folklore als eine besondere Form des Schaffens' in Roman Jakobson, *Selected Writings*, IV (The Hague and Paris 1966), pp. 1–15. (A summary of the argument in Russian is available in *Selected Writings*, pp. 16–19.)

30 Literacy was by no means common amongst members of the dominant classes until at least the end of the seventeenth century, and much literary material (for example hagiography) was transmitted by reading aloud. Even after Westernisation, oral transmission was in common use amongst members of the political and cultural elite: instances which highlight the oral/literary transmission versus cultural hierarchy problem include the dissemination of philosophical or academic ideas via lecture notes, the importance of discussion groups and societies, of private information and of poetry recitations, which were and remain vital in Russian high culture.

31 The two theses, of folklore as independent popular creation and as 'gesunkenes Kulturgut' (sunken cultural material) have gone in and out of fashion at different times. Soviet folklorists were permitted to voice only the first thesis from the mid-1930s on, see Felix J. Oinas (ed.), *Folklore, Nationalism and Politics* (Columbus, Ohio 1978), p. 81; the second has been argued by, amongst others, Antonio Gramsci, who felt that 'folklore has always been tied to the culture of the dominant class': *Selections from Cultural Writings* (London 1986), p. 194. I have chosen the indirect opposition 'high culture' and 'popular culture' (rather than, say, 'popular' versus 'elite' culture) to reflect a process of circulation rather than substitution.

32 Ben-Amos, 'Definition of Folklore', p. 13.

33 Herbert Halpert, *Journal of American Folklore*, 75.

34 Duncan and Linda Williamson, *A Thorn in the King's Foot: Stories of the Scottish Travelling People* (Harmondsworth 1987), biography inside dust jacket; letter in the *Guardian*, 18 October 1988.

35 One of the points voiced by participants in the panel on obscene folklore organised by the American Folklore Society in 1962 (see *Journal of*

American Folklore) was that the 'low' genres were by far the most productive – a state of affairs which inspired regret in some. A. Dundes and R. Georges point out that 'people who transmit and listen to these minor genres of obscene folklore become [ever] more numerous' (JAF 224); for G. Legman, however, these sexual jokes are 'shrill and counterfeit slapstick' (JAF 235). Publication of much Russian-language obscene folklore takes place outside the Soviet Union; see, for example, V. Kabronsky's collection of obscene rhymes, *Nepodtsenzurnaya chastushka* (New York 1987); the 'cruel romance' is one genre branded as vulgar, and under-represented in print: see E. G. Pomerantseva's article 'Ballada i zhestokii romans', in *Russkii fol'klor* XIV (1974), 202–10, which is long on abuse and short on examples. See also Oinas, *Folklore,* p. 80.

36 Williamson and Williamson, *Thorn in the King's Foot*, p. 28.

37 Henry Glassie (ed.), *Irish Folktales* (Harmondsworth 1987), pp. 5–9.

38 Ben-Amos, 'Definition of Folklore', p. 12.

39 ibid., p. 13

40 ibid.

41 Ginzburg, *Cheese and Worms*, p. xxiv.

42 Nekrylova, *Russkie narodnye gorodskie prazdniki*, p. 192; Yu. A. Dmitriev, *Tsirk v Rossii ot istokov do 1917* (Moscow 1977), p. 109 (see also chapter 1); V. A. Sleptsov, *Sochineniya v 2 tt.* (Moscow 1957), II, p. 236; Dmitriev, *Tsirk*, pp. 126, 275; V. I. Lenin, quoted by Klara Tsetkin, *Lenin o literature i iskusstve*, 7th edn (Moscow 1967), p. 665.

43 Peter Stallybrass and Allon White, *The Politics and Poetics of Transgression* (London 1986), p. 4.

44 See, for example, Smirnova, *Sovetskii teatr kukol*, p. 10.

45 A good impression of the raffishness which, happily, still characterises the lower end of the Soviet circus is given by Lyalya Kuznetsova's photographs in Daniela Mrážková and Vladimir Remeš, *Another Russia: Through the Eyes of the New Soviet Photographers* (London 1981), pp. 44–50. But contrast the resistance amongst the management of the elite circuses to innovatory numbers recorded by David Hammarstrom, *Circus Rings Around Russia* (New York 1983), pp. 151–64.

46 Boris and Yury Sokolov, *Poeziya derevni: rukovodstvo dlya sobiraniya* (Moscow 1926).

47 These editions are listed in the abbreviations.

48 RV 11 February 1890, section 'Moskovskaya khronika'. My emphasis.

49 C. Ginzburg, *Cheese and Worms*, p. xvii.

50 Peter Keating, introduction to *Into Unknown England: Selections from the Social Explorers* (London 1976), especially pp. 19–20.

51 C. Ginzburg, *Cheese and Worms*, p. 126. The view that the suppression of folklore would lead to a new Reformation is expressed also by Gramsci, *Cultural Writings*, p. 191. That the effect might more precisely have resembled a new *Counter*-Reformation is suggested by the analogy between the uses of propaganda by the Catholic Church and the Bol-

sheviks made by Peter Kenez, *The Birth of the Propaganda State: Soviet Methods of Mass Mobilization 1917–1929* (Cambridge 1985), p. 10.

52 S. Dreiden in *Teatr kukol: sbornik* (Moscow 1955), p. v.

53 The decarnivalisation of Western society is the subject of Stallybrass and White, *Transgression*, that a *recarnivalisation* might be in progress has been argued by Ann Jefferson, 'Bodymatters: Self and Other in Bakhtin, Sartre and Barthes', in Ken Hirschkop and David Shepherd (eds.), *Bakhtin and Cultural Theory* (Manchester 1989), pp. 152–77.

54 This is Rudnitsky's phrase, from the hymnic conclusion of *Russian Soviet Theatre*, p. 272. The documentary evidence which he gives of cultural planning meetings in the 1920s, at which there was 'unbelievable shouting ... terrible shouting ... so much noise and uproar you can't tell what is being said' (p. 61), is in rather comic contrast to the view that harmony was attained in 1932.

I *PETRUSHKA* AND THE FAIRGROUND

1 Shcheglov, *Narod i teatr*, p. 108. On how the fairgrounds were less elegant than their Italian counterparts, see for example Anon, *Bemerkungen über Rußland*, 2 vols. (Erfurt 1788), II, p. 193.

2 Karl Biedermann, *Unsre Gegenwart und Zukunft*, 8 vols. (Leipzig 1847), VIII, p. 199.

3 A. Benua [= Benois], *Moi vospominaniya*, 2 vols. (Moscow 1980), I, p. 291.

4 Anon, *Bemerkungen über Rußland*, II, p. 193.

5 William Coxe described a disaster on the ice in the late eighteenth century: quoted in A. D. Cross (ed.), *Russia under Western Eyes 1517–1825* (London 1971), pp. 214–15; a similar disaster at the Novgorod Toy Fair in 1864 is cited in *Murrays Handbook for Travellers in Russia*, 5th edn. (London 1893), p. 188.

6 Alekseev-Yakovlev, *Russkie narodnye gulyan'ya*, pp. 13–14. On regulations governing fairground safety, see appendix B, 'Statute on Prevention and Curtailment of Crime' art. 141, part 1 (a); appendix B, Building Statute art. 163, part 1 (b).

7 V. Gilyarovsky, 'Katastrofa na Khodynke', *RV*, 20 May 1896, is a circumstantial account, with explicatory diagrams, of the appalling administrative incompetence which led to the tragedy. Over 1,800 corpses were buried in the Vagankovo cemetery alone.

8 S. R. Mintslov, *Istoriya Peterburga 1903–1910* (St Petersburg 1911), p. 15.

9 *RV*, 29 March 1890, 'Moskovskaya khronika'.

10 Shcheglov, *Narod i teatr*, p. 125.

11 Nekrylova, *Russkie narodnye gorodskie prazdniki*, p. 156.

12 G. Vasilich, 'Moskva 1850–1910', *Moskva v ee proshlom i nastoyashchem*, 11 (1912), 9.

13 On how young bloods would go down on toboggans, see Alekseev-Yakovlev, *Russkie narodnye gulyan'ya*, p. 26.

14 G. Vasilich, 'Ulitsy i lyudi sovremennoi Moskvy', *Moskva v ee proshlom i nastoyashchem*, 12 (1912), 9.

15 Theodore Child, 'The Fair of Nijnii-Novgorod', in *The Tsar and his People: or, Social Life in Russia*, a collection of essays by E. Melchior de Vogüé, T. Child *et al.* (New York 1891), p. 233.

16 *Sanktpeterburg: issledovaniya po istorii, topografii i statistike* (St Petersburg 1870), pp. 155, 157.

17 See appendix B, Statute on Prevention and Curtailment of Crime arts. 136, 137, 142, 143, 144, section 1 (a) (b).

18 *Entsiklopedicheskii slovar'*, XXI, *Obshchestvennaya tishina*, pp. 603–4; vol. IV, *Buistvo*, p. 864.

19 On the coronation festivals see N. A. Belozerskaya, *Tsarskoe venchanie v Rossii* (St Petersburg 1896); on festivals for the Emancipation of the Serfs see RV, 13 February 1911; on the Duma opening see Anon, 'Prazdnik samoobmana', *Volna* 26 April 1906.

20 Belozerskaya, *Tsarskoe venchanie v Rossii*, p. 79.

21 See appendix B, Statute on the General Regulation of the *gubernii* art. 314 section 1 (a)). Ambivalence is evident though in the injunction to the police to be light-handed. On the 1914 disturbances see RV, 12 February 1915, giving a police warning that such disturbances were not to be repeated. There was, conversely, a tendency for political violence to erupt over public festivals and traditional holidays – see Daniel K. Brower, 'Labour Violence in Russia in the Late Nineteenth Century', *Slavic Review* 41:3 (1982), p. 425. It is clear also that labour violence might itself have a carnival character: cf. for example the custom of 'carting out' unpopular foremen in wheelbarrows and suspending them over a canal: S. A. Smith, *Red Petrograd: Revolution in the Factories, 1917–18* (Cambridge 1985), p. 193.

22 See *Entsiklopedicheskii slovar'*, XXI, *Nizhegorodskaya yarmarka*, pp. 40–1.

23 On ground-rent charges, see A. Ya. Alekseev-Yakovlev, 'Vospominaniya' archival document; publication forthcoming; A. Bozheryanov, *Nevskii prospekt 1703–1903*, 2 vols. in 1, (St Petersburg 1902), p. 414; on the ticket levy see appendix B, Statute on Prevention . . . suppl. to art. 139, section 1 (a).

24 Carla Solivetti in Konstantin Miklaševskij, *La Commedia dell'arte*, trans. C. Solivetti (Venice 1981), p. 131.

25 See the studies by Zguta; A. S. Famintsyn, *Skomorokhi na Rusi* (St Petersburg 1889); A. A. Belkin, *Russkie skomorokhi* (Moscow 1975).

26 D. A. Rovinsky, *Russkie narodnye kartinki*, 5 vols. and 'atlas' of illustrations (St Petersburg 1881), IV, p. 210.

27 ibid., p. 212.

28 M. Bakhtin, *Rabelais*, pp. 218–19; see also Introduction, p. 3; on the use of carnival devices by Peter to terrorise, see O. A. Derzhavina, A. S. Demin, A. N. Robinson in V. P. Grebenyuk *et al.* (eds.), *Rannyaya russkaya dramaturgiya: p'esy lyubitel'skikh teatrov* (Moscow 1976), pp. 36–40.

29 Alekseev-Yakovlev, *Russkie narodnye gulyan'ya*, p. 9. The court circular

section of *Sanktpeterburgskii vestnik* in the last quarter of the eighteenth century (1778–91) recorded regular visits by the empress to Italian operas, French comedies, opulent firework displays and masquerade balls. The traditions of popular celebrations undoubtedly continued, but the aristocracy took little part in them. See also I. G. Georgi, *Opisanie rossiisko-imperatorskogo stolichnogo goroda Sanktpeterburga i dostoprimechatel'-nostei v ego okresnostyakh* (St Petersburg 1794), p. 655, which mentions both performances by 'harlequins and fools' and of 'fables and tales' by servants, the latter attended by 'the people' for a fee of 5 kopecks.

30 D. A. Rovinsky reproduces a splendid broadsheet picture of French actresses being expelled from Moscow, in *Russkie narodnye kartinki*, 2 vols. in 1, 2nd edn (St Petersburg 1900), plate XXXVII.

31 Robert A. M. Johnston, *Travels through part of the Russian Empire and the Country of Poland; along the Southern Shores of the Baltic* (London 1815), pp. 163–4.

32 Dmitriev, *Tsirk*, p. 109.

33 On tame dwarves, etc. see Enid Welsford, *The Fool: His Social and Literary History* (London 1935), p. 186.

34 Anon., *An Englishwoman in Russia, by a Lady Ten Years Resident in that Country* (London 1855), pp. 216–17.

35 Dmitriev, *Tsirk*, p. 109; Alekseev-Yakovlev, *Russkie narodnye gulyan'ya*, p. 13–14.

36 A. Yatsevich, *Krepostnye v Peterburge* (Leningrad 1933), p. 56.

37 A. M. Konechny, 'Peterburgskie balagany', *Panorama iskusstv* 8 (1985), 389–90.

38 Anon., *An Englishwoman in Russia*, pp. 214–15.

39 Biedermann, *Unsre Gegenwart und Zukunft*, p. 201.

40 M. Paushkin (ed.), *Staryi russkii vodevil', 1819–1849* (Moscow 1937), p. 24.

41 On the population growth after 1861 see *Entsiklopedicheskii slovar'*, XXVIII, *Sankt Petersburg*, p. 307; ibid., XIX, *Moskva*, p. 937.

42 Visits by the Smol'ny Institute pupils to the St Petersburg *narodnye gulyan'ya* are described by Benois, *Moi vospominaniya*, I, p. 290; by the town governor of Moscow to the Shrove Week Mushroom Market in RV, 15 February 1895, 'Moskovskaya khronika'.

43 N. Vasilich, writing in RV, 21 July 1911, 'Moskva v 50-kh i 60-kh godakh proshlogo stoletiya', comments that the grandeur of the carriages attending the Moscow funfairs had much fallen off in his lifetime.

44 Bronislava Nijinska, *Early Memories*, trans. and ed. I. Nijinska and Jean Robinson (London 1982), pp. 31–2; the international character of the entertainments at the turn of the century is illustrated, for example, by the fact that J. Cartwell Ridley, *Reminiscences of Russia* (Newcastle upon Tyne 1898), p. 43, describes meeting a troupe of African woman dancers in Chelyabinsk whom he had previously encountered in Blackpool.

45 V. Ya. Bryusov, *Sobranie sochinenii v 7 tt.* (Moscow 1973–5), III, pp. 296–7.

46 Vladimir Nabokov, *Speak, Memory* (Harmondsworth 1982), p. 185.

47 G. Vasilich, 'Ulitsy i lyudi', p. 11.

48 Stephen Graham, *Changing Russia* (London 1913), p. 15.

49 Appendix B, Statute on Prevention ... art. 145, section I (a).

50 RV, 3 April 1890, 'Moskovskaya khronika'.

51 Alekseev-Yakovlev, for example, moved to the Mikhailovskii Manège from the *balagans* at this period: see *Russkie narodnye gulyan'ya*, pp. 115–27.

52 Benois, *Moi vospominaniya*, 1, p. 296.

53 *Langenscheidts Sachwörterbücher: Land und Leute in Rußland*, ed. M. L. Schlesinger (Berlin and St Petersburg, *c.* 1910), p. 67.

54 The section 'Moskovskaya khronika' in RV gave regular information on the *gulyan'ya* for Shrove and Easter; it was not always consistent in its reporting, since news on them was treated as a filler item, and might be suppressed to make way for something more interesting; but it does indicate that many traditional celebrations were still going on as late as 1915.

55 Child, 'The Fair at Nijnii-Novgorod', in *The Tsar and His People*, pp. 230–41.

56 On banned times for theatre performances after 1884 and dates for the Nizhnii-Novgorod fair, see appendix B, the Trade Statute: Suppl. to Article 665, section 1 (b).

57 *Gazirovat'* in this meaning is cited by Dmitriev, *Tsirk*, p. 94.

58 Alekseev-Yakovlev, *Russkie narodnye gulyan'ya*, pp. 127–60; see also I. Shcheglov, *Narodnyi teatr*, (St Petersburg 1911), pp. 17–46.

59 Harold Williams, *Russia of the Russians* (London 1914), p. 42.

60 There is a picture of the *grivenniki*, or balcony occupants, in Alekseev-Yakovlev, *Russkie narodnye gulyan'ya*, p. 73 (see also illustration p. 29).

61 These prices are taken from advertisements in RV, 1 January 1890, 4 February 1890, 27 February 1910.

62 The Temperance Society (literally 'Popechitel'stvo narodnoi trezvosti', or 'Trusteeship of the People's Temperance') was one, officially organised, part of the 'rational leisure' movement; often operating on the sites of former state liquor outlets, it offered cheap entertainments, for example 'picture shows' at 5 kopecks entrance fee (RV, 26 February 1902). In 1898 more than 700,000 people attended entertainments organised by the Society in St Petersburg alone: *Entsiklopedicheskii slovar'*, XXVIII, p. 335; the highest attendances were during the traditional festival seasons of Shrove and Easter.

63 Vsevolodsky-Gerngross, *Istoriya russkogo teatra*, II, p. 397. My account here of subordinate class *byt* is necessarily limited: I have concentrated on Moscow and St Petersburg, though Vsevolodsky-Gerngross also classifies Odessa, Khar'kov, Kiev and Rostov as urban centres. Using these cities as a case study, I deal simply with issues relevant to the fairground and to *Petrushka*. More detailed accounts of material culture, especially amongst workers, will be found in Bonnell, *Life and Labour*, Glickman, *Factory Women*, S. A. Smith, *Red Petrograd*, Koenker, *Moscow Workers*, G. Vas-

ilich, 'Moskva 1850–1910' and 'Ulitsy i lyudi', and the articles from *Entsiklopedicheskii slovar'* and *Novyi entsiklopedicheskii slovar'* cited in nn. 64, 68, 69, 70, below.

64 The *sosloviya* are listed in the population statistics given in *Entsiklopedicheskii slovar'*, vol. XXVII, *St. Petersburg*, p. 307.

65 Vsevolodsky-Gerngross, *Istoriya russkogo teatra*, II, p. 397.

66 On surburban life in St Petersburg, see *Entsiklopedicheskii slovar'*, XXVIII, pp. 340–2; in Moscow see G. Vasilich, 'Ulitsy i lyudi', 14–15.

67 This wage comparison is notional – wages of course rose and fell over the nineteenth century; I intend here simply to indicate how little, even in normal circumstances, not during a slump, was left over for clothing, shoes, transport, entertainments and leisure. Figures taken from *Entsiklopedicheskii slovar'*, XXVIII, p. 322.

68 *Entsiklopedicheskii slovar'*, XXVI, *Remeslo*, p. 561.

69 Figures for St Petersburg underground dwellings are given in *Entsiklopedicheskii slovar'*, XXVIII, p. 319; for Moscow, *Novyi entsiklopedicheskii slovar'*, XXVII, *Moskva*, p. 300.

70 These barracks are vividly described by a former factory manager in Bonnell, *Life and Labour*, p. 123. See also *Entsiklopedicheskii slovar'*, XXXV, *Fabrichnoe zakonodatel'stvo*, p. 211.

71 On the night-shelters and plans to replace them, see G. Yaroslavsky, 'Gorodskoe samoupravlenie Moskvy', *Moskva v ee proshlom i nastoyashchem* 11 (1911), 40–1.

72 See *Entsiklopedicheskii slovar'*, XXXV, *Fabrichnoe zakonodatel'stvo*, p. 213; D. D. Christian and R. E. F. Smith, *Bread and Salt* (Cambridge 1984), especially pp. 288–326.

73 *Sanktpeterburg: issledovaniya*, pp. XXI, 105. The unspecified category certainly included prostitutes and beggars, for though a number of people admitted to these two professions, the total was too small to be credible, so it was discounted (p. XXI).

74 On the guild system see *Entsiklopedicheskii slovar'*, XXXVIII, *Tsekhi v Rossii*, p. 133; S. A. Smith, *Red Petrograd*, p. 109, argues that the looseness of guild affiliation had a knock-on effect on the craft unions.

75 *Sanktpeterburg: issledovaniya*, pp. 110–27.

76 The skilled workers insisted on differentiation by title – see Timofeev in Bonnell (ed.), *Life and Labour*, p. 75. On conflicts between temporary and permanent guilded workers, see *Entsiklopedicheskii slovar'*, vol. XXVI, *Remeslo*, p. 561.

77 On the proportion of those born outside St Petersburg, see *Sanktpeterburg: issledovaniya*, pp. 20–9.

78 *Entsiklopedicheskii slovar'*, vol. XXVIII, p. 307; *Novyi entsiklopedicheskii slovar'*, vol. XXX, *Moskva*, p. 300.

79 See *Sanktpeterburg: issledovaniya*, p. 132; for a later period, see S. A. Smith, *Red Petrograd*, pp. 6–7; Glickman, *Factory Women*, pp. 3, 65; Koenker, *Moscow Workers*, pp. 57–8.

80 Details of the protective relationship between *zemlyaki* are give in the memoir by S. Kanatchikov, in Bonnell, *Life and Labour*, p. 38.

81 See for example Williams, *Russia of the Russians*, p. 42.

82 Vsevolodsky-Gerngross, *Istoriya russkogo teatra*, II, p. 398; contrast Soviet estimate cited by S. A. Smith, *Red Petrograd*, p. 19.

83 Gilyarovsky, 'Olsuf'evskaya krepost'', *Sochineniya v 4 tt.* (Moscow 1967), IV, pp. 379–87.

84 G. Vasilich, 'Moskva 1850–1910', 15; Kanatchikov in Bonnell, *Life and Labour*, p. 39.

85 Koenker, *Moscow Workers*, p. 28.

86 The memoirs of S. Kanatchikov are an example of how self-betterment might lead to hostility towards 'frivolity': Bonnell, *Life and Labour*, see especially pp. 42, 59.

87 Krupyanskaya and Polishchuk, *Kul'tura*, p. 87, describe how a literate woman worker in the Urals would read aloud to her illiterate husband from *The Arabian Nights*; he would then re-tell the stories at work. It seems likely that many people in the subordinate classes, like Scottish travellers today, were non-literate, that is, 'some can read and write, but that does not colour their attitude towards oral tradition – they reckon the best stories are not transmitted in print, but by the human voice' (Williamson and Williamson, *Thorn in the King's Foot*, p. 11).

88 *Sanktpeterburg: issledovaniya*, pp. 112–13.

89 On woman's literacy see ibid., pp. 48–9; Glickman, *Factory Women*, p. 112.

90 See S. A. Smith, *Red Petrograd*, p. 92; RV, 16 April 1894, 'Moskovskaya khronika', relates a very unpleasant instance in which a drunken husband cut his drunken wife's throat.

91 The phrase 'creatures of a lower order' was used by a worker quoted in Glickman, *Factory Women*, pp. 172–3, though it should be pointed out that he himself attributed it to a stage of his life preceding enlightenment.

92 Shcheglov, *Narodnyi teatr*, pp. 17–37.

93 One might suppose that the self-improving workers, such as Kanatchikov (see note 87 above), would have despised the fairground; however, there is no evidence for this in memoirs or second-hand accounts.

94 On movements of third-class rail traffic out of Moscow for festivals, see RV, 10 February 1895 and 17 April 1905; Glickman, *Factory Women*, pp. 3, 65, argues that it was normal for male workers to leave at this time; however, Kanatchikov in Bonnell, *Life and Labour*, p. 48, gives a contrary instance of the very rural-seeming 'peasants' in his factory who would sometimes invite their wives to town for festivals.

95 On the dominance of unmarried YAMs (young adult males) see *Sanktpeterburg: issledovaniya*, p. 78; S. A. Smith *Red Petrograd*, p. 6; on their liking for city life, see Koenker, *Moscow Workers*, p. 92.

96 N. Vitengof, *Ocherki moskovskoi zhizni* (Moscow 1842), p. 196.

97 Instances of the use of such terms can be found in *Rassvet*, 30 October 1905; RV, 11 February. 1890; and the article 'Vlast' tolpy' by S. Polozov, *Slovo*, 15 January 1905.

98 Nicholas Bachtin, 'The Russian Revolution as seen by a White Guard', *Alta: the University of Birmingham Review*, 2:10 (Spring 1970), 200.

99 K. D. Kavelin, quoted in Yatsevich, *Krepostnye v Peterburge*, p. 14.

100 L. N. Tolstoy, *Chto takoe iskusstvo?* (Moscow 1985), p. 139 (my emphasis). A similar thesis on the corrupting effects of urban life is argued in *Zhivopisnyi al'bom narody [sic] Rossii* (St Petersburg 1880), pp. 2–3.

101 *Lenin*, p. 202; see also V. E. Gusev, *Marksizm i russkaya fol'kloristika kontsa XIX – nachala XX veka* (Moscow and Leningrad 1961), especially pp. 128–71. The point I am making here is concerned less with the use of class divisions as a divide-and-rule strategy than with the effect of such class divisions in cultural terms; the way they are used to support a circular argument about the superiority of the intellectual view. Kenez, *Propaganda State*, makes some interesting points about condescension and incoherence in Bolshevik reasoning on the subordinate classes, pp. 7, 70, 121–2. On how the subordinate classes might themselves use the generalising term *trudovoi narod* (toiling people), see S. A. Smith, *Red Petrograd*, p. 166.

102 David Mayall, *Gypsy Travellers in Nineteenth-Century Society* (Cambridge 1988), especially pp. 71–93.

103 Gilyarovsky, 'Khitrovka', *Sochineniya v 4 tt.*, IV, pp. 17–41. On the explorer's bravery as a *topos* of social exploration, see Keating, *Into Unknown England*, pp. 15–16.

104 G. Vasilich, 'Ulitsy i lyudi', 9–13.

105 A. V. Druzhinin, *Povesti i rasskazy* (Moscow 1986), p. 279.

106 'A.B.', *Gorodskoe samoupravlenie v Rossii* (Geneva: pub. Soyuz sotsial-demokratov, 1901), p. 23.

107 On regulations against excessive noise, see appendix B, Statute on Prevention ... art. 142, section 1 (a); on audience reaction, see A. V. Leifert, *Balagany* (Petrograd 1922), p. 42.

108 Alekseev-Yakovlev, *Russkie narodnye gulyan'ya*, p. 74, states that the public's interest was 'moral'. The statement may be an over-generalisation based on his own desire to educate, but certainly reflects interested and critical comments from the public. Cf. N. Benkarevich's account of touring Russian villages in the 1890s, *Narodnyi teatr: sbornik* (Moscow 1896), pp. 133–50.

109 Derzhavina, Demin, Robinson *et al.* in V. Grebenyuk *et al.* (eds.), *Rannyaya russkaya dramaturgiya*, p. 33.

110 The survey is cited in S. A. Smith, *Red Petrograd*, p. 97.

111 On performances depicting the Battle of Sinope in the 1850s, see Druzhinin, *Povesty i rasskazy*, p. 279; on the turn of the century, see G. Vasilich, 'Moskva 1850–1910', 11.

112 W. Barnes Steveni, *Petrograd* (London 1915), p. 152.

113 N. Obol'yaninov, *Zametki o russkikh illyustrirovannykh izdaniyakh* (Moscow 1915), p. 5.

114 On the itineracy of small craftsmen, see *Entsiklopedicheskii slovar'*, XVIII, *Remeslo*, p. 561; on the commercial aptitude of showmen, Gilyarovsky,

Sochineniya v 4tt., IV, p. 70, quoting a carnival barker who said 'A crowd's nothing but a herd of sheep. You can do what you like with it.' Another class with which the showmen had something in common were the *raznochintsy – déclassé* persons – to which some theatre workers were assigned. See *Sanktpeterburg: issledovaniya*, p. 40.

115 Unfortunately few philologists bothered to make notes on this central matter. The two *vertep* performers interviewed by Nikolay Vinogradov at the turn of the century were literate: see his 'Velikorusskii vertep', *Izvestiya otdeleniya russkogo yazyka i slovesnosti Imperatorskoi Akademii Nauk* 10:3 (1905), 362. The poet Nikolay Klyuev, who came from a *balagan* proprietor's family, was literate, having been taught to read by his mother: N. Klyuev, *Sochineniya*, 2 vols. (Munich 1969), I, p. 211.

116 On the use of manuscript versions of texts, see Vinogradov, 'Velikorusskii vertep', p. 362; on induction of the illiterate by the literate, see Warner, *Russian Folk Theatre*, pp. 193–4; Krupyanskaya and Polishchuk *Kul'tura*, p. 189; on the use of comic magazines as material for telling funny stories, see Kanatchikov's account of his friend Stepka, in Bonnell, *Life and Labour*, p. 59; it is also likely that the volume listed in Obol'yaninov, *Zametki*, p. 4, called *Rasskazy kosmoramshchika, ili ob"yasnenie k 16 kartinam, nakhodyashchimsya v Kosmorame, izgotovlennye i izdannye Karlom Gubertsom* (St Petersburg 1848), was used by fairground peepshow proprietors for material, since one of the numbers in it, 'The Hot-Air Balloon', is recorded independently as being in use on the fairground. See also A. M. Konechny, 'Raek: narodnaya zabava', *Dekorativnoe iskusstvo*, 346 (1986), 14.

117 On families in the fairground milieu, see Dmitriev, *Tsirk*, p. 247.

118 Alekseev-Yakovlev, *Russkie narodnye gulyan'ya*, pp. 92–4.

119 ibid., p. 58; Leifert, *Balagany*, p. 21.

120 Nijinska, *Early Memories*, p. 44.

121 On living conditions in the fairground, see Dmitriev, *Tsirk*, pp. 246–51; Gilyarovsky, 'Balagan', *Sochineniya v 4 tt.*, II, pp. 47–55, indicates that the showmen sometimes had to perform in the most extraordinary places – in one case, on a scaffold.

122 See appendix B, Statute on Prevention ... arts. 135, 159, Section 1 (a). Over 18,000 people were in fact arrested in St Petersburg on charges of mendicancy in 1898: see *Entsiklopedicheskii slovar'*, XXVIII, p. 331.

123 Dostoevsky, *Prestuplenie i nakazanie*, pt 5, chapter 5, *Polnoe sobranie sochinenii v 30 tt.* VI, (Leningrad 1969–87), p. 328.

124 Simonovich-Efimova, *Zapiski petrushechnika*, pp. 182–3; on the Novinsky fair, see also N. Vasilich, 'Moskva'.

125 Julia Kristeva, *Desire in Language: a Semiotic Approach to Literature and Art*, ed. Leon S. Roudiez, trans. T. George, A. Jardine and Leon Roudiez (Oxford 1981), p. 78.

126 On the *linii* or *ryady* system at fairgrounds, see Alekseev-Yakovlev, *Russkie narodnye gulyan'ya*, pp. 92–4, and the map of the Nizhnii-Novgorod fairground in *Entsiklopedicheskii slovar'*, XXI, *Nizhego-*

rodskaya yarmarka, betw. pp. 40 and 41; in medieval cities, see V. V. Nechaev, 'Ulichnaya zhizn' Moskvy XVI–XVII vv.', *Moskva v ee proshlom i nastoyashchem* 3 (1910), 71; in the nineteenth century see G. Vasilich, 'Moskva 1850–1910', 8.

127 Leifert, *Balagany*, p. 21; Alekseev-Yakovlev, *Russkie narodnye gulyan'-ya*, p. 58.

128 Dmitriev, 'Na starom moskovskom gulyanii', p. 351.

129 Shcheglov, *Narod i teatr*, p. 117.

130 Simonovich-Efimova, *Zapiski petrushechnika*, p. 58. The name of the Zaitsev's theatre was *Teremok Petrushki*, a nearly untranslatable folksy term that could be rendered as 'Petrushka's Little Solar'.

131 Nekrylova, *Russkie narodnye gorodskie prazdniki*, pp. 152–3.

132 Anton Giulio Bragaglia, *Pulcinella* (Rome 1953), p. 401.

133 Georgi, *Opisanie*, p. 656.

134 J. T. James, *Journal of a Tour in Germany, Sweden, Russia and Poland* (London 1817), p. 82 (my emphasis); P. Svin'in quoted in A. M. Konechy, 'Peterburgskie narodnye gulyan'ya' na maslenoi i paskhal'-noi nedelyakh', in *Etnografiya Peterburga–Leningrada: materialy ezhegodnykh chtenii*, forthcoming (Leningrad 1989).

135 James L. Rice, *Dostoevsky and the Healing Art: An Essay in Literary and Medical History* (Ann Arbor 1985), p. 75.

136 Dostoevsky, XXII, p. 180; I, pp. 251–2.

137 Obol'yaninov, *Zametki*, p. 6.

138 The earliest recorded *lubok* text is *Petrushka*, 1887, cited in Eremin's bibliography (TP 181). I have unfortunately been unable to trace this edition. On the others, see my bibliography. The address *moussier* or *musyu* appears in the text translated in appendix A; see also, for example, Dmitriev, 'Na starom moskovskom gulyanii', 350. Its spelling tended to vary, since it was often used to rhyme with another word.

139 G. L. Dain, *Russkaya narodnaya igrushka* (Moscow 1981), p. 143.

140 Jane Grigson, *English Food* (Harmondsworth 1977), p. 264.

141 Adam Olearius, *The Voyages and Travels of the Ambassadors, rendered into English by John Davies of Kidwelly* (London 1662), p. 81; my emphasis.

142 Rovinsky, *Russkie narodnye kartinki*, I, pp. 360–1. The 1900 edn is used here for reference because the material on Petrushka is exactly the same as in the 1881 edn, but is more conveniently collected in one place.

143 See V. N. Peretts, 'Kukol'nyi teatr na Rusi', *Ezhegodnik imperatorskikh teatrov*, Supp. part 1 (1894–5), 84–185; A. Alferov, 'Petrushka i ego predki', *Desyat' chtenii po literature* (Moscow 1895), pp. 175–205; Eremin in (TP); V. D. Kuz'mina, *Russkii demokraticheskii teatr XVIII veka* (Moscow 1958); Belkin, *Russkie skomorokhi*; Warner, *Russian Folk Theatre*; Roberta Reeder, 'Petrushka: a Russian Rogue', *The Puppetry Journal* (Jan.–Feb. 1981), 41–5. Nekrylova, 'Iz istorii formirovaniya', p. 138, voices doubts that Olearius' description refers to *Petrushka*, but does not explore the issue. On genre terms see Zguta, *Russian Minstrels*,

p. 117. Zguta's assertion is based on the idea that *pozorishche*, which meant 'puppet show' in the eighteenth century, must also have meant this in the thirteenth century. As genre terms in drama have displayed remarkable fluidity even over the last two hundred years – a well-known case is the word *komediya* – this argument seems to have little secure foundation.

144 Vsevolodsky-Gerngross, *Russkii teatr ot istokov do serediny XVIII veka* (Moscow 1957), p. 58. When I was in the last stages of preparing this book, George Speaight passed to me A. P. Kulish's article 'Petrushka – "litso nerazgadannoe, mificheskoe"': k voprosu o genezise geroya narodnoi ulichnoi kukol′noi komedii', *V professional′ noi shkole kukol′nikov* 3 (Leningrad 1987), 132–8, which makes this point on technique and one or two textual points also made by me, and which is a good summary of Soviet and East European sources on *Petrushka*.

145 On *mamottes* see M. R. Malkin, *Traditional and Folk Puppets of the World* (New York 1977), p. 18.

146 M. G. Rabinovich, 'K istorii skomorosh′ikh igr na Rusi', *Kul′tura srednevekovoi Rusi* (Leningrad 1974), pp. 53–6.

147 With the exception of brief references in the notes to Savushkina, *Narodnyi teatr* (Moscow 1976), note 19, and Zguta, *Russian Minstrels*, note 117. Zguta does not make much use of the material, however, as he appears to confuse glove puppets and finger puppets, and to have little knowledge of the later tradition of *Petrushka*.

148 Photographs of these toys will be found in Dain, *Russkaya narodnaya igrushka*, plates 16–19.

149 The original German (Olearius, *Vermehrte neue Beschreibung der Muscowitschen und Persischen Reise . . . welche zum andern Mahl heraus gibt Adam Olearius, Schleswig: gedruckt in der Fürstl. Druckerey durch Johan Holwein Im Jahr MDCLVI*), p. 193, uses the verbs 'zeigen', 'einen Possen oder Klucht (wie es die Holländer nennen) agiren', 'Schauplatz machen' and 'die Puppen spielen lassen'. Neither *Posse* nor *klucht* necessarily signifies a verbal text. On this see Catriona Kelly, 'From Pulcinella to Petrushka', *Oxford Slavonic Papers* 21 (1988), 51.

150 Olearius' German text reads, 'und nicht alleine pueros muliebra pati asvetos (wie Curtius redet) sondern auch Männer und Pferde dazu gebrauchen' (p. 193).

151 Peretts, 'Kukol′nyi teatr na Rusi', pp. 92–7.

152 These marionette shows remained in the repertoire of certain puppeteers, for example Zaitsev, albeit in what sounds like a fairly primitive version (Simonovich-Efimova, *Zapiski petrushechnika*, p. 184). But proper analysis of how popular they were cannot be attempted at present: not even one of the texts has been published. It is not clear whether any exist in archives.

153 A. A. Vadimov and M. A. Trivas, *Ot magov drevnosti do illyuzionistov nashikh dnei* (Moscow 1966), p. 48.

154 Peretts, 'Kukol′nyi teatr na Rusi', p. 96.

155 *Esepovy pritchi poveleniem Tsarskogo velichestva napechatany v Sankt-piterburge Let Gospodnya 1717, Aprelya v 5 den'* (a great bibliographical rarity; a copy exists in the Saltykov-Shchedrin library in Leningrad, whose staff kindly dispatched to me a copy of the relevant page).

156 N. Bakhtin, 'Marionetki', *Novyi entsiklopedicheskii slovar'*, xxv, p. 714.

157 On the *vertep* see Vinogradov, 'Velikorusskii vertep'; Warner, *Russian Folk Theatre*, pp. 83–108; Charlotte Pepys, *Domestic Sketches in Russia*, 2 vols. (London 1861), II, pp. 108–15; on the Don puppet theatre see V. Golovachev and B. Lashchilin, *Narodnyi teatr na Donu* (Rostov-on-Don 1947), p. 181; on the Toporets theatre see Peretts, 'Kukol'nyi teatr na Rusi', pp. 174–84.

158 Alferov, 'Petrushka i ego predki', p. 176; *Entsiklopedicheskii slovar'*, XXIII, *Petrushka*, p. 481.

159 On the 1905 carnival, see RV, 20 February 1905.

160 For pictures of a backyard show, see Nekrylova, *Russkie narodnye gorodskie prazdniki*, p. 73.

161 Solomatkin illustration in ibid., p. 79; description from Henry Morley (ed.), *Sketches of Russian Life* (London 1866), pp. 273–4.

162 The poet Innokenty Annensky used to watch *Petrushka* shows near his home in Tsarskoe Selo. See chapter 4 note 103.

163 Smirnova, *Sovetskii teatr kukol*, p. 61.

164 Dain, *Russkaya narodnaya igrushka*, p. 117.

165 The charge of 5 kopecks is specified in the concluding speech of Lashchenko's version (Berkov 123). See also appendix A.

166 Shcheglov, *Narod i teatr*, p. 122.

167 For Gor'ky's view see chapter 2; M. V. Dobuzhinsky, *Vospominaniya*, I (New York 1976), p. 39. It is arguable that children constitute a special section of the popular classes – a view that I accept, though with reservations. We shall see in chapters 4 and 5 how different these children's views of the show might be when they grew up.

168 Benois, *Moi vospominaniya*, II, p. 521.

169 Smirnova, *Sovetskii teatr kukol*, p. 40.

170 Nekrylova, 'Zakon kontrasta', 211.

171 V. Doroshevich, *Sakhalin* (Moscow 1903), p. 130.

172 Sergey Obraztsov, *Moya professiya* (Moscow 1981), pp. 69–71 and 74–6.

173 These statements of theories of diffusion are taken from David L. Clarke, *Analytical Archaeology* (London 1978), p. 426.

2 THE PHYSIOGNOMY OF *PETRUSHKA*

1 Alferov, 'Petrushka', p. 176.

2 V. Ya. Propp, *Russkaya skazka* (Leningrad 1984), p. 38.

3 V. Dal', *Slovar' velikorusskogo yazyka*, reprint of 4th edn, 4 vols. (Moscow 1980), III, p. 106.

4 Alekseev-Yakovlev, *Russkie narodnye gulyan'ya*, p. 59.

5 ibid. Alekseev-Yakovlev almost certainly exaggerated the importance of

'plants': it is unlikely that the smaller outfits could have spared two or three people to shout encouragement from the crowd.

6 Vsevolodsky-Gerngross, *Russkii teatr ot istokov*, p. 58.

7 Alekseev-Yakovlev, *Russkye narodnye gulyan'ya*, p. 60.

8 Eremin (TP 57ff) lists fifteen characters in all: apart from the central ones, the Jew, the Arab, the Turk/Tartar, the Barin, the Soldier's Father, Filimoshka, Aunt Alen'ka, and the Dvornik (Janitor – a person who also often worked hand in glove with the police organisations). Alekseev-Yakovlev, *Russkie narodnye gulyan'ya*, p. 62, refers to the Deacon and the Rag-and-Bone Man; for the Harlequin and the Clown see Tarasov 39. On the prevalence of attacks by dogs on hawkers, etc. see Vitengof, *Ocherki moskovskoi zhizni*, p. 182.

9 This estimate of the length of *Petrushka* performances comes from Krupyanskaya, 'Narodnyi teatr' in P. G. Bogatyrev (ed.), *Russkoe narodnoe poeticheskoe tvorchestvo: posobie dlya vuzov* (Moscow 1954), p. 394.

10 Vsevolodsky-Gerngross, *Russkaya ustnaya narodnaya drama* (Moscow 1959), p. 128.

11 Benois, *Moi vospominanya*, II, p. 522.

12 On assimilation by puppeteers, see chapter 1, p. 44, 58; also Simonovich-Efimova, *Zapiski petrushechnika*, pp. 180–90; on how Zaitsev's wife was also a puppeteer, see ibid., p. 183.

13 Alekseev-Yakovlev, *Russkie narodnye gulyan'ya*, p. 59.

14 *Entsiklopedicheskii slovar'*, XXIII, *Petrushka*, p. 481; Dmitriev, 'Na starom moskovskom gulyanii', 351.

15 M. Gor'ky, *Sobranie sochinenii v 30 tt.*, (Moscow 1949–55), XXIV, p. 494; cf. Dobuzhinsky (quoted in chapter 1, p. 56); contrast Vsevolodsky-Gerngross, *Russkaya ustnaya narodnaya drama*, p. 129.

16 On formulae versus motif variation, see Burke, *Popular Culture*, pp. 128–9.

17 Vsevolodsky-Gerngross, *Russkii teatr ot istokov*, p. 58.

18 Nekrylova, 'The traditional archetectonics', pp. 31–2. The somewhat peculiar tense usage and the mistranslation 'cumulative fairy tale' for *kumulyativnaya skazka* are to be found in the original article, written in English.

19 Nekrylova, *Russkie narodnye gorodskie prazdniki*, p. 81.

20 Vsevolodsky-Gerngross, *Russkaya ustnaya narodnaya drama*, p. 129.

21 Nekrylova, 'Zakon kontrasta', p. 217.

22 The *most* in 'Kuznetskii most' indicates not bridge but paving; Kamennyi Most, on the other hand, is the name of a bridge in Moscow; there is a Kamennostrovskii as well as a Kamennyi Most in St Petersburg; 'the stone bridge' might be a topographical reference more or less anywhere. As Burke notes in *Popular Culture*, bridges were favoured places for quacks and street traders to assemble all over Europe (p. 111).

23 See, for example, Putintsev's version (quoted in chapter 5, p. 184).

24 Doroshevich, *Sakhalin*, p. 131.

25 Nekrylova, 'Severnorusskie varianty', *passim*.

26 Dmitriev, 'Na starom moskovskom gulyanii', 351.

27 A rather perfunctory account of regional variants appears in T. G. Bulak's article, 'Iz istorii komedii Petrushki', *Russkii fol'klor* XVI (1976), pp. 221–7.

28 V. N. Nekrasov, *Komu na Rusi zhit' khorosho*, in *Polnoe sobranie sochinenii v 15 tt.* (Moscow 1982), v pp. 35–6.

29 Henryk Jurkowski, *Dzieje teatru lalek: od romantizma do wielkiej reformu teatru* (Warsaw 1976), p. 151.

30 Shcheglov, *Narod i teatr*, p. 118.

31 Nekrylova, 'Zakon kontrasta', p. 217. The term 'comic oxymoron' goes back to the Russian Formalists. See Bogatyrev, *Cheshkii kukol'nyi i russkii narodnyi teatr* (Berlin and St Petersburg 1923).

32 Nekrylova, 'Zakon kontrasta', p. 216.

33 ibid.

34 ibid., p. 217.

35 See for example Henry Fielding, *Joseph Andrews* (Harmondsworth 1986), p. 26: '[The burlesque] is ever the exhibition of what is monstrous and unnatural, and where our delight, if we examine it, arises from the surprizing absurdity, as in expropriating the manners of the highest to the lowest, or *e converso*.'

36 Lev Losev, *On the Beneficence of Censorship: Aesopian Language and Modern Russian Literature* trans. Jane Bobko (Munich 1984), p. 221.

37 Sigmund Freud, *Der Witz und seine Beziehung zum Unbewußten* (pbk reprint, Frankfurt am Main 1978), p. 72.

38 Rovinsky *Russkie narodnye kartinki*, 2nd edn (1900), I, pp. 363–4.

39 Nekrylova, 'Iz istorii formirovaniya', p. 39.

40 Gor'ky, XXIV, p. 494.

41 Smirnova, *Sovetskii teatr kukol*, p. 37.

42 ibid., p. 25.

43 Vsevolodsky-Gerngross, *Russkaya ustnaya narodnaya drama*, p. 115.

44 Smirnova, *Sovetskii teatr kukol*, p. 30.

45 Vitengof, *Ocherki moskovskoi zhizni*, p. 205: on violence in the subordinate class milieu see chapter 1, pp. 36–8; on holiday fist-fights see Bonnell, *Life and Labour*, p. 41.

46 E. Mandel and G. Novack, *The Marxist Theory of Alienation* (New York 1973).

47 This and other factory laments are collected in A. I. Astakhova and P. G. Shiryaeva, 'Staraya rabochaya pesnya', *Sovetskaya etnografiya* 1–2, (1934), 201–3.

48 Nekrylova, 'The traditional archetectonics', pp. 34, 36, 39.

49 Nekrylova, 'Zakon kontrasta', p. 212. For an explanation of the possible origin of this passage, see chapter 3, pp. 123–4.

50 Nekrylova, 'The traditional archetectonics', p. 39.

51 Olga Freidenberg, *Poetika syuzheta i zhanra* (Leningrad 1936), p. 235. My emphasis.

52 On the rituals associated with conscription, see Krupyanskaya and Polishchuk, *Kul'tura*, p. 165.

53 On the agricultural rituals, see Warner, *Russian Folk Theatre*, pp. 1–80.

54 Dain, *Russkaya narodnaya igrushka*, p. 71.

55 On laughter in fertility cults, see Propp, 'Ritual'nyi smekh v fol'klore', *Uchenye zapiski Leningradskogo gosudarstvennogo universiteta*, third ser., 46 (1939), 151–75; V. V. Ivanov, 'Iz zametok o stroenii i formirovanii karnaval'nogo obraza', in *Problemy poetiki i istorii literatury: sbornik stat'ei* (Saransk 1973), pp. 37–53.

56 As in D. S. Likhachev, A. M. Panchenko and N. V. Ponyrko, *Smekh v drevnei Rusi* (Leningrad 1984).

57 See A. M. Panchenko, 'Smekh kak zrelishche', in ibid., pp. 81–116.

58 Freud, *Der Witz*, p. 193.

59 I am eager not to make an analogy here – as I suspect Freud was doing – with Haeckel's recapitulationary theory of evolutionary biology. On the use of this theory to determinist ends, see Stephen Jay Gould, *Ontogeny and Phylogeny* (Cambridge, Mass. and London 1977), chapter 5.

60 N. N. Beletskaya, 'O pozdnem etape istorii russkoi narodnoi dramy', *Sovetskaya etnografiya* 5 (1963), 28–9.

61 On entertainment and efficacy in literature, and how they appealed to city- and village-dwellers, see J. Brooks, *When Russia Learned to Read*, p. 33.

62 As in 'Pop i batrak', 'Pop i muzhik', A. Afanas'ev, *Russkie zavetnye skazki*, place given as 'Varlaam, god mrakobesiya', actually Geneva (reprint 1975), numbers 40, 44. Moral ambivalence was certainly present in the village too – of which more in chapter 3; I am simply arguing here that it increased in importance in towns.

63 Nekrylova, 'The traditional archetectonics', p. 37.

64 Doroshevich, *Sakhalin*, p. 130.

65 Freud, *Der Witz*, p. 81.

66 M. Bakhtin, *Rabelais*, p. 473. Where Bakhtin's ideas have been absorbed by Soviet scholars, they have been integrated into either formalist or ritualist readings. See, for example, Bogatyrev's chapter 'Khudozhestven-nye sredstva v yumoristicheskom yarmarochnom fol'klore' in his *Voprosy teorii narodnogo iskusstva* (Moscow 1971), pp. 450–96; and V. V. Ivanov's chapter cited in note 55 above.

67 M. Bakhtin, *Rabelais*, p. 146.

68 ibid., p. 473.

69 ibid., p. 26.

70 ibid., p. 281.

71 Warner, *Russian Folk Theatre*, p. 114.

72 Vertinsky, *Zapiski russkogo P'ero*, p. 80.

73 On the Yaroslavl' men in Moscow, see Gilyarovsky, *Sochineniya v 4 tt.*, IV, p. 335; in St Petersburg, on the other hand, identification was not so easy, as *yaroslavtsy* were the largest group of provincials by far, making up 10 per cent of the population in 1868 (*Sanktpeterburg: issledovaniya*,

pp. 28, 121–4); here they were simply the most representative type of YAM.

74 Bakhtin, *Rabelais*, p. 163.

75 Bulak, 'Iz istorii komedii Petrushka', p. 225.

76 On binary and trinary structure in popular culture see Burke, *Popular Culture*, pp. 137–8.

77 Bakhtin, *Rabelais*, p. 81. Stites (Gleason, Kenez and Stites, *Bolshevik Culture*, p. 3) argues for a distinction between 'symbolic retribution' and reversal in subordinate class protest; this distinction is no doubt theoretically convenient, but in carnival texts such as *Petrushka* it was often blurred.

78 'Abjection displacement' in the carnival is argued by Stallybrass and White, *Transgression*, pp. 19, 53.

79 Bulak, 'Iz istorii komedii Petrushka', pp. 223–4.

80 Bakhtin, *Rabelais*, p. 240. Natalie Zemon Davis, *Fiction in the Archives*, has recently indicated some instances in which Frenchwomen of the sixteenth century were more circumscribed in the carnival than men: they were, for example, unable to plead drunkenness or involvement in celebration as a mitigation for crime (pp. 88, 92).

81 An indication of the size of Petrushka is given by the photograph of Sergey Yutkevich holding the puppet in D. Moldavsky, *S Mayakovskim v teatre i kino: khiga o Sergee Yutkeviche* (Moscow 1974), unnumbered illustration in first set of plates.

82 Zoë Brooks, 'Spitting Image', *Animations* 8 (1985), 46–8.

83 For a picture of Zaitsev's Petrushka head, see Nekrylova, *Russkie narodnye gorodskie prazdniki*, p. 75.

84 On the manufacture of puppet costumes by the puppeteers' female relations, see Sergey Obraztsov, *Po stupen'kam pamyati* (Moscow 1987), p. 144.

85 Bogatyrev, 'O vzaimosvyazi dvukh blizkikh semioticheskikh sistem', *Trudy po znakovym sistemam* 6 (Tartu 1973), 306–30; I. N. Solomonik, 'Problemy analiza narodnogo teatra kukol: khudozhestvennyi yazyk narodnogo kukol'nogo predstavleniya', *Sovetskaya etnografiya* 6 (1978), 28–45.

86 Solomonik, 'Problemy analiza narodnogo teatra kukol', 34.

87 V. Meyerhold, 'Balagan', in *Stat'i, pis'ma, rechi*, I, p. 211.

88 Derzhavina *et al.* in V. Grebenyuk *et al.* (eds.), *Rannyaya russkaya dramaturgiya*, pp. 16–25.

89 Rap verse shares with the fairground genres the fact of a musical accompaniment; dub poetry bears considerable formal resemblance to the *raek* in which *Petrushka* is partly composed. It is also tonic verse of irregular line length, rhymed in couplets.

90 Bogatyrev, 'O vzaimosvyazi', 314ff.

91 Dain, *Russkaya narodnaya igrushka*, pp. 138–9.

92 Solomonik, 'Problemy analiza narodnogo teatra kukol', 134.

93 Nekrylova, 'The traditional archetectonics', p. 36.

94 On the associations of the shamans and shamanesses with high-pitched sound, see Jean de Lesseps quoted in Cross *Under Western Eyes*, pp. 241–2; Angela Carter, *Nights at the Circus* (London 1984), pp. 252–70, is an imaginative evocation.

95 Dain, *Russkaya narodnaya igrushka*, p. 45.

96 The term 'ethnographic present' is used by Clifford, *Predicament of Culture*, p. 189.

97 There has been a regrettable tendency for even some feminists to regard oral culture as a better world than literate culture. See, for example, Lissa Paul, 'Dumb Bunnies: a Revisionist Re-Reading of *Watership Down*', *Signal* 56 (May 1988), 119. That popular culture may lead intellectuals into false paths in their search for source material on popular values is suggested by the fact that the version which gives the 'best' and fullest portrait of the submissive plebeian wife, who actually enjoys her beatings and pleads that her husband should be returned from prison, is not any of the street versions but Elena Mitcoff's free variations on the theme of *Petrushka*.

3 PETRUSHKA, PUNCH AND PULCINELLA

1 Pierre Duchartre, *The Italian Comedy* (New York 1966), p. 208.

2 On the possible derivation of Pulcinella from *Pullus Galinaceus*, one of the titles of the Atellan hero Maccus, see Duchartre, *Italian Comedy*, p. 209.

3 Giacomo Oreglia, *The commedia dell'arte* (London 1969), plates 34, 35; the most exact account of Pulcinella's history and dates will be found in K. M. Lea, *Italian Popular Comedy* 2 vols. (Oxford 1934), I, p. 94.

4 Bragaglia, 'Burattino o marionetta', *Pulcinella*, pp. 398–421.

5 The soldier scene and the hanging scene, for example, are found in Germany and Austria as well as Italy: see Anon., *Das neue Kasperltheater* (Sonneberg *c*.1890) and *Das wahrhaftige Kasperltheater in 6 Stücken* (Munich *c*. 1890).

6 'Jan Klaasens leven en heldendaden', *Nederlands volksleren* 18: 4 (Winter 1968–9), 70–82; on Belgium, see R. Guiette, *Marionnettes de tradition populaire* (Brussels 1949), p. 94; Paul Fournel, *Les Marionnettes* (Paris 1982), p. 22.

7 Michael Byrom, *Punch and Judy: Its Origins and Evolution* 2nd edn (London 1978), p. 9.

8 Gustave Doré and Blanchard Jerrold, *London* (Newton Abbot 1971), p. 177.

9 Byrom, *Punch in the Italian Puppet Theatre* (London 1983), p. 44.

10 J. E. Varey, *Historia de los títeres en España*, (Madrid 1957), pp. 95–6.

11 Vsevolodsky-Gerngross, *Istoriya russkogo teatra*, II, p. 340.

12 Zguta, *Russian Minstrels*, p. 119. (My emphasis.)

13 See Alferov, 'Petrushka', *passim*; TP 11–47.

14 Robert Leach, *The Punch and Judy Show: History, Traditions and Meaning* (London 1985), pp. 14–16.

15 Bogatyrev, *Cheshskii kukol'nyi i russkii narodnyi teatr, passim.*

16 Stith Thompson, *Motif Index of Folk Literature* (Bloomington 1957), nos. J.657.1; X.600. This index has to be treated with some caution on account of its gender bias, as Torborg Lundell has pointed out (see Davis, *Fiction in the Archives*, p. 201 n.62). It does indeed suggest that the motif of the 'shrewish wife' is endlessly proliferated in folklore, whilst that of the brutal husband occupies a very modest niche. (Contrast the former, nos. T251–T275, with the latter, S60, S62, S410.)

17 Though discarding the notion of history in folklore or popular culture is useful in that it allows an international perspective and a sense of similarity in historically unconnected cultures, the dangers of biological theories of folklore generation (the latter word is itself suggestive) should perhaps not be underestimated. Now that recapitulatory theory (see chapter 2 p. 250 n.59) is no longer fashionable, some insidious nonsense is being put about that uses garbled versions of genetic theory: one folklorist has argued, for example, that there is a pool of 'creative genes' within a given culture, which emigration may weaken; see Robert Austerlitz, 'Folklore, Nationality and the Twentieth Century in Siberia and the Soviet Far East', in Oinas, *Folklore*, pp. 145–6. The danger with religio-mystical theories of origin (such as Jung's notion of the 'collective unconscious') is that their apparent internationalism tends in fact to be inspired by European and Christian notions.

18 Burke, *Popular Culture*, p. 57.

19 Clarke, *Analytical Archaeology*, pp. 426–7.

20 Only the briefest outline of other European street puppetry traditions can be given here. The following have provided sources and are useful for further information: (1) editions of plays: *Das wahrhaftige Kasperltheater*; Anon., *Das neue Casperltheater*; Anon., *Kasperl und König Mäusebart*; *Kasperl im Räuberwirtshaus* (both Vienna 1950); *Théâtre lyonnais de Guignol* (Lyon 1890): (2) histories: Byrom, *Punch in the Italian Puppet Theatre*, Charles Magnin, *Histoire des marionnettes en Europe* (Paris 1852), Fournel, *Les Marionnettes*, George Speaight, *Punch and Judy: a History* (London 1970), Malkin, *Traditional and Folk Puppets*, Bragaglia, *Pulcinella*. The best way to get an idea of the modern tradition of these texts, that is, to watch a street performance, is unfortunately not available for the earlier tradition.

21 The largest collection of Punch and Judy texts in a single volume is Byrom's *Punch and Judy*, which contains four complete texts as well as quotations from and accounts of others. Besides these, I have used a text from George Speaight's *Punch and Judy: a History*, and my own experiences of the street tradition.

22 Oreglia, *Commedia dell'arte*, pp. 95–108.

23 Lea, *Italian Popular Comedy*, I, pp. 1, 100.

24 Bragaglia, *Pulcinella*, pp. 414–21.

25 Magnin, *Histoire des marionnettes*, pp. 107ff, 160–75; Varey, *Historia de los títeres*, p. 244.

26 On the repertoire of Germany and Austria, see *Das Kasperltheater für Erwachsene* (Frankfurt-am-Main 1978), and the Kasperl collections listed in note 20 above.

27 See Michael Byrom's translation of *The Song of Zeza*, in his *Punch and Judy*, pp. 30–4.

28 Dmitriev, *Tsirk*, pp. 32–3, 44–6.

29 John Payne Collier, *The Tragical Comedy or Comical Tragedy of Punch and Judy* (London 1976), p. 28. A fuller comparison of Grigorovich's version with European tradition will be found in Kelly, 'From Pulcinella to Petrushka', *passim*.

30 Byrom, *Punch in the Italian Puppet Theatre*, pp. 25–6; for the Devil and the Policeman, see Fournel, *Les Marionnettes*, p. 12.

31 Polly appears in Piccini's version (Collier), but rarely in later texts; Katerina appears in Grigorovich and 2 FT texts. A name cognate with 'Katerina' is given to the wife of the hero in the Dutch puppet theatre (Katrijn) in 'Jan Klaasens leven en heldendaden'.

32 See Alekseev-Yakovlev, *Russkie narodnye gulyan'ya*, p. 62; Varey, *Historia de los títeres*, p. 96.

33 'Povest' o Gore-Zlochast'e' (a written text), in N. K. Gudzy, *Khrestomatiya po drevnerusskoi literature*, 8th edn (Moscow 1973), pp. 382–94.

34 J. Brooks, *When Russia Learned to Read*, p. 271.

35 On the Ghost see 'Jan Klaasens leven en heldendaden'; Byrom, *Punch and Judy*, p. 44.

36 Death is found, for example, in Vinogradov's *vertep* text, and here, as usual, Death is feminine. (The gender of the noun is used by Roman Jakobson as an instance of the psychological effects of grammatical gender; see *Selected Writings* (The Hague and Paris 1985), VII, p. 109).

37 *Das wahrhaftige Kasperltheater* includes such a scene with a crocodile. On its arrival in England, see Leach, *Punch and Judy Show*, pp. 81–2.

38 Speaight, *Punch and Judy*, p. 150.

39 Bulak, 'Iz istorii komedii Petrushka', p. 225. She comments: 'The puppeteers might have heard Chinese words from Chinese traders in Russia' – possibly, but by no stretch of the imagination is this Chinese.

40 Speaight, *Punch and Judy*, p. 151.

41 *Das wahrhaftige Kasperltheater*, pp. 3–4.

42 Speaight, *Punch and Judy*, p. 152.

43 See Warner, *Russian Folk Theatre*, pp. 17, 105.

44 Vinogradov, 'Velikorusskii vertep', 373.

45 Such a servant drama performance is described by Gilyarovsky, *Sobranie sochinenii*, IV, pp. 180–3.

46 Grebenyuk *et al.*, *Rannyaya russkaya dramaturgiya*, p. 617. My emphasis.

47 ibid., p. 702.

48 ibid., pp. 524, 620 ff.

49 This is what is asserted by Eremin (TP 59). Rovinsky's collection, *Russkie narodnye kartinki*, lists no Filimoshka, but the 2nd edn (1900), p. 306, has a *lubok* of 'Filat / who is glad / he can sleep in a basket'. Although there is

no etymological connection between *Filat* (from Theophilaktos) and *Filimoshka* (from Philemon), there may be a link in the popular imagination between *Filat* and *Fila* (like *Filimoshka* a diminutive of *Filimon*, Philemon).

50 Oreglia, *Commedia dell'arte*, pp. 8–9, 101–3.
51 Grebenyuk *et al.*, *Rannyaya russkaya dramaturgiya*, p. 669.
52 Nekrylova, 'Zakon kontrasta', p. 213.
53 Vinogradov, 'Velikorusskii vertep', 374.
54 Byrom, *Punch in the Italian Puppet Theatre*, p. 138.
55 For an example of a mummers' horse-sale scene, see Berkov 47–8.
56 J. Brooks, *When Russia Learned to Read*, p. 189. In the rural drama *Lodka* the bandits' wickedness is not curbed (Berkov 146–50), and many ballads about Stenka Razin make no allusion to his death: see L. I. Emel'yaninov (ed.), *Russkaya istoricheskaya pesnya* (Leningrad 1987), nos. 61–70; in three only (nos. 65, 66, 70) is he betrayed or captured.
57 Speaight, *Punch and Judy*, pp. 143–4.
58 As in L. E. E. Duranty's *Pierrot et le Pâtissier*, in his *Théâtre des Marionnettes* (Paris 1880), pp. 199–216.
59 For the Symbolists' view of Petrushka–Pierrot, see chapter 4, pp. 164–5; Ya. Tugendkhol'd, 'Itogi sezona', review in *Apollon* 6 (1911), *chronicle*, p. 74.
60 A. M. Ripellino, quoted by Carla Solivetti in her notes to K. Miklaševskij, *La commedia dell'arte* (Venice 1981), p. 131.
61 Grebenyuk *et al.*, *Rannyaya russkaya dramaturgiya*, pp. 688–9.
62 Gogol', *Mertvye dushi*, part I, chapter 2, in *Polnoe sobranie sochinenii*, 14 vols. (Moscow 1937–52), VI, pp. 19–20. My emphasis.
63 A Sytova (ed.), *The Lubok*, plate 38 (billed by the editor as 'the future Petrouchka [*sic*] of the folk theatre' – but the name Petrushka is not used in the *lubok* text itself).
64 Rovinsky, *Russkie narodnye kartinki* (1881), V, p. 270.
65 Derzhavina *et al.*, in Grebenyuk *et al. Rannyaya russkaya dramaturgiya*, p. 39.
66 Solivetti in Miklaševskij, *Commedia dell'arte*, p. 131.
67 Rovinsky, *Russkie narodnye kartinki* (1881), V, p. 270.
68 Afanas'ev, *Russkie skazki*, 3 vols. (Moscow 1955), III, numbers 383–409.
69 And, *Karagöz*, pp. 102–4.
70 For pictures of the Western European puppet theatre, see illustrations, pp. 115, 117.
71 Malkin, *Traditional and Folk Puppets*, p. 45.
72 And, *Karagöz*, p. 30; on Central Asia see Tsekhnovitser, TP 20.
73 Varey, *Historia de los títeres*, p. 95.
74 'Jan Klaasens leven en heldendaden'; Collier, *Tragical Comedy*, p. 26; Malkin, *Traditional and Folk Puppets*, p. 37.
75 Simonovich-Efimova, *Zapiski petrushechnika*, p. 184.
76 Smirnova, *Sovetskii teatr kukol*, p. 20.
77 Peretts, 'Kukol'nyi teatr na Rusi', 173.
78 M. Bakhtin, *Rabelais*, p. 473.

79 A. M. Panchenko, 'Skomoroshina o chernetse', *Trudy otdela drevnerusskoi literatury AN SSSR* 21 (1965), 92.

80 M. Bakhtin, *Rabelais*, p. 218.

81 J. W. von Goethe, *Hanswursts Hochzeit*, in *Jugendwerke 2: Dramen und dramatische Skizzen 1774–5* (Berlin 1953), pp. 289–95. Hanswurst was a traditional clown who appeared in farces, usually of a rather gross kind.

82 And, *Karagöz*, pp. 71, 79.

83 Byrom, *Punch in the Italian Puppet Theatre*, p. 153. One can, of course, take the national specificity argument too far, as I think Darnton, *Great Cat Massacre*, does when he argues that French popular heroes were specially streetwise (p. 62). It would hardly be possible to be more streetwise than the glove-puppet heroes of *any* European or indeed non-European tradition.

84 Lea, *Italian Popular Comedy*, I, p. 98.

85 See especially the obscene folk-tales issued by Afanas'ev in his 'Secret Tales' (*Russkie zavetnye skazki*).

86 See Kabronsky, *Nepodtsenzurnaya chastushka*, nos. 91, 122, 127, 129.

87 Afanas'ev, *Russkie skazki*, III, nos. 395–6.

88 C. Carey (ed.), *Les Proverbes érotiques russes: études de proverbes recuellis et non publiés par Dal' et Simoni* (The Hague and Paris 1972), nos. 49, 51.

89 Afanas'ev, *Russkie skazki*, III, no. 523. The icon of *Vremennaya Pyatnitsa* was an icon of St Paraskeva, so called because the feast fell occasionally (*vremenno*) on a Friday (see Propp's 'note', ibid., p. 445).

90 ibid., no. 406.

91 ibid., no. 384; on the 'primitive' perceptions of the universe as a series of unconnected moments in time–space, see V. Toporov, 'On the cosmological origins of early historical descriptions', *Russian Poetics in Translation* 3 (1976), 38–81.

92 The exception is an anecdote on the 'pound of flesh' principle in which, in order to revenge himself on an avaricious tavern-keeper, a peasant purchases from him a *lopatka* (shovel, *spade*) and then reveals that he has actually purchased another sort of *lopatka* – the man's shoulder *blade* (Afanas'ev, *Russkie skazki*, III, no. 498).

93 This argument ignores the possibility of folklore professionals in villages; but even in these cases it seems likely that they were integrated into a mutual aid system (i.e., rewarded in barter or services), rather than paid. The *vertep* puppeteers whom Charlotte Pepys encountered were, for example, rewarded with 'a few coins' during the play, but with vodka and food after it, *Domestic Sketches*, II, pp. 108–15. How far the villages were affected by contact with town commerce is another possible point of debate; a possible comparative model is given by Hugh Brody's study of migrancy in Ireland, *Inishkillane: Change and Decline in the West of Ireland* (London 1982).

94 Doroshevich, *Sakhalin*, p. 130.

95 'Povest' o Frole Skobeeve', Gudzy, *Khrestomatiya po drevnerusskoi literature*, pp. 412–21.

96 Grebenyuk *et al.*, *Rannyaya russkaya dramaturgiya*, pp. 676–81.
97 ibid., pp. 614–16.

4 *PETRUSHKA* AND *PETROUCHKA*; FAIRGROUND AND
CARNIVAL IN HIGH LITERATURE

1 On the import of roundabouts from Germany and America into other
countries see Frederick Fried, *A Pictorial History of the Carousel* (New
York 1964). A good sense of the international character of fairground and
circus is given also by Grock's two volumes of autobiography, *Life's a
Lark* (London 1931) and *King of Clowns* (London 1957), and by George
Speaight's *A History of the Circus* (London 1980).
2 See Bragaglia, *Pulcinella*, Lea, *Italian Popular Comedy*, Oreglia, *Commedia dell'arte*, Duchartre, *Italian Comedy*.
3 David Braithwaite, *Fairground Architecture* (London 1968); Ian Starsmore (ed.), *The Fairground*, catalogue to an exhibition at the Whitechapel
Art Gallery (London 1977).
4 The prologue of Jonson's *Bartholomew Fair* states the play's purpose as
a polemic with 'the jealous noise / Of your land's faction, scandalized at
toys, / As babies, hobby horses, puppet plays ...' (cited from E. M.
Waith's edition, New Haven and London 1963, p. 23).
5 E. A. Baratynsky, *Tsyganka*, in *Polnoe sobranie stikhotvorenii* (Leningrad
1951), p. 279.
6 N. G. Pomyalovsky, 'O tom, kak porechane lupyat po puti progressa',
Polnoe sobranie sochinenii v 2 tt. (Leningrad 1935), II, pp. 262–5; A. I.
Levitov, 'Tipy i tseny sel'skoi yarmarki', in *Rasskazy i ocherki* (Voronezh
1980), pp. 23–63; V. A. Sleptsov, 'Pod verbami' and 'Balagany na
Svyatoi', in *Sochineniya v 2 tt.* (Moscow and Leningrad 1933), II,
pp. 461–4; V. Garshin, 'Medvedi', in *Rasskazy* (St Petersburg 1909),
pp. 304–23; S. El'patevsky, 'Yarmarochnye kartinki', *Russkoe bogatstvo*
12 (1896), 7–21; see also Nekrylova, 'Ocherkisty-shestedesyatniki', *Russkaya literatura i fol'klor: vtoraya polovina XIX veka* (Leningrad 1982),
pp. 152–9; Michael Pursglove, 'D. V. Grigorovich's "Gutta-percha
Boy"', *Quinquereme: New Studies in Modern Languages* 9:1 (1986),
46–62. A similarly disapproving attitude is taken by Goncharov, whose
hero Oblomov's descent into vulgarity is marked, amongst other things,
by visits paid to the fairground (*Oblomov* pt 4, chapter 9, *Sobranie
sochinenii v 6 tt.* (Moscow 1959), IV, p. 397).
7 Gleb Uspensky, *Polnoe sobranie sochinenii*, III (St Petersburg 1908),
p. 300. A story in a similar vein, though from a later date (1915), is
Gor'ky's 'Teatral'noe' (Theatre Stuff) in *Sobranie sochinenii v 30 tt.*, XIV,
pp. 180–6.
8 Korney Chukovsky in Nikolay Uspensky, *Sochineniya v 2 tt.* (Moscow
and Leningrad 1933), I, p. 7.
9 A. S. Pushkin, 'O narodnoi drame i drame Marfa-posadnitsa', in *Polnoe
sobranie sochinenii v 10 tt.* (Leningrad 1977), VII, p. 147.

10 Gogol', in 'Peterburgskie zapiski 1836 goda', *Polnoe sobranie sochinenii*, VIII, pp. 179–90, and 'O teatre ...', ibid., pp. 267–77, expresses his concern that theatre should be moral and follow the high-theatrical traditions of Shakespeare and Schiller, not the popular *obez'yanstvo* (apery) of vaudevilles and melodramas. But there is no doubt that Gogol's own writing draws on at least the first of these two genres, as on the *vertep* and Ukrainian comedies of his youth, on which see V. Gippius, *Nikolai Gogol'*, trans. R. Maguire (Ann Arbor 1981), pp. 31–2; it also bears a generic, if not direct, relationship to the carnival plays and acts of the capital.

11 On the 'circulation of social energy' between Elizabethan theatres and society see Stephen Greenblatt, *Shakespearian Negotiations* (Oxford 1988), chapter 1. That the provincial theatres were less elevated is indicated by B. A. Babochkin *et al.* (eds.), *Russkii provintsial'nyi teatr: vospominaniya* (Leningrad 1937).

12 See the *Teatral'naya entsiklopediya*, ed. P. A. Markov, 6 vols. (Moscow 1963–7), III, *Monopoliya imperatorskikh teatrov*, pp. 905–7. On censorship after 1882 (still very heavy) the most neutral source is *Entsiklopedicheskii slovar'* XXXII, *Teatr* pp. 743–4.

13 On censorship of the *balagans* before 1882 see Alekseev-Yakovlev, *Russkie narodnye gulyan'ya*, pp. 11–12, 80.

14 On the People's theatre movement see 'Chastnye i lyubitel'skie teatry stolits. Narodnyi teatr', *Istoriya russkogo dramaticheskogo teatra*, ed. E. G. Kholodov (Moscow 1982), VI, pp. 238–90.

15 B. V. Varneke, 'Chto igraet narod', *Ezhegodnik imperatorskikh teatrov*, 4 (1913), 1.

16 *Istoriya russkogo dramaticheskogo teatra*, VI, p. 289.

17 Alekseev-Yakovlev, *Russkie narodnye gulyan'ya*, pp. 75–115.

18 Alferov, 'Petrushka i ego predki', p. 716. This process was exactly similar to the changes which happened in Western Europe rather earlier, around 1800, of which Stallybrass and White, *Transgression*, write: 'As the realm of Folly was being restructured within bourgeois consciousness as precisely that *other realm* inhabited by a grotesque body which it repudiated as a part of its own identity and disdained as a set of real life *practices and rituals*, so it seemed to become more and more important as a set of *representations*' (p. 103).

19 A. P. Chekhov, 'Yarmarka', in *Polnoe sobranie sochinenii i pisem v 30 tt.* (Moscow 1975), I, pp. 247–52.

20 A. Blok, 'Predislovie k Vozmezdiyu', in *Stikhotvoreniya* (Leningrad 1955), p. 524.

21 Meyerhold, *Stat'i, pis'ma, rechi*, I, p. 309.

22 I. F. Annensky, 'Shariki detskie', in *Stikhotvoreniya i tragedii* (Leningrad 1959), p. 141.

23 Vyacheslav I. Ivanov, 'Esteticheskaya norma teatra', *Sobranie sochinenii* (Brussels 1974), I, p. 207.

24 With the exception of Annensky's *Famira-kifared*, which does use dog-

gerel verse and is an adaptation of the Greek satyr-play owing something
to the *balagan* tradition: see Kelly, 'Bacchic Revels? Annensky's *Famira-
kifared* and the Satyrs', *Essays in Poetics* 10:2 (1985), 77–95. On the
neo-classical tragedies of Ivanov and Annensky, see also Kelly, 'Classical
Tragedy and the "Slavonic Renaissance"': the Plays of I. F. Annenskij and
Vjačeslav Ivanov Compared', *Slavic and East European Journal*,2 (1989),
235–54.

25 Bryusov's 'Nenuzhnaya pravda' does have a reference to the 'factory
   theatre', but only in terms of staging, not of text, *Sobranie sochinenii v 7 tt.*
   VII, p. 73.
26 A. Bely, 'Teatr i sovremennaya drama', *Teatr: kniga o novom teatre*
   (St Petersburg 1908), p. 274.
27 Ellis, 'Chto takoe teatr?', *Vesy* 4 (1908), 88.
28 F. Sologub, 'Teatr odnoi voli', in *Teatr: kniga o novom teatre*, pp. 179,
   185.
29 ibid., p. 192; my emphasis.
30 Meyerhold, *Stat'i, pis'ma, rechi*, I, p. 218; my emphasis.
31 Chekhov, *Chaika*, act IV, *Polnoe sobranie sochinenii*, XIII, p. 49.
32 A. M. Remizov, *Tsar' Maksimilian* (Berkeley 1988, reprint of Petersburg
   edn of 1920; his own postscript states his method: to 'throw out the barracks and emphasise the chorus' (p. 117), and choric effects resembling
   those in Symbolist neo-classical tragedy rather than the theatre of Russian
   soldiers and villagers have indeed been used. In Remizov, *Plyas Irodiady*
   (Berlin, n.d.), he adapts the Herodias motif known in *vertep* in a manner
   owing much to Oscar Wilde's *Salome*.
33 Sologub, *Van'ka-klyuchnik*, in *Dramaticheskie proizvedeniya*, VIII
   (St Petersburg 1908), pp. 157–221; Remizov, *Rusal'nye deistva* (reprint,
   Munich 1971).
34 J. Frazer, *The Golden Bough*, abr. edn (London 1970), ch. 27, sect. 9,
   pp. 424–5; one way in which Frazer's text could have filtered through to
   those knowing no English was via Vyacheslav Ivanov's monumental essay
   'Ellinskaya religiya stradayushchego boga' *Novyi put'*, 1904, which
   reiterates many central themes from it, with acknowledgements.
35 Blok, 'Balagan', in *Stikhotvoreniya*, p. 220.
36 V. Khodasevich, 'V Petrovskom parke', in *Sobranie sochinenii*, (Ann
   Arbor 1983), I, p. 83; 'Akrobat', in ibid., p. 77.
37 M. Voloshin, 'Tsirk', in *Stikhotvoreniya*, 2 vols. (Paris 1982–4), I, p. 22.
38 Blok, *Balaganchik*, in *Teatr* (Leningrad 1981), pp. 59–72.
39 Benois, *Moi vospominaniya*, I, pp. 294–5.
40 Blok, *Teatr*, p. 70.
41 T. M. Rodina, *Aleksandr Blok i russkii teatr nachala XX veka* (Moscow
   1972), p. 132.
42 This example of literal-mindedness in the popular theatre is taken from
   Dmitriev, *Tsirk*, p. 285; Pierrot discovers that Columbina is made of
   cardboard: Blok, *Teatr*, p. 71.
43 Blok, *Teatr*, p. 70.

44 Blok, 'Balaganchik', in *Stikhotvoreniya*, p. 189.

45 The agitprop theatre will be discussed in chapter 5.

46 E. Zamyatin, *Blokha: igra v 4-kh deistviyakh*, in *Sochineniya* (Munich 1982), II, p. 373.

47 Dmitriev, *Tsirk*, p. 133.

48 L. Leonov, *Vor* (Moscow 1965).

49 Vsevolod Ivanov, *Pokhozhdeniya fakira*, in *Sobranie sochinenii v 8 tt.* (Moscow 1973–87), IV.

50 M. Zoshchenko, 'Karusel'', in *Sobranie sochinenii* (Leningrad 1931), I, p. 30.

51 Zoshchenko, 'Teatr dlya sebya', in *Tsarskie sapogi* (Riga 1924), p. 66.

52 S. A. Esenin, *Sobranie sochinenii v 5 tt.* (Moscow 1962), III, pp. 59–60.

53 Yury Annenkov, *Dnevnik moikh vstrech: tsikl tragedii*, 2 vols. (New York 1966), I, p. 267; on Kustodiev, see *Kustodiev v teatre: katalog* (Moscow, 1979), Central Theatre Museum.

54 Moldavsky, *S Mayakovskim v teatre i kino*, p. 15.

55 V. B. Shklovsky, *Eizenshtein* (Moscow 1973), p. 45.

56 *Pokhozhdeniya fakira* was not republished between 1935 and 1959. The circus-inspired second and third volumes received much hostile criticism in the 1930s, unlike the Gor'ky-esque first volume. See notes, in Vsevolod Ivanov, *Sobranie sochinenii v 8 tt.* IV, 714–19.

57 *Kino: entsiklopedicheskii slovar'*, ed. S. Yutkevich (Moscow 1986), p. 508.

58 Vertinsky, *Zapiski russkogo P'ero*, p. 80.

59 Leonid Askol'dov, *Za kulisami tsirka: sbornik rasskazov* (Paris 1962).

60 Alla Golovina, 'Sochel'nik', in *Lebedinaya karusel'* (Paris 1935), p. 36; a fairground is given similar treatment in 'Lebedinaya karusel'', in ibid., p. 22.

61 Doré and Jerrold, *London*, p. 178.

62 The remarkably rich materials associated with *Punch and Judy* can be seen in the studies of Speaight, Byrom and Leach (see bibliography), as well as in the collections of the Bethnal Green Museum, London, the Museum of London and the Puppet Centre Trust, London.

63 See Magnin, *Histoire des Marionnettes*; Bragaglia *Pulcinella*; Fournel *Les Marionnettes*; Jaroslav Bartoš, *Loutkařské hry českého obrožení* (Prague 1952). An example of literary use of popular puppetry outside Western Europe is Y. Vlachoyannis', 'The Bitter-Sweet Art', in Rom Gudas, *The Bitter-Sweet Art; Karaghiozis, the Greek Shadow Theatre* (Athens 1986), pp. 25–90.

64 Duranty, *Théâtre des marionnettes*; Alfred Jarry, *Tout Ubu* (reprint, Paris 1980); Federico García Lorca, *La tragicomedia de Don Cristóbal*, in *Obras III: Teatro I* (Madrid 1980), pp. 81–152; *El retablillo de Don Cristóbal*, in ibid., pp. 153–81.

65 Lorca, *El retablillo de Don Cristóbal*, pp. 156–7; Jarry, *Ubu sur la butte*, in *Tout Ubu*, pp. 261–4.

66 Duranty, 'Polichinelle retiré du monde', in *Théâtre des marionnettes*, pp. 257–72.

67 Sleptsov, 'Peterburgskie zametki', in *Sochineniya v 2 tt.*, II, p. 331.
68 V. A. Kurochkin, *Prints Lutonya*, in *Sobranie sochinenii* (Moscow 1947), pp. 462–503; *Amerikanskii prints i afrikanskaya printessa*, in ibid., pp. 425–7. Both are translations of plays by the French author Marc Monier. Some interesting observations on the theory of puppetry are made in the introduction by Kurochkin to the former play.
69 N. S. Gumilev, *Ditya Allakha: arabskaya skazka* (Berlin 1922).
70 Nekrasov, *Polnoe sobranie sochinenii v 15 tt.*, p. 35.
71 G. N. Zhulev, 'Petrushka', in I. Yampol'sky (ed.), *Poety Iskry*, 2 vols. (Leningrad 1955), II, p. 697.
72 *Petrushka*, illustrated journal, ed. N. Kholodny, no. 1 (only one published) (St Petersburg 1905).
73 Dostoevsky, *Polnoe sobranie sochinenii*, XXII, p. 180.
74 ibid., p. 181.
75 Leach, *Punch and Judy Show*, pp. 35–9.
76 N. N. Evreinov, 'Dan' marionetkam', *Teatral'nye novatsii* (Petrograd 1922), p. 99.
77 Andrey Bely, *Kotik Letaev*, facsimile of Petrograd edn of 1922 (Munich 1964), p. 89. The hyphenation precisely reproduces the original.
78 Z. Ashkenazi, 'Bessmertnyi Petrushka', *Ezhegodnik Imperatorskikh teatrov* 4 (1914), 7.
79 ibid., 8.
80 ibid., 17.
81 Duchartre, *Italian Comedy*, p. 251.
82 Welsford, *The Fool*, pp. 303–10. See also Robert Storey, *Pierrot: A Critical History of a Mask* (Princeton 1978), which is a detailed study of French and English literary appropriations.
83 Sologub, 'Na nem iznoshennyi kaftan', *Stikhotvoreniya* (Leningrad 1979), p. 198.
84 Peter Lieven, *The Birth of the Ballets Russes*, trans. L. Zarine (London 1936), p. 145. Ya. Tugendkhol'd called *Petrouchka* 'the real masterpiece of the Russian season': 'Itogi sezona', *Apollon* 6 (1911) chronicle, 74; responses were just as enthusiastic when it was premiered in the Soviet Union in the 1920s: see Igor Glebov's review in *Sovetskii teatr: dokumenty i materialy* (Leningrad 1968) I, pp. 202–3.
85 Lieven, *Ballets Russes*, p. 153.
86 ibid., p. 130.
87 S. Karlinsky, 'Stravinsky and Russian Pre-Literate Theatre', *Nineteenth Century Music* 6 (1983), 233. The only exceptionable factor in this fascinating article is the use of the term 'pre-literate', since many of the genres which Karlinsky describes in fact date from a period when Russia was a secondary oral culture, that is, had been exposed to literacy.
88 Lieven, *Ballets Russes*, p. 136; Nijinska, *Early Memories*, p. 31. Amongst recent evidence of the confusion in the West over *Petrushka/Petrouchka* is the programme for the 1988–9 Sadlers Wells Royal Ballet season, which announced that *Petrouchka* was 'a poignant adaptation of an old Russian

folk tale', and a broadcast on BBC Radio Three, 21 November 1988, which stated that it was 'based on a scenario from the Russian puppet theatre'.

89 For a full account of the *Petrouchka* scenario, see Sandy Posner, *Petrouchka: the Story of the Ballet* (London 1946); for a technical account, see Cyril Beaumont, *The Complete Book of Ballets* (London 1937), pp. 717–22.

90 Benois, *Moi vospominaniya*, ii, p. 522.

91 E. Gordon Craig, 'The Actor and the Über-Marionette', *On the Art of the Theatre* (reprint, London 1980), pp. 56–94. The book, first published in German in 1905, was translated into Russian in 1906. See Edward Braun, *The Theatre of Meyerhold: Revolution on the Modern Stage* (London 1979), p. 91. On possible precedents for Craig's ideas in German Romantic aesthetics, see H. von Kleist, 'Über das Marionettentheater', *Werke und Briefe in 4 Bänden*, ed. Siegfried Streller (Berlin 1978), iii pp. 473–81; in Ancient Greek philosophy, see Richard Gregory, *Mind in Science: a History of Explanations in Psychology and Physics* (London 1981), p. 69; in 'primitive' notions of puppets as fetishes and symbols of demonic power, see Frazer, *Golden Bough*, ch. 49 sect. 2, p. 647; ch. 57 sect. 2, p. 740.

92 Sologub, 'Teatr odnoi voli', p. 188.

93 Craig, *Art of Theatre*, pp. 82–3.

94 ibid., p. 83.

95 Photographs of the exquisite puppets are reproduced in Yu. Slonimskaya, 'Marionetka', *Apollon* 3 (1916), 1–42.

96 ibid., p. 1.

97 Benois, *Moi vospominaniya*, ii, p. 522.

98 ibid., 521. The production to which Benois refers is probably a play called *Petrushka* by Petr Potemkin, the text of which I could not trace in either published or unpublished form. The backdrop by Dobuzhinsky, showing a street in St Petersburg, is reproduced in M. Dobuzhinsky, *Zhivopis', grafika, teatr*, ed. A. Gusarova (Moscow 1982), plate 94. I have found one review of the production, which took place in Meyerhold's 'Strand' cabaret for one night between 30 December 1908 and January 1909. The piece was a satire on contemporary literary life which 'had borrowed its humour from town squares', to the reviewer's disapproval – he said it had the character of a 'strained forced grimace': S. Auslender in *Zolotoe runo*, 1 (1909), 104–5.

99 On the tunes which Stravinsky used, see Karlinsky, 'Stravinsky', 234; on Benois' use of his 'uncle's etchings', see Leifert, *Balagany*, p. 17.

100 G. Kozintsev, 'Glubokii ekran', *Novyi mir* 3 (1961), 153.

101 Reproduced in Moldavsky, *S Mayakovskim v teatre i kino*, between pp. 16 and 17.

102 On Mayakovsky's *Banya* done on film with puppets, see Sergey Yutkevich, *Kino – eto pravda 24 kadra v sekundu* (Moscow 1977), pp. 128–58.

103 An example of the Symbolists' different attitudes is the reaction of the poet Innokenty Annensky to *Petrushka*: a memoirist who had known

him well as a child observed that she had only ever seen him genuinely amused when watching a *Petrushka* show in the street, but his writings on humour and comedy bear no trace of the experience. See A. V. Lavrov and R. D. Timenchik, 'Innokenty Annensky v neizdannykh vospominaniyakh', *Pamyatniki kul'tury. Novye otkrytiya. Ezhegodnik 1981* (Moscow 1983), p. 78.

104 O. Mandelstam, *Sobranie sochinenii*, 4 vols. (Washington DC, New York and Paris 1967–81), III, p. 64.

105 ibid., II, p. 101.

106 A. Akhmatova, *Poema bez geroya*, in *Stikhotvoreniya i poemy* (Leningrad 1977), p. 363.

107 B. Privalov, *Petrushka – dusha skomorosh'ya* (Moscow 1963).

108 Ivan Elagin, 'Petrushka', *Perekrestki: al'manakh* 3 (1979), pp. 33–9; references henceforth in text.

109 The Russian word *efreitor*, 'corporal', is a borrowing from the German *Gefreiter* (the soft *g* is a characteristic of Prussian dialect). Since there is no English equivalent military term borrowed from the German, it seemed appropriate simply to keep the original, here transliterated as *Jefreiter*.

110 Keating, *The Working Classes in Victorian Fiction* (London 1979), p. 8.

111 Kristeva, *Desire in Language*, p. 79.

112 Frazer, *Golden Bough*, p. 424.

5 SANITARY PETRUSHKA AND SANITISED *PETRUSHKA*

1 Speaight, *Punch and Judy*, p. 145.

2 Simonovich-Efimova, *Zapiski petrushechnika*, p. 181.

3 Ibid., p. 182.

4 Vsevolodsky-Gerngross, 'Nachalo tsirka v Rossii', p. 71.

5 Sergey Obraztsov, 'O narodnom iskusstve', *Pravda*, 15 May 1927, p. 6.

6 *Sovetskii teatr*, p. 185. That there was increasing pressure to state this view at the end of the 1920s is suggested by a comparison of Vsevolodsky-Gerngross' *Istoriya russkogo teatra*, II, pp. 376–8, harping on the inadequacy of pre-revolutionary popular culture, and his 'Nachalo tsirka v Rossii', *O teatre: sbornik stat'ei*, *Vremennik otdela istorii i teorii teatra Instituta istorii iskusstv* II (Leningrad 1927), pp. 66–107, published two years earlier (1927), which is entirely free of such homilies.

7 Leon Trotsky, *Literature and Revolution* (Ann Arbor 1960), p. 204.

8 On the Proletkul't drama theories see Robert Russell, 'People's Theatre and the October Revolution', *Irish Slavonic Studies* 7 (1986), 65–84. The *intsenirovki*, or massed spectacles, which are described here were carefully orchestrated and performed on the basis of scenarios written by intellectuals; they were very far from the oral history-based spectacles of the modern British community theatres.

9 A. Lunacharsky, 'O tsirkakh', in *O teatre i dramaturgii: izbrannye stat'i v 2-kh tt.* (Moscow 1958), I, p. 458.

10 Lunacharsky, 'O narodnykh prazdnestvakh', in ibid., I, pp. 191, 193.
11 Alekseev-Yakovlev, *Russkie narodnye gulyan'ya*, p. 164.
12 Obraztsov, 'O narodnom iskusstve'.
13 *Bol'shaya sovetskaya entsiklopediya* 3rd edn, 31 vols. (Moscow 1969–81), xxx, *Yarmarki* cols. 1643–5; on the roundabouts, see appendix B, section II,(b).
14 *Malen'kaya entsiklopediya: Tsirk*, ed. A. Ya. Shneer and R. G. Slavsky (Moscow 1973), pp. 16–17, 94, 96, 272–3, 295, 312.
15 Alekseev-Yakovlev, *Russkie narodnye gulyan'ya*, p. 22.
16 Sergey Obraztsov soon regretted his early interest in folk culture. In *Moya professiya* (first published 1940) he writes: 'How moribund and false are the works of those amongst our contemporaries who imitate the primitives in their painting and sculpture' (p. 74). In the English edition of her book, Simonovich-Efimova states that Zaitsev did not perform with glove puppets at the Central Puppet Theatre: *Adventures of a Russian Puppet Theatre* (Birmingham, Michigan 1935), p. 173.
17 Eugene Lyons, *Modern Moscow* (New York, 1935), p. 255.
18 Yury Sokolov, *Russkii fol'klor* (Moscow 1941), p. 378; Cyril Beaumont, *The Puppet Stage* (London 1938), p. 28, writes that the *Petrushka* showmen had carried on 'until recently'.
19 Two Russian informants in their fifties recalled *Petrushka* shows in the 1930s in Leningrad; a third recalled shows in Odessa at this date, but given with marionettes, not glove puppets.
20 Vero Roberti, *Moscow Under the Skin* (London 1969), pp. 176–80.
21 ibid., p. 176.
22 Some legal prohibitions against petty hooliganism and mendicancy are listed in appendix B, section 2, (a).
23 Leach, *Punch and Judy Show*, pp. 148–9.
24 Braithwaite, *Fairground Architecture*, p. 20; for more recent information on the activities of fairground artistes in Britain see Starsmore, *The Fairground*; Harry Whewell, 'A Fair Exchange', *Guardian* 18 April 1987.
25 Tim and Amanda Webb, 'The Puppet Theatre in China Today', *Animations* 9:1 (1985), 9.
26 I owe this information to George Speaight.
27 Bakhtin, *Rabelais*, p. xi.
28 On the carnivals of 1918 and 1919 see Smirnova, *Sovetskii teatr kukol*, pp. 122, 149; a photograph of the Efimovs' *agitfurgon* is reproduced in *Les Cahiers de la marionnette*, 3 (1985). For a description of the street decorations, see Arthur Ransome, *Six Weeks in Russia in 1919* (London 1919), p. 23.
29 František Deák, 'Blue Blouse', *Drama Review* 17:1 (1975) 43; Warner, *Russian Folk Theatre*, p. 198.
30 E. A. Uvarova, *Estradnyi teatr: miniatyury, obozreniya, myuzik-kholly 1917–1942* (Moscow 1983), p. 42. The account here is fuller and less condescending than that given in Rudnitsky.
31 Uvarova, *Estradnyi teatr*, p. 42.

32 ibid., p. 41. On the agitprop theatre see also Peter Yershov, *Comedy in the Soviet Theatre* (New York 1956), pp. 5–54.

33 Alekseev-Yakovlev, *Russkie narodnye gulyan'ya*, p. 162; Deák, 'The Agit-Prop and Circus Plays of Vladimir Mayakovsky', *Drama Review* 17:1 (1975), 47–52.

34 Lunacharsky, 'Budem smeyat'sya', in *Teatr i revolyutsiya* (Moscow 1924), p. 61.

35 Smirnova, *Sovetskii teatr kukol*, p. 249.

36 ibid., p. 74.

37 For example, E. Demmeni, *Za petrushechnoi shirmoi* (Leningrad 1930); E. Demmeni and V. Kachalin, *Kak ustroit' petrushechnyi teatr* (Leningrad 1927); V. Stepanov, *Derevenskii Krasnyi Petrushka*, etc. (all cited by Tarasov 140–1).

38 V. Markov and N. Nadezhdin manufactured sets of ten puppets which could be adapted by individual clubs (see Smirnova, *Sovetskii teatr kukol*, p. 273).

39 Smirnova, *Sovetskii teatr kukol*, p. 258.

40 Uvarova, *Estradnyi teatr*, p 132 (Deák's article 'Blue Blouse' mistakenly gives the date as 1928).

41 Varlam Shalamov, 'Lagernaya svad'ba', in *Kolymskie rasskazy* (London 1978), p. 692.

42 Smirnova, *Sovetskii teatr kukol*, p. 261.

43 Obraztsov, *Moya professiya*, pp. 199–200.

44 Losev, *Censorship*, p. 100.

45 See 'Raeshnik po vsem frontam' in *Krasnoarmeiskii fol'klor: sbornik* (Moscow 1938). An interesting but not very traditional 'revolutionary *vertep*', with a boozy Archangel Michael and a blustering ineffectual God, can be found in P. Gorbenko, *Revolyutsiinii lyal'kovii teatr* (Kiev 1924), pp. 33–40.

46 Simonovich-Efimova, *Zapiski petrushechnika*, p. 130.

47 See chapter 2, note 43 above.

48 Obraztsov, *Moya professiya*, pp. 198–9.

49 For pictures of the agitprop Petrushkas, see also *Les Cahiers de la marionnette*, 3; only that of the *Teatr detskoi knigi* recalls the prototype.

50 On the exclusion of women from military life, see Cynthia Enloe, *Does Khaki Become You? The Militarisation of Women's Lives* (London 1983), *passim*. Kenez, *Propaganda State*, p. 180, quotes a Komsomol leader's statement advocating the 'use' of women in combating antisocial male behaviour. Gor'ky in 'O proletarskom pisatele' likewise described women as 'faithful helpers' (*Sobranie sochinenii v 30 tt.*, XXIV, p. 333).

51 Simonovich-Efimova, *Zapiski petrushechnika*, p. 129.

52 ibid., p. 152.

53 S. Marshak, *Skazki, pesni, zagadki* (Moscow 1981), p. 175.

54 Henriette Pascar, 'Petrushka, notre Guignol', *Mon théâtre a Moscou* (Paris 1930), p. 89.

55 ibid., p. 86.

56 On the use of violence in folklore to political ends, see Maureen Perrie, *The Image of Ivan the Terrible in Russian Folklore* (Cambridge 1987).

57 Oinas, *Folklore*, p. 83.

58 Ibid., pp. 84ff.

59 Afanas'ev's collection of obscene folk-tales, *Zavetnye skazki*, has still not been published in the Soviet Union; the concerts, records and graphic materials which I have come across have always been of the most unimpeachable character. On didactic uses for folklore, see Terence Wade, 'Russian Folklore and Soviet Humour', *Journal of Russian Studies* 54 (1988), 3–20, though it should be pointed out that by no means all the examples here are properly described as folkloric.

60 On the historical development of propaganda and on the ideological problems of discussing it, see Kenez, *Propaganda State*, pp. 2, 13.

61 Clifford, *Predicament of Culture*, has some very telling examples of how flexible traditional genres can be in adopting new material; he describes, for example, a cricket match fought in New Guinea in traditional masks, whilst an umpire eats nuts out of a bright blue plastic carrier bag (p. 148). Dain, *Russkaya narodnaya igrushka*, records that village women in the Soviet Union were astounded by her interest in old peasant toys, which they considered vastly inferior to new plastic ones (p. 9). In two parts of rural Europe which I myself know, Achill Island in the West of Ireland, and the Mani in the Southern Peloponnese, old stone dwellings are spurned by villagers in favour of tidy new concrete bungalows. Anyone who has spent a winter in the former may feel their regrets tempered.

62 Smirnova, *Sovetskii teatr kukol*, p. 62.

63 See Dana Polan's contribution, 'Bakhtin, Benjamin, Sartre: Toward a Typology of the Intellectual Cultural Critic' in Catriona Kelly, Michael Makin and David Shepherd (eds.), *Discontinuous Discourses in Modern Russian Literature* (London and New York 1989), p. 16.

64 Gary Friedman, 'Puppets against Apartheid', *Animations* 9:3 (1986), 48–9.

65 Susie Cornfield, 'Battered Wife Lands a Punch', *Sunday Telegraph Magazine* 28 September 1986, p. 11; Lorca, *El Retablillo de Don Cristóbal*. The pitfalls of wholesale adaptations done from the outside have been humourously represented in Colin Hayden-Evans' radio play *All Done in A Squeaky Voice*, broadcast on BBC Radio Four, 28 September 1988, in which a well-intentioned local council tries to force a Punch and Judy showman to bring his act into line with accepted educational principles.

66 Kenez, *Propaganda State*, p. 70.

67 Obraztsov, 'O narodnom iskusstve'.

68 'Even the outward attributes of the *oprichnina* had some carnival aspects' (M. Bakhtin, *Rabelais*, p. 270). The same could be said of the ghastly ritual humiliations of prisoners which were central to interrogations under Stalin, whilst the behaviour of Stalin himself was a classic example of the Lord of Misrule at his worst. In a very interesting article on labour politics under Stalin, D. Filtzer has pointed to similar systematic humiliations of

workers on the shop floor during the 1930s in 'Labour and the Contradictions of Planning under Stalin: the Working Class and the Regime
during the First Years of Forced Industrialisation', *Critique* 20–1 (1987),
91. The use of filthy abuse and insults in the show trials is an area which
also illustrates the instrumental populism of the Stalin period. That such
populism is not confined to the political elite, or to Soviet official culture,
is illustrated by the laddish misogyny of such writers as Mayakovsky,
Vysotsky, Eduard Limonov and Dmitry Savitsky. On this, see, for
example, A. Zholkovsky: 'O genii i zlodeistve, o babe i vserossiiskom
masshtabe', in *Mir avtora i struktura teksta*, (Tenafly NJ 1986),
pp. 255–79.

69 The contradictions in Stalinist policy are illustrated by the artificial revival
of the Leningrad *narodnye gulyan'ya* in the late 1940s, (personal information). On the contradictions inherent in using the critical discourse of
Marxism as an instrument of terror and legitimation, see Jean-François
Lyotard, *The Postmodern Condition: a Report on Knowledge* (Manchester
1984), p. 37; on the contradictions of socialist realism itself, see Régine
Robin, *Le Réalisme socialiste: un ésthétique impossible* (Paris 1986).

CONCLUSION

1 Even the observations of the tsarist censors at the most repressive period,
prior to the 1862 reforms, reveal, besides the famously idiotic suppositions
that printed music might contain treacherous messages in code, concerns
with educational purpose and usefulness in literature: *Sbornik postanovlenii i rasporyazhenii po tsenzure*, pp. 249, 255, 279.

2 The Stalinist manipulation of folklore at its height is represented by the
collection of essays *Ocherki russkogo narodnogo poeticheskogo tvorchestva
sovetskoi epokhi* (Moscow and Leningrad 1952), which, besides containing sections on the images of Stalin and Lenin in folklore, is heavily
based towards rural, ritual and heroic genres.

3 These examples are taken from *First Russia, Then Tibet* by Robert Byron,
who visited the Soviet Union in the early 1930s (Harmondsworth 1985),
p. 44.

4 Boris Gasparov has written that ethnographical research is not carried on
in the Soviet Union, which is actually a mis-statement, in Lotman *et al.*,
The Semiotics of Russian Cultural History, p. 28; but Krupyanskaya and
Polishchuk's description, in *Kul'tura*, of the way research was organised
for their book, with heavy reliance on printed questionnaires which
directed the replies of those who filled them in, is indicative that the results
of research may not be much subject to control by the informants.

5 The mistrust of street culture is matched by mistrust of street language on
the part of many Soviet intellectuals. 'You don't campaign hard enough
against dialect words and expressions', a teacher wrote to Korney
Chukovsky, a rebuke which he accepted; *Zhivoi kak zhizn'* (Moscow
1963), p. 177. He was hostile also to youth slang (p. 110).

6 This stanza from a song by the Soviet rock group Aquarium is taken from an unpublished talk by Irina Pond, an expert on Soviet popular music, given at the Oxford Russian Seminar in spring 1987. On popular re-creation of 'guitar poetry', an intellectual and high-cultural genre as far as its creation goes, see G. S. Smith, *Songs to Seven Strings: A History of Russian Guitar Poetry* (Bloomington 1985).

7 A recent story by Arkady Arkanov about popular clowning uses only figures from Western European tradition, such as Pulcinella; see Elena Moszenin, 'Arkady Arkanov's "I Dream of a Carnival": a Perspective on Clowns in European Culture', *Australian Slavonic and East European Studies* 1:1 (1987), 17–30). When a Soviet puppeteer called in 1987 for a return to *balagan* traditions, he was inspired by Lorca's puppet plays rather than by Russian or other indigenous street traditions, *Teatr* 7 (1987), 132.

8 Vitaly Vitaliev, 'Once Upon a Time in Amur', *Guardian* 28 October 1988.

9 This new-style social exploration can be found, for example, in the film *The Burglar*, as well as in the short stories of Sergey Kaledin and to a lesser extent Lyudmila Petrushevskaya.

10 The genre of 'village prose', for example, is in the first place an evocation of Soviet village life for an intellectual audience, whose supposed educated and urbanised world-view is called into question by the depiction of peasant wisdom and transcendental values, such as Orthodoxy or harmony with the natural world; see, for example, Leonid Borodin's novel *Partings*, trans. David Floyd, London 1987.

Bibliography

Though the Russian carnival has received relatively little attention, the issues which it raises are wide-ranging. This bibliography is primarily a list of source materials used in my book, but I have attempted also to suggest further reading on certain subjects (such as Soviet studies of the sociology of 'mass festivals'), which it has been possible only to touch on here.

'A.B.', *Gorodskoe samoupravlenie v Rossii*, Geneva, izdanie Soyuza sotsialdemokratov, 1901.

Afanas'ev, A., *Russkie skazki*, 3 vols., Moscow 1955.

[as *Filobib*] *Russkie zavetnye skazki*, 'Valaam, god mrakobesiya' – [actually Geneva] (reprint, Geneva 1975).

Akhmatova, Anna, *Stikhotvoreniya i poemy*, Leningrad 1977.

Alekseev-Yakovlev, A. Ya., *Russkie narodnye gulyan'ya*, Leningrad and Moscow 1948.

'Vospominaniya', archival document, forthcoming.

Alferov, A., 'Petrushka i ego predki', *Desyat' chtenii po literature*, Moscow 1895, pp. 175–205.

And, Metin, *Karagöz: Turkish Shadow Theatre*, Istanbul 1980.

Annenkov, Yury, *Dnevnik moikh vstrech: tsikl tragedii*, 2 vols., New York 1966.

Annensky, I. F., *Stikhotvoreniya i tragedii*, Leningrad 1959.

Ashkenazi, Z., 'Bessmertnyi Petrushka', *Ezhegodnik imperatorskikh teatrov*, 4 (1914), 1–18.

Askol'dov, Leonid, *Za kulisami tsirka: sbornik rasskazov*, Paris 1961.

Astakhova, A. I. and Shiryaeva, P. G., 'Staraya rabochaya pesnya' *Sovetskaya etnografiya* (1934), 1–2, 201–3.

Auslender, S., 'Petersburgskie teatry', review, *Zolotoe runo* I (1909), 104–5.

Babochkin, B. A. *et al.* (eds.), *Russkii provintsial'nyi teatr: vospominaniya*, publ. by Vserossiiskoe teatral'noe obshchestvo, Leningrad 1937.

Bachtin, N., 'The Russian Revolution as seen by a White Guard', *Alta: the University of Birmingham Review*, 2:10 (Spring 1970), 197–208.

Baddeley, John F., *Russia in the 'Eighties': Sport and Politics*, London 1921.

Bakhtin, M. M., *Rabelais and His World*, trans. Hélène Iswolsky, Bloomington, 1984.

Bakhtin, N., 'Marionetki', *Novyi entsiklopedicheskii slovar'*, xxv, pp. 712–17.

Baratynsky, E. A., *Polnoe sobranie stikhotvorenii*, Leningrad 1951.

Barnes Steveni, W., *Things Seen in Russia*, London 1913.
Petrograd, London 1915.
Bartoš, Jaroslav (ed.), *Loutkařské hry českého obrožení*, Prague 1952.
Beaumont, Cyril, *The Complete Book of Ballets*, London 1937.
The Puppet Stage, London 1938.
The Diaghilev Ballet in London, London 1940.
Beletskaya, N. N., 'O pozdnem etape istorii russkoi narodnoi dramy', *Sovetskaya etnografiya* 5 (1963), 20–31.
Belkin, A. A., *Russkie skomorokhi*, Moscow 1975.
Belozerskaya, N. A., *Tsarskoe venchanie v Rossii*, St Petersburg 1896.
Bely, Andrey, 'Teatr i sovremennaya drama', *Teatr: kniga o novom teatre*, pp. 263–89.
Kotik Letaev (reprint of Petrograd 1922 edn), Munich 1964.
Anon., *Bemerkungen über Rußland*, 2 vols. Erfurt 1788.
Ben-Amos, Dan, 'Toward a Definition of Folklore in Context', in A. Paredes and R. Bauman (eds.), *Toward New Perspectives in Folklore*, Austin and London 1972, pp. 3–16.
Benua, Aleksandr [= Alexandre Benois] *Moi vospominaniya*, 2 vols., Moscow 1980.
Biedermann, Karl, *Unsre Gegenwart und Zukunft*, 8 vols., Leipzig 1847.
Blok, A. A., *Stikhotvoreniya*, Leningrad 1955.
Teatr, Leningrad 1981.
Bogatyrev, P. G. *Cheshskii kukol'nyi i russkii narodnyi teatr*, Berlin and St Petersburg 1923.
(ed.) *Russkoe narodnoe poeticheskoe tvorchestvo: posobie dlya vuzov*, Moscow 1954.
Voprosy teorii narodnogo iskusstva, Moscow 1971.
'O vzaimosvyazi dvukh blizkikh semioticheskikh sistem', *Trudy po znakovym sistemam*, 6 (Tartu 1973), 306–30.
'Stage Setting, Artistic Space and Time in the Folk Theatre', trans. L. M. O'Toole, *Russian Poetics in Translation*, 3 (1976), 33–8.
Böhmer, G., *Puppets through the Ages*, London 1971.
Bol'shaya sovetskaya entsiklopediya, 3rd edn, 31 vols., Moscow 1969–81.
Bonnell, Victoria E. (ed.), *Life and Labour under the Tsarist Regime*, Berkeley, Los Angeles and London 1983.
Bor'ba za realizm v iskusstve 20-kh godov, Moscow 1962.
Borodin, Leonid, *Partings*, trans. David Floyd, London 1987.
Bowlt, John, E., *The Silver Age: Russian Art of the Early Twentieth Century and the 'World of Art' Group*, Newtonville, Mass. 1979.
Bozheryanov, A., *Nevskii prospekt 1703–1903*, St Petersburg 1901.
Bragaglia, Anton Giulio, *Pulcinella*, Rome 1953.
Braithwaite, David, *Fairground Architecture*, London 1968.
Braun, Edward, *The Theatre of Meyerhold: Revolution on the Modern Stage*, London 1979.
Brody, Hugh, *Inishkillane: Change and Decline in the West of Ireland*, London 1982.

Brooks, Jeffrey, *When Russia Learned to Read: Literacy and Popular Literature, 1861–1917*, Princeton 1985.

Brooks, Zoë, 'Spitting Image', *Animations*, 8:3 (1985), 46–8.

Brower, Daniel K., 'Labour Violence in Russia in the Late Nineteenth Century', *Slavic Review*, 41:3 (1982), 417–31.

Bryusov, V. Ya., *Polnoe sobranie sochinenii i perevodov*, xv, *Teatr*, St Petersburg 1914.

Sobranie sochinenii v 7 tomakh, Moscow 1973–5.

Bulak, T. G., 'Iz istorii komedii Petrushka', *Russkii fol'klor*, xvi (1976), pp. 221–7.

Burke, Peter, *Popular Culture in Early Modern Europe*, London 1978.

Byrom, Michael, *Punch and Judy: Its Origins and Evolution*, 2nd edn, London 1978.

Punch in the Italian Puppet Theatre, London 1983.

Byron, Robert, *First Russia, then Tibet*, Harmondsworth 1985.

Les Cahiers de la marionnette, 3, 1985.

Carey, C. (ed.), *Les Proverbes érotiques russes: études de proverbes recueillis et non publiés par Dal' et Simoni*, The Hague and Paris 1972.

Carter, Angela, *Nights at the Circus*, London 1984.

Cartwell Ridley, J., *Reminiscences of Russia*, Newcastle upon Tyne, 1898.

Chamot, Mary, *Gontcharova*, Paris 1972.

Chekhov, A. P., 'Yarmarka', in *Polnoe sobranie sochinenii i pisem v 30 tomakh*, Moscow 1974– , i, 247–52.

Child, Theodore *et al.*, *The Tsar and his People: Social Life in Russia* (collection of essays), New York 1891.

Christian, D. D. and Smith, R. E. F., *Bread and Salt*, Cambridge 1984.

Chukovsky, K. I., *Zhivoi kak zhizn'*, Moscow 1963.

Clarke, David L., *Analytical Archaeology*, London 1978.

Clifford, James, *The Predicament of Culture: Twentieth-Century Literature, Ethnography and Art*, Cambridge, Mass. and London 1988.

Collier, John Payne, *The Tragical Comedy or Comical Tragedy of Punch and Judy*, paperback reissue of London 1828 edn, London 1976.

Cornfield, Susie, 'Battered Wife Lands a Punch', *Sunday Telegraph Magazine*, 28 September 1986, p. 11.

Coward, Rosalind, *Patriarchal Precedents*, London 1983.

Craig, E. Gordon, 'The Actor and the Über-Marionette', *On the Art of the Theatre* (reprint), London 1980, pp. 56–94.

Cross, Anthony D. (ed.), *Russia under Western Eyes, 1517–1825*, London 1971.

Dain, G. L. *Russkaya narodnaya igrushka*, Moscow 1981.

Dal', V., *Slovar' velikorusskogo yazyka*, 4 vols., reprint of 4th edn, Moscow 1980.

Darnton, Robert, *The Great Cat Massacre and Other Episodes in French Cultural History*, Harmondsworth 1985.

Davis, Natalie Zemon, *Fiction in the Archives: Pardon Tales and their Tellers in Sixteenth-Century France*, Oxford 1988.

Deák, František, 'The Agit-Prop and Circus Plays of Vladimir Mayakovsky', *Drama Review*, 17:1 (1975), 47–52.

'Blue Blouse', *Drama Review* 17:1 (1975), 35–46.

Dmitriev, Yu. A., 'Na starom moskovskom gulyanii', *Teatral'nyi al'manakh VTO*, 6 (Moscow 1947), 345–57.

Tsirk v Rossii ot istokov do 1917, Moscow 1977.

Dobuzhinsky, M. V., *Vospominaniya*, 1 [only one published], New York 1976.

Zhivopis', grafika, teatr, ed. A. Gusarova, Moscow 1982.

Doré, Gustave, and Jerrold, Blanchard, *London*, reprint of London 1871 edn, Newton Abbot 1971.

Doroshevich, V., *Sakhalin*, Moscow 1903.

Dostoevsky, F. M., *Polnoe sobranie sochinenii v 30 tomakh*, Leningrad 1969–87.

Druzhinin, A. V., *Povesti i rasskazy*, Moscow 1986.

Duchartre, Pierre, *The Italian Comedy*, reprint of London 1929 edn, New York 1966.

Duranty, L. E. E., *Théâtre des Marionnettes*, Paris 1880.

Elagin, Ivan, 'Petrushka', *Perekrestki: al'manakh*, 3 (1979), 33–40.

Ellis [= L. Kobylinsky], 'Chto takoe teatr?' *Vesy*, 4 (1908), 85–91.

El'patevsky, S., 'Yarmarochnye kartini', *Russkoe bogatstvo* 12 (1896), 7–21.

Emel'yaninov, L. I. (ed.), *Russkaya istoricheskaya pesnya*, Leningrad 1987.

Anon., *An Englishwoman in Russia, by a Lady Ten Years Resident in that Country*, London 1855.

Enloe, Cynthia, *Does Khaki Become You? The Militarisation of Women's Lives*, London 1983.

Entsiklopedicheskii slovar' izd. Brokgauza i Efrona, ed. I. Andreevsky, 42 vols and 4 supp. vols., St Petersburg 1890–1907.

Esenin, S. A., *Sobranie sochinenii v 5 tomakh*, Moscow 1962.

Evreinov, N. N., 'Dan' marionetkam', in *Teatral'nye novatsii*, Petrograd 1922.

Evstigneeva, L. A. (ed.), *Poety Satirikona*, Moscow and Leningrad 1966.

Famintsyn, A. S., *Skomorokhi na Rusi*, St Petersburg 1889.

Fedotov, A. Ya., *Sekrety teatra kukol*, Moscow 1963.

Fielding, Henry, *Joseph Andrews*, Harmondsworth 1986.

Filtzer, D., 'Labour and the Contradictions of Planning Under Stalin: the Working Class and the Regime during the First Years of Forced Industrialisation', *Critique* 209–1 (1987).

Fokin, M. M., *Protiv techeniya: vospominaniya baletmeistera*, Leningrad and Moscow 1962.

Fournel, Paul, *Les Marionnettes*, Paris 1982.

Frazer, J. G., *The Golden Bough: a Study in Magic and Religion*, abr. edn, London 1970, reprint of London 1922 edn.

Freidenberg, Olga, *Poetika syuzheta i zhanra*, Leningrad 1936.

Freud, Sigmund, *Der Witz und seine Beziehung zum Unbewußten*, reprint, Frankfurt on Main, 1978.

Fried, Frederick, *A Pictorial History of the Carousel*, New York 1964.

Friedman, Gary, 'Puppets Against Apartheid', *Animations* 9:3 (1986), 48–9.

Garshin, Vsevolod, *Rasskazy*, St Petersburg 1909.

Georgi, I. G., *Opisanie rossiisko-imperatorskogo stolichnogo goroda Sankt-peterburga i dostoprimechatel' nostei v ego okresnostyakh*, St Petersburg 1794.

Gilyarovsky, Vladimir, 'Katastrofa na Khodynke', *Russkie vedomosti* 20 May 1896.

Sochineniya v 4 tomakh, Moscow 1967.

Ginzburg, Carlo, *The Cheese and the Worms*, trans. J. and A. Tedeschi, London 1980.

Gippius, V., *Nikolai Gogol*, trans. R. Maguire, Ann Arbor 1981.

Glassie, Henry (ed.), *Irish Folktales*, Harmondsworth 1987.

Gleason, Abbott, Kenez, Peter and Stites, Richard, *Bolshevik Culture: Experiment and Order in the Russian Revolution*, Bloomington 1985.

Glickman, Rose, L., *Russian Factory Women: Workplace and Society 1880–1914*, Berkeley, Los Angeles and London 1984.

Goethe, J. W. von, *Das Jahrmarktsfest zu Plundersweilen: ein Schönbartsspiel*, in *Goethes Poetische Werke: Vollständige Ausgabe*, III, Stuttgart 1953, pp. 637–73.

Hanswursts Hochzeit, in *Jugendwerke 2: Dramen und dramatische Skizzen 1774–5*, Berlin 1953, pp. 289–95.

Gogol', N. V., *Polnoe sobranie sochinenii*, 14 vols., Moscow 1937–52.

Golovachev, V. and Lashchilin, B., *Narodnyi teatr na Donu*, Rostov-on-Don, 1947.

Golovina, Alla, *Lebedinaya karusel'*, Paris 1935.

Goncharov, I. A., *Sobranie sochinenii v 6 tomakh*, Moscow 1959.

Gorbenko, P., *Revolyutsiinii lyal'kovii teatr*, Kiev 1924.

Gor'ky, Maksim, *Sobranie sochinenii v 30 tomakh*, Moscow 1949–55.

Gould, Stephen Jay, *Ontogeny and Phylogeny*, Cambridge Mass. and London, 1977.

Graham, Stephen, *Changing Russia*, London 1913.

Gramsci, Antonio, *Selections from Cultural Writings*, London 1986.

Grazhdanskii kodeks RSFSR, Moscow 1948.

Grebenyuk, V. *et al.* (eds.), *Rannyaya russkaya dramaturgiya: p'esy lyubitel'skikh teatrov*, Moscow 1976.

Greenblatt, Stephen, *Shakespearian Negotiations*, Oxford 1988.

Gregory, Richard, *Mind in Science: a History of Explanations in Psychology and Physics*, London 1981.

Grigson, Jane, *English Food*, Harmondsworth 1977.

Grock [= Wettach, K. A.], *Life's a Lark*, London 1931.

King of Clowns, London 1957.

Grushin, B. A., *Problems of Free Time in the USSR: a Sociological Study*, Moscow 1969.

Gudas, Rom, *The Bitter-Sweet Art: Karaghiozis, the Greek Shadow Theatre*, Athens 1986.

Gudzy, N. K., *Khrestomatiya po drevnerusskoi literature*, 8th edn, Moscow 1973.

Guiette, R., *Marionnettes de tradition populaire*, Brussels 1949.

Gumitev, N. S., *Ditya Allakha: arabskaya skazka*, Berlin 1922.

Gustev, V. E., *Marksizm i russkaya fol'kloristika kontsa XIX – nachala XX veka*, Moscow and Leningrad 1961.

Hammarstrom, David, *Circus Rings Around Russia*, New York 1983.

Istoriya russkogo dramaticheskogo teatra, vol. 6, Moscow 1982.

Ivanov, Vsevolod, *Sobranie sochinenii v 8 tomakh*, Moscow 1973–87.

Ivanov, Vyacheslav I., 'Ellinskaya religiya stradayushchego boga', *Novyi put'* (1904), 1, 110–34 [part 1]; 2, 48–78 [part 2]; 3, 38–61 [part 3]; 5, 28–40 [part 4]; 9, 46–70 [part 5].

'Esteticheskaya norma teatra', *Sobranie sochinenii*, 1, Brussels 1974, pp. 205–15.

Ivanov, Vyacheslav V., 'Iz zametok o stroenii i formirovanii karnaval'nogo obraza' in *Problemy poetiki i istorii literatury: sbornik stat'ei* Saransk 1973, pp. 37–53.

Anon., *Iz rabochego dvizheniya za Nevskoi zastavoi: vospominaniya starogo rabochego*, Geneva, pub. Soyuza sotsialdemokratov, 1900.

Jakobson, Roman, *Selected Writings*, IV, The Hague and Paris 1966; VII, The Hague and Paris 1985.

James, J. T., *Journal of a Tour in Germany, Sweden, Russia and Poland*, London 1817.

'Jan Klaasens leven en heldendaden', *Nederlands volksleren*, 18:4 (Winter 1968–9), 70–82.

Jarry, Alfred, *Tout Ubu*, reprint, Paris 1980.

Jefferson, Ann, 'Bodymatters: Self and Other in Bakhtin, Sartre and Barthes', in Hirschkop, Ken and Shepherd, David (eds.), *Bakhtin and Cultural Theory*, Manchester 1989, pp. 152–77.

Johnston, Robert A. M., *Travels through Part of the Russian Empire and the Country of Poland; along the Southern Shores of the Baltic*, London 1815.

Jonson, Ben, *Bartholomew Fair*, ed. E. M. Waith, London and New Haven 1963.

Journal of American Folklore (JAF), Panel on Folk Literature and the Obscene, July–Sept. 1962.

Jurkowski, Henryk, *Dzieje teatru lalek: od romantizma do wielkiej reformy teatru*, Warsaw 1976.

Kabronsky, V. (ed.), *Nepodtsenzurnaya chastushka*, New York 1978.

Karlinsky, Simon, 'Stravinsky and Russian Pre-literate Theatre', *Nineteenth-Century Music*, 6 (1983), 232–40.

Russian Drama from its Beginnings to the Age of Pushkin, Berkeley, Los Angeles and London 1985.

Anon., *Kasperl und König Mäusebart*, Vienna 1950.

Anon., *Kasperl im Räuberwirtshaus*, Vienna 1950.

Das Kasperltheater für Erwachsene, Frankfurt on Main 1978.

Keating, Peter, *Into Unknown England: Selections from the Social Explorers*, London 1976.

The Working Classes in Victorian Fiction, London 1979.

Kelly, Catriona, 'Bacchic Revels? Annensky's *Famira-kifared* and the Satyrs', *Essays in Poetics*, 10:2 (1985), 77–93.

'From Pulcinella to Petrushka', *Oxford Slavonic Papers* 21 (1988), 41–63.

Kelly, Catriona, Makin, M. and Shepherd, D. (eds.), *Discontinuous Discourses in Modern Russian Literature*, London and New York 1989.

Kenez, Peter, *The Birth of the Propaganda State: Soviet Methods of Mass Mobilization 1917–1929*, Cambridge 1985.

Khodasevich, V., *Sobranie sochinenii*, I, Ann Arbor 1983.

Kholodov, E. G. (ed.), *Istoriya russkogo dramaticheskogo teatra*, VI, Moscow 1982.

Kino: entsiklopedicheskii slovar', ed. S. Yutkevich, Moscow 1986.

Klapisch-Zuber, Christiane, *Women, Family and Ritual in Renaissance Italy*, trans. Lydia G. Cochrane, Chicago 1985.

Kleist, Heinrich von, 'Über das Marionettentheater', *Werke und Briefe in 4 Bänden*, ed. S. Streller (Berlin 1978), III, pp. 473–81.

Klyuev, N., *Sochineniya*, 2 vols., Munich 1969.

Koenker, Diane, *Moscow Workers and the 1917 Revolution*, Princeton 1981.

Kohl, J. G., *Russia*, London 1842.

Konechny, A. M., 'Peterburgskie balagany', *Panorama iskusstv*, 8 (1985), 383–95.

'Raek: narodnaya zabava', *Dekorativnoe iskusstvo*, 346 (1986), 13–14, 34–5.

'Obshchestvennye razvlecheniya i gorodskie zrelishcha v Tsarskom Sele (XVIII-nachalo XX v.)' in *Etnografiya Peterburga – Leningrada: materialy ezhegodnykh chtenii*, ed. N. V. Yukhneva, part 2, Leningrad 1988.

'Peterburgskie narodnye gulyan'ya na maslenoi i paskhal'noi nedelyakh' in *Peterburg i guberniya: istoriko-etnograficheskie issledovaniya*, forthcoming, Leningrad 1989.

Kozintsev, G., 'Glubokii ekran', *Novyi mir*, 3 (1961), 141–72.

Krasnoarmeiskii fol'klor: sbornik, Moscow 1938.

Kristeva, Julia, *Desire in Language: a Semiotic Approach to Literature and Art*, ed. and trans. Leon S. Roudiez, Oxford 1981.

Krivonosov, V. and Kulakovsky, L., 'Tsar' Maksimilian', *Sovetskaya muzyka* 7 (1939), 32–43.

Krupyanskaya, V. Yu., 'Narodnyi teatr', in Bogatyrev, *Russkoe narodnoe poeticheskoe tvorchestvo*, pp. 382–414.

Krupanskaya, V. Yu. and N. S. Polishchuk, *Kul'tura i byt rabochikh gornozavodskogo Urala konets XIX-nachalo XX v.*, Moscow 1971.

Kulish, A. P., 'Petrushka – "litso nerazgadannoe, mificheskoe": k voprosu o genezise geroya narodnoi ulichnoi kukol'noi komedii', *V professional'noi shkole kukol'nikov* 3 Leningrad 1987, 132–8.

Kurochkin, V. S., *Sobranie sochinenii*, Moscow 1947.

Kustodiev v teatre: katalog, Central Theatre Museum, Moscow 1979.

Kuz'mina, V. D., *Russkii demokraticheskii teatr XVIII veka*, Moscow 1958.

Langenscheidts Sachwörterbucher: Land und Leute in Rußland, ed. M. L. Schlesinger, Berlin and St Petersburg n.d. [c. 1910].

Lavrov, A. V. and Timenchik, R. D., 'Innokenty Annensky v neizdannykh vospominaniyakh', *Pamyatniki kul'tury. Novye otkrytiya. Ezhegodnik 1981*, Moscow 1983, pp. 61–81.

Lea, K., M., *Italian Popular Comedy*, 2 vols., Oxford 1934.

Leach, Robert, *The Punch and Judy Show: History, Traditions and Meaning*, London 1985.

Lederman, Minna, *Stravinsky in the Theatre*, New York 1975.

Leifert, A. V., *Balagany*, Petrograd 1922.

Lemke, Mikhail, *Epokha tsenzurnykh reform*, St Petersburg 1904.

Lenin o literature i iskusstve, 7th edn, Moscow 1967.

Leonov, Leonid, *Vor*, Moscow 1965.

Levitov, A. I., *Rasskazy i ocherki*, Voronezh 1980.

Lieven, Peter, *The Birth of the Ballets Russes*, trans. L. Zarine, London 1936.

Likhachev, D. S., Panchenko, A. M. and Ponyrko, N. V., *Smekh v drevnei Rusi*, Leningrad 1984.

Lorca, Federico García, *La tragicomedia de Don Cristóbal*, in *Obras III: Teatro I*, Madrid 1980, pp. 81–153; *El retablillo de Don Cristóbal*, in ibid., pp. 153–81.

Losev, Lev, *On the Beneficence of Censorship: Aesopian Language and Modern Russian Literature*, trans. Jane Bobko, Munich 1984.

Lotman, Iu. M., Ginsburg, L. Ia., and Uspenskii, B. A., *The Semiotics of Russian Cultural History*, Ithaca, New York, London 1985.

Lunacharsky, A. V., *Teatr i revolyutsiya*, Moscow 1924.

O teatre i dramaturgii: izbrannye stat'i v 2-kh tomakh, Moscow 1958.

Lyons, Eugene, *Modern Moscow*, New York 1935.

Lyotard, Jean-François, *The Post-Modern Condition: A Report on Knowledge*, trans. Geoff Bennington and Brian Massumi, Theory and History of Literature 10, Manchester 1984.

Mackenzie Wallace, D., *Russia*, 2 vols., London 1877.

Macluhan, Marshall, *The Mechanical Bride: Folklore of Industrial Man*, London 1967.

Magnin, Charles, *Histoire des marionnettes en Europe*, Paris 1852.

Malen'kaya entsiklopediya: Tsirk, ed. A. Ya Shneer and R. E. Slavsky, Moscow 1973.

Malkin, M. R., *Traditional and Folk Puppets of the World*, New York 1977.

Mandel, Ernest and Novack, G., *The Marxist Theory of Alienation*, New York 1973.

Mandelstam, Osip, *Sobranie sochinenii*, 4 vols., Washington, New York and Paris 1967–81.

Marshak, S., 'Petrushka-inostranets' in Marshak, *Skazki, pesni, zagadki*, Moscow 1981, pp. 174–89.

Mayall, David, *Gypsy Travellers in Nineteenth-Century Society*, Cambridge 1988.

Mazaev, A. I., *Prazdnik kak sotsial'no-khudozhestvennoe yavlenie*, Moscow 1978.

Mesto massovogo prazdnika v dukhovnom zhizni sovetskogo obshchestva, Leningrad 1981.

Meyerhold, V. E., *Stat'i, pis'ma, rechi, besedy*, 2 vols., Moscow 1968.

Miklaševskij, K. [= K. Miklashevsky], *La commedia dell'arte*, trans. (into Italian) and ed. Carla Solivetti, Venice 1981.

Mintslov, S. R., *Istoriya Peterburga 1903–1910*, St Petersburg 1911.

Moldavsky, Dmitry, 'Mayakovsky i fol'klor' in *Perekrestok stikhov i trass*, Leningrad 1972, pp. 4–72.

S Mayakovskim v teatre i kino: kniga o Sergee Yutkeviche, Moscow 1974.

Morley, Henry (ed.), *Sketches of Russian Life*, London 1866.

Moser, Charles A., 'Jeffrey Brooks: *When Russia Learned to Read*', review, *Slavic and East European Journal*, 30:4 (1986), 568–9.

Moszenin, Elena, 'Arkady Arkanov's "I Dream of a Carnival": a Perspective on Clowns in European Culture', *Australian Slavonic and East European Studies*, 1:1 (1987), 17–30.

Mražková, Daniela and Remeš, Vladimir, *Another Russia: Through the Eyes of the New Soviet Photographers*, London 1981.

Murrays Handbook for Travellers in Russia, 5th edn, London 1893.

Muzei teatral'nykh kukol pri Gosudarstvennom tsentral'nom teatre kukol: Putevoditel', Moscow *c*. 1982.

Nabokov, Vladimir, *Speak, Memory*, reprint, Harmondsworth 1982.

Narodnyi teatr: sbornik, Moscow 1896.

Nechaev, V. V., 'Ulichnaya zhizn' Moskvy XVI-XVII vv.', *Moskva v ee proshlom i nastoyashchem*, 3 (1910), 56–96.

Nekrasov, N. A., *Komu na Rusi zhit' khorosho* in *Polnoe sobranie sochinenii v 15 tomakh*, v, Moscow 1982.

Nekrylova, A. F., 'Genezis odnoi iz stsen Petrushki', *Sovetskaya etnografiya*, 4 (1972), 126–31.

'Severnorusskie varianty Petrushki' in *Fol'klor i etnografiya russkogo severa*, Leningrad 1973, pp. 242–9

'Stsenicheskie osobennosti narodnogo kukol'nogo teatra Petrushka' in *Narodnyi teatr*, Leningrad 1974, pp. 121–40.

'Zakon kontrasta v poetike russkogo narodnogo kukol'nogo teatra Petrushka', in *Russkii fol'klor*, XIV (1974), pp. 210–18.

'Iz istorii formirovaniya russkoi narodnoi kukol'noi komedii Petrushka' in *V professional'noi shkole kukol'nikov*, Leningrad 1979, pp. 137–47.

'Ocherkisty-shestedesyatniki' in *Russkaya literatura i fol'klor: vtoraya polovina XIX veka*, Leningrad 1982, pp. 131–78.

'The traditional archetectonics of folk puppet street comedy' (in English), *Proceedings of the UNIMA Symposium*, Moscow 1983, pp. 26–40.

Russkie narodnye gorodskie prazdniki, uveseleniya i zrelishcha, Leningrad 1984 (reissued with several new illustrations and some new textual material, Leningrad 1988).

Anon., *Das neue Kasperltheater*, Sonneberg *c*. 1890.

Nijinska, Bronislava, *Early Memories*, trans. and ed. I. Nijinska and Jean Robinson, London 1982.

Novyi entsiklopedicheskii slovar' Brokguaza i Efrona, ed. K. K. Arsen'ev, 29 vols., St Petersburg 1911–1916 [edn never completed].

Obol'yaninov, N., *Zametki o russkikh illyustrirovannykh izdaniyakh*, Moscow 1915.

Obraztsov, Sergey, 'O narodnom iskusstve', *Pravda*, 15 May 1927, 6.

Moya professiya, Moscow 1981.

Po stupen'kam pamyati, Moscow 1987.

Ocherki russkogo narodnogo poeticheskogo tvorchestva sovetskoi epokhi, Moscow and Leningrad 1952.

Oinas, Felix J. (ed.), *Folklore, Nationalism and Politics*, Columbus, Ohio 1978.

Olearius, Adam, *Vermehrte neue Beschreibung der Muscowitschen und Persischen Reise ... welche zum andern mahl heraus gibt Adam Olearius*, Schleswig: gedruckt in der Fürstl. Druckerey durch Johan Holwein Im Jahr MDCLVI.

The Voyages and Travels of the Ambassadors, rendered into English by John Davies of Kidwelly, London 1662.

Oreglia, Giacomo, *The commedia dell'arte*, London 1969.

Panchenko, A. M., 'Skomoroshina o chernetse', *Trudy otdela drevnerusskoi literatury AN SSSR*, 21 (1965), 89–93.

Pascar, Henriette, *Mon théâtre à Moscou*, Paris 1930.

Paul, Lissa, 'Dumb Bunnies? A Revisionist Re-Reading of *Watership Down*', *Signal* 56 (May 1988), 113–22.

Paushkin, M. (ed.), *Staryi russkii vodevil', 1819–1849*, Moscow 1937.

Pepys, Lady Charlotte, *Domestic Sketches in Russia*, II, London 1861.

Peretts, V. N., 'Kukol'nyi teatr na Rusi', *Ezhegodnik imperatorskikh teatrov* (1894–5), Supplement, Part 1, 84–185.

Perrie, Maureen, *The Image of Ivan the Terrible in Russian Folklore*, Cambridge, 1987.

Petrushka, illustrated journal, ed. Kholodny, 1 [only one published], St Petersburg 1905.

Pinkerton, Robert, *Russia: or Miscellaneous Observations on the Past and Present State of that Country and its Inhabitants, compiled from Notes made on the Spot, during Travels at different Times, in the Service of the Bible Society, and a Residence of many Years in that Country*, London 1833.

Polozov, S., 'Vlast' tolpy', *Slovo*, 15 January 1905.

Pomerantseva, E. G., 'Ballada i zhestokii romans ...', *Russkii fol'klor*, XIV (1974), pp 202–10.

Pomyalovsky, N. G., *Polnoe sobranie sochinenii v 2 tomakh*, II, Moscow and Leningrad 1935.

Popov, Oleg, *Russian Clown*, London 1970.

Posner, Sandy, *Petrouchka: the Story of the Ballet*, with decorations by Joyce Millieu, London 1946.

Anon., 'Prazdnik samoobmana', *Volva* 26 (April 1906).

Privalov, B., *Petrushka – dusha skomorosh'ya*, Moscow 1963.

Propp. V. Ya., 'Ritual'nyi smekh v fol'klore', *Uchenye zapiski Leningrad-skogo gosudarstvennogo universiteta*, 46 (1939), 3rd series, 151–75.

Russkaya skazka, Leningrad 1984.

Pursglove, Michael, 'D. V. Grigorovich's "Gutta-percha Boy"', *Quinquer-eme: New Studies in Modern Languages*, 9:1 (1986), 41–62.

Pushkin, A. S., 'O narodnoi drame i drame Marfa – posadnitsa', *Polnoe sobranie sochinenii v 10 tomakh* vii, Leningrad 1977, pp. 146–52.

Rabinovich, M. G., 'K istorii skomorosh'ikh igr na Rusi' in *Kul'tura srednevekovoi Rusi*, Leningrad 1974, pp. 53–6.

Ransome, Arthur, *Six Weeks in Russia in 1919*, London 1919.

Reeder, Roberta, 'Petrushka, a Russian Rogue', *The Puppetry Journal* (Jan–Feb. 1981), 41–5.

Remizov, A. M. *Tsar' Maksimilian*, Berkeley 1988, facsimile reprint of Petersburg 1920 edn.

Plyas Irodiady, Berlin n.d.

Rusal'nye deistva, reprint, Munich 1971.

Reynolds, Rothay, *My Russian Year*, London c. 1907.

Rice, James L., *Dostoevsky and the Healing Art: An Essay in Literary and Medical History*, Ann Arbor 1985.

Ritter, Helmut, *Türkische Schattenspiele*, i, Hanover 1924.

Roberti, Vero, *Moscow Under the Skin*, London 1969.

Robin, Régine, *Le Réalisme socialiste: un ésthétique impossible*, Paris 1986.

Robinson, A. (ed.), *Novye cherty v russkoi literature i iskusstve XVII- nachala XVIII v.*, Moscow 1976.

Rodina, T. M., *Aleksandr Blok i russkii teatr nachala XX veka*, Moscow 1972.

Rovinsky, D. A., *Russkie narodnye kartinki*, 5 vols. plus atlas of pictures, St Petersburg 1881; 2nd edn, 2 vols., St Petersburg 1900.

Rudnitsky, Konstantin, *Russian Soviet Theatre*, London 1988.

Russell, Robert, 'People's Theatre and the October Revolution', *Irish Slavonic Studies* 7 (1986), 65–84.

Sanktpeterburg: issledovaniya po istorii, topografii i statistike, pub. MVD: Tsentral'nyi statisticheskii komitet, St Petersburg 1870.

Savushkina, N. I., *Narodnyi teatr*, Moscow 1976.

Sbornik postanovlenii i rasporyazhenii po tsenzure s 1720 po 1862 g., St Petersburg 1863, pub. Ministerstvo narodnogo prosveshcheniya.

Shalamov, Varlam, *Kolymskie rasskazy*, London 1978.

Shapovalova, G. G., 'Samodeyatel'nyi narodnyi teatr i fol'klor', in *Fol'klor i khudozhestvennaya samodeyatel'nost'*, Leningrad 1968, pp. 122–44.

Shcheglov, Ivan, *Narodnyi teatr*, St Petersburg 1898.

Narod i teatr, St Petersburg 1911.

Shklovsky, V. B., *Eizenshtein*, Moscow 1973.

Simonovich-Efimova, N. Ya., *Zapiski petrushechnika*, abr. reprint of Leningrad 1925 edn, Leningrad 1981 [also published in English as *Adventures of a Russian Puppet Theatre*, Birmingham, Michigan 1935].

Skabichevsky, A. M., *Ocherki istorii russkoi tsenzury 1700–1863*, St Petersburg 1892.

Sleptsov, V. A., *Sochineniya v 2 tomakh*, Moscow and Leningrad 1933.
Sochineniya v 2 tomakh, Moscow 1957.
Slonimskaya, Yu., 'Marionetka', *Apollon*, 3 (1916), 1–42.
Smirnova, N. I., *Sovetskii teatr kukol 1918–1932*, Moscow 1963.
Smith, G. S., *Songs to Seven Strings: A History of Russian Guitar Poetry*, Bloomington 1985.
Smith, S. A., *Red Petrograd: Revolution in the Factories, 1917–18*, Cambridge 1985.
Sokolinsky, E. K., 'Smert' Tarelkina A. V. Sukhovo-Kobylina i russkaya narodnaya komediya, russkaya demonologiya', *Russkii fol'klor*, XVIII (1978), pp. 42–60.
Sokolov, Boris and Yury, *Poeziya derevni: rukovodstvo dlya sobiraniya*, Moscow 1926.
Sokolov, Yury, *Russkii fol'klor*, Moscow 1941.
Sologub, Fedor, 'Teatr odnoi voli' in *Teatr: kniga o novom teatre*, pp. 179–98.
Dramaticheskie proizvedeniya, VIII, St Petersburg 1909.
Stikhotvoreniya, Leningrad 1979.
Solomonik, I. N., 'Problemy analiza narodnogo teatra kukol: khudozhestvennyi yazyk narodnogo kukol'nogo predstavleniya', *Sovetskaya etnografiya*, 6, (1978), 28–45.
Sovetskii teatr: dokumenty i materialy, I, Leningrad 1968.
Speaight, George, *Punch and Judy: a History*, London 1970 (abr. reprint of London 1955 edn).
A History of the Circus, London 1980.
Stallybrass, Peter and White, Allon, *The Politics and Poetics of Transgression*, London 1986.
Starsmore, Ian (ed.), *The Fairground*, catalogue of exhibition held at the Whitechapel Art Gallery, 1977.
Storey, Robert, *Pierrot: a Critical History of a Mask*, Princeton 1978.
Svod zakonov Rossiiskoi Imperii, ed. I. D. Mordukhay-Boltovsky, 16 vols and index, St Petersburg 1912.
Svod zakonov RSFSR, 8 vols., Moscow 1985.
Svod zakonov SSSR, 11 vols., Moscow 1985.
Sytova, A. (ed.), *The Lubok*, Leningrad 1984.
Teatr: kniga o novom teatre, St Petersburg 1908 (collection of essays by Lunacharsky, Bely, Sologub, Bryusov and others; relevant items listed separately).
Teatr kukol: sbornik, Moscow 1955.
Teatral'naya entsiklopediya, ed. P. A. Markov, 6 vols., Moscow 1963–7.
Anon., *Théâtre lyonnais de Guignol*, Lyon 1890.
Thomas, Keith, *Religion and the Decline of Magic: Studies in Belief in Sixteenth- and Seventeenth-Century England*, Harmondsworth 1978.
Man and the Natural World: Changing Attitudes in England 1500–1800, Harmondsworth 1984.
Thompson, Stith, *Motif Index of Folk Literature*, Bloomington 1957.
Tolstoy, L. N., *Chto takoe iskusstvo?*, Moscow 1985.

Toporov, V. N., 'On the Cosmological Origins of Early Historical Descriptions', *Russian Poetics in Translation*, 3 (1976), 38–81.

Trotsky, Leon, *Literature and Revolution*, Ann Arbor 1960.

Tsirkovaya entsiklopediya, Moscow 1980.

Tugendkhol'd, Ya., 'Itogi sezona', *Apollon*, 6 (1911), chronicle, 65–74.

Uspensky, Gleb, *Polnoe sobranie sochinenii*, 6th edn, 6 vols., St Petersburg 1908.

Uspensky, Nikolay, *Sochineniya v 2 tomakh*, I, Moscow and Leningrad 1933.

Uvarova, E. D., *Estradnyi teatr: miniatyury, obozreniya, myuzik-kholly 1917–1945*, Moscow 1983.

(ed.), *Russkaya sovetskaya estrada*, 3 vols., Moscow 1976–81.

Vadimov, A. A. and Trivas, M. A., *Ot magov drevnosti do illyuzionistov nashikh dnei*, Moscow 1966.

Varey, J. E., *Historia de los títeres en España*, Madrid 1957.

Varneke, B. V., 'Chto igraet narod', *Ezhegodnik imperatorskikh teatrov*, 4 (1913), 1–40.

Vasilich, G., 'Moskva 1850–1910', *Moskva v ee proshlom i nastoyashchem*, 11 (1912), 3–28.

'Ulitsy i lyudi sovremmenoi Moskvy', *Moskva v ee proshlom i nastoyashchem*, 12 (1912), 3–18.

Vasilich, N., 'Moskva v 50-kh i 60-kh godakh proshlogo stoletiya', RV, 21 July 1911, 2–3.

Vertinsky, Aleksandr, *Zapiski russkogo P'ero*, New York 1982.

Veselovsky, A. N., *Starinnyi teatr v Evrope: istoricheskie ocherki*, Moscow 1870.

Vinogradov, Nikolai, 'Velikorusskii vertep', *Izvestiya otdeleniya russkogo yazyka i slovesnosti Imperatorskoi Akademii Nauk*, 10:3 (1905), 360–82.

Vitaliev, Vitaly, 'Once Upon a Time in Amur', *Guardian*, 28 October 1988.

Vitengof, P., *Ocherki moskovskoi zhizni*, Moscow 1842.

Voloshin, M., *Stikhotvoreniya*, 2 vols., Paris 1982–4.

Vsevolodsky-Gerngross, V. N., 'Nachalo tsirka v Rossii', *O teatre: sbornik stat'ei, Vremennik otdela istorii i teorii teatra Instituta istorii iskusstv* II, Leningrad 1927, pp. 66–107.

Istoriya russkogo teatra, 2 vols., Leningrad and Moscow 1929.

Russkii teatr ot istokov do serediny XVIII veka, Moscow 1957.

Russkaya ustnaya narodnaya drama, Moscow 1959.

Wade, Terence, 'Russian Folklore and Soviet Humour', *Journal of Russian Studies*, 54 (1988), 3–20.

Das wahrhaftige Kasperltheater in 6 Stücken, Munich c. 1890.

Warner, Elizabeth, *The Russian Folk Theatre*, The Hague and Paris 1977.

Webb, Tim and Amanda, 'The Puppet Theatre in China Today', *Animations*, 9:1 (1985), 9.

Welsford, Enid, *The Fool: His Social and Literary History*, London 1935.

Whewell, Harry, 'A Fair Exchange', *Guardian*, 18 April 1987, back page.

Williams, Harold, *Russia of the Russians*, London 1914.

Williamson, Duncan and Linda, *A Thorn in the King's Foot: Stories of the Scottish Travelling People*, Harmondsworth 1987.

Yampol'sky, L. (ed.), *Poetry Iskry*, 2 vols., Leningrad 1955.

Yaroslavsky, G., 'Gorodskoe samoupravlenie Moskvy', *Moskva v ee proshlom i nastoyashchem*, 11 (1912), 17–48.

Yatsevich, A., *Krepostnye v Peterburge*, Leningrad 1933.

Yershov, Peter, *Comedy in the Soviet Theatre*, New York 1956.

Yutkevich, Sergey, *Kino – eto pravda 24 kadra v sekundu*, Moscow 1977.

Zamyatin, E., *Blokha: igra v 4-kh deistviyakh*, in *Sochineniya*, Munich 1982, II, pp. 341–89 (see also Zamyatin's comments on the play, pp. 503–18).

Zemtsovsky, I. I. (ed.), *Poeziya krest'yanskikh prazdnikov*, Leningrad 1970.

Zguta, Russell, *Russian Minstrels: a History of the Skomorokhi*, Oxford 1978.

Zhivopisnyi al'bom narody [sic] Rossii, St Petersburg 1880.

Zholkovsky, A., 'O genii i zlodeistve, o babe i vserossiiskom masshtabe' in *Mir avtora i struktura teksta*, Tenafly NJ 1986, pp. 255–79.

Zoshchenko, Mikhail, *Tsarskie sapogi*, Riga 1924.

Sobranie sochinenii, I, Leningrad 1931.

Index

abjection displacement, 99, 251 n. 78
acculturation, 37, 38–9
Aesop, 53
Aesopian narrative, 83–4
Afanas'ev, A: *Forbidden Tales*, 266 n. 59
agitprop theatre, 2, 13, 154, 189–208; *see also* Red Petrushka; Blue Blouse; propaganda
Akhmatova, Anna: *Poem without a Hero*, 173–4
Alekseev-Yakovlev, A. Ya., 61, 68, 192: organises Entertainment and Benefit theatre, 144
Alferov, A., 59
alienation, 86–7
anarchism, 195–6
anecdotes, 8, 134, 213, 256 n. 92; *see also* folk-tales
Anna, Empress, 17, 127
Annenkov, Yu., 158
Annensky, I.: and classical drama, 146, 247 n. 162, 258 n. 24; and *Petrushka*, 262 n. 103
'Children's Balloons', 145, 258 n. 22
Arab, the (character in puppet theatre), 65, 66, 67, 104, 105, 113, 114; (or Moor, character in *Petrouchka*), 168–9
archives, *see* popular culture: sources for study of
Aristotle, 80
Arkanov, A., 268 n. 7
Armenian, the (character in *Petrushka*), 74, 95, 99, 136
Ashkenazi, Zigfrid, 164
'attractions', 17
Auslender, S.: review of Potemkin's *Petrushka*, 262 n. 98
Austerlitz, R., 253 n. 17

Baby, the (character in Western European puppet plays), 116
Bakhtin, M. M., 3, 92–3, 131, 132, 178, 189, 211

Bakhtin, N., 40
balagans, xiii, 24, 31, 33
adaptations of: in agitprop, 191–2; in high literature, 151–2
life in, 44–5, 142–3, 154, 158
Petrushka in, 46–7
plays in, 42, 144;
see also funfairs, carnival, popular theatre
Baratynsky, E. A.: 'The Gypsy', 141–2, 172
Barin, the (or 'Toff', character in *Petrushka*), 65–6, 72, 98, 121, 122, 124
bears, dancing, 24, 50, 179, 186, 192
beggars, 36, 41, 45, 188, 216, 241 n. 73, 244 n. 122
Bely, Andrey: *Kotik Letaev*, 163–4; views on popular theatre, 146
Ben-Amos, D., 8, 9, 10
Benois, A.: as co-creator of *Petrushka*, 167–72; views on fairground 1, 2, 19, 32, 145; on *Petrushka*, 56, 167
Berkov, P., 85
biological determinism, 92, 250 n. 59, 253 n. 17
Blok, A.: views on wrestling, 145
'Balagan', 148–9
The Little Balagan (play), 151–3
'The Little Balagan' (poem), 153–4
Blue Blouse, 191, 194
body, the
in the carnival, 127–33; deformation of, 132–3; functions of, 127–8, 132
in *Petrushka*, 92–8; praised, 92–3; used in insults, 95; used in puns, 96; used topographically, 97–8
see also carnival; drinking and drunkenness; food; sex
Bogatyrev, P. G.: on Czech theatre, 110; on fairground theatre, 250 n. 66; on puppets, 103; *see also* Jakobson, R.
Bombov, I. (clown), 27

283

subordinate classes: attitudes of ruling
classes to, 15, 39–41; composition
of, 34–6; Freud on, 92; living
conditions amongst, 35–7, 240
n. 63; occupational diversity of, 35;
political radicalism amongst, 37;
population growth amongst (after
1861), 29; reactions to fairground
theatre of, 27, 42, 134–5; reactions
to *Petrushka*, 1, 11, 86–90;
representation of, in high culture,
141–2, 148, 154, 177–8; in
Petrushka, 84, 87, 92; *see also*
proletariat
Svin'in, P., 48
swazzle, the (squeaker device in puppet
theatre), 102, 106, 129, 163
swings, 18, 23, 24
Symbolism, 3, 145–53, 163–72

'Tale of Frol Skobeev, The' (written
popular tale), 137
'Tale of Misery and Misfortune, The'
(written popular tale), 116
Tarasov, G., 192, 195, 196
technology: and *Petrushka*, 77; popular
views of, 30, 43
temperance movement, 32, 55, 56, 240
n. 62
terror: under Peter I, 25, 127; under
Stalin, 210, 266 n. 68
theatrical monopoly, 143
Thompson, S., 110
Todd, Sweeney, 83
Tolstoy, L., 6, 8, 27, 40–1
tooth fairy, the, 9
topicality: in fairground genres, 42–3; in
Petrushka, 71, 77
toys: compared to puppets, 51; functions
of, in towns, 89; sale of, at fairs,
23; theatrical forms of, 105
toy theatre, 49
trade fairs, 16, 186; *see also*
Nizhnii-Novgorod
tradition, 9, 54, 59, 88, 139, 188–9,
209–10
tragedy: Attic, 145, 259 n. 32; Jacobean,
95; Symbolist views, of, 3, 145–7,
168
Trotsky, Leon, 184
Tsar' Maksimilian, 135, 191;
literary versions of, *see*
Remizov, A. M.
Tsekhnovitser, O., 110, 112

Über-marionette, the, 169, 262 n. 91
urbanisation, 36–8, 89; *see also* Moscow;
St Petersburg
Uspensky, B. A., 5
Uspensky, G., 142
Uspensky, N., 142–3
Utenkov, M. D., *Witch-Doctory*,
197–204

Van'ka, *see* Petrushka
Van'ka-Kain, 24
Vasilich, G., 37, 41
Vasilich, N., 239 n. 43
vaudevilles, 28, 258 n. 10
vertep (Ukrainian puppet theatre),
xiv, 54, 61, 112, 121, 123–4, 265
n. 45
Vertinsky, A., 94
village prose, 268
Vindusaka, 110
violence: in agitprop theatre, 177, 203;
domestic, 38, 69–70, 98–100; in
glove-puppet theatre, 106; amongst
labourers, 238 n. 21; played down
in *lubok* texts, 74; in *Petrushka*,
62, 98–100, 177; amongst
subordinate classes, 19, 24, 249
n. 45
Vitengof, P., 39, 86
'Vixen and the Puppets, The', 53
Vlachoyannis, Y., 260 n. 63
Voloshin, M., 150
Vol'pin, M.: *An Amateur Performance*,
197–204
Voronezh, 179
Vysotsky, V., 267 n. 68
Vsevolodsky-Gerngross, V. N., 4, 34, 37,
51, 63, 72, 73, 86, 110, 179, 195
'vulgar sociologism', 214

Warner, E., 6, 94
White, A., 237 n. 53
Williamson, D. and L., 10
women: in agitprop theatre, 203–4, 265
n. 50; in books, 234 n. 21; in
fairground audiences, 39; literacy
amongst, 232 n. 5; in towns, 38; in
Western European tradition,
117–18; *see also* gender;
Petrushka's fiancée; rape; sexual
harassment; violence, domestic

yarmarka, 16: *see also* trade
fairs

CAMBRIDGE STUDIES IN RUSSIAN LITERATURE